Palgrave Studies in European Union Politics

Edited by: **Michelle Egan**, American University USA, **Neill Nugent**, Manchester Metropolitan University, UK, **William Paterson**, University of Birmingham, UK

Editorial Board: **Christopher Hill**, Cambridge, UK, **Simon Hix**, London School of Economics, UK, **Mark Pollack**, Temple University, USA, **Kalypso Nicolaïdis**, Oxford UK, **Morten Egeberg**, University of Oslo, Norway, **Amy Verdun**, University of Victoria, Canada, **Claudio M. Radaelli**, University of Exeter, UK, **Frank Schimmelfennig**, Swiss Federal Institute of Technology, Switzerland

Palgrave Macmillan is delighted to announce the launch of a new book series on the European Union. Following on the sustained success of the acclaimed *European Union Series*, which essentially publishes research-based textbooks, *Palgrave Studies in European Union Politics* will publish research-driven monographs.

The remit of the series is broadly defined, both in terms of subject and academic discipline. All topics of significance concerning the nature and operation of the European Union potentially fall within the scope of the series. The series is multidisciplinary to reflect the growing importance of the EU as a political and social studies, international relations, political economy, public and social policy and sociology

Titles include:

Katie Verlin Laatikainen and Karen E. Smith (*editors*)
THE EUROPEAN UNION AND THE UNITED NATIONS

Esra LaGro and Knud Erik Jørgensen (*editors*)
TURKEY AND THE EUROPEAN UNION
Prospects for a Difficult Encounter

Paul G. Lewis and Zdenka Mansfeldová (*editors*)
THE EUROPEAN UNION AND PARTY POLITICS IN CENTRAL AND
EASTERN EUROPE

Hartmut Mayer and Henri Vogt (*editors*)
A RESPONSIBLE EUROPE?
Ethical Foundations of EU External Affairs

Lauren M. McLaren
IDENTITY, INTERESTS AND ATTITUDES TO EUROPEAN INTEGRATION

Christoph O. Meyer, Ingo Linsenmann and Wolfgang Wessels (*editors*)
ECONOMIC GOVERNMENT OF THE EU
A Balance Sheet of New Modes of Policy Coordination

Frank Schimmelfennig, Stefan Engert and Heiko Knobel
INTERNATIONAL SOCIALIZATION EUROPE
European Organizations, Political Conditionality and Democratic Change

Justus Schönlau
DRAFTING THE EU CHARTER
Rights, Legitimacy and Process

Palgrave Studies in European Union Politics
**Series Standing Order ISBN 1-4039-9511-7 (hardback) and
ISBN 1-4039-9512-5 (paperback)**

You can receive future titles in this series as they are published by placing a
standing order. Please contact your bookseller or, in case of difficulty, write
to us at the address below with your name and address, the title of the series
and one of the ISBNs quoted above.

Customer Services Department, Macmillan Distribution Ltd, Houndmills,
Basingstoke, Hampshire RG21 6XS, England

Constitutional Politics in the European Union

The Convention Moment and its Aftermath

Dario Castiglione
Reader in Political Theory
University of Exeter, UK

Justus Schönlau
PES-Group Secretariat
Committee of the Regions, Belgium

Chris Longman
Deputy Director of the Centre for European Studies
University of Exeter, UK

Emanuela Lombardo
Research Fellow
Complutense University of Madrid, Spain

Nieves Pérez-Solórzano Borragán
Senior Lecturer in European Politics
University of Bristol, UK

and

Miriam Aziz
Associate Professor
University of Siena, Italy

First published 2007 by
PALGRAVE MACMILLAN
Houndmills, Basingstoke, Hampshire RG21 6XS and
175 Fifth Avenue, New York, N.Y. 10010
Companies and representatives throughout the world

PALGRAVE MACMILLAN is the global academic imprint of the Palgrave Macmillan division of St. Martin's Press, LLC and of Palgrave Macmillan Ltd. Macmillan® is a registered trademark in the United States, United Kingdom and other countries. Palgrave is a registered trademark in the European Union and other countries.

ISBN-13: 978-1-4039-4523-5   hardback
ISBN-10: 1-4039-4523-3   hardback

This book is printed on paper suitable for recycling and made from fully managed and sustained forest sources. Logging, pulping and manufacturing processes are expected to conform to the environmental regulations of the country of origin.

A catalogue record for this book is available from the British Library.

A catalog record for this book is available from the Library of Congress.

10   9   8   7   6   5   4   3   2   1
16   15   14   13   12   11   10   09   08   07

Printed and bound in Great Britain by
Antony Rowe Ltd, Chippenham and Eastbourne

Contents

Preface and Acknowledgements

This book was first planned at the time when the 'Convention on the Future of Europe' was drawing to its conclusion. Most of its chapters were drafted during the IGC period and the half-interrupted ratification process. It was finally completed at the beginning of 2007, when the 'reflection period' seemed to come to a close, and the German presidency of the European Council manifested the intention to inject new life into the moribund 'Treaty establishing a Constitution for Europe', even though this may eventually be presented as a treaty on institutional reform rather than as a constitution.

The book, like the Constitutional Treaty itself, has therefore gone through several phases and upheavals (more, perhaps, than we might have wished). Indeed, it is always difficult to write with a moving object in view. But, as we hint in the title and make clear in the rest of the book, rather than being concerned with the EU Constitution as an end-product, in this book we focus on the political process through which the EU has attempted to give itself a formal and comprehensive *constitutional text* – though in the form of a *treaty*. Our real object of study is not the EU Constitution, but EU constitutional politics, and in particular the Convention as a 'moment' in the ongoing constitutionalisation of the EU.

As we suggest throughout the book, this 'Convention moment' has a meaning of its own, albeit a contested meaning, but one that should not be overlooked, even though it may end in a 'defeat' of the Constitutional Treaty. The EU does not (yet) have a formal constitutional text, but, warts and all, it has had its first public constitutional debate. In this respect, the 'Convention on the Future of Europe' represents an important 'moment' in the ongoing constitutionalisation of the European Union, and as such deserves being studied in its own right. This book is a contribution to that study.

Authorship

This book aims to be a co-ordinated study of the Convention moment from different perspectives. Throughout the phases of conception, drafting and revising, we have collectively discussed its shape and content. As a book, it has therefore six authors. But its parts are the responsibility of the individual authors, as indicated in each chapter. Although the scope and the underlying argument of the book have a fundamental unity and coherence, in treating different aspects of the Convention, of its context, and of its aftermath, individual authors have followed different approaches and occasionally taken different positions. We make no apology for this, since imposing a single line of argument might have prevented us from exploring our subject in full, and from different perspectives. Hopefully, the overall effect succeeds in offering a broadly unitary picture, as that produced by the differently coloured pieces of a mosaic, rather than by the neat brushstrokes of a hyper-realistic painting.

The book originated as part of a European research project financed by the Fifth Framework Programme of the European Commission. The general theme of the project was 'Citizenship and Democratic Legitimacy in the European Union' (CIDEL), and was co-ordinated by ARENA at the University of Oslo. As part of this project, a number of researchers from various countries worked on constitutional issues and constitution-making in the EU. This book is one of the products of that research, and emerges from the work done by a group of researchers connected at different times to the University of Exeter, and co-ordinated by Dario Castiglione. Although not formally linked to Exeter, two of the authors, Emanuela Lombardo and Nieves Pérez-Solórzano Borragán, also shared an interest in the research, and agreed to join in the production of a collective book.

A note on terminology

Although this book is part of a specialised literature on European constitutionalism and constitution-making, its presentation and terminology are easily accessible to the general reader. Most of the more specialised terminology is easily accessible from the context, and reproduces standard understandings available in the literature. However, a few clarifications on how we use this terminology may be in order.

For a general clarification of the different meanings attributed to specific terms, within the general family of concepts of 'constitution/constitutionalism', we refer to what is said in Chapter 1. Most of these terms are contested, so there is no agreed definition. The context will usually indicate the precise sense in which they are meant in different chapters. The sense in which we use 'constitutional politics' in the title of this book has already been indicated at the beginning of this Introduction and is further discussed in Chapter 1. A number of chapters refer to the more specific opposition between *normal* and *constitutional* politics in a normative sense. This distinction has become common currency in the constitutional literature thanks to the influential work of Bruce Ackerman (1991); its normative purchase is discussed in Chapter 2, though in other parts of the book it is used as shorthand for a broad distinction between a more 'deliberative' and an interest-based kind of politics. By 'documentary' constitution, an expression which appears in a number of chapters, the more narrow sense of the constitution as a 'document' is meant. Given that part of the argument about the 'constitutionalisation' of Europe relies on a broader sense of the constitution as an organising norm/structure of either the polity or the legal order, the reference to a move towards a 'documentary' constitution in the EU refers to the more specific attempt to fix that norm/structure in a single text.

The title of this book refers also to a 'Convention moment'. In some of the constitutional literature, the idea of a 'constitutional moment' is closely associated with that of 'normative' politics, and the way in which political mobilisation in and through a particular *moment* gives political action a *constituent* force. The relevance of the idea of a 'moment' (as opposed to a more diffuse idea of constitutional foundations through time) is discussed in both Chapters 2 and 11. These chapters refer to ideas of an 'embedded' constitution and the 'living law' respectively, as understandings of the constitution as developing through time, rather than foundational events. (The expression 'living law' tends also to suggest an intrinsic correlation between the constitutional and the legal order.) When we refer to the 'Convention moment', therefore, we wish to indicate the possibility that the Convention on the Future of Europe worked, or might have worked, as the central event in a European constitutional moment. This, however, is only a suggestive use of the idea, for there is no a priori assumption on our part that this was indeed the case. Most of the book is meant to investigate whether such an interpretation stands scrutiny.

Throughout the book we also use expressions such as 'Convention experiment' (occasionally 'experience') and 'Convention method'. The former is usually meant as a more 'descriptive' way of referring to what the Convention meant as part of the EU constitutionalisation process. Although it makes implicit reference to the more normative use of 'Convention moment', it mainly wishes to indicate that the Convention represents a particular experience/experiment in the history of European integration. 'Convention method' is used in a more generic sense, as the combinations of methods and principles associated with the use of a 'convention' as a way of either writing or drafting a constitutional text. Part of the intention of this book is to explore whether the 'Convention experiment' either produced or followed a 'Convention method' that may have wider significance for the future constitutionalisation of the EU.

When in the book we talk about the 'Convention' we refer to the 'Convention on the Future of Europe' established at Laeken. (For a more precise history of how this came about, see Chapter 3.) But in a number of places (and particularly in Chapters 3, 7 and 10) we also talk in some detail of the previous Convention, the one that drafted the 'Charter of Fundamental Rights of the European Union', eventually proclaimed at Nice, but not as yet officially integrated within the EU official legal provisions. In such cases, we refer to the former as the 'Constitutional Convention' and to the latter as the 'Charter Convention'.

Finally, we normally refer to the members of the Constitutional Convention as the *conventionnels* (as they themselves did) rather than the clumsier 'members of the Convention'. We use a variety of expressions to refer to the 'Treaty establishing a Constitution for Europe', including '(European) Constitution' and 'Constitutional Treaty'. The use of one or the other expression has no particular meaning, apart from a stylistic choice, depending on the context. All of them refer to the same document, approved by the IGC and signed by the heads of states and governments and the foreign ministers in October 2004 (see Chapter 12). When this document is quoted, it is referred to as 'TCE'. This document is different (as argued in more detail in the concluding chapter) from the text elaborated by the Convention, which is normally referred to as the 'Draft (Constitutional) Treaty' or the 'Draft Constitution'. This is abbreviated as DCT when quoted in our book. In general, when discussing issues of substance, we have preferred to quote from the TCE, unless we were making a specific point on the text or provisions agreed in the Convention. When quoting documents prepared by or submitted to the Convention, we refer to the Conv. Docs as accessible for the time being through the web-site (www.european-convention.eu.int). The decision to keep a variety of terms reflects common usage in the literature and in more popular publications. Indeed, it also reflects the inherent ambiguity of these documents, half 'treaties' and half 'constitutions', a point germane to both this book and our analysis.

Interviews and questionnaires

Part of the research for this book is based on interviews with *conventionnels* and other participants in and observers to the Convention. This concerns Chapters 3, 4, 5, 6 and 8 in particular.

The analyses for Chapters 3–5 (and to a certain extent Chapter 6) are in part based on twenty-four semi-structured interviews with Convention members, as well as background conversations with several other actors involved in the process of drafting the EU Constitution in the Convention. All but one of the twenty-four interviews with Convention members (list available from the authors) were carried out during the lifetime of the Convention in the context of the EU-supported research project, Citizenship and Democratic Legitimacy (CIDEL). The interviews were based on a flexibly adapted set of open questions which were aimed at inducing the interviewee to communicate his or her visions on a broad range of issues connected with the role and purpose of the Convention, its working methods, the interviewee's own role in the process, and his or her evaluation of a number of issues related to the draft EU Constitution. The general aim in selecting the interview partners was to include as broad a balance of views as possible from within the Convention. The choice of interviewees also reflects the effort to ensure, within the limits of the overall small number of interviewees, a rough proportionality among the three Convention delegations (national parliaments, national governments and the European Parliament), between party groups, between small and large countries, and to reflect a wide spread of nationalities.

The empirical research for Chapter 6 was partly based on the interviews discussed above (in which questions about the language regime were asked), and supplemented by five further interviews in December 2003 with key actors in the Convention secretariat, including two of the eleven Convention *redacteurs* (drafters), one of the principal language service organisers, and experts in translation and interpretation. These interviews were semi-structured, and focused around themes such as trade-offs between ideals and pragmatism, as well as detailed questions about assumptions, organisation and problems encountered.

In relation to the methods employed in the chapter on civil society (Chapter 8), an internet questionnaire was circulated at the beginning of 2003 targeting organisations that contributed to the Forum on the Future of Europe, in particular individuals who acted as representatives of Contact Groups in the Public Hearings on civil society that the Convention organised on 24 and 25 June 2002. The aim of the questionnaire was to gather information coming from direct participants in the Forum and Hearings, both on the type of interaction that the Convention had been able to establish with them and on their own satisfaction with the process and outcome of the consultation. The questionnaire included twelve open-ended questions, and was sent to forty organisations belonging to the following Contact Groups of civil society: social sector, environment, academia and think tanks and citizens and institutions, regional and local authorities, human rights, development, and cultural sector. Six people answered the questionnaire on behalf of their organisations.

Acknowledgements

As a group, and particularly Castiglione, Schönlau, Aziz and Longman, we acknowledge the financial support of the Fifth Framework Programme of the European Commission. In this connection, we thank all the people at ARENA involved in CIDEL, and in particular Erik O. Eriksen, John E. Fossum and Agustín J. Menéndez, with whom we have passionately discussed most of the issues covered by this volume – and although we are aware that they may not fully agree with some of our analyses and conclusions, we hope that they can see the extent of the debt we owe to them, as a result of our common deliberations over several workshops. A very similar debt we owe to other researchers involved in CIDEL and working with us on constitutional issues, in particular Carlos Closa, Michelle Everson and Christian Joerges. Furthermore, we greatly benefited from discussions at two CIDEL workshops (in Albaraccín and London), with other scholars who were not part of the project itself. These included Richard Bellamy, Jo Shaw, Johannes Pollack, Ben Crum, Jürgen Neyer, Paul Magnette, Kalypso Nicolaides, Daniel Göler and Mattias Kumm.

There are also a number of personal acknowledgements from each of us separately. Castiglione and Aziz greatly benefited from their involvement (in different capacities) in the EUI 2003–4 European Forum on 'Constitutionalism in Europe', and particularly from the very interesting exchanges with two of the directors, Neil Walker and Bruno de Witte. Castiglione also benefited from conversations and exchanges with James Bohman and Ulrich Preuss, and from participation in various conferences at Oxford, Montreal, Indiana University and Berlin. Schönlau is particularly grateful to all those working in and around the Convention, who were willing to share information and exchange ideas. Longman would like to thank the organisers and participants of the workshops at which he presented ideas for his two chapters: the CIDEL workshop 'One EU – Many Publics? at Stirling University; the symposium, 'The Re-/Constructions of Europe/EU' at Lancaster University; and the conference, 'Language and the Future of Europe' at Southampton University. He would also like to thank the members of the Convention secretariat who agreed to be interviewed as part of the research for Chapter 6. Lombardo wishes to thank the Spanish *Secretaría de Estado de Educación y Universidades* for supporting her research, and Carlos Closa as director of the research project in which she was involved at the University of Zaragoza. She also wishes to thank those members of NGOs who participated in the forum and public hearings and kindly answered her questionnaire: Pawel Krzeczunowicz, Claire Godin, Birgit Hardt, Paloma Saavedra, Nicolas Beger and Sophia Spiliotopoulos. Pérez-Solórzano is extremely grateful to Stijn Smismans for his detailed and constructive comments on earlier versions of her chapter. Aziz, on her part, wishes to thank Sabino Cassese, Giuliano Amato, Bernardo Giorgio Mattarella and Lorenzo Gaeta for their help. Castiglione and Lombardo, finally, are grateful to the editors and publishers of a number of publications in which they had developed themes and arguments that are re-elaborated in their contribution to the present book. These include *Constellations*, Palgrave, and Sage for Castiglione; and *Social Politics*, and its guest editor Sylvia Walby, for Lombardo.

We would regard ourselves as very fortunate if our prospective readers are as tolerant of our failures and limitations as the people whose help we have here acknowledged were generous with their time and disinterested advice. As always, however, the responsibility for what we have written remains with us – either collectively or separately.

Our final word of thanks must go to an anonymous reader for the publisher, whose comments helped us to improve the very last version of this book, and to our editors at Palgrave, Alison Howson, Amy Lankester-Owen and Gemma d'Arcy Hughes, whose patience and unstinting support have been remarkable by any standard.

Introduction: a Convention Without a Constitution?

This is a book about European political constitutionalism and the 'Convention on the Future of Europe' (hereafter, Convention). This may require some explanation both on the approach of this book and on its purpose. We start with the latter, since the main object of our analysis – the setting up of the Convention, the way in which it worked, and its significance and impact – may strike readers as a 'historical' rather than a 'political' topic. Moreover, it may seem as if this is the history of a failure. For, at least at the time of writing, the Convention's efforts have not materialised into a Constitution.

So, this was a Convention without a Constitution. Does it matter? Part of the purpose of this book is to show that it may not, or at least not in the sense that many think. It is one of the central contentions of this book that the end product is not all that matters in the story of the Convention, and that, indeed, what the Convention in itself represented and how it operated are very much part of this story. Besides, and this is another central contention of the book, this is a story in progress. The Constitution's obituaries may have been rather premature in the aftermath of the French and the Dutch referendums. As we argue in the Conclusion, these were powerful blows to the project of giving the EU a written constitution, while raising significant issues for the European integration project as a whole, but at the time of writing there is plenty of evidence that the question of the European Constitution has not gone away, and that a political battle is being fought over it. Indeed, there are signs that, in spite of remarkable political difficulties faced, the attempt to provide the EU with a constitutional text is still on the political agenda – albeit in the likely form of a more traditional 'treaty', playing down its more 'constitutional' features. This was one of the declared objectives of the German presidency of the European Union for the first semester of 2007, as also agreed by the member states in the Berlin Declaration signed on the occasion of the 50th Anniversary of the Treaty of Rome.

Moreover, recent European polls show that in countries where the 'Treaty establishing a Constitution for Europe' has not yet been approved, the majority of citizens (53 per cent) are in favour of an EU Constitution. This is also true in France and the Netherlands, where the percentages of those in favour of the EU giving itself a Constitution have increased since the referendums that rejected the Treaty took place (Eurobarometer 66: Autumn 2006). Although these figures do not guarantee that the Constitution will be eventually approved, they are a general indication that the constitutional issue is an important aspect of the European *political* agenda in ways that it was not before the establishment of the 'Convention on the Future of Europe'. In this sense, the Convention represents a watershed in the history of constitutional politics in the EU.

Constitutional politics

But there is another sense in which the Convention matters, and cannot be dismissed as a kind of 'non-event'. This is because, regardless of whether or not it achieved its ostensible purpose of producing a Constitution, the Convention represents an important moment in European constitutional politics. Indeed, the other main purpose of this book is to analyse the Convention as such a moment. This requires some words of explanation of our approach, and of what we mean by 'constitutional politics'. As further explained in the section on terminology in the Preface to this book and in Chapter 1, the phrase 'constitutional politics' has various meanings, with overlapping empirical and normative connotations. Most of these meanings are relevant to various parts of our analysis, but, as a whole, the book approaches the question of 'constitutional politics' by taking it in the sense of the 'political' process through which constitutions are made. This is the meaning in which we intend the title of this book to be understood, for we study the Convention as a 'moment' of European constitution-making. From this perspective, as the rest of the book will demonstrate, the study of the Convention as a particular process, with its own internal and external dynamics, is an important part of the history and politics of European integration regardless of whether the Constitution in its present form is eventually ratified.

Most of the chapters in this book analyse the way in which the Convention operated, how it related to its external referents, and what it meant for the European constitution-making process. Most of the questions it addresses have an empirical and analytical dimension, but because of the particular 'foundational' elements that are associated with the 'constitutional' dimension of politics, it is inevitable that our analysis deals with normative issues. This is done more consistently in Part I of the book, and intermittently in Chapters 10, 11 and 12. But such a dimension is never completely absent from the horizon of the other chapters. There are two important normative considerations that underlie our study of the Convention and how this has contributed to shaping constitutional politics in the EU. One concerns the nature of the European Union itself, the other the form that constitutional politics has taken. With regard to the nature of the European Union, our analysis of the

Convention engages with the analytical, but also normative, question of whether the EU is still predominantly an international organisation, or whether it has entirely constitutionalised itself as a 'polity'. With regard to the form of constitutional politics, we address the parallel question of whether the way in which the EU is giving itself a 'constitution' reflects (or should reflect) an intergovernmental method based on separate sovereign powers, or a more democratic and deliberative method, which presupposes some commonality of purposes and interests.

As already said, the book as a whole offers both an empirical and a normative analysis of the Convention. But, overall, the message that the book conveys about these two questions is that the Convention represents a further moment in the transition of the EU from an international to a more supranational entity, from an intergovernmental to a more deliberative way of conceiving constitutional politics. And yet – and this is also part of the message that the book seeks to convey – these transitions are neither completed nor uncontested. In fact, the Convention is part of a longer and ongoing story, and this is why a study of it matters.

Fifty years on from the Treaty of Rome

It is perhaps significant that the current phase of European constitutional politics, and the 'crisis' it has generated, comes more or less at the time of the 50th anniversary of what could be considered as the first 'constitutional' text of the European Union/Communities, this being the Treaty of Rome of 25 March 1957. From such a perspective, the Convention may be considered as part of a broader process of change and continuity in EU constitutional politics.

The anniversary of the signature of the two Treaties of Rome (the EEC Treaty and the Euratom Treaty) may also remind us that, in its fifty-year history, the European integration process has gone through several crises. The period between 1954 and 1957 was characterised by an ambitious attempt, which eventually came to nothing because of French resistance, to move to a more integrated Europe via the development of the European Defence Community. At the time, as now, fundamental questions about the aim and purposes of integration were asked. The ensuing debate focused on whether integration should be about grand projects or consist of smaller pragmatic steps; and whether European integration should be pursued more as part of a liberal economic project or through an increase in social protection. Perhaps not surprisingly, some of the political objectives which were eventually formulated during the Messina intergovernmental conference in 1955 sound very similar to those of today's EU agenda: 'a united Europe . . . seems indispensable . . . if Europe is to preserve the standing which she has in the world, to restore the influence and her prestige, and to improve steadily the living standards of the population'.

From today's perspective, it may be interesting to speculate on how quickly things changed: from the failure of the EDC project, to the signing of the Treaty of Rome. It may also be intriguing to look at the role of political leadership at both national and supranational levels then and now, and how various international contingencies helped to shape the course of events. During the negotiations at Messina and Venice in 1955 and 1956, it became possible to reconcile different views so as to arrive at a broadly shared view of the main purposes of the integration process as set out in the Treaty of Rome. Nevertheless, the 'historical' significance of the Rome Treaty in March 1957 was hardly noticed at the time, while the Treaty itself was met with substantial levels of scepticism (Brunn, 2005: 117–18).

Here perhaps the parallels should end, since, as we argue in the Conclusion, but also in other chapters of the book, one of the main questions raised by the Convention, and as yet unresolved by the present constitutional phase, is the place of European citizens in this process. Indeed, an important question that we raise at various stages of our argument is whether the circumstances and forms of European integration have now changed sufficiently for the citizens of the enlarged European Union to have both a more distinctive voice and role in its constitutionalisation process, and whether ultimately the Convention has contributed to creating the conditions for this to happen. This is not the same question as whether Europe should or should not have a written constitution, but whether the institutional consolidation of the integration process should be the subject of public debate, or confined to member state governments and the institutions of the Union.

A brief overview of the book's arguments

The latter is a question for the future. Most of the book is an analysis of the Convention and of its place in EU constitutional politics. In Part I we try to define what constitutional politics means in the EU, and whether the Convention contributed to the resolution of what can ultimately be described as the legitimacy crisis, which *de facto* started at Maastricht. Chapter 1 outlines different perspectives from which to judge the constitutionalisation of the European Union, and poses the problem of whether the more self-consciously open form of constitutional discourse and constitution-making embodied by the Convention experiment can be justified. Chapter 2 addresses the more specific problem of the nature of the 'Constitution' and constitutional legitimacy in the EU, and whether the Convention should be conceived as a moment of founding of the EU polity or as part of a more diffuse process of constitutionalisation. Part I is therefore an attempt to contextualise the Convention in the broader discourse of European constitutionalism. In doing so, it argues two things. First, that seeing the Convention as an isolated moment, as many of the critics and some of the supporters tend to do, misses the point that constitution-building in Europe has been an ongoing process for some time, and that this is only one of the forms that it takes. Second, however, that there is no inevitability to formalising the constitutional *acquis* in a written document, but that such a move inevitably carries an interpretation of the future of the integration process, which in Europe remains a deeply contested issue.

Part II is more directly an analysis of the Convention itself. Chapter 3 offers a more historical contextualisation of the Convention, by showing how it relates to previous episodes of constitution- (and treaty-) making in the European Union/Communities. Such a foreground of the Convention experiment allows us to understand it as a moment of continuity with the past history of political integration, but also to appreciate the way in which it operates as a rupture of that same history. Chapters 4 and 5 analyse the formation of the Convention and the way in which it operated. Chapter 4 concentrates on the way in which the Convention gave body to the political interests of the various components of the European polity, and how this embodiment allowed it to operate politically in between the supranational and intergovernmental institutions of the EU. In spite of falling short of many standards of democratic representation, it is suggested that the Convention offered the opportunity for the process of constitution-making in Europe to become more open and more responsive to a wider range of interests and opinions in European society. Chapter 5 turns the attention to the so-called 'Convention method' both by describing the way in which the Convention deliberated and arrived at its conclusions, and by trying to find out whether such a 'method' has something distinctive in it, which makes the Convention different from past experiences of constitution-making in the EU. In many respects, the 'Convention method' reflects a shift towards a more deliberative and majoritarian, as opposed to bargain-based and intergovernmenal, way of conceiving the constitutionalisation process in the EU. However, its practical application and the political conditions in which the Convention operated were fraught with difficulties and contradictions. Overall, the picture that emerges is one of cautious innovation. The 'Convention method' may have made a mark in the European constitutionalisation process, but it has not yet changed it dramatically.

Part III looks at how the Convention related more generally to European society. It focuses in particular on some of the aspects of diversity characterising the EU, comprising, as it does, many different nations, histories, cultures, religions and languages. The latter is at the centre of Chapter 6, which looks at how the multilingual nature of the EU affected the operations of the Convention, and the behaviour or attitudes of its members. Chapter 7 asks similar questions about the role of gender in the Convention, although it focuses as much on problems of substance as of process, by looking at some of the constitutional provisions discussed in the Convention, which have relevance to the gender issue. Chapters 8 and 9 look at the role that civil society and business organisations played as part of the Convention. Although there were no official members of these organisations in the Convention, the Convention itself provided for some form of representation for such organisations with the aim both of increasing its visibility to European society, and of better reflecting the interests and views of society at large. These chapters assess how successful the Convention was in these two objectives. The final chapter (Chapter 10) of Part III looks at how the Convention dealt with the tricky problem of the values embodied by Europe, and the implications of engaging in this kind of discourse within the present process of constitution-making, insofar as it has the potential of both uniting and dividing the EU polity. From a more substantive perspective, all chapters of Part III offer as much of a mixed assessment of both the operating methods and the results of the Convention as that offered in Part II. Indeed, because of its relative openness and transparency, the Convention better reflected the diversity of European society within the constitutionalisation process, but ultimately this remained a process directed and controlled by the institutional players. Its capacity for innovation remained circumscribed to the form rather than affecting the substance of the Constitution or the democratic legitimacy of the entire process.

Part IV, finally, concludes the book by making an assessment of both the legal and political impact of the Convention. Chapter 11 looks at the way in which the particular moment of constitution-making relates to the more diffuse way in which the EU legal corpus has developed. This chapter returns to some of the problems discussed at the beginning of the book, by raising the question of whether a written constitution is all that there is to the constitutionalisation process. In fact, it suggests that even in its draft form the Constitution interacted with the way in which community legislation and judicial interpretation shape the 'living law' of the EU. The suggestion is that the constitutionalisation process is a fluid and dynamic one, which depends as much on its constitutional formalisation as on the way in which the law is shaped and interpreted by the judges. Chapter 12 deals more directly with the immediate aftermath of the Convention, by analysing the relationship between the Convention and the IGC, and the following (and more dramatic) phase of ratification. It looks at how the work of the Convention impacted on these later phases, and what all this may mean for constitutional politics in the EU. The overall assessment is that in the course of moving from the Convention phase to the IGC, more traditional and intergovernmental practices came to the fore. This was partly inevitable and also a reflection of the mixed nature of the EU, still divided between intergovernmental and supranational *modi operandi*. More ominously, the ratification process highlighted the still unresolved issue of democratic legitimacy in the EU, and how this can be addressed, if at all, at a more constitutional level. This, of course, is an issue on which future events will shape our understanding of the past. We hope, however – and this is partly the rationale for this book – that our understanding of the present may give us some of the intellectual instruments through which to shape the events of the future.

Part I
The Convention as a Moment of EU Constitutional Politics

Introduction to Part I

During the last ten years at least, a considerable literature on constitutional politics and constitutional law has emerged as part of the academic research on the European integration process, contributing to a continuing focus of attention on issues of legitimacy and on the normative underpinnings of the political, legal and administrative system comprising the EU and its Communities. But only in the last four to five years has the issue of constitutional politics become a real political issue in the EU. The decision to establish a Convention for the drafting of the EU Constitution seemed at the time the beginning of European constitutionalism's end-game. Although everyone was aware that there were a number of formidable obstacles along the path – the British referendum being the most obvious candidate for this role – it seemed that the Constitution, or the Constitutional Treaty as it came to be called, would eventually be approved. With the advantage of hindsight, we now know that the path of EU constitutional politics is far more complex than even sceptics were predicting several years ago. Indeed, as already suggested in the Introduction to the book as a whole, it is the intention of this book to show that the Convention should be considered as a 'moment' in a longer and far from linear process of constitutionalisation. The EU 'documentary' constitution may be moribund, and indeed the EU may never have a constitution in its most traditional sense, but the issues that lie behind it and the discussions that have surrounded both its drafting and the halted ratification process are very much alive in Europe.

The main object of Part I is therefore to provide the context within which we can make sense of the 'Convention moment'. This requires a discussion of the nature of constitutional politics in the EU. Chapter 1 starts by addressing the conceptual difficulties that are intrinsic to constitutional politics, particularly in a transnational setting such as that of the European Union. It then goes on to sketch various narratives of how 'constitutional politics' has emerged in the EU. At the centre of these narratives of constitutionalisation there is the question of the *emergence* of a constitutional order and what this entails. Indeed, the identification of what is meant by 'constitutional order' and its main characteristics provides a meaningful battleground for what can be called constitutional politics. The concluding part of Chapter 1 sets up the question of the legitimacy of the constitutional order at a European level. This question is inevitably bound up with the issue of divided sovereignty, which is still the stumbling block for any discussion of legitimacy and democracy in the EU. Whereas many believe that giving a 'documentary' constitution to the EU is a way of cutting the Gordian knot of sovereignty in Europe, this chapter suggests that there is a certain circularity between sovereignty and legitimacy in the EU, and that the very exercise of writing a constitution needs some form of legitimacy.

The issue of what makes the EU constitutional order legitimate is discussed in more detail in Chapter 2, which engages with both the idea of the 'supranational constitution', and that of the normative character of the constitutionalisation process. This implies a discussion of the distinction between *constitutional* and *normal* politics in the European context, and of the sources of constitutional *normativity*. In particular, Chapter 2 focuses on whether the normative force of the constitutional order is the result of the *generative* properties of a certain form of constitutional politics, or whether it depends on the general *nature* of the constitutional order itself. In other words, whether a legitimate constitution for Europe is the direct result of the actions and intentions expressed through a constituent *moment*, or of the *process* through which the constitution (and its application) affects the life of a polity.

The main conclusion at which Chapter 2 arrives is that the constitutional order is the result of the complex way in which 'constitutional moments' and 'constitutional process' interact, and ultimately correct each other. Indeed, the very distinction between 'constitutional' and 'normal' politics is problematic, so that the Convention experiment in the EU cannot be seen as a 'foundation' moment with a legitimacy of its own, but should be judged both according to external criteria of legitimacy, and according to its capacity to contribute to the generation of a European constitutional order. These are the normative grounds against which it may then be possible to analyse the Convention experiment, its genesis, its characteristics, its internal and external dynamics, and its *dénouement*.

1
Constitutional Politics in the European Union

Dario Castiglione

One of the problems, perhaps the main problem, that the 'Convention on the Future of Europe' had to face when it set out to draft a constitution was not so much whether it would succeed in writing a constitution that might satisfy the majorities of European citizens and all member states; but whether it *could* write a constitution at all. The original sin of European constitutionalism is that it tries to apply categories (those of the constitutional discourse) that have been developed for polities which have a fundamental element of political 'unity', even though they can take the form of either centralised or federal states. The European Union and its preceding institutional expressions started life, instead, as a form of international co-operation. As such, there is an underlying resistance to the very idea of a fundamental political 'unity' between the different members of such an organisation. In this sense, the challenges that the Convention faced were both practical and theoretical, empirical and normative.

Indeed, for some time legal philosophers, political theorists, theoretically inclined lawyers and political scientists have contributed to shaping a normative vocabulary and sharpening the analytical tools for coming to terms with the fundamental ambivalence of political integration. The central question, as already indicated, is that the European integration process has come to symbolise the crisis of one of the central categories on which modern political theorising has rested since Hobbes's time, namely the distinction between the kinds of relationships that apply *within* a state and those that apply *between* states. The partial breaking down of such a distinction has important consequences for how we think of politics itself and of its interlocking domains.

It is for these reasons that an understanding of the Convention consists not only in questioning whether writing the EU constitution was a way of making the European Union more legitimate, efficient and democratic; but also whether the very writing of an EU constitution was either possible or legitimate in the first place. We start, accordingly, by trying to clarify some of the central categories that apply to constitutional politics in the EU.

11

The meaning of constitutional politics

If one examines the current uses circulating in the different academic branches of literature on the European Union, one finds that 'constitutional politics' has no settled meaning. One of the available meanings takes constitutional politics to be an aspect of 'judicial power' (Stone Sweet, 2000). This derives from the defining role that the written constitution and the process of judicial review of legislation have acquired in many modern democracies, following in particular the American model, but with reference also to a number of European *Rechtsstaat* traditions. The role that constitutional courts and the process of constitutional interpretation and adjudication play in limiting and redirecting legislation and policy-making can be considered intrinsically *political*, and studied as a form of *politics*. This understanding of constitutional politics therefore focuses on the way in which political issues and policy-making are influenced by the judicial process and by judicial actors, through means and modes of arguing that are typical of the judicial process and system, but that, insofar as they operate on substantive policies, can be considered political in the narrow sense, as determining the substance of the decisions and not just offering a 'frame' or the 'rules of the game' for arriving at the decisions themselves.

A second meaning of constitutional politics takes a reverse view of the relationship between constitutional reality and politics by looking at ways in which political action contributes to the creation of a stable structure of rules, norms and expectations within which ordinary politics operates. The focus here is on the capacity that political decisions and circumstances have to determine a higher order of rules and to produce a constitutional structure, even when this is not formalised as such.

A third meaning, finally, identifies constitutional politics with the more specific processes of constitution making and constitutional transformation, and it looks at the particular qualities and normative purchase that political action has, or needs to have, in order to produce a higher set of rules and laws.

These three meanings of constitutional politics are not in complete opposition to each other; indeed, they occasionally tend to coincide. For instance, the exercise of judicial power can be seen as a form of constitution making. In its turn, constitution making is considered to be successful only if and when political action generates the background conditions within which a more formalised document or set of norms acquire true constitutional status. As we shall see in the course of our discussion, all three meanings are at play in the way in which the EU has become consolidated in some kind of polity.

The ambiguous meaning of 'constitutional politics' partly reflects ambiguities in the use of ideas of 'constitutionalism' and the 'constitution'. In one sense, constitutionalism is a modern political doctrine. It refers to a series of principled arguments for the limitation of political power in general and of a government's sway over the life and rights of citizens in particular. Although one may conceive the means for the limitation of political power in many different ways, in the course of the last two centuries these limitations and their underlying principles have been embodied in the institutions and practices of the modern constitutional state, with a written constitutional text at their centre (Castiglione, 1995, 1996). By constitutionalism, in a second sense, one can thus refer to the complex of institutions that characterises a constitutional regime; a form of state, and an organisation of government, that is, that embodies the principles of constitutionalism. This double meaning is very similar to that which applies in the case of the term 'socialism', which is used to indicate either the ideology or the political regime – and occasionally both at the same time. There remain, however, some important differences between the analytical use of constitutionalism as a regime, and its normative meaning, so that discussions of European constitutionalism and its transformations (Weiler, 1999), may be taken to refer to either the introduction of some kind of constitutional charter and constitutional law in the EU system of governance, or to a discussion of what kind of public philosophy should guide such a form of governance.

Although it would at first appear less evident, the ambivalence in the uses of the term 'constitutionalism' also applies to the understanding of the constitution itself. In a more obvious sense a constitution is, as Paine said, 'a thing . . . in fact': something that has 'a visible form', and can be quoted 'article by article' (1989: 81). But of course, Paine was here making a point against the ancient and unwritten tradition of English constitutionalism. Even though, in its modern sense, the constitution is usually intended as a document setting out the higher law (or 'constitutive' rules) of a state, by reference to the constitution a number of other 'things' are also intended, such as the act through which something is constituted, the basic norm according to which other laws and legislation can be judged, and the structure or inner characteristics defining a political order.

Such a variety of meanings suggests that different roles are attributed to the constitution within organised legal and political systems, and that such roles can be looked at either analytically, as having a *function* within the system, or normatively, as determining how the system *ought to* work. Thus, to agree on what a constitution is or does may not be that easy, even when one takes it to be the linchpin on which the modern constitutional state rests. This distinction between the functional and normative role of the constitution is partly the basis of the two narratives of constitutional politics identified in this chapter, one more concerned with the way in the which the EU has acquired a constitutional order, the other more attentive to the legitimacy of such a constitutional order.

There is, of course, as mentioned at the beginning, the added complication that the EU, and the other institutional forms in which European integration has temporarily crystallised over the past fifty years, cannot readily be conceived as having state properties. At least, this is true when we think of the state in a traditional way, as consisting (in broadly Weberian terms) in a unified territorial entity, where the central authority exercises a legal monopoly of power, and the citizenry accepts such an exercise as having some form of legitimacy (i.e. where power does not rest on force alone). In modern constitutional democracies, the constitution (in its various meanings) is said to play a number of important roles. One such is that of legitimating power, insofar as it seems to authorise it. A second one is that of conferring unity to the legal and political system, by acting as the crucial link between these two systems of social organisation (Luhmann, 1996). A third one is that of ensuring the loyalty of the citizens, by offering itself as a cultural and normative point of reference for the citizens' allegiance to the political system and their identification with the political community.

In each of these three roles, however, the capacity of the constitution to perform those functions is seen as dependent on the fact that there is some form of unified structure of power that the constitution helps to put together and organise in a hierarchical arrangement. This is precisely what is understood to be lacking at the European level, where certainly at the beginning of the integration process, and arguably still nowadays, authorisation, legitimacy, integration, allegiance and enforcement are fundamentally mediated by the member states. Because of this, the EU reflects the fragmented structure of power typical of the international system, and not (or not yet) the more unified and homogeneous one of the constitutional state. In order to talk meaningfully of constitutional politics in the EU (in either its functional or normative version), it is therefore necessary to make some sense of the divided image of the EU, as both an international organisation and a polity in the making. This is the issue which EU constitutional politics cannot avoid.

The emergence of the European constitutional order

One way, the most obvious one, of telling the story of constitutional politics in the EC/EU is to look at how the European constitutional order has come to life. Or, as Alec Stone Sweet has put it, how has it happened that the EC/EU has metamorphosed 'from an international regime, founded on the precepts of international law, into a multi-tiered, quasi federal polity' (2000: 160)? This is hardly an uncontested fact, but even those who embrace the view that EU politics still operates as an international law regime (Grimm, 1995), or that EU decision-making is in essence intergovernmental (Moravcsik, 1999), must offer some account of the consolidated nature of the Community legal and institutional order, and of what Weiler has described as the virtual foreclosure to member states of the *exit* option from Community obligations (1999: 31).

Weiler himself has illustrated the emergence of European constitutionalism, meant as a constitutional regime, by looking at its 'geology', at how it was first conceptualised from a number of practical and theoretical perspectives

(1999: 221–37). Following, in a slightly modified form, Weiler's own characterisation of what he considers the three main approaches during the foundational phase, we here distinguish between historical (an adaptation of what Weiler calls a 'doctrine' approach), legal and political narratives of the emergence of the European constitutional order. These three narratives offer a complex view of European constitutionalisation. We shall look at them in reverse order.

The neo-functionalist narrative of the European supranational order

The political science narrative is probably the least self-consciously constitutional of these three readings, but it offered the first sustained attempt to identify a new kind of order, as this was emerging from the European integration process. This version of the constitutionalisation narrative developed through a series of, often competing, 'grand theories' of European integration, starting with the intellectual breakthrough represented by neo-functionalism (Haas, 1958). This is not the place to reassess that theory and its intellectual history, but from a more specific constitutional perspective, its contribution can be summarised under several aspects.

Neo-functionalism entrenched the idea that there was a new, supranational dimension to politics. Interest formation and mediation were no longer taking shape exclusively within the two distinct, but mutually supportive sites of national statehood and the international arena. Moreover, the supranational dimension was not characterised by domination, as in the cases of imperial and colonial relationships, but it was emerging from the interactions of separate social and institutional actors. Such actors operated with a certain degree of autonomy from the national context, and they found it convenient to think of their interests and of the scope of their actions as something reaching beyond the nation-state. As part of their actions, they developed a series of connections with other groups and institutions from other nations, who were similarly operating with a more regional political context in mind. Furthermore, neo-functional theories and analyses propped up the idea of the new supranational dimension by suggesting that it had a dynamic of its own based on the concept of 'spillovers', and that its emergence was further reinforced by the very fact that it produced (and empowered) new institutional actors operating at the supranational level. Finally, both the mechanisms of functional development and adaptation, and the relative autonomy attributed to the supranational institutions overseeing integration, became part of a minoritarian, but self-conscious, federal strategy for the promotion of the supranational level as an important, if not the dominant, political arena.

The partial demise of neo-functionalism, following a number of sustained attacks on some of its central tenets (Moravcsik, 1999; Milward, 2000) and the realisation that its teleology of integration was not consistently and unequivocally sustained either by empirical analysis or general political developments, should not detract from the fact that neo-functionalism contributed to the conceptualisation of the integration process, making this and the European institutions specific objects of analysis. Such analysis has since been carried forward through other methodological perspectives which, though rejecting some of the fundamental premises and guiding concepts of neo-functionalism, have nonetheless taken seriously the emergence of a supranational space and the autonomous role played by some of the European institutions. Neo-institutionalism, multi-level governance, and in a way constructivism, have offered a more nuanced way of conceiving the interactions between the national and the supranational levels, and how it is this mixture of levels, of institutional and normative constraints, and of competing constructions of political meaning that determines the constitutional underpinning of politics in the EU and the countries comprising it.

Judicial constitutionalisation

In spite of the increasing attention showed by political scientists to the structural elements in European integration and politics, a constitutional discourse was relatively slow to emerge in this literature. This may have something to do with the general inattention towards constitutional matters in much of political science and political theory for several decades after the middle of the twentieth century (Bellamy and Castiglione, 1996). Not so amongst the lawyers. The second, and arguably the most influential constitutional narrative, is the one focused on the emergence of a new legal order at the European level, and how particularly the European Court of Justice was instrumental in fixing both its character and the way in which such a supranational legal order related to that of the member states.

The story of the so-called 'judicial constitutionalisation' has been told many times, and in a variety of forms, but its basic outline is undisputed (though its significance remains contested). At the centre of this narrative of constitutionalisation there is the action of the European Court of Justice (ECJ) and how this, in the often quoted words of Eric Stein, 'fashioned a constitutional framework for a federal-type structure', while working in 'benign neglect' from its basis in 'the fairyland Duchy of Luxembourg' (1981: 1). The constitutional order, in this case, is not (at least on the face of it) the product of a slow evolutionary process, as conceived from a neo-functionalist perspective; nor is it the sedimentation of institutional logics and the way in which these both constrain and produce path-dependency. The constitutional order emerges instead as the by-product of a piecemeal, but purposive process of rationalisation of the legal system through case law, in which the Court plays a pivotal role in its dealings with private litigants and national courts.

The assumption here is that the *de facto* legal system emerging from the integration process, the *acquis communautaire*, was given constitutional shape by the establishment of a series of ordering principles of European jurisprudence. These principles are usually identified as the *supremacy*, and the *direct effect* doctrines (De Witte, 1999); though one may also add *pre-emption* and the protection of human rights (Mancini, 2000: 7–14; Weiler, 1999: 22–5), and in a later period *indirect effect*, and *governmental liability* (Stone Sweet, 2000: 163). Most of these doctrines are associated with particular legal cases and how the ECJ's rulings over them have become the cornerstones of the new constitutional order.

To deal only briefly with *supremacy* and *direct effect*: the doctrine of *supremacy*, first established in *Costa v ENEL* (ECJ, 1964), maintains that community law has primacy over national law in view of the obligations that member states have incurred through agreements signed with other member states at the European level, and that national legislators cannot therefore legislate in a manner that is inconsistent with such agreements, while national judges have a 'duty to disapply' (De Witte, 1999: 190) laws that may undermine such binding agreements. The doctrine of *direct effect*, first formulated in the *Van Gend en Loos* case (ECJ, 1963) just before the *Costa* case, established instead the applicability at the national level of various Community legislative and regulative acts ('regulations', 'treaty provisions' and 'directives'). This would hold true even in those cases where national authorities either failed to make provisions for such application in a reasonable time, or where the national law clashed with the spirit of the directives and regulations. Although the two rulings of the ECJ (and others that have followed along the same path) remain controversial in their justification, their combined effect has been to suggest that there is a common legal order at the European level and that this has a kind of hierarchical structure that makes it similar to that which applies at the national level.

There is an interesting ambivalence in this understanding of the judicial constitutionalisation of the EU. On the one hand, it is clear that the constitutional order so conceived, as a coherent system organised around a number of key principles and doctrines, is the product of 'judicial creativeness'; on the other hand, the action of the ECJ is presented as nothing more than the rational interpretation and coherent systematisation of principles already included in the acts and intentions of the national governments and the political actors who promoted and signed the EC/EU founding Treaties, thus giving form and direction to the process of integration. The fact, of course, is that the difference between judicial 'creativeness' and judicial 'rationalisation' depends on how one interprets what Stein called 'benign neglect', and on whether one assumes that such neglect has persisted over time, from the foundational phase of the 1960s and 1970s until nowadays (cf. also Weiler, 1999: 191–2; De Witte, 1999: 194–8).

The relationship between the kind of constitutional jurisprudence defined by the ECJ, and the way in which this has been viewed by member states' governments and parliaments, as well as by ordinary and constitutional courts at the national level, is an exceedingly complex story; but posing the problem in these terms makes it clear that the view of judicial constitutionalisation as the single-handed product of the ECJ is an over-simplification into which both supporters and critics occasionally tend to fall. In any case, the view of the Court as the actor unpacking the logical implications of the intentions of the Treaties' signatories, and of the 'fact' that the Treaties themselves have created 'a Community of unlimited duration', with 'real powers stemming from a limitation of sovereignty or transfer of powers from the States to the Community' (ECJ, 1964: 593), is something that must necessarily rest on a particular reading of the history of treaty-making in the EC/EU. This is indeed the third narrative that was referred to at the beginning – the one dealing with the chronicle of the formal and political acts through which member states have locked themselves into the integration process.

From the treaties to the constitution?

At the centre of this narrative there is the conceptual distinction between *treaty* and *constitution*, an issue to which we shall return later from a more theoretical perspective. For the time being, we may look at the issue from a more historical perspective. Indeed, such a historical reconstruction is at the centre of Chapter 3.[1] Here, we shall only attempt a summary overview to assess its broad significance. The historical view seems to suggest that constitutional development in the EU/EC should be conceived as a linear evolution from 'treaty' to 'constitution', as the effect of cumulative developments from economic to political integration. In fact, a closer examination of the various phases seems to undermine such an image, offering a much more complex picture of changes and continuities.

The nature of the organisational structure within which to frame the process of European peaceful co-operation after the Second World War was a matter of contention and experiment from the very beginning. The rhetorical appeal to the idea of a 'constitution' was there from the outset. This emerged in between the lines of numerous official documents and declarations, and motivated a number of failed attempts to establish a more solid ground for political co-operation. In spite of the difficulty that the more radical federal project encountered in the Europe of the 1950s, the Treaty of Rome made explicit reference to the aim of an 'ever closer union', thus making the point that its underlying aspiration went beyond that of a common international treaty. Such a reading of the early beginnings paints a picture of competing projects rather than slow piecemeal evolution, as indicated by the neo-functionalist narrative. One the one hand there was the consolidation of federal aspirations, which had already emerged in interwar Europe; and on the other, the political realism of member states' governments and political elites at large, who by the end of the 1950s saw with increasing scepticism some of the federal ambitions underlying co-operation, which they also perceived as a threat to their own positions of power.

The evident impracticability of a federal project contributed to the shifting of the focus of economic co-operation towards more functional instruments and piecemeal agreements. This, however, did not stop the formation of a basic institutional structure mixing intergovernmental and supranational institutions, a structure that has remained in place to the present day. Increasingly, the process of treaty-creation saw the involvement of other political actors besides national governments. This process acquired a somewhat self-reflexive nature, and gave voice to supranational interests as these became progressively embodied by the European institutions. So, both the institutional structure and the way in which the integration process progressed became a site for the redefinition of the public interest from an exclusively national basis to one where supranational elements started intruding.

Although for a long period throughout the 1970s and part of the 1980s no new major 'constitutional' initiative seemed to emerge, the period was one of development and consolidation of the supranational dimension. Issues like the extension of qualified majority voting, the role played by the more distinctively elected institutions such as the Parliament, the more explicit recognition of a solidaristic component in the enlargement of the communitarian institutions to other European countries, or the increasing perception that the integration project needed to get closer to the citizens – all such issues testify to the fact that there was more to the EC than a series of intergovernmental treaties. The very logic of market integration seemed to require the (partial) abandonment of the unanimity principle, and the construction of a European-wide collective interest in a number of policy areas. As a consequence of such attempts at redefining the boundaries within which to consider common interests and hence common policies, the question of the democratic nature of representation in the European institutions started to emerge as a widely discussed issue. Moreover, the introduction of direct elections to the European Parliament in 1979 rather paradoxically made it more, rather than less, evident that there were unresolved questions both of political representation and political competence within the institutional structure of the Community. Paradoxically, the more a constitutional dimension was put in place, the more it seemed that there was a constitutional gap (hence a gap of legitimacy) at the centre of the EU/EC.

By the end of the 1980s, the introduction of the Single European Act, and the rapidly changing geo-political configuration of Europe, with the collapse of the Soviet regimes, significantly accelerated the series of intergovernmental conferences and treaty reforms, which in the past two decades have profoundly changed the relationship between the EU, the member states and European citizens. From the perspective of the more historical narrative that we are here considering, the intergovernmental conferences became, or at least started to be perceived as, the true markers of constitutional development in the EU. Over time, the IGCs have become events where some form of genuine negotiation and confrontation over different visions of the future of Europe have started taking place amidst the more traditional – yet inevitable – low-level bargaining and log-rolling. By the time the upheavals of 1989 and the foundation of a new 'European Union' in the early 1990s had forced a more open 'constitutional' phase onto the European agenda, European integration had finally (and perhaps irrevocably) become an issue of genuine political contestation in almost all member states. In this context, the Maastricht ratification crisis marked the end of the permissive consensus, and output legitimacy as the quasi-exclusive basis for an elite-driven integration process, even though, as had happened in previous occasions, this did not produce a clear move towards a more defined constitutional project. At Maastricht, and at the following IGCs, the contours of the project for political integration remained undefined; even though monetary unification, the formation of a definite common framework for macro-economic policy, and enlargement to the post-communist countries provided a historical opportunity for doing so.

In spite of all this, and in spite of the more cautious attitudes triggered by the popular reactions to Maastricht, the age of constitutional politics seemed to have finally dawned on Europe. Thus, a *political* debate on the 'future of Europe' became inevitable, something that was reflected in the not always successful attempts to broaden participation in the process of institutional reform of the Union. Such an attempt could be considered as a way of finding new forms of ex-ante legitimacy for constitutional politics in the EU. This move led to the Cologne Summit, in 1999, to set up a new body (later called a 'Convention') to draft the EU Charter of Fundamental Rights; and eventually to the Laeken Declaration setting up the 'Convention on the Future of Europe', with the task of defining the EU's constitutional agenda. One of the key moments of this more 'historical' narrative of European constitutionalisation remains of course Joschka Fischer's speech at the Humboldt University in May 2000, when the then German Foreign Minister forcefully proposed an overtly 'constitutional' path for the future of Europe. This was followed by a series of other political speeches along the same lines, making sure that the Constitution had become a political, and not simply an academic issue.

Fifty years after the early discussions about some form of political integration, the European political debate had come full circle and acknowledged the need for an explicit 'constitution' within which to inscribe the integration process. The main difference, this time, was the recognition, at least in the public rhetoric, that such a development would need some form of direct democratic legitimacy. This could partly be achieved ex-ante, through the Convention process; and ex-post through popular or parliamentary ratification. With the Laeken Declaration, the EU entered into the most explicitly constitutional phase of its development yet. It is at this juncture – meant here in conceptual rather than merely historical terms – that the issue becomes no longer that of the nature and effects of the constitutionalisation process, but that of its legitimacy. It is to this that we now turn.

The supranational constitution and its legitimacy

As the 'historical' reading of the constitutionalisation narrative suggests, the ideas of constitutionalism and of the constitution were present in the political debate from the very beginning of the integration process. Nevertheless, it took some time for the notion that the EC/EU had acquired some kind of, at least functional, constitution to be accepted. Weiler (1999: 3–9), for one, has remarked on this inversion of the traditional way of conceiving modern constitutionalism (but not, of course, of 'ancient' ideas of the constitution), by figuratively making use of the biblical passage in Exodus 24:7, where the people of Israel are said to have declared their acceptance of the book of Covenant with the words: 'we will do, and hearken'. There would seem to be some incongruence in ante-posing the deeds ('we will do') to the act of listening and declaring one's willingness to obey ('and hearken'). In Weiler's metaphor, the 'doing' stands for the process of material constitutionalisation, while the 'hearkening' represents the legitimate way in which a constitutional order is established: 'the deliberative process of listening, debating, and understanding' (1999: 5). This debate over the sources of legitimacy is at the core of the much debated question on whether a 'supranational constitution' is possible.

Such a question overlaps with the debate on the 'democratic deficit' (for a recent statement on this, cf. Føllesdal and Hix, 2005) and with what has become the standard account of the way in which the democratic deficit in the EU has emerged as a consequence of the partial exhaustion, or inadequacy, of its output form of legitimacy (Scharpf, 1999; Beetham and Lord, 1998). Indeed, the idea of legitimacy has played an increasingly important role as a way of linking the theoretical-normative debates with the reality of ongoing integration (Bellamy and Castiglione, 2003).

At least since the early 1970s the question has been asked of how the current system or even further integration could be justified, in particular in the face of decreasing public support as measured by opinion polls. The realisation grew that, apart from successful policy delivery (output legitimacy), democratic input and probably some kind of social recognition (identification) were also needed to maintain the legitimacy of the emerging European polity. Informal constitutionalisation (through the ECJ or the gradual institutionalisation of certain practices) was increasingly seen as playing an ambiguous role in the EU's 'quest for legitimacy' (De Búrca, 1996). On the one hand, it was seen as necessary to develop and consolidate the system, thus ensuring its continuous functioning. On the other hand, it was criticised for excluding and further alienating the citizens from the process of integration, also provoking the occasional backlash from the member states as the guardians of the democratic interests of their citizens. As more questions were raised on how to ensure that a European-wide polity could be normatively legitimate, the very idea of democratic legitimacy in supranational conditions came under scrutiny. The same question obviously applied to democratic constitutionalism and the constitution. Indeed, the debate over the nature of democratic legitimacy in the EU has inevitably got entangled with the question of whether Europe needed a written constitution (Habermas, 2001).

Does Europe need a constitution?

In a strange way, the discussion about writing the European constitution took over from where the narrative of the neo-functionalists floundered, offering a moment of closure to the integration process as it had been described by the neo-functionalists. The constitution was an obvious, and theoretically unproblematic, aim for those who conceived the future of Europe in federal terms. Indeed, the constitution seemed to provide some 'meaning and purpose' (Nuotio, 2004) to the integration process, determining once and for all what has been called its *finalité* (to this, we shall return in the next chapter). Since many identified the *finalité* of the European integration process with the establishment of a new form of statehood at a supranational level, the constitution was conceived as the sanctioning of the idea that political integration was, on the whole, complete. By fixing the structure of internal power, assigning precise competences at national and supranational level, and between the various European institutions, the constitution would establish a new architecture of sovereignty within the EU and its member states. From such a perspective, the constitution would contribute to making the EU more legitimate, efficient and democratic. But if the constitution is meant to confer legitimacy to the EU as a state-like entity, where does the legitimacy of the constitution itself come from? The normative narrative of constitutional politics becomes therefore embroiled with the discussion of what is the nature and legitimacy of the 'constitution' in supranational conditions.[2]

This discussion has developed along two parallel lines of dispute, two sides, so to speak, of the same coin, involving, on the one hand, the identification of the 'constituent power' in the EU constitutional order, and, on the other, the characterisation of the nature of the foundational document of such an order: whether this should be regarded as a 'treaty' between states, or as a 'constitution' of the European people. The German jurist Dieter Grimm has perhaps been the most authoritative and consistent voice arguing against the view that the European Union can, at this stage of its development, meaningfully give itself a constitution (Grimm, 1995). Grimm remarks that the emergence of modern constitutions is intrinsically linked to the way in which positive law operates at two levels over the public domain. The first level establishes the legitimate source of state power and regulates the operations of government. The second level follows from the exercise of state power itself, but it acquires force insofar as state power has been bound by the rules set down at the first level. Grimm argues that this is not the way in which Community law has operated over the years, and that any attempt to constitutionalise it comes up against the intractable question of who are the 'masters' of the Treaty, the ultimate repositories of sovereignty in the EU legal and political system, i.e. the true constituent power. According to Grimm, the 'constituent power' remains with the member states, who, as actors within an international system, are not subject to the constitutional discipline typical of first- and second-order positive law, as it applies in constitutional states, where instead the constituent power dissolves itself into the 'constituted powers' as a result of the creation of a constitutional order. Grimm's argument here is that, due to the dominance of the separate state actors, the EU legal space lacks the distinctive structural properties of constitutional law. Attempts to introduce some form of constitutionalisation remain partial and superficial until the EU can claim some form of self-sufficient statehood *independently from the member states*. According to this view, the European constitution cannot legitimate European statehood and democracy, since it itself presupposes some form of established statehood.

Even if we assume that Grimm is right in his analysis of the structural limits to be overcome in order for the EU to have a constitution, it could be argued that the post-Laeken process and the 'Treaty establishing a Constitution for Europe' were meant to create the background political conditions for constitutional politics and constitutional law. This raises the other point of controversy, intriguingly captured by the decision made in the Convention to mix the languages of international and constitutional law by referring to the agreed document as both a 'treaty' and a 'constitution', or as they put it: a treaty establishing a constitution, where it remains unclear where the 'text' of the treaty ends and that of the constitution starts. This linguistic solution, however, only highlights the problem. As suggested by De Witte (2004a), a close exegetical analysis of the language of the approved text, and of the formal status of the document itself, seems to support the case that the way in which the document was both conceived and formulated is entirely within the tradition and language of international treaty-making, showing the clear intention of the drafters to confirm, rather than weaken, the position of the member states as the 'High Contracting Parties', who have the power to bind themselves to the agreements set up in the Treaty, within the limits set by their own *separate* constitutional orders. Such evidence, however, does not in itself seem conclusive, for there is nothing to prevent the possibility that a treaty may become the basis for a self-contained constitutional order, as happened in the German case towards the end of the nineteenth century. In this respect, the intentions of the framers are of limited guidance. In fact, it is part of the 'constitutionalisation' thesis to suggest that the passage from an international regime to a constitutional order has been on the whole unintended.

But there is another way of putting the sceptical argument against a federal Europe and against the idea that the EU is already in the position to give itself a constitution. This is generally known as the 'No-demos' thesis (Weiler, 1999). Simply put, this argument suggests that without some kind of unified people there cannot be democracy – and therefore that any European state without a European people would necessarily be undemocratic. The issues commonly raised in relation to the 'No-demos' thesis are of three kinds. One concerns the deliberative presuppositions for democracy to operate. Such presuppositions comprise a diffuse and fairly integrated European public sphere, a working representative system at the European level, and even more obviously the ability to communicate and understand each other through a shared language. Although in some limited and/or rudimentary forms, these elements are already present in the EU, it is difficult to see how such conditions can operate beyond the narrow circle of European elites, something that would make it difficult for a European-wide political system to have a genuine popular character.

The second issue raised by the 'No-demos' thesis concerns the way in which, in a democracy, people are prepared to accept collective decisions that have redistributive implications out of a sense of solidarity with the other members of the community. The nature and boundary of such solidarity are strongly contested, but historically in Europe democratic citizenship has developed in parallel to a solidaristic conception of the national community. A working democracy at the European level would therefore need some form of connective solidarity to ensure that people were willing to accept as legitimate the application of the majoritarian principle across a series of important policy decisions.

The third issue, finally, is that of cultural diversity. Whereas the experience of democracy within the nation-state has tended to coincide with a certain homogeneity of the people[3] – or, more often, with a nation-building project, which relied on processes of democracy- and citizenship-formation in order to get firmly established – in the EU, cultural and national diversity is both pervasive and tends to be considered a value worthy of being preserved rather than overcome.

In each of its forms, the 'No-demos' thesis once again proposes the question of sovereignty and the unresolved (perhaps unsolvable) question of the nature and role of the constituent power.[4] In the experience of national constitutionalism, the ultimate appeal to the demos, as both a unitary and self-constituting subject ('We, the people'), has played an important role as the alleged source of, and the legitimating influence over, the exercise of power by the political and legal institutions – the 'constituted powers'. The question is whether this self-constituting model can be reproduced at a European level, in a situation in which the national demoi still cling both to the separateness of their interests and to demands for the recognition of their socio-cultural differences.

It is here that the issue of the 'supranational constitution' comes into its own. In other terms, if one does not start from the assumption that a quasi-federal structure is the natural *telos* of the integration process, how is it possible for constitutional politics to operate at a supranational level?[5] The answer to this question has taken two main forms, which represent the two divergent readings of the 'supranational constitution'. One reading concentrates on the idea that the making of the constitution is the result of a *constitutional moment*; the other reading emphasises the idea of the constitution as the result of a *process* of continuous negotiation and interpretation of constitutional law and of the underlying constitutional order – a process that requires time and that operates at different levels. The issue of the legitimacy of the European constitution must therefore confront the crucial question regarding the legitimate way of arriving at such a constitution under the conditions of supranational politics.

Notes

1. For this reconstruction, I am indebted to Justus Schönlau.
2. From a federalist perspective, the legitimacy of the constitution is not a real problem, or at least its legitimacy is no different from that one may attribute to the constitution of a state. There is here a difference between those who think that European statehood can be easily disjointed from nationhood, and that European democracy and constitutionalism therefore require a federal-like structure (Mancini, 2000: xxvi), and those who take more seriously the conundrum of constitutionalising a supranational entity.
3. This homogeneity is very often idealised and there are many examples of states in Europe which do not follow this model, such as Belgium, Switzerland, Spain and the UK.
4. The circularity that the issue of 'constituent power' poses to constitutionalism is similar to that raised by the possibility of establishing a democracy according to democratic means. In either case, something prior and *discontinuous* seems to be presupposed in order to establish a constitutional or a democratic regime.
5. This does not exclude the possibility that Europe's supranational constitution may resemble traditional federal constitutions. In fact, this is very likely. The issue here is not one of substance but of legitimacy. Discussions about the supranational constitution, even when they are in favour of a European constitution, start from the assumption that this cannot be justified on the basis of an already established statehood at the European level.

2
Constitutional Moment or Constitutional Process?

Dario Castiglione

The European Union at a 'crossroads' has been a recurrent image in the European constitutional debate at least since Maastricht. It was used in the Laeken Declaration – and of course it has been used since, particularly during the 'reflection period' after the French and Dutch 'no' to the Constitutional Treaty. It is obviously meant to imply that the European Union has reached a point at which it urgently needs to decide on its future institutional path.[1] Miguel Maduro (2003: 74–102) has ironically evoked a very similar image by comparing Europe to Alice in Wonderland, when she asks the Cheshire Cat what road to take: 'That depends on where you want to go' is the Cat's answer. The question is indeed whether Europe knows where it wants to go.[2] In the eyes of many, the Constitution was intended to give such a direction.

But in truth the crossroads image is a misleading one, for it implies the need to march on in some direction, besides assuming that each of these directions will lead to some definite destination. Both assumptions are contested. With regard to the former, the idea of a continuous march forward is generally known as the 'bicycle theory', for which to stop pedalling means falling. From a socio-economic perspective, there may be a grain of truth in this; for the single economic market and the introduction of a common currency have created a context that requires both increasing convergence on a number of rules and conditions, and common management policies (Hirst, 1995: 47). But in a broader sense, increasing forms of political integration are neither inevitable nor unequivocally desirable.

From an analytical perspective, and in contrast with the bicycle analogy, it can be argued that the European Union has already acquired a more or less definite institutional shape, which can be sustained in time – or at least for a considerable amount of time. From a more normative perspective, it is not unreasonable to maintain that there are as many dangers as opportunities in the Union's eventual evolution towards a more definite state-form.[3] Such a transformation may be unfeasible, as supporters of the 'no-demos, no democracy' theory clearly imply. And even if feasible, it may be considered undesirable; for it may risk both weakening the institutions of democratic

26

accountability, and undermining valuable differences between countries, while ultimately paving the way for commercial homogenisation and over-bureaucratic centralisation.

No less contestable and contested are the assumptions made on the possible end-states of the process of European integration. These are often imagined as either a federal or a con-federal state. But, so far, the European process has been both open with regard to the forms of integration, and indeterminate in relation to its historical movement. This reinforces the impression, partly discussed in the previous chapter, that some of the traditional concepts and categories of our political language have exhausted their usefulness, with the effect that, while we struggle to understand the nature and direction of the European march – or in some people's view, of the present status quo (Weiler, 2003a; Moravcsik, 2002b) – we ought to revise the conceptual instruments through which we interpret it.

As indicated in Chapter 1, this is the case with the idea of a 'supranational constitution', and with whether its legitimacy depends more on a 'constitutive' act as expressed in a constitutional moment, or in the more processual ways in which constitutional law offers a normativity framework for the functioning of a polity. Such different interpretations of the intrinsic legitimacy of the constitution in a supranational context naturally affect our interpretation of what the Convention was meant to do and what it actually achieved. They are therefore part of the normative context within which to make sense of what we have called the Convention moment, and as such they are discussed in this chapter.

The idea of *finalité*

It is probably best to start our discussion from the much used, and abused, idea of *finalité politique*. This was at the core of Joschka Fischer's Humboldt University speech, which, as we mentioned in the previous chapter, gave *political* credibility to the constitutional debate. There are different senses in which this idea of 'finality' is deployed in the European debate. Neil Walker has distinguished seven of them. He suggests, however, that each sense refers to different processes, appealing to overlapping normative principles and values (2003). Walker distinguishes between territorial, political, institutional, purposive (of purpose), social, legal and constitutional finality. At least conceptually, territorial finality is easy to understand. There are, of course, disagreements on where to draw Europe's borders. Such disagreements depend as much on geo-political considerations as on different conceptions of the European Union itself. But there is no disputing that for both functional and historical reasons the European Communities first, and the European Union later, were conceived as 'expansive' projects, whose concrete dynamics, however, need halting at some stage.

The other applications of the idea of finality are more problematic. Ideas of finality in both the institutional and legal domains, for instance, are clearly overdrawn. In the European context, both domains have grown piecemeal as the functional outgrowth of a complex series of international treaties and ad hoc policy agreements. The European Union has increasingly developed its own self-referential 'order' (the legal and institutional *acquis*). As this has progressively been rationalised and acknowledged by an increasing number of social and political agents, it has become obvious that some kind of 'final' reorganisation (of the institutional architecture) and simplification (of the large number of legal documents and treatises) are in order. And yet, there is no political society that can fix its political institutions and the power balance between them once and for all; nor is there any democratic society that can fully rationalise and co-ordinate the plurality of legal orders operating within its own borders. Both institutional and legal domains are continuously in flux, determining and being determined by the changing relationships between the polity and the regime aspects of the political community (Bellamy and Castiglione, 2003).

In fact, there seems to be an intrinsic contradiction in the 'language of finality', particularly when one looks at its application to the social and political domains, and to the alleged purposes of the European Union. These three areas of application are intrinsically linked and they cover what is often, and more broadly, intended as *finalité politique*.

In Walker's classification, their respective meaning is more circumscribed. By social finality, he intends the question of whether the different peoples (and nations) of Europe may be able to unite into a single demos. By political finality, he refers to the question of the state-form of the Union, of whether this should be functioning as a confederacy (*Staatenverbund*) or a federation (*Föderation*). This was, after all, the main problem posed by Fischer in his Humboldt speech, echoing the most common understanding of 'finality'. By the finality of purpose, instead, Walker refers both to the general objectives and ideals attributed to the Union, and to its specific areas of policy competence.

The problem with these three kinds of 'finality' is that they present a paradox. On the one hand, the 'language of finality' seems to imply that the quest for either a 'final point' or an encompassing 'aim' is part of the attempt to change the European Union into a self-standing 'state' or political community. On the other hand, it is apparent that in our common understanding of political communities we make reference to neither a 'final point' nor a particular set of 'aims'. The claim that political communities make on their citizens' allegiance is not based on having reached a particular 'point' in their own evolution, nor do they appeal to 'aims' that are extrinsic to their own existence as political communities. Their demand for political and legal obligation is indeed part of them being, either *de facto* or by tacit consent, the 'social unions' and 'communities of fate' within which their citizens are born and engage in viable forms of social and political co-operation.[4] The point here is neither about the grounds for political legitimacy, nor the conditions for a well-ordered society. More narrowly, it is here suggested that there is an inherent contradiction in advocating the evolution of the European Union into a fully-fledged political community while adopting the 'language of finality'. For the latter attributes to the Union instrumental qualities, which are usually associated with secondary associations, whose scope and purposes are subordinate to those of the political community.

This conundrum is perhaps better explained by paying closer attention to a linguistic point, also raised by Walker in a footnote to his piece (2003: 1, n. 2). There is, in fact, a difference of meaning between 'finality' as it is used in the English language and the equivalent term (*finalité, Finalität, finalità*) in most of the other European languages. The latter meanings refer to an 'ultimate aim or purpose', while in the English language 'finality' refers to the 'quality of being final'. Walker suggests that the English meaning has recently intruded into what was the more traditional, and mainly continental debate on the 'ultimate aims and objectives' (*finalité*) of the integration process, by adding to it the sense that the question of integration is now 'apt for final resolution – or . . . as having reached the end game' (2003: 1, n. 2). In his view, this '(mis)translation' has created some equivocation, thus contributing to the polarisation of the debate.

All this is probably true, but the mistranslation also points to something more conceptual. The English meaning of 'something final' carries with it the idea that something is also 'complete and definite'. Moreover, a subordinate meaning of 'finality' in English is that of being a 'final cause'. With respect to this, less colloquial, sense, the difference between English and the other European languages is less marked. Thus, the various meanings seem to combine and reinforce each other, giving to the idea of the 'finality' of the integration process (its aim, its final and functional causes, its definite and most complete state) a distinctively teleological undertone, which turns out to be the truthful philosophy behind the 'language of finality' itself.

There is a further paradox here. It regards the way in which the demands for democratic legitimacy, when presented through the 'language of finality', turn out to be based on the very same premises on which the functionalist method – the Monnet method of making Europe through practical policies and their spillover effects – rested. Although it is now generally agreed that more direct legitimacy should partly substitute the output-based forms of legitimacy associated with the functionalist method, the ends of the integration process remain the same, confirming the impression that these are intrinsically (hence teleologically) inscribed in the process of integration itself. In other words, it is assumed that there was a *telos* driving the European integration process from the very beginning. Direct and functional forms of legitimacy turn out to be different means of an unchanging philosophy of history (Friese and Wagner, 2002). Such an operation tends to idealise, and partly to misrepresent, the nature and history of the functionalist 'method' (Dehousse, 2000). Besides, it proposes a curious view of democratic legitimacy, which forecloses citizens' options by fixing the political agenda in advance of the democratic debate, and predetermines their decision by putting in front of them the stark alternative between either integration or decline (J.H.H. Weiler, 2000: 235–8).[5]

The reason for this paradoxical continuity between functionalism and 'finalist' federalism lies perhaps in the erroneous foreshortening of the view of the various phases of the 'integration' experience, into a single process. This approach fails to distinguish between the conditions and the socio-legal dynamics characterising different phases of the formation period of the European Communities and the Union, particularly those applying to the post-Maastricht period. The latter is inscribed in a new geo-political scenario, which follows from the collapse of the Soviet regime in Eastern and Central Europe, and poses new political demands to the nations and peoples of Europe.[6] As a consequence of this over-compressed view of European integration, the vocabulary of *finalité* (in the more instrumental sense of aims and purposes), which was originally applied to the evolutionary, and functionally determined process of socio-economic integration, has uncritically been grafted onto issues of direct and democratic legitimacy concerning the new demands for greater political co-operation and social solidarity. It is this confusion that lies at the basis of the unresolved paradoxes of the 'language of finality'.

A constitutional moment?

So far, we have not discussed the last type of 'finality' mentioned by Walker: constitutional finality. One reason is that, in a sense, this is derivative from the others, particularly from the central group of social, political and purposive finality. In another sense, constitutional finality – meaning by this the achievement of a constitutional settlement – is, as Walker aptly shows, both a focus and a catalyst for all other forms of finality. It is not surprising, therefore, that the idea of a constitution of Europe has been at the centre both of federal projects of Europe and of the 'language of finality'. And yet, as is obvious, a constitution is a 'beginning' or a foundation moment, rather than a point of arrival. The only sense in which it can be considered as the end of a process is when looked at from a pre-constitutional perspective, as a document or a moment made possible by the coming to maturation of certain historical and political conditions. To be fair, in his Humboldt speech, Fischer did not duck the issue. When talking of the main reforms that the Europe Union needed in order to confront the challenges of the new century, he abandoned the language of finality for that of renewal: 'These . . . reforms . . . will only be able to succeed if *Europe is established anew constitutionally*. In other words, through the realisation of the project of a European constitution' (Fischer, 2000: 27).[7]

We shall return to the temporal ambivalence – as end-results and new beginnings – of constitutions and constitutional moments. For the moment, we shall concentrate on the process of making a constitution from a normative perspective. In other words, we shall move from the question of whether

Europe *needs* a constitution, to what making a constitution *means* for Europe. The political and constitutional debate surrounding the work of the European Convention developed its own dominating image. This was no longer abstract and generic, like the crossroads, but concrete and historically situated: Philadelphia. Was the European Convention the new Philadelphia? The question normally points at two other distinct questions. More directly: Can the European Convention have the same kind of impact that Philadelphia had on the making of the United States? Somewhat implicitly: Can the European Constitution start a new constitutional model, as the American Constitution did more than two hundred years ago? Here we shall concentrate on the former question, but, as will emerge below, the answer one gives to it partly depends on issues that have to do with the latter.

But to proceed in order, we need first to clear the ground of a number of confusions that the comparison with Philadelphia gives rise to. The comparison invites two types of judgements that, though understandable from a political and rhetorical perspective, may be misleading. One concerns the *historical* impact, the other the *product* of the European Convention. The first comparison is misleading because it asks us to compare events of which we already have historical knowledge, and whose effects we are able to judge with hindsight, with other events, of which we can only make a judgement based on the aspirations of the participants.

Moreover, many of the comparisons are usually based on an idealised view of Philadelphia as seen through the eyes of successive American generations. These have often looked back at the work done by the 'founding fathers' at Philadelphia, in the light of the ongoing political process, reshaping constitutional history in their own self-image in the attempt to find a narrative for American political identity. The 'meaning' of Philadelphia is therefore a *historically* constructed meaning, which transcends the events of the time, while the 'meaning' of the European Convention is still in the making. The second comparison, that between the text of the American Constitution as it was approved at Philadelphia and the Constitutional Treaty drafted by the European Convention, is also misleading from a historical perspective. The two texts emerge from different sets of circumstances and operate in very different institutional, legal and cultural contexts: both geographically and historically. To assume that texts so far apart in time, space and purpose should have similar systemic properties is rather naive.[8] It reflects a purely idealistic conception of the 'constitution', while overlooking the nature of the specific challenges posed by the constitutionalisation of the European Union.[9]

This said, there are ways of making more meaningful comparisons. These are neither historical nor textual, but normative in character, and mainly concerned with the process of constitution making. Of course, constitution making itself can be examined historically, by paying attention to its originating conditions and to the socio-political dynamics that drive it. It can also be studied descriptively, by analysing the agents involved in it, the instruments and procedures adopted to pursue it, the arguments deployed throughout, and the kind of documents produced by it. Both perspectives offer valuable insights for a normative analysis, but in themselves are inconclusive. Nor are all normative perspectives equally interested in constitution making. Those that resolve the validity of constitution making into either the unmediated exercise of ultimate sovereignty (*pouvoir constituent*), or in the codification of a superior rationality (rightful norms), have little concern for the normativity of the constitution-making process itself. In order to establish a normative framework within which to assess and compare different constitution-making experiences, one needs to start from a more procedural and open-ended conception of constitutional principles and legitimacy. Such a conception takes the constitution-making process more seriously, by assuming that it makes a difference to the normative force (if any) of the constitution.

One particular normative framework through which to judge constitution making is that recently suggested by Bruce Ackerman (and partly endorsed by Rawls) in his interpretation of the American experience as a dualist form of democracy with a two-track law-making process, one for 'normal' and the other for 'constitutional' politics (Ackerman, 1991; Rawls, 1993; Bellamy and Castiglione, 1997). This is a partial re-elaboration of the distinction between 'constituent power' and 'constituted powers' which was elaborated during the constitutional debates during the French Revolution.[10] According to Ackerman, normal politics is mainly oriented towards substantive policy-making, while constitutional politics sets the general legal and constitutional framework within which the polity functions. But for Ackerman the difference is not exclusively, and indeed not particularly, one of substance. There are other important characteristics that need to be in place throughout the various phases of constitutional politics for the higher law-making function to be discharged legitimately and with full credibility. These include a deep, broad and decisive popular mobilisation, capable of articulating its transformative project in the language of public reason; a sustained period of public deliberation; and the elaboration of a coherent set of principles, which can function as a credible guide for normal policy-making for an extended period (Ackerman, 1991: 290). These characteristics derive from Ackerman's own view of the quality of participation in modern democratic societies.[11] According to him, though democracies cannot rely on the full commitment of their citizens in the ordinary political process, they must nonetheless expect the citizens to make their own clear (and sovereign) voice heard in important and decisive moments of politics. These are the *moments* of constitution making, the legitimacy of which can be tested in relation to their ability to meet the criteria for higher law-making suggested by Ackerman.

Although his framework is mainly an interpretation and rationalisation of American constitutional history, at a certain level of abstraction, and as a first approximation, it can be used to assess whether Europe is living through a constitutional moment.[12] Neil Walker has suggested that what is characteristic of constitutional moments, as defined by Ackerman, is the fact that they are 'marked both by *discontinuity* and by *transformation*' (Walker, 2004b: 368). This would seem to imply a mere consequentialist approach to constitution making. On the one hand, constitutional moments are events that *mark* and *make* the difference between two different periods of normal politics; on the other, they need to make a *significant* difference. Both elements can only be judged a posteriori. Moreover, as Walker also remarks, the discrete and transformative character of constitutional politics implies that these moments should be both relatively rare and brief in duration: moments, indeed.

This characterisation is certainly correct, but perhaps over-stylised. The duration of the constitutional moments, for instance, may vary greatly. Indeed, Ackerman notices that the phase of 'mobilised deliberation' requires that the 'movement's transformative proposals [be] tested time and again'.[13] More generally, in his own characterisation of Ackerman's position, Walker concentrates on the 'effects' of constitutional politics, while giving less consideration to its 'properties', which, as he nonetheless says, are an important part of Ackerman's theory of dualist democracy. Such properties, which as already mentioned mark off constitutional from normal politics, can be judged as events unfold, even though they may need to be validated by their capacity to produce certain kinds of effects for the constitutional moment to succeed. In fact, Ackerman also contemplates the possibility of constitutional moments ending in failure, something that occurs in those cases in which the proposed transformations do not reach the codification phase (1991: 267).

Thus the normative validity of constitutional moments is not merely consequential. Constitutional politics is legitimate not merely because it produces something new and distinctly different, but because it is able to express, at particular moments, the generative force of democratic sovereignty. Its validity needs therefore to be fully inscribed in Ackerman's more general vision of dualist democracy as a system of legitimate government. This assumes that ('We') the people are able to engage in a higher form of law-making at certain historical junctures, thus making it possible for the citizens to conduct the normal (and less demanding) business of interest-driven politics in between such junctures.[14]

Constitutional deliberation in constitutional moments

When seen in its entirety, Ackerman's framework offers a number of procedural criteria for the evaluation of the present phase of constitution making in Europe. As John Erik Fossum and Agustín Menéndez (2002) have attempted to do, there is scope for assessing the pre- and post-Laeken process of writing the European Constitution in terms of the signalling, proposal, mobilisation and formulation phases outlined by Ackerman. Of course, the tests through which we can put the current constitutional process are mainly interpretative. First, we need to decide whether the public debate has been both deep and broad. Second, we need to consider whether the proposal on the table has what Ackerman calls 'decisiveness'. In other words, whether it commands a decisive majority against any likely alternative, or instead if it is only supported by a relative majority, which lacks 'decisiveness'.[15] Third, we need to establish whether the way and the channels through which the proposal has been formulated make it worth constitutional consideration. This is a rather intricate issue, which is particularly intertwined with the constitutional history of a country and the way in which some of its institutions may come to acquire a particular role as conduits towards constitutional transformation. Fourth, we need to assess whether the mobilisation of public opinion in support of transformation is extended over time, so as to gain an intertemporal and decisive majority. Finally, we need to evaluate whether the proposal is capable of legal codification, so as to act effectively as a constitutional guideline for normal legislation.

In short, a constitutional moment is such if it is capable of bringing into being the fundamental elements that give legitimacy to a polity and to its political regime. Here views may diverge on whether what matters is more an outcome-based assessment of legitimacy – a constitutional moment is therefore assessed on the kind of constitutional order it produces and on the substance of the constitutional document; or whether legitimacy is seen in more procedural terms – if, for instance, the constitutional moment succeeds in either mobilising the citizenry or producing public deliberation and a higher form of consensus.

The Constitutional Convention has offered an interesting terrain for developing and debating the validity of the more procedural approach, and particularly the normative and socio-psychological basis for a deliberative approach to democracy and constitutionalism. A number of authors have engaged with the issue of the nature of discourse and agreement in politics, and what normative force principled deliberation and agreement (as opposed to contractual bargaining) may carry with them (see many of the contributions in Eriksen et al., 2004; and Eriksen, 2005). By applying certain aspects of Habermas's communicative theory, they see the prolonged phase of institutional discussion and transformation in Europe since Maastricht as a way of constructing the unity of the European polity on the basis of a reflexive form of problem solving which appeals to shared norms and progressively entrenched commitments. From such a perspective, the introduction of the 'Convention method' can be seen as a decisive improvement on the IGC, for it would seem to introduce a more dispassionate way of arguing about the organisation of the European institutions, appealing to general reasons, instead of taking narrow national interests as the basis for logrolling and the bargaining-type of intergovernmental politics dominating the signing of previous treaties in the history of European integration.

But this position presents some problems, for it offers an idealised view both of what happens in discussions on constitutional issues, and of the 'Convention' experience itself, besides suggesting a somewhat artificial separation between constitutional questions and fundamental policy issues, thus assuming that the former are a better ground on which to build consensus at the European level. The normative quality of constitutional deliberation can be questioned from two distinct perspectives. The first does not necessarily imply a rejection of the analytic and normative contentions made by advocates of the superiority of constitutional deliberation. According to this view, although it is difficult to prove empirically that particular agreements are the result of rational deliberation, or that they reflect a rationally motivated consensus, it may still be true that the contextually induced restraints of constitutional deliberation create incentives through which agents are motivated to reach agreements based on more dispassionate principles and reasoning, and that such agreements have a strong 'integrative' function, establishing something stronger than a simple *modus vivendi*.

From such a perspective, the work of the constitutional Convention looks like a genuine attempt at substituting a more deliberative and supranational style of constitutional politics to the bargaining model based on strong national interests as instantiated in the practice of the IGCs. However, even though the process may look distinctive, it remains to be seen whether the outcome of the constitutional Convention – i.e. the kind of constitutional document that it managed to produce – went beyond the kind of substantive compromises that have characterised much treaty-making in the EU (Magnette, 2004b). Indeed, as further discussed in Chapters 5 and 12, the very fact that the constitutional draft prepared by the Convention needed approval by the IGC may cast some doubt on the idea that the writing of the Constitutional Treaty represents a real break with past experience. Moreover, the stalling of the ratification process can be cited as further proof that the deliberative character of the process does not guarantee a consensual outcome.

Constitutional deliberation can also be questioned from a second, and normatively more radical, perspective. For, it can be argued that the negotiations in the constitutional Convention showed that a number of key constitutional questions can only be settled by 'normal' political means, and by trade-offs between policy issues within a wider context; and that indeed such a bargaining style of politics is both unavoidable and justifiable, since political compromises are intrinsic to all forms of democratic politics. Compromises are not to be rejected because they may fall short of some idealised form of consensus, but judged contextually and according to their capacity to favour social and political integration, besides producing some distributive outcomes accepted by those involved. Compromise, and not consensus, is the form of agreement that better reflects political pluralism in modern times, and this is no different in either normal or constitutional politics (Bellamy and Schönlau, 2004b).

In the case of the present European constitutional moment, since, arguably, the debate over the European Constitution has not yet concluded, it may be premature to formulate a definite opinion on whether this has manifested the 'properties' of deliberation and decisiveness that Ackerman attributes to successful (or even failed) constitutional moments. Indeed, the rest of this book is an attempt to discuss in depth the way in which the Convention contributed to produce those normative 'properties', but the application of Ackerman's framework to the European context presents two more fundamental difficulties. First, as we have already observed, the legitimacy criteria outlined by Ackerman are parasitic on his general theory of dualist democracy. Thus it would appear that the application of his evaluative framework to the European Union depends on whether this can be considered to be a kind of dualist democracy – which it would not yet seem to be – or whether at least we think it should aspire to become one. In either case, and specifically in the latter one, the European Constitution cannot so much be conceived as a constitutional moment *in between* two phases of ordinary politics, but as a more *foundational* moment, from which a dualist democracy may eventually emerge.

The second difficulty concerns the emphasis that Ackerman places on the sovereign subject ('We, the People') in the process of constitutional politics. This is particularly cogent if one assumes that the European Constitution is a *foundational* moment, standing at the beginning of a series of cycles of ordinary and constitutional politics. The adoption of Ackerman's model therefore requires the solution of what is still a very open question in the European debate: who is the *subject* of the European Constitution? This is no other than the much discussed question of the European demos: whether it is possible to envisage the formation of a European people, or whether differences between European peoples can not and should not be completely overcome. In considering these two difficulties, it must be concluded, as Walker does, that Ackerman's dualist framework is not immediately applicable to the European situation. We must find some other normative framework in order to judge constitution making in Europe.

Normative and institutional disagreements

It is possible to identify a number of other approaches to constitution making. Andrew Arato lists three such approaches, besides Ackerman's (Arato, 2000). Two of them – the classical European tradition, which places the constituent power in a normative vacuum (revolutionary democracy); and the liberal tradition, which is primarily interested in the substance of the constitutional arrangements (liberal democracy) – limit the importance of the constitution-making process by emphasising respectively the radical break with the past and the outcome of the process. The other two approaches (Ackerman's and Hanna Arendt's) conceive democracy as a dualist process, harnessing the vitality of democratic power to some kind of process or rule of law.

This list is probably not exhaustive, but has the advantage of suggesting a link between the democratic principles underlying each approach and the institutional solutions characterising different historical models of constitution making. The latter are distinguished depending on who the main agent directing the process of constitution making is: a constitutional convention, a constituent assembly, a normally elected legislature, the executive powers, or an evolutionary process. Opting for one or the other of these institutional solutions tends to reveal the implicit theory of democratic sovereignty enshrined in a historical experience. But, according to Arato, there is no one-to-one relationship between normative approaches and historical solutions; rather, each democratic approach favours different rankings of the institutional options, thus suggesting a more complex relationship between democratic theories and constitutional processes.

There are advantages in considering the European experience by combining the institutional and normative perspectives. For it would appear that the post-Laeken phase of constitution making in Europe has so far opted for a mix of institutional solutions, and that this is one terrain of confrontation between different normative positions. Neil Walker suggests as much when he considers four constitutional narratives in competition with the 'constitutional moment' hypothesis, comprising constitutional scepticism, historical contextualism, serialism and processualism (Walker, 2004b). Each of these positions either denies that the European Constitutional Convention can produce a proper constitution or defends a more gradualist conception of the constitutionalisation process. More significantly, all these perspectives are presently operating in the very process of constitution making, leaving, as Walker puts it, 'practical "traces" in the process of the Convention and the body of the Constitutional text' (Walker, 2004b).

From what has been said, it would seem that, in the present phase of constitution making, both the institutional and the normative games are still wide open, suggesting that the debate on the European Constitution is more fragmented than often assumed. Disagreements are not mainly on whether we need some kind of constitutional document. Nor are disagreements limited to the content of the eventual constitutional document: the kind of values, rights and 'power map' this may enshrine – something which is still very much open to discussion, as a result of the ratification failure so far. There are also disagreements on the nature of constitutional legitimacy, and whether a constitutional moment is really the way of giving legitimacy to a constitutional order.

Normal and constitutional politics

This challenge undermines the *categorical* distinction between constitutional and normal politics, denying that they can be easily distinguished on the basis of their normative value. In the European case, some commentators go even further and question whether the recent phase of constitutional politics, which has focused discussion on the EU institutional framework, and on what the EU is, or should become, may be the best ground on which to build consensus at a European level. Andrew Moravcsik, for instance, maintains that talks on the constitution, far from consolidating the integration process, have opened up a Pandora's box, risking destabilising the 'constitutional settlement' reached throughout the 1990s (Moravcsik, 2002b and 2005b). This position, however, denies that there is a crisis of legitimacy in the EU, while assuming that its *de facto* supranational constitutional order needs no explicit normative basis, for it ultimately rests on the democratic legitimacy of the member states.

Even allowing for Moravcsik's point on political prudence, it would seem difficult to maintain that the emergence of an explicit constitutional discourse in Europe is a largely manufactured event, particularly when one considers that it has developed within the context of an unprecedented process of enlargement, and that it follows from a phase of profound changes in the nature and extent of the economic integration process. If anything, the constitutional debate testifies to the need for finding a new balance between the EU institutional structure and its policy-making ambitions. Arguably, Europe's constitutional moment should not be identified with the Laeken process of writing a documentary constitution, but with the new phase of political integration that started at Maastricht (Weiler, 1999: 3–4). From such a perspective, the Convention and the Constitutional Treaty look more like the concluding acts of a protracted constitutional moment, whose fundamental features are not those enshrined in the articles of the constitutional text, but momentous political decisions such as enlargement, the introduction of a common currency and an independent European Central Bank, and the Stability Pact. It is partly ironic that such decisions are not regarded as 'constitutional', and that they have been taken with very little popular involvement, without a European-wide discussion (Weiler, 2002).

But as the ratification crisis of 2005 shows, in the eyes of the European public there is very little difference between what the EU *is* and what it *does*, so that at the moment of considering the ratification of the Constitutional Treaty many voters found it problematic to distinguish between what the Constitution *says* (i.e. what is in the actual text of the Constitution) and what, in their view, it *stands for* (i.e. how they consider the European Union and its impact upon their everyday lives). It is not surprising, therefore, that present and future enlargement, immigration, and social and economic policies – all issues that are hardly affected by the introduction of the Constitutional Treaty – have played such an important part in the way in which people voted in the French and Dutch referendums. It is a sign that constitutional politics cannot be limited to institutional matters, but is inevitably entangled with some of the substantive issues associated with normal politics.

This raises two general questions. One is the question of the relevance of the issues at the centre of constitutional debates, and the other is the precise impact that constitutional politics makes when compared to ordinary politics. On the issue of relevance, Joseph Weiler (2002) has been particularly critical of the way constitutional mobilisation has diverted attention from the really momentous changes that, as we noted, have occurred in the European Union, and which have instead been managed either pragmatically or taking decisions by default, *de facto* excluding the citizens from debating and deciding on such issues. On the hard choices confronting Europe the formal constitutional process seems to have made little or no impact.

Weiler's argument on the 'irrelevance' and timidity[16] of the European constitutional debate can lead to two different conclusions. One, of more local consequence, is that there has been a failure in the European political class to decide on which issues to put at the centre of the public debate. The other, of a more widely ranging nature, would suggest that there is no difference between constitutional and ordinary politics, and that the latter can have effects as momentous as the former. From this one can conclude that the main difference between normal and constitutional politics is more *strategic* than *categorical*. In a broader sense, constitutional politics is the kind of action that a series of favourable circumstances converge to create by offering a 'window of opportunity' within which it is possible to operate so as to determine the character of a polity and of its regime for a relatively long period of time. From this perspective, constitutional politics can only be judged consequentially, as was discussed earlier.

But there are a number of other important elements that follow from this 'strategic' sense, which should also be noticed. First, that constitutional politics is not tantamount to producing a formal constitution, a document, that is, that has the formal qualities of constitutional law, distinct from ordinary legislation. The object of constitutional politics is more often the interconnection between the political (the more substantive organisation of power) and the formal constitution. At times, it may concern changes in the 'material' constitution, by which one should understand important pieces of legislation or of organisation of the state, which do not need to be part of the formal constitution itself. In view of this, it is impossible to define the province of constitutional politics in a way that excludes ordinary politics. Secondly, because of its partly consequentialist character, constitutional politics finds its validation in the way in which ordinary politics makes it its own point of reference.

In relation to the more 'intrinsic' properties of constitutional politics, these can be seen as a possible effect of the 'window of opportunity' contingency and of the capacity of both leaders and citizens to operate in such a way to exploit the moment by organising political attention and activating mechanisms of broader acceptance and allegiance within the community (Olsen, 1997a: 217–20; Castiglione, 1995). In the modern conditions of democratic societies, sustained public debate and the mediation of 'strong publics' make an important contribution to the emergence of broad forms of principled and strategic agreement, and practical convergence, at least in the long term (Eriksen and Fossum, 2002). But all this does not necessarily require a higher level of consensus, which is almost impossible to achieve even between reasonable citizens, in view of their diversity of values, interests and empirical assessments, besides considerations on the complexities of social choice and its subject matter. Agreements in constitutional politics, as in ordinary politics, are points of equilibrium often reached through a variety of considerations and strategies, involving arguments, bargaining and negotiating processes, compromises, incomplete theorisation, and strategic arguments (Elster, 1996; Bellamy, 1999; Bellamy and Schönlau, 2004b; Castiglione and Schönlau, 2006; Magnette, 2002).

What is sometimes considered as the binding character of constitutional consensus is at its origins – even when it emerges from truly exceptional moments of collective crisis and mobilisation, which are indeed rare – the product of a number of more or less principled compromises. At first, these compromises result in a *modus vivendi*. Over time and by the effect of common and continuous engagement both in the business of ordinary politics and in ongoing deliberative and decision-making experiences, such a *modus vivendi* may consolidate in a shared framework, always open, however, to different interpretations or to sudden collapse – as the experience of constitutional democracies amply testifies. To conclude on this point, if constitutional and ordinary politics cannot be clearly and categorically distinguished from each other on either their substance or because of their properties, and if nonetheless there is a more strategic sense in which such a distinction can occasionally become operative, there is no simple way of saying whether constitutions, and their normative appeal, are either the product of extended processes or decisive events. Indeed, it is probably safer to assume that both aspects tend to contribute to the making of a constitution.

There is, however, another side to the idea that the normative character of constitutional politics needs a constitutional moment, something that breaks the routine of normal politics. This is connected with the importance of symbolism as part of constitutional politics. The point has been made forcefully by Jürgen Habermas, when he intimates that 'as a political collectivity, Europe cannot take hold in the consciousness of its citizens simply in the shape of a common currency. The intergovernmental arrangement at Maastricht lacks that power of symbolic crystallization which only a political act of foundation can give' (2001: 6). According to Habermas, the constitution can act as a catalytic point in the 'circular creation' of Europe as a political community, coming as the constitution does at the end of an already advanced process of social, economic and political integration, and, in turn, helping to put in motion the construction of a European-wide civil society, a common public sphere, and a shared political culture (2001: 16–21). Underpinning this operation there is what Habermas calls 'constitutional patriotism', a form of allegiance to the political community, which rests on abstract and universal principles of a civic kind. A lively debate has developed around this idea and whether it may rightfully become part of a

European identity (Friese and Wagner, 2002; Lacroix 2002; Kumm 2005), but from Habermas's perspective the main question is whether the focus on the constitution could help in fostering such an allegiance. In other words, the writing of the constitution would be part of a constitutional project aimed at enlarging our circle of solidarity at a European level and at creating the conditions for a 'federation of nation-states' (Habermas, 2001: 15).

In Habermas's and other supporters' view of the need for a constitution, as a strong normative and symbolic statement, the constitution is part of a constructivist gambit intended as the beginning of the process of construction of a political demos in Europe. But, as Neil Walker has argued (2003, 2004a, 2005), the way in which the Constitutional Treaty has taken shape did not reflect one single project or conception of the EU Constitution and European constitutionalism. For Walker, a number of very different influences have shaped both the text and the form taken by the drafting process of the Constitutional Treaty, comprising positions expressing various shades of scepticism against constructive and documentary constitutionalism, and even extending to those who were in principle hostile to it. From such a perspective, the Constitutional Treaty reflects a compromise between different views, and is the basis for future political and intellectual battles. Thus the current debate on whether its text may be rescued after the defeats in the French and Dutch referendums is beside the point. The real issue is whether the halting of the constitutional moment simply signals a temporary retreat of constructivist and federalist constitutional projects, or whether it is the sign of a process of reversion to the broader constitutional agenda set at Maastricht.

The 'processual' constitution

The fuzzy definition of a European constitutional moment highlights the difficulties besetting any attempt to reproduce the traditional concepts of national constitutionalism at a European level. One of the key ideas of those who tend to emphasise the post-national character of the constitutional path in the EU is that constitution making in it cannot be characterised as an *event*, but as a *process* (Shaw, 2003a). This is no trivial disagreement. It takes us back to some of the themes discussed *apropos* finality and constitutional moments. In point of substance, there may be no difference between a constitutional order achieved through a gradual process and one agreed at a particular moment. Indeed, many who throughout the years have applauded the role of the European Court of Justice in upholding the existence of a new European constitutional order now welcome the fixing of the Constitution by the Convention. According to them, after a period of *de facto* constitutionalisation, we have entered a phase when a more definite constitutional settlement needs to be formalised in view of the profound changes introduced by the single market, monetary unification and enlargement. Moreover, both legitimacy and democratic deficits need urgent attention, something that may only be achieved by fixing Europe's institutional architecture and the rights of the European citizens.

This kind of argument, however, presents two problems. By accepting that a constitution of sorts was already in place, it makes the present moment less foundational, thus posing the problem of what the relationship is between the past and the future constitutional order. By emphasising the legitimacy deficit of the European institutions, it becomes vulnerable to the counter-argument that fixing the European Constitution at this particular moment risks freezing the status quo, making it less acceptable to the European citizens. A more gradual process, instead, may be better at tracking and directing the political sentiments of the European peoples as they are asked to widen their sense of solidarity. It may also be more flexible and therefore better equipped at developing institutional arrangements so to make them seem relevant to policy projects and policy objectives in which citizens can more immediately recognise their interests and for which they may more readily mobilise.

This argument about a more 'processual' understanding of constitution making has many facets, involving different elements of constitutional politics. One is concerned with the relationship between formal and informal moments in the making of the constitutional order, emphasising, for instance, how treaty reform in Europe cannot be seen as a simple succession of different treaties each amending the other, and characterised by intergovernmental bargaining (Greve and Jorgensen, 2002; Farrell and Héritier, 2003). A second element consists in a more systemic understanding of how both law and politics operate, but also of how they interact by producing a 'structural coupling' between them, so that constitutional politics is the result of various institutional dialogues and the way in which they come to interact (Greve and Jorgensen, 2002). A third element concerns the way in which the development of European community law has changed the structural context in which different branches of law operate at the national level, forcefully impacting on the relationship between private and public law in the member states' legal systems, contributing to redrawing some of the boundaries between them, whilst in particular problematising the relationship between private and public autonomy. This process is part and parcel of the open constitutionalisation of the EU legal system (Joerges, 1997; Joerges and Everson, 2004).

Conclusion: European constitutionalism as work in progress

One manifestation of the disagreement over whether the Constitution should be conceptualised as either an event or a process is on how to consider the present Constitutional Treaty, an issue already touched upon in Chapter 1. Giuliano Amato has put this question in a humorous way, by talking of the Constitutional Treaty in terms of the 'gender' of this document.[17] He wished, or so he says, that the newly born text were a 'girl' (*una femmina*), but has to acknowledge that, in fact, it was a 'boy' (*un maschio*). In his view, the Convention did not produce a 'constitution' (*costituzione*, a feminine noun in Italian), but a 'treaty' (*trattato*, masculine). Amato is convinced that the real point of difference lies in the power of revision that the Draft attributes to the national governments and not to the European institutions, thus favouring an interpretation of the nature of the EU as still an international organisation operating according to intergovernmental principles. And yet, the Draft does not present itself as a simple 'treaty', but as a 'constitutional treaty', or, in other contexts as a 'treaty establishing a constitution'. This would seem to signal that the process of constitutional definition of the European Union is still very much open and in the making.

Moreover, and perhaps more importantly, the nature of the European Constitution is in doubt. Indeed, many believe that the idea of the constitution as traditionally applied to the national context is no longer adequate in the transnational and multilevel context characterising European governance. Such inadequacy has two sources. One is in the very conception of the constitution as an overarching document at the apex of a unified legal and political system. Such a conception has been said to be no longer tenable even at the national level, because it would be unable to capture in a few general principles the normative pluralism of modern societies, their sociopolitical differentiation, and the more particularistic nature of social legislation (Fioravanti, 1992).

The other source of inadequacy is the changing nature of constitutionalism, which in the European context needs to accommodate the national forms and practices of constitutional law. According to many, this gives to European constitutionalism a plural character, which needs to make a virtue of the necessity of entering into dialogue with diverse traditions and also find forms of accommodation between parallel legal and constitutional orders. One of the formative principles of European constitutionalism is therefore that of being tolerant, as Weiler maintains,[18] or as Maduro (2000) says: 'we have to start reasoning in the realm of what could be called couterpunctual law . . . The discovery that different melodies could be heard at the same time' (De Witte, 2002; Shaw, 2003a). From such a perspective, writing the constitution now as a more traditional text may risk jeopardising what may be construed as perhaps the greatest achievement to date of the European constitutional order, that of allowing for an ongoing political and constitutional conversation to go on across Europe.

This idea of constitutional toleration and of a constitutional conversation is closely connected to the recognition of the fact that there are different demoi at the heart of the construction of the EU as a polity (Maduro, 2003). For Weiler (2001) the *Sonderweg* of European constititutionalism consists of renouncing the desire to look for a 'positive' common constitutional culture, but accepting that there are different national constitutional cultures. Similar echoes can be found in other authors (Nuotio, 2004; Shaw, 2003a), applying to EU constitutionalism an open-textured and continuously negotiated (both internally and externally) method of constitution building. The principles that guide it, however, are still very much a matter of experiment and contention and may apply beyond the EU experience (Slaughter, 2004). The basic intuition, however, is that the European constitutional order is a plural one, operating both at the supranational and at the national level, and encompassing both the national and the EU constitutions (Pernice and Kanits, 2004). As Neil MacCormick says: 'a pluralistic analysis . . . shows the systems of law operative on the European level to be distinct and partially independent of each other, though also partially overlapping and interacting' (1999: 119). In itself, this is not a difficult state of affairs to perceive and analyse. The problem is how to conceive and operationalise conflict resolution in the context of such radical pluralism. This is indeed the challenge for constitutional politics in the EU. In this sense, European constitutionalism is still work in progress.

Notes

1. The title of the first section of the Laeken Declaration is 'Europe at a crossroads', and the text maintains: 'The European Union is a success story . . . Fifty years on, however, the Union stands at a crossroads, a defining moment in its existence'. The Preface to the Draft Constitutional Treaty, signed by the President (Valéry Giscard d'Estaing) and the Vice-Presidents (Giuliano Amato and Jean-Luc Dehaene) of the Convention, echoes the same argument by using the related image of Europe being at a 'turning point'. For earlier uses of the 'crossroads' image, cf. Hirst (1995) and Furet (1995).
2. This was the question at the basis of Joschka Fisher's Humboldt University lecture several years ago: *Quo vadis Europa?* Both German, French and English versions of the text can be found in Joerges et al. (2000).
3. For a sustained argument in favour of Europe becoming a 'unitary' state (or a 'superstate', as the author maintains), see Morgan (2005).
4. The expressions 'social union' (used by Rawls and other liberals) and 'community of fate' (which has a more communitarian flavour) are here purposefully mixed in order to indicate, as the following sentence in the main text does, that the argument does not depend on accepting either of these perspectives.
5. Weiler suggests that the European elite is relying on sleight-of-hand tactics when they present a number of options (in his colourful example: different types of flavoured milk) to the European peoples, while in fact taking away from them the most important decision of all (whether or not they want milk). Weiler is perhaps carried too far in his criticism by his own rhetoric, but his suggestion that no real democratic choice has been given to European citizens is substantially right. On this, see below. On the rather alarmist aspect of the alternative between integration and decline, see Albert Hirschman's cautionary advice that reformers should be wary of the force and persuasiveness of the 'impending-disaster' arguments (1993).
6. The continuity between the 'functionalist' and the 'federal' phase is self-consciously maintained by Fischer in his own speech. More generally, such continuity is embraced by most supporters of the federal option.
7. Emphasis added. This quote is, of course, from the English translation, which is here slightly changed to reflect the original German, where the first sentence talks

of 'Europe's constitutional renewal' (*konstitutionelle Neugründung Europas*), which needs to be achieved by writing a 'European constitution' (*europäische Verfassung*). The English translation uses 'constitution' in both parts of the sentence, making them look too much alike, whereas the German implies a difference between the objective of 'constitutional renewal' and the means, a 'constitution' as a document, through which to achieve this.

8. This is not meant as a defence of the draft text prepared by the Convention. There were certainly other (probably more effective and certainly more elegant) ways of writing it. But direct comparison with the American Constitution, and the kind of criticisms that point out that the European draft is neither as short, nor elegant, nor memorable as the text of the American Constitution miss the point of what the European Constitution is *meant to do* in the present circumstances. This is part of the 'illocutionary act' of the constitutional text, which in the European case may be very different from the one that applies to the American Constitution when it was written.

9. On both these issues, see below.

10. See Castiglione (1996: 15–16) for a brief discussion of the historical and theoretical context of the distinction.

11. For a critical (though partly sympathetic) discussion of Ackerman's vision of citizenship, cf. Castiglione (2000).

12. Ackerman himself has generalised what he sees as the American experience of dualist democracy into a more general model that other political societies can follow (Ackerman, 1992).

13. Ackerman says that this phase may take years. Moreover, this phase needs to be distinguished from what he calls the 'signalling phase', which can also be long and protracted. Cf. Ackerman (1991: 266).

14. As it is clear from the main text, this is not a criticism of Walker's general characterisation of Ackerman's idea of constitutional moments, which is both correct and perceptive. There is instead a difference of emphasis on the importance to be attributed to the procedural aspects. In talking of the 'property' of Ackerman's constitutional politics, Walker refers to the 'quality and inclusiveness of the debate'. This seems to refer to the extent and depth of public participation, but tends to glide over the 'public reason' elements that (more controversially) Ackerman's position would seem to endorse.

15. This is a condition difficult to apply to the present circumstances in Europe, but a possible way of operationalising this condition would be that proposed by Philippe Schmitter, who suggests putting two different constitutional texts to the vote and to apply each of them to the European countries whose citizenry supports them. Cf. Schmitter (2000).

16. Such 'timidity' can be connected to a more general timidity on the importance of promoting and recognising citizens' participation at the European level. On this, cf. Bellamy and Castiglione (2002).

17. Cf. G. Amato, 'Prefazione', in Ziller (2003: 9). Ziller discusses Amato's distinction in the main text at pp. 47–8.

18. Cf. Weiler, 'In Defence of the Status Quo' (2003a). Weiler's argument about the plural nature of the European constitutional order is clear, but his use of the idea of 'toleration' as applied to the interrelation between different constitutional orders is rather confusing, unless it is meant as a generic attitude to intercultural dialogue. On the difficulties raised by recent debates on toleration, see McKinnon and Castiglione (2003).

Part II
The Convention Experiment

Introduction to Part II

Part I has offered a general picture of European constitutionalism and of constitutional politics in the EU. The picture it has portrayed is one of contested narratives and antagonistic understandings of the European polity and of its constitutionalisation. Within such a picture, the Convention on the Future of Europe has become a site for constitutional experiment.

Part II explores the meaning of the Convention experiment by subjecting it to closer analysis. The three chapters comprising Part II give an account of the historical genesis of the Convention as a 'method' for treaty and constitutional reform, explore the particular mechanisms through which the Convention was composed and through which it claimed to have legitimacy as an instrument for constitution making, and finally illustrate the way in which the Convention operated.

Chapter 3 reconstructs a number of key passages in the history of treaty-making and treaty-reform in the European Union/Communities. It does so by focusing in particular on the relationship between the drafting process and the decision-making process. The delicate nature of this relationship is not always understood, particularly when it concerns complex organisations, comprising different agents with separate interests. In such cases, bodies that are appointed to draft framework rules for the co-ordination of the actions and behaviour of states and individuals are given an important 'negative' power (the power of excluding issues or solutions from the agenda), even though they might not have the power to make the final decision. The pre-history of the Constitutional Convention, as seen through the history of previous drafting bodies, is therefore of some significance. From a more substantive perspective, the chapter argues that there is both continuity and rupture in such a history, and that though one can find precedents for the kind of mandate and powers accorded to the Convention by the Laeken mandate, ultimately the emergence in the last eight years or so of the Convention as a privileged instrument for drafting a document of primary political importance represents a new turn in the constitutionalisation of the EU. In this case, the *method* of constitutional politics is the message.

Chapters 4 and 5 are more specifically about the Constitutional Convention and the way in which it worked. Both chapters present a mixed picture. On the one hand, they tend to show the shortcomings of the Convention, when this is considered from the perspective of the great expectations raised by its supporters as a more democratic, more deliberative, and more legitimate method of constitution making, if compared to the intergovernmental procedures characterising the IGCs. On the other hand, they stress the fact that, even taking into account such shortcomings, the 'Convention method' has proposed a different way, and different standards for looking at constitution making in the European Union. In this respect, the Convention's enduring legacy may lie more in the 'method' that it has embodied, rather than in its 'output.'

The 'Convention method' is analysed first from the point of view of the nature of the Convention itself. Chapter 4 gives a detailed account of the composition of the Convention's membership, of how the *conventionnels* were selected, and of how they interpreted their mandate. This is not just a descriptive exercise, for issues of selection, representativeness and accountability imply important normative questions on what is the proper role for such drafting bodies, on the scope and extent of their powers, and on whose interests and opinions the representatives of the Convention were meant to embody. From all such perspectives, the Convention certainly showed great limitations, some of which were due to the fact that the Convention itself comprised different 'forms' of representation, which implied different conceptions of the way in which the members of the Convention represented their respective 'constituencies'.

The second angle from which the 'Convention method' is analysed is that of its internal working. Chapter 5 provides an analysis of the internal organisation of the Convention, of its methods of discussion and deliberation, and of the different phases which the various drafts of the Constitution underwent. This chapter is particularly attentive to some of the internal dynamics, often dominated by the Presidium and its President, and constrained by the time factor, which operated both as a spur towards reaching agreement, but also as an important limit to the quality of deliberation. Such an analysis is of particular importance to assess some of the claims often made in support of the 'Convention method' as reflecting a more democratic and deliberative style of constitution making, and hence a better way of giving legitimacy to the Constitution itself. This chapter, as the other chapters in Parts II and III, offers some ground for a cautious optimism, but, ultimately, the jury is still out both on the normative claims in support of the 'Convention method' in general, and on whether the Constitutional Convention interpreted its role effectively.

3
The Convention on the Future of Europe and its Antecedents

Justus Schönlau

European integration and its structures have been constantly evolving since the beginning; the basic texts of the European Treaties themselves have undergone several rounds of revisions and additions. Although, as argued in Part I of this volume, the constitutionalisation process of the EU cannot be reduced to the making and revising of treaties, it is at this level that change has become both most visible and politically contested. This chapter concentrates on the successive rounds of negotiation and treaty revision since the early 1950s. In this sense, it outlines 'constitutional politics' in its most immediate sense, that of political actions involved in making a constitution.

This chapter looks in particular at how changes to the EC/EU Treaties were negotiated over the first five decades of the integration process, and how the 'Convention method' first emerged for the drafting of the EU Charter of Fundamental Rights, and was later adopted for the drafting of the Constitutional Treaty. Obviously, there were important differences between the two Conventions. The Charter Convention was more of an experiment, and its members were given free rein in the way in which to organise themselves and their procedures, even though their mandate was comparatively narrower in scope. The Constitutional Convention was a larger body, on which political actors exercised a tighter control, but to which they gave a wider remit, something that made it a more political body. In spite of these differences, there were important structural similarities, as we will show in this and subsequent chapters. In doing so, we shall also examine the role of the European Council, which established the Conventions in the first place, determined their composition, their agenda and working method, and retained the power to sanction the results of their deliberations.

This chapter, however, is mainly intended to develop an understanding of the Convention phase in the wider context of the EU's institutional development. It does so by emphasising the continuities with some of the previous methods and attempts in the history of EC/EU institution building, but also by arguing that the Conventions represent a new development, due both to their internal structures and to their (potential) capacity to broaden the

51

debate, thereby involving the European public at large. The second part of the argument, concerned with the novelty of the method, will be discussed at greater length in the following chapters.

In the beginning, there were the committees

Even though the history of European integration is frequently told as an endeavour of brave, far-sighted individuals who took lonely decisions (Dinan, 1994), it is also true that there have always been larger or smaller *groups* of people who were involved in the strategic planning and who devised the political and legal framework for what was to become the EU. While Jean Monnet and his role in shaping the first steps of European integration certainly suggest that there was a crucial part to be played by a strong-minded individual whose success was partly due to his ideological and political independence, the concrete follow-up (the Schuman declaration of 9 May 1950) saw the establishment of the 'Schuman-Plan Conference' (Monnet, 1976: 409) to discuss the details – the first European intergovernmental conference.[1] The conference consisted of representatives of six national governments with several advisers each, under the leadership of Jean Monnet himself. Altogether this first IGC included about sixty individuals, though Monnet underlined in his memoirs how he realised, early on, that in order to achieve rapid progress he had to divide the conference into working groups while he kept the delegation leaders of each country in an upper circle to discuss the institutional problems in an open atmosphere 'without consideration for technical advisers and without being bound by an agenda' (Monnet, 1976: 410, translation provided). It was this body which wrote, on the basis of an original draft which Monnet and his closest advisers had prepared, the original Treaty of the European Coal and Steel Community, which was signed on 18 April 1951, after about ten months of what Monnet insisted was 'co-operation' within the conference rather than 'negotiation' (Monnet, 1976: 409).

The ECSC Treaty established, as one of the institutions of the new structure, a parliamentary body, the Common Assembly. When talks began, even before the ECSC Treaty was signed, about the parallel setting up of a European Defence Community (EDC), the idea of a parliamentary assembly was replicated. Moreover, the Treaty on the EDC (signed by the member states in May 1952) included a commitment to some kind of political authority to supervise and direct the new defence community and called on the parliamentary assembly of the ECSC to '. . . study: a) the creation of an assembly of the European Defence Community elected on a democratic basis; b) the powers which might be granted to such an assembly; c) the modifications which should be made to provisions of the present treaty relating to the other institutions of the Community, particularly with a view to safeguarding the appropriate representation of the States' (cited from Fondation Spaak I, 1984: 37).

In response to this provision, the parliamentary assembly of the Council of Europe, the other parliamentary structure at European level, passed a resolution which called upon the governments of the six signatories of the ECSC and EDC Treaties to entrust either the ECSC parliamentary assembly, or alternatively a body of members of the Council of Europe assembly belonging to the states in question, to draft a constitution for a supranational European Political Community (EPC) (Schröder, 1994: 267). Thus, at this early stage, there were two bodies of delegated national parliamentarians competing for the task of drafting a 'constitutional' text for the future EC.

It was at this point that the foreign ministers of the six member states, perhaps because – in Dinan's words – of '[the] indifference towards the proposed EPC and doubts that it would ever come to anything' (Dinan, 1994: 27), gave the constitutional task to a special committee of the ECSC assembly rather than to either of the two assemblies as a whole. This new body became known as the 'ad hoc committee' and made far-reaching proposals to the conference of foreign ministers a couple of months later. This early predecessor to the Conventions is little known and has only recently been placed appropriately on the European constitutional continuum (Griffith, 2000) – clearly because of the lack of lasting impact of the proposals made. The ad hoc committee's proposals did not survive, firstly because in the course of subsequent meetings of the foreign ministers and their representatives (in 1953–4) the more federalist proposals were watered down, and secondly because the whole project of a European political community was shelved after the failure of the Defence Community Treaty at the French National Assembly in August 1954. Nevertheless the idea of a more comprehensive constitutional settlement for European integration had become an issue for the European institutions themselves, as well as discussed by outsiders such as the federalist movements or individual heads of states or governments.

Moreover, in reaction to this failure, the 'Monnet method', that is the idea of achieving more encompassing integration through a series of smaller, pragmatic steps of functional integration, gained prominence. The Coal and Steel Community survived the failure of the more far-reaching constitutional project and served as the basis for subsequent, less ambitious but still important steps: the foundation of the European Economic Community and Euratom in 1957. To promote these new initiatives which were to prove crucial for the further development of the integration project, two specially constituted bodies were instrumental: Monnet's 'Action Committee for a United States of Europe' and the Spaak Committee. The former was a creation of Jean Monnet himself in reaction to the vote against the European Defence Community in the French National Assembly. In 1955, Monnet resigned from the presidency of the High Authority of the Coal and Steel Community, and used his newly acquired freedom of initiative to form a committee of thirty eminent personalities from the main political parties and trade unions of the six member states. The Committee's role was to issue declarations of common intent for further integration, putting pressure on national politicians, and supporting those who spoke in favour in further integration. According to Monnet, the Committee met eighteen times in its twenty-year existence, providing many ideas that later became common currency and found application as part of the integration process (Monnet, 1976: 538–42 quotes, for example, the idea of a European reserve fund, and of free movement of capital). The Committee worked on the basis of unanimous declarations. These were agreed ahead of the plenary meetings through some form of shuttle diplomacy co-ordinated by Monnet and his closest collaborators. The effectiveness of such declarations depended on the Committee members acting as multipliers within their own organisations and national debates.

The Spaak Committee, on the other hand, was a product of the intergovernmental level of European integration. It was created by the ministerial meeting at Messina in June 1955 which discussed possible plans for further integration at the initiative of the Benelux countries who were getting weary of being sidelined by closer Franco-German co-operation. The Messina conference thus set up a committee of national government delegates who would be assisted by experts and who would work under the chairmanship of a 'political figure' (Fondation Spaak II, 1984: 21). It is important to note that this committee was 'to call on the assistance of the High Authority of the ECSC, the general secretariat of OECE, of the Council of Europe and of the Conference of European Transport Ministers' (Fondation Spaak II, 1984: 21). Thus the Spaak Committee was an early precedent for the attempt to combine political and technical expertise by bringing all the important players at European level into the debate about the future of integration. This concept is important because it began to turn the reflection about the European Community from an issue which was discussed only outside the Community institutions, into a process that received (and continues to receive) impulses from within the European structures in a self-sustained attempt to improve and develop.

Nevertheless it was clear in the case of this new committee that it would propose texts for a future treaty, on which the heads of states and governments in an intergovernmental conference would take the decisions. Moreover, the Committee, which the Belgian Foreign Minister Paul-Henri Spaak was then designated to chair, had to present proposals on a number of quite detailed questions which had been set by the Messina conference, by 1 October 1955 – a mere three months after it was set up. The Spaak report was in fact finally presented to the foreign ministers only on 29 May 1956 at their meeting in Venice and was a detailed draft for the Treaties to establish Euratom and the European Economic Community. The intergovernmental conference accepted them after further negotiations (which led to substantial changes, such as the inclusion of a common agricultural policy in the Treaty) and the Treaties of Rome were consequently signed on 25 March 1957. It is difficult to reconstruct here the precise relation between the Spaak Committee's proposals and the final result of the intergovernmental negotiations, but the mix of political weight and expert knowledge in the Committee, together with the important contribution of the high authority in the Committee, significantly shaped the outcome.

Despite the examples of treaty drafting and change discussed so far, it would be mistaken to present the history of European integration as one of an uninterrupted line of successful initiatives to revise and reform the European Treaties by means of committees. On the contrary, often these very endeavours sparked controversy and reactions, which drove European co-operation in a different direction. The example of the failed European defence and political integration initiative of the early 1950s is a case in point. Yet, even the less successful attempts to shape and reshape European integration are instructive for the present purpose. One such an attempt was the so-called 'Fouchet plan', named after the French chairman of a small committee of national ambassadors, which drafted a plan for a European confederation shortly after the signing of the Treaty of Rome. It was aimed at institutionalising intergovernmental co-operation in foreign policy matters as a way to counterbalance both the existing systems of interstate co-operation such as NATO, and more federalist visions of Europe. Symptomatically for the contents of the plan, its origin was intergovernmental, and negotiations about it took place between the foreign ministers of the six member states, without involving the existing European institutions. This attempt to institutionalise European interstate co-operation failed essentially because no agreement could be reached between a minority Franco-German position and the other four EC partners, but Gerbet also notes that 'if the basic disagreements played a more important role than the actual details of the negotiations, the latter also contributed to failure. The absence of a Community framework made itself felt. The negotiations were conducted according to the norms of classic diplomacy, with its deals, manoeuvres, and attempts at intimidation' (Gerbet, 1987: 125).

While it is not clear how much of this analysis was shared by the other actors involved in the process, and thus what was its impact on subsequent initiatives, it is striking to note that it took nearly twenty years until the next major attempt to deepen European political integration and to tackle the constitutional question of the European Communities. At the request of the European Council of 1974, Leo Tindemans, Prime Minister of Belgium, was given the task of elaborating a report on the question of how to make European union a reality. This initiative came after a decade in which intergovernmentalism seemed to prevail at the European level, due to Charles de Gaulle's stance on, amongst other things, majority voting in the Council of Ministers. This eventually led to the Luxembourg compromise, and the institutionalisation of the European Council itself under the leadership of Valéry Giscard d'Estaing. The first enlargement of the Community in 1973 raised fresh concerns about the constitutional nature and purpose of the co-operation arrangements and their effectiveness, while at the same time, the legal 'constitutionalisation' of the European polity continued (see, Chapter 1 above, and for a fuller analysis: Weiler, 1999).

For his report on European Union, Tindemans originally proposed a body of three wise men, whose task would be to canvas the various European political options. He suggested that at least one should be an acting high level politician. In the end he was given the task himself, with the mandate to formulate his proposals on the basis of 'reports received from the institutions and of consultations which he is to have with the Governments and with a wide range of public opinion in the Community' (European Summit, 7–8 December 1974, EC Bulletin 12/1974, quoted in Vandamme, 1987: 152). This mandate set the stage for the first popular consultation on the future of Europe. Tindemans proceeded on the basis of a questionnaire elaborated by a group of academic experts, which was distributed amongst the representatives of organised interests and of governments in all member state capitals. Vandamme speaks of 'a thousand individuals and groups consulted' by Tindemans (1987: 152) in the space of more than one year, which shows the scale of the undertaking. On the basis of both this research and the extensive reports he received from the European Commission, the European Parliament and the European Court of Justice, Tindemans drafted his own proposals. He insisted that they were not intended as a draft European Constitution but rather were to 'state the objectives and the methods whereby Europe can be invested with a new vitality and current obstacles can be overcome' (Tindemans's letter to the Council, cited in Vandamme, 1987: 159). The report was thus not an institutional or constitutional blueprint, but a general assessment of the status quo and of possible changes. Yet even as a broad policy document the report became the subject of controversy, and produced little by way of immediate, tangible 'constitutional' follow-up. Nevertheless it was to become an important point of reference for the ongoing debate about European integration, not least because of the comparatively broad consultation on which it was based.

The European Parliament: a new constitutional player

In the couple of years following the Tindemans report, there was a truly constitutional breakthrough in the form of the agreement, reached in 1975, to hold the first direct elections to the European Parliament in 1979. Albeit with some delay, this move profoundly affected the institutional balance within the European Community, and had an important impact on future constitutional initiatives (Corbett et al., 2003). The new directly elected Parliament soon started to play a central role in the European constitutional debate with a first prominent example being the initiative, at the insistence of Altiero Spinelli, to propose a draft European Constitution in 1984. Another 'constitutional' contribution had come in 1981 from the bilateral Genscher–Colombo initiative and had led to the creation of an ad hoc working group of diplomats who 'negotiated' the plan. This initiative did not produce much in terms of results because of disagreement among member states and ended up as a rather generic declaration on European Union (at the 1983 Stuttgart Council meeting). Nonetheless, as far as the method is concerned, the Genscher–Colombo plan is interesting, since it recognised the growing legitimacy of the European Parliament, while the 'ad hoc working group' was kept in order to regularly inform the Parliament.

Yet, the directly elected Parliament was no longer content with its role as a bystander. Many of its members saw the Parliament as a European 'constituent assembly' (Schmuck, 1987: 189), and in 1982 they decided to set up an 'institutional committee' with the aim to prepare a comprehensive proposal for a 'constitution'. The newly appointed committee designated six rapporteurs, one for each specific aspect of a draft Treaty, with Altiero Spinelli as their 'co-ordinator'. Four full-scale plenary debates were organised on the Draft Constitution, which was finally adopted with a large majority on 14 February 1984. The EP's Draft Treaty was a far-reaching and self-consciously 'constitutional' initiative, aiming at the 're-foundation' of the European Community/Union. It included, for instance, a clause on the implementation of the Constitution if a majority of member states representing two-thirds of the EU's population ratified it, thus clearly making the transition from an international treaty, based on unanimous agreement among sovereign states, to a genuine federation. While the Parliament's hope to by-pass national governments in the drafting of a constitution did not materialise (Schmuck, 1987: 207), the initiative prompted national governments to resume their debate about institutional reform, and to set up two more ad hoc working groups in preparation for what was to become the 1986 IGC, which eventually produced the Single European Act.

The IGC-age: the Single European Act

The Fontainebleau summit meeting of June 1984 established two committees to tackle the constitutional questions: the Adonnino Committee, tasked to make proposals on practical steps to create a 'people's Europe', and the Dooge Committee on institutional reform, which became known as the 'Spaak II Committee'. The Dooge Committee comprised representatives of the heads of states or governments. Unlike the first Spaak Committee it was not headed by one of the members of the Council, but by an Irish diplomat: James Dooge. It was expected to come up with some general proposals for political change, but its mandate was nothing like the 'Messina questions' in terms of institutional reforms (Keatinge and Murphy, 1987: 220). The Dooge Committee comprised a mix of politicians and national officials, plus a representative of the European Commission, and was supported by a small secretariat. Significantly, it included an 'informal' representation of the European Parliament's Institutional Affairs Committee in the form of three of its members (Keatinge and Murphy, 1987: 224); more formally it was meant to consult with the Institutional Affairs Committee's chairman (Spinelli), the European Parliament's president, and the president of the Economic and Social Committee. Keatinge and Murphy describe the Committee's working method as '(s)trictly speaking [. . .] not engaged in negotiations' (Keatinge and Murphy, 1987: 223). This was because its members were not plenipotentiaries of their respective states, a fact that led to the adoption of a somewhat novel approach to making decisions: 'Although it was agreed to aim at unanimity, this was not to be an overriding principle; where views differed from the majority position they were expressed in the form of reservations appearing as footnotes in the main text' (Keatinge and Murphy, 1987: 224). Even though the Committee's proceedings were supposed to be confidential, the European news agency, Agence Europe, reported them extensively thus contributing to the creation of a small critical public.

Having concluded its deliberations, and in preparation for the Milan Summit of 1985, the Committee presented its final report to the heads of states or governments in bilateral meetings, and at a conference of foreign ministers at which alternative proposals were also put forward by individual member states. The Summit itself, as Keatinge and Murphy comment, was the 'first occasion in which the European Council gave the best of its attention to a general consideration of the future of European integration' (Keatinge and Murphy, 1987: 229). In spite of this, there was no agreement on concrete reforms, while the Dooge report itself remained contested even as a basis for further reflections. Nevertheless, for the first time in the history of the European Council a majority decision was taken (with the UK, Denmark and Greece in the minority) in favour of convening an intergovernmental conference on institutional reform and on the formalisation of European political co-operation.

The intergovernmental conference began on 22 July 1985 on the basis of the national positions, which the Dooge Committee's work had at least contributed to clarify. The Luxembourg presidency opened the IGC with a list of issues to discuss in order to arrive at particular reforms of the Treaties. In fact, this introduced a new way of conducting affairs in an IGC, since 'previous revisions of the Treaty [had been] negotiated within the Council, often in close association with the other institutions, and the IGC had provided merely formal assent' (Corbett, 1987: 239, who quotes the IGC on the merger Treaty, 1965, and the 1970/75 negotiations on the budgetary procedure as examples). It was also decided to hold one single IGC at foreign minister level on institutional reform, rather than two separate ones, on European political co-operation and institutional reform respectively. The IGC was prepared by meetings of national diplomats and the permanent representatives to the EU, under the leadership of the Luxembourg member of the Dooge Committee, Jean Dondelinger.

Throughout the works of the 1985 IGC, the European Parliament fought to be given a greater role in the proceedings. However, only limited progress was made on this. A two-person 'delegation' of the Parliament (the EP president and the chairman of the Institutional Affairs Committee) was received by the IGC, the Parliament was 'informed' by the presidency and the Commission on debates in the IGC, and it made its own views known, but the only real chance for direct impact on the results by the EP was the Italian government's assurance that it would veto proposals in the IGC which were not acceptable to the Parliament. In the event, such a threat was never carried out, and the IGC was concluded despite criticisms from the European Parliament as well as from the Danish and Italian delegations (Corbett, 1987: 242). Even though negotiations in the diplomatic working parties and among the ministers covered nearly all aspects which had been raised by the European Parliament's Draft Treaty on European Union, thus reflecting the overall need for reform and, possibly, the EP's role in setting the agenda for the IGC, the final result was only achieved in the bargaining between the heads of states or governments at the Luxembourg Summit in December in what was to become the IGC tradition of long hours of haggling.

Although it disappointed the EC institutions and the supporters of a more federal Europe, the Single European Act (SEA) represented at the time a significant change to the original Treaties, changing the direction of European integration by introducing new areas of competences (environmental policy, research, regional policy, etc.), new decision-making procedures (limited extension of qualified majority voting, assent and co-operation procedures), and by formalising European political co-operation. In the end, all member states signed the Act and even the European Parliament, though recording its unhappiness, supported it as 'better than nothing'. Part of the reason for this acquiescence might be sought in the fact that this was the first major treaty revision initiated 'by an elected Parliament' (Corbett, 1987: 267). For this reason, and though still filtered through the IGC process, to which the European Parliament remained effectively extraneous, the Single European Act marks an important step towards the broadening of the constitutional base for the European integration process.

The Maastricht Treaty

With the deadline of 1992 for the completion of the single market and Jacques Delors's determined efforts to meet this deadline, the Community concentrated on pragmatic progress based on the Single European Act until the events of 1989 dramatically changed the political landscape. The core of integration politics in those years was the move towards European Monetary Union (EMU), where an important role was played by another body of experts in the form of the Delors Committee comprising the national central bankers. The Committee envisaged another IGC to see to the necessary Treaty changes for the implementation of its recommendations, which would lead to the introduction of a single currency in three stages. This was an interesting example of a 'technical' committee with a political mandate, proposing far-reaching changes without much involvement from either the national or European parliamentarians, but that an IGC was supposed to rubber-stamp. The advent of German unification at the end of 1989 changed this scenario, however, by creating a strong incentive for a substantial deepening of European integration. At the Strasbourg Summit in December 1989 'the [Council] president merely announced that a majority existed to hold a new IGC [on EMU]' (Dinan, 1994: 163) with Margaret Thatcher being opposed but not formally outvoted.

Throughout early 1990, there was renewed pressure from some member states (Belgium, Italy) as well as from the Commission and the European Parliament, to make use of the new IGC as a vehicle for political union. These efforts culminated in a letter from Mitterand and Kohl to the Irish Council presidency arguing for a *second* IGC on political integration. In the end, this line prevailed, so that at the Dublin Summit in June 1990 it was decided to have another IGC on the reform of the Treaties, with a wide range of aims, from the improvement of the EC's legitimacy to making its institutions more efficient, from creating a coherent economic and monetary policy to establishing a common foreign and security policy. This was scheduled to begin at the same time as the IGC on EMU and the two IGCs started in Rome in December 1990, against a backdrop of growing concerns as to the ability of the Community to react to a number of burning issues, such as the continuing uncertainty in Central and Eastern Europe, the first Gulf crisis, and, later on, the breakout of war in Yugoslavia. Both IGCs took more than one year to complete their business. The General Affairs Council was given the task of ensuring the 'parallelism' (Dinan, 1994: 169) between the two conferences. In particular the Commission was keen on a strong link being established between them, since in this way it could guarantee to extend its central role in the EMU IGC to the political IGC, in which it would otherwise play only a marginal part.

While the EMU negotiations were based on the Delors report, the IGC on political union – differently from previous occasions – had no background document on which to rely. The initial negotiations for the 1991 IGCs were conducted at the usual three levels: the European Council; the specific ministers involved in the negotiations (mainly finance and foreign ministers); and the permanent representation officials. The intergovernmental nature of the negotiations, as Dinan notes, was partly offset by the fact that the Commission participated in all different levels of negotiations, even though 'it lacked the authority to veto a final agreement' (Dinan, 1994: 170). In truth, the Commission was often on the defensive in the EPU debates, while the European Parliament's involvement was marginal, its presence being limited to the 'regular contact between the presidents of the Council, the Commission and the Parliament and [to] allowing the president of the Parliament to address ministerial sessions of the conference' (Dinan, 1994: 181).

The lack of a background document, and the prevalence of interstate bargaining with a limited role for supranational actors, meant that a central role was played by the presidencies of 1991 (Luxembourg and the Netherlands) and by the general secretariat of the Council. This became visible in the proposal of the Luxembourg 'non-paper' of April 1991, a complete draft Treaty based on extensive bilateral consultations, which introduced the idea of a pillar structure for the European Union. The Dutch presidency of the second half of 1991 proposed a more federally inclined text, which was, however, widely rejected by the other member states, so that the final text was indeed closer to that originally proposed by the Luxembourg presidency. Negotiations on both EMU and political union were difficult and characterised by frequently changing alliances and coalitions, and they culminated in a bargaining-marathon at Maastricht. In the event, the Treaty introduced numerous important changes, but many of them only in embryonic shape (such as CFSP and CJHA) which, together with the technical nature of the document, gave rise to widespread disappointment. What followed, of course, were the ratification crises over the Maastricht Treaty with a nearly negative referendum in France and a first negative referendum in Denmark, some patchy changes to the Treaty agreed at the Edinburgh summit, another Danish referendum and eventual ratification in mid-1993.

After Maastricht: the concept of 'leftovers'

Crucially, Clause N of the new Treaty on European Union prescribed another IGC within a few years in order to review the functioning of the new European structures. This institutional automatism made the 1996 IGC, which led to the Amsterdam Treaty, different from previous ones, which had instead at least partly been caused by external events. True, the commitment made at the 1993 Copenhagen summit to a substantial enlargement of the Union, including a number of countries from Central and Eastern Europe, besides the three countries that had joined in 1995 (Austria, Finland and Sweden), made institutional adjustments necessary. Nonetheless, it is unlikely that the IGC would have been called so soon after Maastricht without the inbuilt revision clause (Dinan, 1999: 170).

Because of the ratification problems that had marred the Maastricht Treaty, and because it was felt that the Maastricht IGCs (especially the one on political union) were badly prepared, much more effort went into the preparation of Amsterdam, so much so that some observers maintain that 'if anything, the 1996 IGC was over-prepared' (Dinan, 1999: 170). There was also a growing pressure for more transparency, due not only to the Maastricht effect, but also to the entry of two Scandinavian countries with long-standing commitments to transparent governance. All this resulted in the Amsterdam IGC being conducted in a more open way. As part of its preparation, a high level reflection group was formed, which included not only representatives of national governments but also a Commissioner and two representatives of the European Parliament. Moreover, each of the three EU institutions (Council, Commission and Parliament) prepared a detailed report on the functioning of the TEU. In the case of the European Parliament, the preparation of its report sparked a (short-lived) flurry of consultative activities with NGOs and civil society, as well as the so-called 'assizes' between the European Parliament and national parliaments.

The resulting reports, however, mainly assessed the status quo of integration and made limited proposals for changes to the institutional structure. The reflection group itself, made up of representatives of the member states' governments, and chaired by the Spanish state secretary for foreign affairs Carlos Westendorp, was launched in June 1995 at Messina (to commemorate the fortieth anniversary of the Messina conference). It proceeded by collecting contributions from the EU institutions and the member states, as well as from political parties (both national and European), the academic world, interest groups and international organisations. Its main achievement was to clarify the IGC agenda and to identify several areas of consensus.

Divisions among the member states, and in particular British opposition to many of the proposed reforms, meant nevertheless that the reflection group's final report was rather weak, reiterating the three general areas in need of reform: making the EU more relevant to the citizens; improving the EU's efficiency and accountability; and increasing its capacity to act at the international level. Thus, 'buried under more preparatory documents than had been generated by all previous treaty reforms, member states launched the IGC at a special summit in Turin on March 29, 1996' (Dinan, 1999: 175). As in the past, the negotiations themselves took place at three levels, involving respectively high ranking diplomats (meeting more or less weekly), the foreign ministers (in the General Affairs Council), and the heads of states or governments (during the successive summits, and in particular at the concluding one in Amsterdam in June 1997). The roles of the Commission and the European Parliament remained unchanged, with the former having a formal place at the summits, but no veto power; and the latter being 'regularly informed' by the presidency and invited to comment on the work of the conference.

The resulting Amsterdam Treaty brought some important changes but failed in its main task: to prepare the institutional structure for a significantly enlarged EU. In particular, the questions of the weighting of votes in the Council of Ministers and of the size of the European Commission were left unsolved and known thereafter as the Amsterdam 'leftovers', something that required yet another IGC before the EU could admit the new applicant countries into its fold. This was actually stated in a protocol attached to the Amsterdam Treaty itself (see Dinan, 1999: 180–1). As enlargement became the EU's central preoccupation in the years following Amsterdam, so the need for further institutional reform became more pressing. Once enlargement negotiations were opened in March 1998, it was felt that the 'leftovers' problem needed to be tackled urgently. Only five months after the entry into force of the Amsterdam Treaty, the Cologne summit of June 1999 decided to call a new IGC for the following year, meant to deal with the institutional agenda once again. The way in which preparatory works were conducted before Maastricht and Amsterdam offered an easy blueprint to follow. The newly formed European Commission under Romano Prodi was charged with preparing a report outlining the reform options, which would function as the basis for the IGC. The report itself was drafted by 'three wise men' (Jean-Luc Dehaene, Lord David Simon and Richard von Weizsäcker), who were asked to act freely and independently in their work, with the proviso, however, that they would not make explicitly drafted Treaty proposals. On the basis of the three wise men's paper, which argued for comprehensive reforms of the whole EU institutional system, the Commission submitted its own contribution to the IGC.[2]

A new method is born: the Charter Convention

As well as calling for another IGC, the Council at Cologne took what proved to be a seminal decision. It decided to set up a special body to draft a catalogue of Fundamental Rights for the European Union in parallel with the work of the intergovernmental conference. Both processes were to be concluded before the end of 2000. The 'body' to elaborate the Charter of Fundamental Rights, however, was to be a very different kind of animal from the IGCs. The origin of the idea to set up an assembly comprising, for the first time in the EU's history, delegates from national governments, from national parliaments, from the European Commission and from the European Parliament, all nominally equal, seems to have been in the German administration. The need for a European document dealing with Fundamental Rights was of particular significance in Germany, because of the cases brought before the German constitutional court on the compatibility of successive EU Treaties with the guarantee of fundamental rights under the German Constitution (the so-called 'Solange decisions' of 1974 and 1986).[3] There had already been calls for such a document during the Maastricht negotiations, which had also been referred back to the EP's Spinelli draft constitution. The Bundestag had raised the issue in the mid-1990s, and when it became clear that there would not be a majority in favour of such a move at the Amsterdam IGC, the issue became a priority for the German EU presidency of the first half of 1999. A public commitment to such a document was made by Joschka Fischer in his inaugural speech of the German presidency programme to the European Parliament in January 1999. It was supported by a report prepared for the European Commission by another 'group of wise men', under the chairmanship of Professor Spiros Simitis, arguing in favour of a system of fundamental rights for the EU (Simitis et al., 1999).

The link between the project of a fundamental rights catalogue and a new, more inclusive procedure, different from that used for previous treaty drafting, developed during the first couple of months of 1999. The German Minister of Justice, Hertha Däubler-Gmelin, who took responsibility for the project, together with the foreign minister, invited a large number of constitutional and fundamental rights experts, as well as representatives of the member states for a brain-storming conference in March, where 'procedural as well as substantial issues were discussed' (interview: H. Däubler-Gmelin, 9 March 2004). The idea of creating a body including national parliament representatives and European parliamentarians, based on the earlier Bundestag debates, was then tested in bilateral talks with key European partners. It reflected a common understanding that the process 'could not be just an IGC, and it could not just be a body of experts, but had to combine elements of the two' (interview: H. Däubler-Gmelin, 9 March 2004).

The summit meeting at Cologne adopted the conclusions drafted by the two ministries. The provisions regarding the assembly to draft the EU Charter were, according to one source close to the presidency, accepted without much debate (interview: German foreign ministry official, 9 August 2000). The lack of resistance from those member states who were sceptical both of the idea of the Charter of Fundamental Rights, and of the need for a special body to draft it, may need some explanation. One reason for this can be found in the contemporary political international context characterised by the war in Kosovo, which had started a couple of weeks earlier. This required the EU heads of states or governments to present the Union as both determined and united in its defence of fundamental and human rights (Merlingen et al., 2001). Another reason is that the Charter was seen as a pet project of the German presidency, and probably perceived as an easy way of allowing the newly established German government to claim some kind of success for its presidency, in an otherwise difficult period, amongst controversies over Kosovo and the EU's financial prospects. In 1999, Chancellor Schröder was a newcomer to the European Council (the SPD-Green government took office in October 1998), and he needed a positive initiative to make his mark. In this sense it was 'lucky for us [the supporters of the Charter project] that at Cologne there were not many other big issues on the agenda' (interview: H. Däubler-Gmelin, 2004). Finally, the decision to make Roman Herzog (former president of Germany and of its constitutional court, and an internationally recognised expert on fundamental rights) the main German representative in the drafting body gave credibility to the entire project both within Germany and in the EU at large.

Against this backdrop, the Cologne mandate not only set out the task for the new body and the sources from which it should draw, but also established the basic structure of the Convention's four main representative components: from national parliaments, from national governments, from the European Parliament, and from the Commission. It omitted, however, to decide the size of their respective representation. Following Cologne, an 'ad hoc' working group of the Committee of Permanent Representatives (Coreper) was set up with the task of drafting more detailed provisions for the new body, which were eventually taken to the Tampere summit in October 1999. The Tampere Conclusions stipulated that the heads of states or governments would send one personal representative each to the new body, the national parliaments would send two emissaries each, the president of the European Commission would send one, and the European Parliament would be represented by sixteen of its members. The latter provision on the number of EP representatives is interesting because apparently an earlier draft of the working group had proposed a lower number of MEPs to be involved, but it was agreed that the Parliament should at least have as many representatives as the member states, and in fact one more, to underline that the Parliament delegates were not representing member states (interview: Finnish presidency official, 7 February 2001). The Tampere Council Conclusions are also significant because they added a significant number of observers (two from the European Court of Justice and two from the Council of Europe, including one from the European Court of Human Rights) to the Convention. The same conclusions established that a number of other institutions such as the Economic and Social Committee, the Committee of the Regions and the European Ombudsman should be consulted; that the views of the candidate countries should be listened to; and, last but not least, that the proceedings of the new body should be public.

With these provisions some of the most important characteristics of what was to become the 'Convention method' were established. These comprised the inclusion of all core EU institutions as well as the member states on a nominally equal basis; the commitment to a wider dialogue with interested parties; and the general principle of transparency and openness. Although some of the elements of the Constitutional Convention were different, the main principles remained unchanged. These principles, however, left a number of aspects unspecified: most notably what was the status of the document to be drafted, and what were the decision-making procedures to be followed. In this context, it is important to note that the Tampere mandate made clear that, contrary to earlier drafts envisaging a rotating presidency, the body would elect its own president for the full duration of the deliberations, and that the two parliamentary delegations would elect one representative each to the executive body of the assembly. The first Convention's Presidium was thus made up of three elected members plus the Commission representative and the representative of the acting Council presidency on behalf of the national government delegates. The body elected Roman Herzog as its chairman and decided to call itself 'Convention' at the first meeting in December 1999.

On the crucial question of how decisions would be reached in the Convention, the Tampere text contained the formula 'When the chairperson, in close concertation with the vice-chairpersons, deems that the text of the draft Charter elaborated by the body can eventually be subscribed to by all the parties, it shall be forwarded to the European Council through the normal preparatory procedure' (European Council, 1999b). This procedural hint was interpreted by the Convention's Presidium as excluding decisions by majority votes. It was instead taken to warrant a more 'consensus-building' procedure, by allowing this to develop in the course of the Convention's debates, leading eventually to 'generally accepted' conclusions. This resulted in the final draft of the Charter being approved by acclamation by 60 out of the 62 members of the Convention in October 2000, marking an important difference between the 'Convention method' and that normally employed by either the intergovernmental conferences, based on unanimity, or the Council of Ministers, based on a sophisticated system of qualified majority. According to minister Däubler-Gmelin, the ambiguity in the provision on the decision-making was deliberate because other possibilities (unanimity or some kind of qualified majority) had been discussed with the experts beforehand and rejected as too divisive. 'We therefore decided to pursue our double strategy of using this diplomatic language on the decision-making [to allow for flexibility] and to exercise pressure [to reach decisions] through the timing of the Convention' (interview: H. Däubler-Gmelin 2004).

In retrospect, the judgement on the Charter Convention can be positive, and most commentators have regarded it as a successful experiment, in so far as it favoured a broad agreement on some limited, yet at times controversial, sets of questions, comprising not only the listing of well-established human rights, but also issues that touched upon a wide range of sensitive issues concerning the nature and scope of the integration process (Eriksen et al., 2003; Schönlau, 2005). Arguably this was possible partly because the very status of the Charter remained undecided throughout the work of the Convention, thus making the link between it and the final decision-makers in the IGC somewhat unclear. Nonetheless, both the Convention president and the majority of its members worked under the assumption that they had to produce a draft 'as if' this was eventually to become a legally binding document. This self-imposed restraint provided the rationale for how the Convention worked, and motivated the members of the Convention to produce a text that could not easily be unpicked by the heads of states or governments. Despite the fact that the Nice IGC did not ratify the Charter formally, but merely 'proclaimed' it as a 'political' declaration, and in spite of some questions which can be raised about the transparency and openness of the Convention's process, the Charter Convention was considered by many as a success and as having established an alternative to the traditional IGC.

The Charter Convention and the Nice débâcle: more of the same?

This positive perception was reinforced in particular because the 2000 IGC was run along the same lines as the previous ones, albeit with a more direct involvement of two observers from the European Parliament, and ended in a bad-tempered and not very successful summit in Nice in December 2000. As on previous occasions, lengthy preparations had been done by the so-called 'preparatory group' consisting of personal representatives of the foreign ministers, one Commissioner and the two European Parliament observers. The twelve applicant countries had been invited to make statements to the IGC. The foreign ministers and two European summits had also debated the controversial IGC issues (in particular the extension of qualified majority voting, the issue of flexibility or 'enhanced co-operation' and the size of the Commission and the European Parliament), and the Parliament itself had submitted detailed proposals for reform (European Parliament Leinen/ Dimitrakopoulos report 2000).[4] Nevertheless the IGC itself progressed slowly and concentrated more and more on the key institutional questions on which agreement remained distant.

It was in such a context that Joschka Fischer's speech at Humboldt University in Berlin in May 2000 succeeded in changing the political agenda by bypassing the narrow questions of institutional engineering, and opening up the debate on the wider issue of the future of Europe. This call was taken up by a number of key players in different member states, so that at the Biarritz Council meeting, i.e before the IGC 2000 was even concluded, a consensus emerged on the opportunity to have another IGC in 2004 where issues such as the division of competences between the EU and its member states, the status of the Charter of Fundamental Rights, and the simplification of the European Treaties, could be finally solved. This was partly due to intense pressure on some governments (in particular from the German Länder and other regions) to fix clearer limits to the EU's competences, which were seen as both increasing and entrenched. The rather disappointing compromises on institutional matters arrived at in Nice, in spite, or perhaps because of some hard-fought interstate bargaining, were generally regarded as inadequate for the kind of challenges posed by enlargement.

So, it was at the Nice summit itself that it was agreed to hold yet another IGC on the wider questions raised by Fischer and others. Despite the fact that the Nice Treaty was presented as having prepared the EU for enlargement, a declaration attached to it acknowledged that 'a deeper and wider debate about the future of the European Union' should be launched in 2001 by the Swedish and Belgian presidencies 'in cooperation with the Commission involving the European Parliament' (European Union, 2001: Declaration 23, point 3). The declaration also included a list of interested parties to be consulted, such as the 'representatives of national Parliaments and all those reflecting public opinion namely political, economic and university circles, representatives of civil society etc.', and it stated that '[t]he candidate States will be associated with this process in ways to be defined.' A debate between all these parties was supposed to lead to an IGC in 2004, but was not supposed to 'constitute any form of obstacle or pre-condition to the enlargement process' (ibid.).

Based on this declaration and in a context of widespread disappointment with the Nice experience not only for the insufficient results as far as institutional reform was concerned, but also because of the obvious shortcomings of the method of intergovernmental negotiation and its tendency to produce lowest common denominator solutions, the Swedish and in particular the Belgian presidency in 2001 started to explore the options for a different process for the new round of EU debate. Numerous national parliaments, the European Parliament, several national governments as well as outside actors continued to lobby for a conference based on the experience from the Convention which had successfully drafted the EU Charter of Fundamental Rights. The general agreement to set up a Convention with a similar composition (four components, majority of parliamentarians, etc.) to the Charter Convention, albeit including the candidate countries on a more or less equal basis, was taken in October 2001 at the European Council meeting in Genval following a proposal from the Belgian presidency. At this stage, however, there was still disagreement among member states on the nature of the new Convention mandate, and on how the Convention would be related to the IGC. The Belgian presidency, and in particular Prime Minister Verhofstadt, made it his priority to reach an agreement on these issues at the Laeken summit (Ludlow, 2002).

The Laeken mandate and the new Convention

Once again, a group of wise men (this time five of them) was set up by the Belgian presidency to feed their ideas into the process of setting the wider debate in motion. The group consisted of former prime ministers Giuliano Amato and Jean-Luc Dehaene, former Commission president Jacques Delors, former Polish foreign minister Bronislav Geremek, and David Miliband 'a British MP and confidant of Tony Blair' (Ludlow, 2002: 53). In Verhofstadt's mind, this group 'was [probably] not so much to advise him, as to enhance the credibility of the Laeken project as a whole' (Ludlow, 2002: 56). The real decisions were yet again taken in the European Council, on the basis of documents prepared by the General Affairs Council and the Committee of Permanent Representatives of the Member States who, together with the Belgian presidency, drafted the declaration that set up the Convention on the Future of Europe. It is interesting how this way of proceeding, involving some shuttle diplomacy on the Belgian prime minister's part, both before and at the Laeken summit in December 2001, built in part on the experience leading to the Charter Convention, but was also markedly different.

Even though the European Council at Laeken did propose the same kind of basic composition of the Convention (of two national parliament representatives per country, one representative of the head of state or government of each country and sixteen from the European Parliament), it changed the internal balance of the Convention by, firstly, extending its size with the inclusion of the 'accession candidate countries', and, secondly, by choosing the president and two vice-presidents for the new Convention. This latter change was quite clearly an attempt to build safeguards into the system, limiting the independence of the Convention. Agreement on the presidency, however, was not easy. And the decision to appoint Valéry Giscard d'Estaing as the Convention's chairman was only reached after protracted behind-closed-door discussions at the Laeken meeting (Ludlow, 2002).

As part of the compromise reached on the Convention president, it was also decided to increase the size of the Presidium of the Convention from five (as it was for the Charter Convention) to twelve members. The Presidium of the Constitutional Convention therefore comprised two national parliamentarians, two Commission representatives, two European parliamentarians, the Convention's president, two vice-presidents, and the representatives of the three heads of states or governments holding the presidency of the Union during the lifetime of the Convention. Eventually, under pressure from the Convention and in particular from the applicant and candidate countries, a representative chosen by the applicant countries was added on as a permanent observer (this was Alojz Peterle, representative of the Slovenian government). This composition of the Presidium gave it a more definite intergovernmental bias, while at the same time making it less cohesive than the smaller Presidium of the Charter Convention. Moreover, Giscard d'Estaing's own personality, and his strongly privileged position (alongside that of his two vice-presidents), somewhat affected the internal dynamic of the Constitutional Convention's Presidium when compared to that of the Charter Convention (Norman, 2003). These changes were important because they allowed even those member states who were less than enthusiastic about a Convention to accept it, first at Coreper level and then at the Laeken summit itself. According to Ludlow, 'the principal reason that they eventually acquiesced was that, during the summer and autumn, Coreper installed several significant safeguards regarding the composition, functions and organisation of the assembly, which appear to have convinced them that the Convention was "safe as well as sexy" ' (Ludlow, 2002: 59).

Of course, in this context it was also crucial to reach agreement on the aims of the Convention and on its relation with a future IGC. During the discussions in Coreper, strong feelings were expressed that the Convention's mandate should not make it a replacement for the IGC as the ultimate decision-making body. Coreper therefore proposed that the Convention should work on 'options' for reform. The formula was subsequently changed several times. Interestingly, a comparison between the draft conclusions which Guy Verhofstadt took on his 'tour des capitales' in November 2001 (Council Document SN 4663/03, reproduced in Ludlow, 2002: 218ff.) and those finally adopted at Laeken shows that the Convention's mandate was strengthened rather than weakened in the redrafting. Indeed, the earlier version stated that the Convention's final document 'may set out a number of options, to be shown in order of preference, and any comments deemed of assistance for readier understanding of the text' (European Council 2001a; Ludlow, 2002: 225). The adopted document reads: 'It [the Convention] will draw up a final document which may comprise either different options, indicating the degree of support which they received, or recommendations if consensus is achieved' (European Council, 2001b; Ludlow, 2002: 234). At the same time, while the early draft underlined that the result of the Convention would 'provide the basis for further work, without formally binding the parties involved in the future Intergovernmental Conference', the Laeken text stresses that the Convention's report would 'provide a starting point for discussions in the Intergovernmental Conference, which will take the ultimate decisions' (ibid.). These provisions are important because they encouraged the Convention to decide early on that it would attempt to produce a single draft so as to exercise maximum influence on the IGC.

The elements of the Laeken declaration just quoted are significant because, unlike the Cologne mandate for the Charter Convention, they made explicit reference to the consensus method as the decision-making procedure in the Convention. Whereas the November draft was closely modelled on the Cologne formula, since it stated that '[i]t will be for the Convention Chairman, in close consultation with the Presidium, to find a sufficient consensus on the document within the Convention' (European Council, 2001a; Ludlow 2002: 225), the Laeken text did not mention this as the explicit prerogative of the Chairman. Nevertheless the condition that recommendations could only be made 'if consensus is achieved' and the fact that no further provisions were made for establishing when this was the case, meant that the Convention president *de facto* decided when discussions had produced a consensus – in the same way as this happened at the Charter Convention (Bellamy and Schönlau, 2004a on the Charter; Closa, 2003 on the Laeken Convention). Finally, it is important to note that both the earlier draft, and the final document explicitly linked the Convention's work to the possibility of a European Constitution because the provisions on the working method of the body come after a paragraph headed 'Towards a Constitution for European citizens' under which four core questions are listed for the Convention to tackle. This heading seems to have remained unchallenged in the negotiations at Laeken – possibly because it was seen as a sufficiently distant prospect by those who had a more sceptical position, and because they perhaps relied on the safeguards built into the Convention's own mandate. Perhaps by default, the 'constitutional' question had now become central to the EU political debate.

One other issue, however, proved rather controversial both before and at the Laeken summit. This was the question of the timing of the Convention's work. As mentioned earlier, the debate occurred in a framework set by two existing deadlines. According to declaration 23 attached to the Treaty of Nice, 'a new Conference of the Representatives of the Governments of the Member States will be convened in 2004, to address the aforementioned items with a view to making corresponding changes to the Treaties.' Yet, the Nice IGC had also made clear that this new conference would 'not constitute any form of obstacle or precondition to the enlargement process' (point 8) – which was already scheduled to see the first accessions in time for the new member states to participate in the (June) 2004 elections to the European Parliament. This created a problem because some member states, in particular the UK, insisted that there should be a 'cooling off' period after the end of the Convention to allow them to explain (and possibly mitigate) the Convention's results in their national contexts before having to make a final decision about them in the IGC. At the same time, Italy was very keen to be able to start the IGC under its presidency (July–December 2003) in the hope that it would gain prestige from setting the stage for a 'second Treaty of Rome'. Because of the disagreement on this issue, the final version of the Laeken Declaration was somewhat unclear, mentioning a start date (1 March 2002), but only saying that its proceedings will be 'completed after a year', without any mention of a cooling off period. This lack of clarity meant that several actors in the Convention process tried to influence its timetable, so as to extend its mandate and to reduce the cooling off period (the Convention officially finished in July 2003, i.e. after sixteen months) (Ludlow, 2002: 71). Nevertheless the Convention worked under considerable time pressure given the scale of its task, something that had an important impact on the kind of debates which developed (Schönlau, 2004). The IGC opened less than three months after the end of the Convention, on 4 October 2003, only to fail to reach an agreement after two more months.

Other issues such as the precise role of the two vice-presidents and whether they would 'count' as part of their national government's representation, or the inclusion of Turkey as one of the candidate countries in the same way as Bulgaria and Romania, continued to be discussed even after the Laeken summit, though they were eventually resolved by the time the Convention held its inaugural meeting on 28 February 2002 (Hummer, 2002). But even then, procedural uncertainties and divisions remained. First, there were issues regarding the financing of the Convention in general, but also Giscard d'Estaing's own financial and personal claims, which were the object of negative press coverage (Norman, 2003: 40–1). Secondly, Giscard's own draft of the rules of procedure for the Convention sparked controversy even before they were made officially public on 27 February (CONV 3/02), mainly because they were seen as giving excessive powers to the president and seemed to exclude the alternate members. After numerous amendments and intensive debates in the Presidium and the Convention plenary, the issues were eventually resolved with a compromise on 22 March (on this, see Chapter 4). Thirdly, the role of the applicant and candidate countries created some tensions. The Laeken mandate formulated their special status as 'not-yet-member states' by stressing that they 'will be able to take part in the proceedings without, however, being able to prevent any consensus which may emerge among the Member States' (European Council, 2001b; Ludlow, 2002: 233). This implied a clear division of status between 'old' and 'new' member states, which reflected some fears from the old member states, but which in the event proved to be unfounded, to the extent that later on in the process most *conventionnels* seemed to accept the representatives of the new member states as full equals – a view borne out, of course, by the inclusion of the ten new member states which were to join on 1 May 2004, as equal partners with a right of veto in the intergovernmental conference. Nevertheless, this equal status was not clear at the beginning of the process and the exclusion of the applicant countries from the Presidium and from some preparatory meetings before the Convention started led to early doubts about the fairness and equality of the 'Convention method' (Norman, 2003: 43).[5]

Conclusion: a new method for a new constitutional phase?

The Convention, which convened for the first time in a solemn ceremony on 28 February 2002, was in many ways a first in EU history. With 105 full members and 102 alternates it was larger than any body which had so far been working to prepare constitutional/Treaty changes in the EU before. While by no means fully 'representative', the Convention, with a majority of elected parliamentarians (56 national and 16 European MEPs) was very different from the preparatory or working groups constituted by high ranking national diplomats or by appointed eminent political figures in the past. Given the repeated emphasis on the Convention's dependence on a wider public debate and the commitment to open and transparent proceedings of the body itself, it was constituted as the 'opposite' of secretive IGCs where deals are made in the early hours among weary national leaders. Finally, the leeway given to the Convention by its principals (the heads of states or governments united in the European Council at Laeken) regarding the decision-making method, coupled with the reference to a (possible) constitutional document, meant that the Convention could see itself as an assembly drafting a Constitutional Treaty, which would not depend on unanimous agreement but rather on the more flexible notion of consensus.

And yet, the Convention was not a complete break with the EU/EC history of treaty-making. There are clear continuities in the way in which the constitutional development of the European polity has progressed. While the early days after the setting up of the European Coal and Steel Community had seen ambitious plans for a constitutional document for a European political community to be drafted by a 'constituent assembly' composed of elected parliamentarians (drawn, however, from the ranks of the appointed national parliamentarians in the Council of Europe or ECSC parliamentary assemblies), the early failure of these plans had led to a much more cautious approach in which technocrats and diplomats became the central players of constitutional change for many years. The growth and institutionalisation of intergovernmental co-operation in the day-to-day running of European integration also meant that it was the IGC method which came to dominate even the fundamental decision-making about changes to the Treaties and the overall direction of the European project.

Nevertheless there has been a long-running debate amongst academic commentators and European political elites (both at national and supranational level) about the obvious deficiencies of this method of functional integration exclusively conducted through the executives at the expense of democratic control (Warleigh, 2003). In particular, ever since the early 1970s the danger of alienation between the integration project and 'the people' has been on the agenda of the core decision-makers and has been both trigger and crucial challenge for attempts to adapt the political-legal framework of integration. Increasingly, debates about the European Treaties have focused on how to bring the European Community/Union closer to its citizens and how to make it more democratic. After the watershed first direct elections in 1979, these concerns have found an additional channel in the European Parliament which has become increasingly influential over the years.

Importantly for the present analysis, this debate has increasingly focused on the process of Treaty change itself. From the IGC on the Single European Act in response to the European Parliament's draft constitution of 1984, via the Maastricht ratification crises towards the 2002 Convention project, a gradual opening up of the closed IGC procedures can be observed. The questions of whether individual steps in this process are sufficient or not, and whether the trend will continue after the experience of the 2003 IGC, will be further explored in the Conclusion of this book. Nevertheless it is significant that the idea of a broad and structurally representative Convention was first tested and then repeated in the context of the EU's impending enlargement in response to a growing concern that unanimity among member states will be much more difficult to achieve among twenty-five or more very different players. The two Conventions therefore mark a new 'phase' in the EU's constitutional history.

Notes

1. It should be noted that the term 'intergovernmental conference' was not used at this time.
2. Available at http://europa.eu.int/igc2000/repoct99_en.pdf
3. BVerfGE 37, 271ff., of 1974 and BVerfGE 73, 339ff., of 1986.
4. In two parts, A5-0018/2000 and A5-0058/1999.
5. See Chapter 6 for a discussion of the inequalities between the member states and applicant states in the language regime of the Convention.

4
Membership, Representation and Accountability

Justus Schönlau

In Chapter 3 it has been argued that, in spite of the fact that the Convention has a certain family resemblance with other specific bodies appointed in the past to prepare important treaty revisions, the Convention and its 'method' represent a significant departure in European constitution-making. This and the next chapter are more directly interested in discussing how much the Constitutional Convention lived up to the expectations of offering a new means for more democracy and participation.

In particular, this chapter deals with the issue of the composition of the Constitutional Convention, drawing some comparisons with the Charter Convention, and assessing both its representativeness and accountability. Such issues are of particular significance in view of the fact that the 'Convention method' is considered as an improvement on the intergovernmental method characterising the IGCs, because it was deemed to be more inclusive, open and democratic, and hence ultimately more legitimate, as a way of reaching decisions of a constitutional nature at the European level. Arguably, the Convention structure offered a broader basis for legitimacy; nevertheless a number of issues such as the equality of status of the *conventionnels*, the process through which they were selected, the mechanisms of feedback and accountability to their natural constituencies, and questions of openness and transparency of the proceedings need to be looked at more closely in order to formulate a precise judgement on how well the 'Convention method' worked. This chapter and the next will therefore examine these issues in an attempt to determine in what sense the Convention experiment opened a new phase of constitutional politics in the European Union.

As we saw in the previous chapter, the Convention on the Future of Europe was set up to prepare either a series of options or a single proposal for changes to be made to the EU Treaties. These were eventually to be decided by member states at an intergovernmental conference. Early on during its proceedings, the Convention opted to prepare a single draft for a Constitutional Treaty, with the intention of forcing the hand of the IGC, to sanction the text more or less unchanged. In this way the Convention body acted less as a technical body and more as a quasi-constitutional assembly or, indeed, as a constitutional convention. This makes the issue of the composition of the Convention and of its representativeness particularly important in order to judge its legitimacy and the legitimacy of its output.[1]

Yet, such a self-representation of the Convention did not go unchallenged either within or outside of it (Bonde, 2003; Stuart, 2003; Arnull, 2003). Many *conventionnels* were aware that they were not entirely free in their decisions, and that, paraphrasing Magnette (2004b), they acted under 'the shadow' of the IGC, where the 'representatives of the governments of the member states' would determine 'by common accord the amendments to be made to the Treaties' (Art. 48 TEU). The *conventionnels* were therefore caught between the limited and somewhat ambiguous nature of the mandate given to the Convention of the Future of Europe, and their own individual and/or collective ambitions and claims of legitimacy. In fact, while the Convention's proceedings were arguably more open and internally democratic than those normally taking place at the IGCs, their democratic credentials need to be examined more closely before they can be judged superior to those of the Council, which represents democratically elected and nationally accountable governments. In the following, the Convention and its membership will therefore be explored through the lens of representation and accountability (Pollak and Slominski, 2004).

The analysis will focus first on the composition of the Convention in order to show how the mix of different institutional actors contributed to give a broad representative basis to the body itself. Yet the hybrid nature of its composition also meant that the mechanisms for the selection and accountability of the *conventionnels* differed widely across the membership. This had repercussions on the status of the *conventionnels*, depending on what 'constituency' they represented, a fact which was recognised early on by the Convention's president, who therefore concluded that the body could not formally function on a majority principle by voting on decisions, since different members' votes would have to be 'counted' differently depending on whether they had been delegated by a national parliament, a national government or a European institution. The decision to eschew voting as a procedure contributed to a search for 'consensus' and thus to a more deliberative style of debate in the Convention, something which will be discussed further in the following chapter. In certain respects, this was a positive feature of the way in which the Convention was both structured and operated, but it also highlights the problematic nature of its representativeness.

The membership of the Convention

With 102 full members, the Convention on the Future of Europe was a rather large body, certainly in comparison with the frequently invoked Philadelphia Convention which had 55 members. Moreover, the Convention on the Future of Europe had a corresponding number of substitute members and a triumvirate of presidents, bringing its total membership to 207 plus thirteen permanent observers from the Committee of the Regions, the Economic and Social Committee, and the European Ombudsman. Following the example of the Charter Convention, it was expected that substitute members would be fully involved in the Convention's work. Yet, the role of the substitutes was one of the issues over which controversy broke out at the very beginning of the Convention's work (Dauvergne, 2004: 52–3). The Laeken mandate itself had stated that *conventionnels* could only be replaced by substitutes if they were not present, and that substitutes had to be appointed in the same way as full members. Early proposals for a set of rules of procedure for the Convention, drafted by Giscard d'Estaing and his secretariat (CONV 3/02), adopted a strict reading of this provision and limited the rights and role of substitute members by stating that they could only participate in Convention meetings if the absence of the full member had been announced to the secretariat two days in advance.

In the words of one analyst, this 'antipathy to the alternates' on the part of Giscard 'partly reflected [his] concern that the full Convention members would be less than diligent in attending the plenary sessions and so fail to develop the necessary *esprit de corps*, if the alternates were practically their equals' (Norman, 2003: 44). In response to pressure from the Convention, however, and in particular from a large group supporting alternative proposals for rules of procedure drafted by Andrew Duff, a member of the European Parliament delegation, a more flexible attitude was adopted, which allowed substitute members to attend all Convention meetings and to speak if the respective full member was absent for a full day (CONV 9/02, 14 March 2002). Moreover, in the ensuing debate Giscard promised that the rules of procedure would be applied 'flexibly', which allowed him to state that there was a 'consensus' on the revised rules of procedure (Norman, 2003: 45). Due to these changes, which moved the Convention's internal rules much more towards a 'typically parliamentary logic' (Floridia, 2003: 80), the substitute members did play an increasingly important role as the Convention progressed.

The role of the substitutes was particularly important in relation to the representativeness of the Convention, by making sure that different voices were heard (Pollak and Slominski, 2004: 47–50). This was so because in many cases of national parliaments, for example, the two full members came from the main forces of government and opposition respectively, with the substitutes 'covering' other parties (for example, Austria, Belgium or Finland). Many two-chamber parliaments were represented by one full Convention member for each chamber (for example, the German Bundestag and Bundesrat or French or Italian Chambers and Senates respectively), but in other cases, like the British Parliament, the House of Lords was represented only by two alternates, while the House of Commons appointed both full members (Norman, 2003: 44). Thus in the 'delegation' from the national parliaments, a number of different models of representation manifested themselves, and the substitutes played a crucial part in broadening the representative basis of the assembly as a whole.

In the case of the European Parliament delegation, its representation was mainly focused on providing an image of the balance of political power, and less on territorial or other criteria. Its sixteen full members were selected on the basis of a rough calculation (based on the d'Hondt criteria) of the relative size of political groups within the EP. Each political group chose its own substitutes. This resulted in a delegation composed of six EPP-ED members, five PES members, and one each of ELDR, EDD, GUE-NGL, Greens and UEN and a mirror-image substitute delegation. The EP caucus thus represented the seven party groups present in the EP at the time among members and substitutes, but did not include any member of the so-called 'group of non-aligned' independent MEPs. Within the party delegations, allocation was based on complex horse-trading in relation to other posts and entitlements because the setting up of the Convention coincided with the so-called 'mid-term review', where Committee positions are redistributed among parties half way through a legislature in the EP. One important factor in selecting the particular individuals was their experience in Constitutional and Convention matters. This resulted in a sizeable number of the *conventionnels* from the EP – seven out of a total of sixteen full members, and five out of the sixteen substitutes – who had already served in the Charter Convention in 1999. Furthermore, ten of the sixteen full members of the Convention and eleven of sixteen substitutes of the EP delegation were either full or substitute members of the EP's Constitutional Affairs Committee.

With regards to nationalities, the EP delegation was much less representative, comprising three representatives for Britain and Germany, two for France and Italy, and one each for Denmark, Spain, Holland, Portugal and Austria. None of the other six nationalities of the fifteen EU countries were represented as part of the full members of this delegation. Even considering the substitute members, the EP delegation had no member from Sweden, Luxembourg or Ireland. In terms of gender equality, the European Parliament delegation – with five women out of the sixteen full members, and seven out of the sixteen substitutes – fared much better than the Convention as a whole (as will be further illustrated in Chapter 7), but it obviously underrepresented women given their numbers in the general European population. Overall, however, the EP delegation was broadly representative of a number of social, political and national cleavages of European society.

Looking at the group of national representatives it is important to remember that, technically speaking, they were 'personal representatives of the respective heads of government' even though they were frequently referred to as '(national) government representatives'. By definition this group had a very different kind of representational role to fulfil. As a body they included an interesting mix of different profiles and the membership of this delegation saw some of the most important changes during the lifetime of the Convention, partly due to governments changing after national elections, partly reflecting changing strategies or priorities with regard to the Convention itself. While several governments chose initially to be represented by individuals with an academic rather than a political profile (notably Finland's Teija Tiilikainen and Germany's Peter Glotz) or by nominally non-partisan individuals (mainly among candidate countries such as Cyprus, Lithuania, Malta or Poland), this changed in some cases as the Convention process unfolded: the entry of the foreign ministers of both Germany and France in the autumn of 2002, which was followed by similar moves by Greece, Slovenia and Latvia, was seen by many as a recognition of the (growing) political significance of the Convention and marked the transition into a new phase of the Convention's work. Alain Dauvergne notes, moreover, that this change in representation coincided with a changing role of the applicant country representatives who became more assertive after the Copenhagen summit in December 2002 had definitely set the date for their accession to the EU at 1 May 2004 (Dauvergne, 2004: 125).

Altogether thirteen government representatives were replaced during the Convention, with Turkey and Spain changing government representative twice. It is noteworthy that, besides president Giscard himself, the Convention comprised a significant number of former heads of states or governments, such as Jean-Luc Dehaene, Giulio Amato, John Bruton, Alojs Peterle and Jacques Santer, and a number of serving ministers.[2] This situation was clearly different from the Charter Convention where a much greater number of representatives were experts in the field of human rights or European law rather than prominent politicians. This was partly due to the fact that the Charter Convention had a more restricted mandate and was seen, especially at the beginning, as a more 'technical' exercise. Nonetheless, the Constitutional Convention was similarly characterised by a high number of members with a professional or educational background in law (Kleger, 2004: 74).

As for the two representatives of the Commission in the Convention, they played a separate role as part of the representative structure of the Convention. Technically, Commissioners Vitorino and Barnier represented the Commission president, in his role as the head of the 'college of Commissioners', which is regarded as the guardian of the general interest of the European Union. As such, they did not form part of any particular 'caucus' in the Convention; nor were they a proper 'delegation' – in fact, it was not always clear whether they spoke on behalf of either the Commission as a whole or of its president. In most accounts of the Commission's performance in the Convention it is noted that, despite the high quality of the two individuals concerned, the Commission as an institution did not play as important a role as could have been expected because of a lack of internal unity, and weak leadership from Prodi (Dauvergne, 2004: 52; Norman, 2003: 322). In particular, the Commission's contribution to the Convention was marred by co-ordination or communication problems between the two *conventionnels* and their 'home' institution (Beach, 2003).[3]

Finally, the Presidium of the Convention was interesting from the point of view of representation. It had been stipulated by the Laeken Council decision that the Presidium would be composed of the president and his two vice-presidents (appointed rather than elected, as had been the case for the Charter Convention), and nine other *conventionnels*, including representatives of all governments holding the EU presidency throughout the Convention, plus two representatives of the Commission, and two each of the European Parliament and the national parliaments. Only the four latter of the twelve Presidium members were elected to their posts by the relevant delegation, while the others were members *ex officio*. Interestingly, even though the Presidium was not thought out as a representative body in itself, the failure to include the future member states in it sparked controversy. In the end, a thirteenth member was invited as 'permanent observer' to the Presidium, chosen by the national government and parliament representatives of the thirteen candidate countries. Similarly, there were criticisms of the clear political bias represented in the Presidium. A group of eight *conventionnels* who failed to support the final Draft of the Constitutional Treaty (DCT) criticised the Presidium for not including 'one single Eurosceptic or Eurorealist person' and comprising members from three political families only (CONV 851/03 para. 14; Arnull, 2003). Although, technically speaking, the Presidium 'represented' the four delegations comprising the Convention, only the members of the national parliamentarians and the MEPs who were part of the Presidium seemed to regard their position as 'accountable' to their own groups of origin. In the absence of a coherent view of the national government caucus, the envoys of the rotating presidency of the EU ended up representing their countries – while the president and vice-presidents represented no one but themselves.[4] On the whole, the Presidium therefore forms the weakest link in any claim about the representativeness of the Convention (Stuart, 2003; Arnull, 2003).

The status of the *conventionnels*

The Laeken mandate had set out criteria of membership of the Convention along institutional and territorial lines (through the member states), which led to a 'potentially uneven structure of presence' (Pollak and Slominski, 2004: 50). It had not explicitly envisaged a balancing (or representative structure) along party political, demographic, sociological or other criteria, even though some institutions attempted to select their representatives by paying attention to some of these criteria. As Closa notes, territorial representation was envisaged by the patrons of the Convention (the drafters of Laeken) only at two levels (European and national), but not at the sub-national level which was only indirectly involved through the six observers from the Committee of the Regions (Closa, 2004b: 189). The Convention structure thus stressed the principle of equality of states within the EU to a much greater degree than is the case in the daily administrative and political practice of the EU. In 'normal' EU politics, the Commission takes on the common European interest, while the European Council, at least when deciding by qualified majority, relies on a system according to which national votes are weighted in relation to the population of the member states, in order to balance equality between nations with equality between individual citizens. This does not seem to have transferred fully to the constitutional level, where state-based representation is still dominant. It is no surprise, therefore, that discussions about voting issues, concerning the degrees to which to extend 'qualified majority' decisions, turned out to be controversial.

The territorial logic, however, was not applied consistently across the structure and working of the Convention, as was clear from the case of the applicant and candidate countries, which, as discussed in the previous chapter, were regarded as 'not-yet-member states', and therefore given reduced rights at the outset. More generally, the Laeken mandate produced a number of ambiguities in the way in which the *conventionnels* were meant to 'represent' their respective institutions. On the one hand, all *conventionnels* were formally equal not only as envoys of a certain country, but also as individual members of the Convention. On the other, as Giscard stressed in his inaugural speech, the *conventionnels* 'must not regard themselves simply as spokespersons for those who appointed them' and furthermore, they were not 'equal enough', so that it was unreasonable to arrive at decisions within the Convention by simple majority voting (Giscard, 2002c; Floridia, 2003: 83). In this context it is also noteworthy that the 'European' representatives, that is the members of the European Parliament and the European Commission, were in a clear minority. As mentioned, the number of representatives of the EP had been sixteen in the Convention on the Charter to counterbalance fifteen government representatives, but had not risen in parallel to the number of government representatives in the Convention on the future of Europe which went from fifteen to twenty-eight because of the inclusion of the applicant and candidate countries. The Commission was, however, given a second representative where in the Charter Convention it had only had one.

The lack of *de facto* equality of status between the *conventionnels* was further underlined by the fact that the Constitutional Convention (unlike the Charter body) did not elect its own leadership. Giscard and his two vice-presidents were appointed after much internal bickering in the European Council (Ludlow, 2002) by the patrons of the Convention. The three were thus obviously 'different' from the rest, and played key roles in the work of the Convention without having any additional representative legitimation from their peers. The governmental envoys as a group were also in a 'privileged position' because their opinions could be backed up by the threat of their governments using the veto power at the IGC (Magnette, 2004b). Some government representatives used such a threat more often than others, a fact that was not lost on the other members of the Convention. In some cases (notably in the case of Peter Hain, the British representative), this tactic seemed to backfire slightly, for his frequent reference to his particular position as the representative of the British government produced a certain weariness on the part of many of the other *conventionnels*, so much so that after a while Peter Hain changed strategy, and rather than using threats, became more amenable to discussion in an attempt to either convince his interlocutors in the Convention or to build coalitions within it (Crum, 2004b). This could be cited as an interesting example of what Elster has called the 'civilizing force' of public deliberation (see Magnette, 2004b: 214, who cites Elster, 1998).

Another crucial challenge to the concept of equality in terms of the individual Convention member's ability to influence the debate was the greatly varying degrees of knowledge of, and previous experience in, EU affairs, in particular among the 56 national parliament representatives. While many of them had become *conventionnels* because of previous EU-level activity, others had no or little experience. They were clearly disadvantaged *vis-à-vis* their counterparts. For them in particular the Convention fulfilled an important function as a 'crash-course' in European issues. This had also been the case in the Charter Convention, but because of the clearer focus and the more limited scope of the latter, the lack of EU experience on the part of some of the *conventionnels* was more easily compensated for by their knowledge as experts on human rights. The experience from the Charter Convention also seems to have been considered as an asset and consequently twenty-two members of the Charter Convention came back for the Constitutional Convention.

Finally, the differing degree of logistical and other support they received from their originating institutions constituted another element of inequality among the *conventionnels*. A number of them, when asked which groups they saw as most influential in the Convention, named, after the Presidium, the caucus of the European Parliament – because of the MEPs' access to offices and assistants in Brussels, and because of their familiarity with the EU system both at a theoretical level and in its practical application. The national parliamentarians, by contrast, were the least supported in this sense, many of them coming to Brussels on their own and only for the meetings of the Convention. Many national parliaments did not provide additional secretarial support for their envoys to the Convention and some national parliament *conventionnels* felt overwhelmed by the amount of work and the lack of support (interview: Caspar Einem, 24 April 2003). The Convention secretariat of some twenty-two members (on its composition, see Norman, 2003: 37), which nominally was supporting all *conventionnels*, was in fact working for the Presidium and was indeed busy enough producing background papers and draft texts, and later on processing thousands of written amendments tabled by the *conventionnels*. National government representatives on the other hand did often have a whole staff of advisers and experts, either from the permanent representations of their countries to the EU, or from the foreign ministries, in particular towards the end of the process when more and more high-profile politicians entered the arena to put 'national' points across.

The mandate of the *conventionnels*

In spite of some of the reservations discussed in the previous section, the Convention was more representative of the body politic of the European Union than had been the case with preparatory bodies of previous treaty and constitutional reform. Because of its combination of different institutional-territorial levels of representation, the Convention marked a decisive innovation in EU 'constitutional politics' (Closa, 2004b: 204). At the same time, the issue of democratic representation does not only raise questions of presence and delegation, but crucially also of accountability and responsiveness (Müller et al., 2003). The Convention was conceived as a response to the secretive and unaccountable way of EU constitutional politics in the IGCs. Therefore, its overall legitimacy also depended on its members' mandate and how their interaction with their constituencies was organised. When assessing the Convention's merits in this context, it has to be borne in mind that the mandate of the body as a whole was ambiguous and probably deliberately so: the Convention was more than a preparatory group, but clearly less than a constituent assembly. As such, its members were neither directly elected nor bound to a precise mandate. According to some commentators, such an uncertainty in the scope of the Convention's mandate was in itself an important element of freedom, setting one of the conditions for the debate to be more 'deliberative' in style (Fossum, 2003). The ambiguity of the mandate also speaks to the fundamental need for constituent bodies to strike a balance between freedom of initiative, on the one hand, so as to come up with innovative solutions that are acceptable to the different parties involved in the process; and accountability to the principal parties represented in the constituent body, on the other, so that the agreements and/or compromises reached by the body have a realistic chance of being adhered to (Elster, 1998).

From this point of view, it is understandable that none of the participating institutions seems to have established binding mandates for its representatives in the Convention. Its members were therefore generally free in their action in most cases, and the way in which they 'accounted' for them was 'ex post' through reports to their sending institutions. Moreover, there were significant differences in the process of selecting the *conventionnels* and in the degree of 'supervision' which they were subject to in their own contexts, and these differences also affected their 'equality' as participants in the deliberations of the Convention. As has been noted, for example, a large number of key members of the Convention were appointed (rather than elected) to their positions: the Presidium, the national government representatives and to a certain degree the Commission representatives. The procedures by which other members were chosen were also not in all cases fully democratic and transparent.

In several national parliaments, for instance, *conventionnels* were often not voted on because they 'emerged' or were appointed as quasi-default candidates for the job because of experience as chairpersons of the committees on European or foreign affairs, or because of previous EU experience. In some cases, there were several candidates for the post, but a vote was unnecessary either because agreement was reached through negotiations or other candidates eventually withdrew (as in the German Bundestag's case), or the vote took place only within the relevant parliamentary committee rather than in the parliamentary assembly as a whole (as it was for the Dutch first chamber). In other cases the candidates were selected directly by their own parliamentary party within the framework of a pre-arranged share-out between the parties (the UK House of Commons), or the task of selection was given to some special body within the Parliament (the presidents or the presidia of parliaments, for example in the Slovenian Parliament or the Dutch Senate). Interestingly, despite the wide variety of structures in which national parliaments nowadays debate issues of European integration, apparently nowhere were there broader consultations within the parliaments or even beyond on the specific tasks of the Convention *prior to* the selection of a parliamentary envoy. This resulted in unclear structures for *conventionnels* to inform and be accountable to their 'sending' institutions.

The representatives of national governments, or more precisely of the heads of states or governments in contrast had to report to their patrons and seem to have been in some cases under quite tight control (for example Britain's Minister for Europe, Peter Hain or Spanish Foreign Minister Ana Palacio). On the other hand, in some cases where the government representative was a senior cabinet minister and had an independent political power base (as for example in the cases of Germany's Joschka Fischer or Belgium's Louis Michel), they had considerable freedom to shape their own governments' policy on the Convention. In particular Joschka Fischer's secretive bilateral meetings on the fringes of the Convention were noted, and to many *conventionnels*, they were in clear contrast to the Convention's aspirations to openness (Dauvergne, 2004: 132). It is interesting, though not surprising in this context, when Ben Crum notes that the government representatives very often acted on their own in submitting proposals, or at most together with their alternates, and in any case 'engaged little or not at all with their party-political groups' (Crum, 2004b: 3). Since their position was based on a more or less 'personal' link of representation between the Convention member and the respective head of state or government, this was of course a feedback-link removed from public scrutiny. In this sense they were accountable in many cases directly only to the heads of government and, only if they were members of the government themselves, before national parliaments.

The members of the European Parliament delegation in contrast did have a mandate from the Parliament as a whole which consisted of a package of resolutions and reports since the Nice Treaty negotiations covering most issues before the Convention. Moreover, the EP delegation was closely followed by the European Parliament's Constitutional Affairs Committee (AFCO) with whom the delegation membership widely overlapped (see above). Moreover, the Constitutional Affairs Committee timed its own work in many cases not only to allow for frequent hearings of *conventionnels* and the Convention president, but also to supply specialised reports on specific issues 'in time' to influence the debate in the Convention.[5] The European Parliament also had several plenary debates on the Convention's work and received continuous reports from its two representatives in the Convention Presidium. Since all the political parties and the party political groups in the European Parliament followed the developments around the Constitution with interest, a number of additional layers of accountability to different parliamentary and extra-parliamentary bodies developed at EP level.

As far as the national parliamentarians' feedback links are concerned, the situation was somewhat different. In many cases the interest in the Convention at national parliament level during the early stages hardly went beyond those who were already dealing with European affairs in the relevant committees. The interest of most national chambers increased as soon as the Convention started to take shape and in particular once it started debating the role of national parliaments, but overall the national parliamentarians were somewhat more loosely connected to their institutions in most cases. Most of them did report on their work (often monthly) to special committees, and most assemblies had at least two special debates, organised parliamentary hearings or prepared extensive reports on the Convention. Nevertheless, the members of the national parliament delegation as a whole had the least clear-cut link to their 'patron' institutions because of the sheer diversity of parliamentary cultures, political forces involved and procedures employed. This also meant that there was only limited transparency as far as the accountability of national parliamentarians was concerned. Thus, the fact that national parliaments were involved via their representatives in EU constitutional politics was, of course, one of the key novelties of the 'Convention method', but this was not immediately appreciated everywhere.

Finally, the two European Commission representatives occupied a special position because, as mentioned above, technically speaking they were accountable to the Commission president and through him to the college of Commissioners. It appears that the Commission did have regular reports from, and debates about the Convention, and that individual proposals to the Convention were debated in the college. At the same time, however, the Commission president had his own 'project for an EU Constitutional Treaty' prepared apparently without consultation with the college of Commissioners or his two representatives. When this document was presented in the

Convention, it took even the two Commission envoys by surprise and left them looking (and feeling) isolated, which, in the overall assessment, weakened the Commission's influence. It can only be inferred that the accountability-link between the Commission president and his two representatives was weak at best after this episode (i.e. from October 2002 onwards) (Dauvergne, 2004: 117–18).

Accountability: how, for what, and to whom?

The structures and practices of feedback between the participant institutions and their representatives varied greatly and in many cases seem to have been, at least at the outset, up to the individual imagination or good-will of the *conventionnels*. When asked in individual interviews how they reported back to their 'home' institutions, many *conventionnels* quoted meetings of parliamentary bodies like the European Affairs Committees (in case of national parliamentarians), but also meetings with special structures set up to bring all the national Convention representatives together with the governments (Grabowska, Heathcote), party structures within the national parliaments or governing coalitions (Meyer, Fayot), special hearings organised by their parliaments on the Convention or a national forum (Einem, Fayot, de Rossa) or even academic and other conferences (Altmaier, Meyer, Voggenhuber). In the case of one Presidium member, the feedback mechanisms also included a responsibility to report to 'their' delegation of national parliamentarians (Bruton). At the same time, however, in particular the two Presidium members from the national parliament delegation (Stuart and Bruton) were criticised for not adequately 'representing' what was, admittedly, often not a very clear position of the delegation as a whole (Einem, 2004: 254)

A number of *conventionnels* were then asked with whom they co-operated most closely in their work, to establish which channels of information and influence existed at a practical level. A rather varied picture emerges: some *conventionnels* claimed to have had most contacts with academics and outside advisers or NGOs, others worked most intensely within their own parties, or within their own institutions, while others again had close working relationships with members of their own nationality in other institutions. The latter answer (close contact with other institutions) was mainly given by members of national parliaments who felt that they relied on members of the European Parliament or their national representations to the EU on expertise in European affairs or logistical support, while closest contact with representatives from the same institution and the same party was strongest among members of the European Parliament delegation. This fact confirms the general assessment of the EP group being the most cohesive despite its internal political divisions.

The reasons for this relative cohesion of the EP delegation, which replicates similar findings concerning the Charter Convention (Leinen and Schönlau,

2001), probably lie in the institutionalised habit of co-operation between the MEPs as much as in the formal structures of exchange. It became particularly important in the final phase of the Convention's work (see the next chapter) when the EP and the national parliaments did manage to adopt a number of important common positions under the determined leadership of (mainly) the members of the EP delegation. Yet, while the Convention itself did a lot to improve the links between national parliaments and the European Parliament in particular, the process was not enough for the national parliamentarians to catch up with the already existing links within the EP. In any case it seems that contacts both within the institutions and within the party groups grew in importance as the Convention went on, partly because of the differing styles of debate (see the next chapter), and partly because of the gradual development of mutual acquaintance of the *conventionnels*.

With regard to the role of political parties as a channel for accountability, it is important to underline the diverse and evolving nature of links between the *conventionnels* and their respective parties. Given that very often the division lines on core issues of European policy cut across parties in the national arena, it was not to be expected at the outset that party affiliation would be a clear-cut marker of belonging in this novel body. The Charter Convention had already shown, however, that political parties did become more important as time went on and open deliberation gave way to bargaining and power politics in the later phases (Schönlau, 2005). Moreover, given the task of the Constitutional Convention of animating a 'general' debate about the future of Europe, at least the political party families at European level tried to provide additional channels of information for their counterparts in the member states, as well as increasingly becoming tools in the political game in the Convention. In this sense, the responses from *conventionnels* from national parliaments in particular reflect the dual linkage to party *and* institution. At the same time, it seems that this was in most cases a link to feed information from the Convention to the national parties rather than for the national party to directly influence the Convention.

Conclusion: a positive balance sheet?

For an assessment of the representativeness and accountability of the Convention, the open and often loose structures described above pose several problems. Firstly, the Convention has to be understood (and evaluated) in the context of the institutional development of EU constitutional politics. Thus, the unclear role of the Convention between preparatory expert circle and *assemblée constituante* raised different expectations and prompted different responses in the various institutional, political and national contexts which were not always easily comparable or compatible because of different political (and democratic) traditions in the different member states (this issue is further discussed in Chapters 11 and 12). Secondly, the structures and practices within and around the Convention changed over time and according to the issues that were debated. Finally, if we consider the Convention as a proto-constituent assembly and look at its work from the angle of a deliberative approach to decision-making (Closa and Fossum, 2004), it becomes clear that strict accountability criteria cannot be applied. The *conventionnels* needed a certain degree of freedom to be creative and innovative, not least in order to interpret and broaden the mandate they were given. At the same time, the opaque nature of the way *conventionnels* became representatives, and the lack of clear structures of accountability do raise questions about the legitimacy of the process as a whole which have been asked both by *conventionnels* (Bonde et al., CONV 851/03; Stuart, 2003) and by observers of the process (Arnull, 2003; Closa, 2004b), albeit mainly with hindsight.

Even if one does not go as far as Gisela Stuart in claiming that the Convention brought together merely a 'self-appointed elite', and that 'those who were directly accountable to their electorate . . . were in a minority', while the MEPs 'spoke for the institution of the European Parliament, not for the people who elected them' (Stuart, 2003: 17–19), there remain questions on how the Convention could be made more accountable and representative. From a purely formal point of view, this is no grave problem, since the Convention was not making binding decisions, but was only drafting proposals for the intergovernmental conference to consider, so that ultimate accountability should be both looked for and found in the latter. Yet, this answer is unsatisfactory not only because of the Convention's manifest (and widely shared) aspiration to be more than another preparatory body, but also because of the frequently expressed hopes to use the 'Convention method' to improve or even replace the deficient IGC method. In this sense, the Convention with its peculiar mix of different levels of representation and a diverse, flexible structure of individual members' allegiances and cleavages between different component groups did have a structural legitimacy which made it at least an equal partner to an IGC. Moreover, as the discussion of the Convention's working method attempted in the following chapter may show, the 'output legitimacy' (Scharpf, 1999) of the Convention compares favourably with the IGCs, in particular those of Amsterdam and Nice.

Yet another criticism levelled at the Convention by the group of eight *conventionnels* who tabled the 'minority opinion' (CONV 851/03 Annex), concerns the representation (or lack thereof) of a particular view on European integration: according to the signatories of the minority report, the 'Convention had no Members from that half of the population, which rejected the Maastricht Treaty in France or the Nice Treaty in Ireland' and 'not one single Eurosceptic or Eurorealist person was allowed to observe or participate in the work in the Presidium' (quoted in Arnull, 2003: 574). While the first part of the allegation (the non-inclusion of people voting no in previous referendums) is difficult to verify and seems to be proven wrong by the very existence of the minority report (whose three Danish, one Irish and one French authors can be safely assumed to have voted 'no' in the relevant referendums), it raises a more general point. In the absence of a clearly defined representative structure beyond the mere institutional aspect, how can 'fair' representation be guaranteed, in particular along dimensions such as 'attitude to European integration' which has not found institutional expression apart from the presence of anti-European or Euro-critical forces in the European Parliament? In fact, the eight signatories of the minority report (four full and four substitute members) do seem a roughly fair representation of these views in the Convention context, if compared to the size of the Union for a Europe of Nations and the Europe of Democracy and Diversities Eurosceptical groups in the European Parliament who had a combined membership of thirty-eight (out of 626 MEPs) in the 1999–2004 Parliament. The second criticism, regarding the Presidium, also raises an important question because it points to the fact that the Presidium worked in secrecy and thus questions its overall 'legitimacy'. In fact, it challenges the Presidium's role in general, including its composition, its mandate and its working method. These are serious problems which will have to be addressed if the 'Convention method' as a whole is to claim independent legitimacy as an addition, or even alternative, to the IGC.

This is also true for some aspects of the Convention's 'input legitimacy' mentioned above, i.e. the composition of the Convention and its members' accountability. To improve the Convention's score in this respect, any future body of this kind should be based on clearer standards as to who will participate, how they are selected and how they will be accountable to their constituencies. An issue that remains problematic is of course the role of the representatives of the national executives – partly because of the open question about what the precise relationship a future Convention would have to the IGC and/or the European Council. Obviously, making the national envoys representatives of the governments (rather than of the heads of states or governments) would increase the transparency of their role and would at least make them accountable before a wider audience than under the system adopted in the Constitutional Convention.

Despite these problems, according to the vast majority of observers and participants, the Convention can be considered an overall success, mainly because it opened up the behind-closed-doors process of treaty preparation and agreement, a process traditionally dominated by diplomats and national bureaucracies.

Notes

1. The Convention president, amongst others, was keen to pursue the analogy between the Convention on the Future of Europe and other historical examples of constituent assemblies, and notably the Philadelphia convention.
2. Kleger counted nine national ministers at the beginning of the Convention's work, in February 2002 (Kleger, 2004: 74).

3. This problem was epitomised by the uncoordinated way in which two different proposals regarding the structure of the future Constitution were presented by the Commission to the Convention; see also Chapter 5.

4. There had been an argument early on whether Amato and Dehaene would 'count' as Italian and Belgian government representatives respectively, but especially the Italian prime minister (Berlusconi) had insisted on having his own choice (Fini) as representative in addition to Amato (Hummer, 2002).

5. Convention and AFCO member Alain Lamassourre quotes his own report on the division of competences, the Bourlanges report on the hierarchy of norms, the Napolitano report on the regions and the Duff report on the incorporation of the Charter of Fundamental Rights (Lamassourre, 2004: 53).

5
The 'Convention Method'

Justus Schönlau

As already discussed in Chapter 3, part of the rationale for calling a Convention on the Future of Europe was to find an adequate public space for the constitutional debate on the European Union, one that would enhance the legitimacy of the constitutional process itself, thus strengthening the Union's own political legitimacy. The idea to call a Convention was in part born out of frustration with the results of previous intergovernmental conferences (IGCs), and in particular with what appeared to be the meagre results of the IGC at Nice, made even worse by the seemingly undignified late-night horse-tradings between governments. Even though 'there was no immediate agreement about how things might be done better in the future . . . the idea of a Convention was widely spoken about from the beginning' (Ludlow, 2002: 52). There was thus an important emphasis on the 'process' of the Convention as an alternative to classical diplomatic negotiations. As discussed in the previous chapter, the 'Convention method' was innovative in terms of the actors involved in it; but, as we shall further examine in this chapter, it was not less novel in its working methods. On the whole, this second experiment with the 'Convention method', after the one for the Charter of Fundamental Rights, can be considered as a success. Part of the reason for this 'success' is the way in which the Convention managed to produce a broad consensus among a heterogeneous group of political actors on a large number of highly controversial issues. It did so by developing its own peculiar 'method' of consensus building, a particular dynamism, and some 'genuine, very personal networks' amongst its participants (Einem, 2004: 269).

This chapter sets out to examine critically both the working methods and the formal, as well as informal, practices which governed the Convention. The analysis will focus on the way in which the 'Convention method' managed to provide a favourable framework for public deliberation and consensus building. The elements on which the success or otherwise of this method is judged comprise the final product (that is, mainly the Draft Constitutional Treaty, rather than the text eventually amended by the IGC), and the quality of the decision-making process, with particular reference to issues of openness and transparency, to the influence exercised by groups and individuals, to the procedures of decision-making adopted at various phases, and to the way in which the process developed over time. An examination of these factors reveals that the Convention was far from an ideal instance of deliberative democracy at work, due to many contingencies and limitations, but that the process as a whole was successful both in itself and when compared to other forms of constitution-making and treaty revision attempted in the history of the EU/EC (Göler, 2006, and for a more critical assessment, see Pollak, 2005).

What the *conventionnels* did

From a purely quantitative perspective, the Convention was an impressive exercise. The 105 *conventionnels* and 102 substitutes met 27 times between 28 February 2002 and 10 July 2003 and each meeting lasted one and a half to three days. The Convention produced more than 850 working documents, while the *conventionnels* submitted 386 contributions, and more than 5900 written amendments to the Presidium's drafts. The Convention's drafting body, the Presidium, met 50 times, while the eleven working groups of the Convention met 86 times (Deutscher Bundestag, 2003). Given the magnitude of the questions to be discussed, and the diversity of the individuals involved, the logistical challenge of these debates (including the issues of translation and interpretation, see Chapter 6) was considerable. The plenary meetings took place in the European Parliament in Brussels and were supported by the Convention's 22-strong secretariat, European Parliament staff (translation, security, meeting support) and a great number of other individuals working for either political parties, or European institutions, or individual *conventionnels*.

The Convention also triggered a great number of parallel meetings and activities, mainly taking place on the margins of the body's plenary sessions. First, at an official level, there were the hearings of the civil society Forum on 25–26 June 2002, and the so-called 'Youth Convention' on 10–12 July of the same year. Secondly, the constituent groups of the Convention (the 'delegations' of *conventionnels* from national and the European parliaments, and from national governments) often met in advance of the plenary sessions and sometimes independently of them. This was also true of *conventionnels* from the same political groupings at European level, of groups of like-minded members of the Convention, or indeed of other organisations involved in the process. Such meetings had the purposes of preparing the Convention meetings and providing input for them, as well as publicising the Convention's work and linking it with the general public debate in Europe. While this more general link between the debate within and outside the Convention is further explored in Parts III and IV of this book, this chapter concentrates on the way in which the debate internal to the Convention was organised.

How they operated

The ground rules for the Convention were set out by the Laeken mandate. After announcing the appointments for president and vice-presidents, the overall composition of the Convention, the role of substitute members, and the composition of the Presidium, the European Council specified the duration and likely timetable of the process:

> The Convention will hold its inaugural meeting on 1 March 2002, when it will appoint its Presidium and adopt its rules of procedure. Proceedings will be completed after a year, that is to say in time for the Chairman of the Convention to present its outcome to the European Council.
>
> (European Council, 2001)

This apparently clear time frame turned out to be crucial in driving the Convention's work along, even though the one-year limit was eventually extended by an extra three months.

The time constraints in which the Convention worked, and the particular role played by the Convention's president in timetabling matters has been commented upon as one of the key factors in understanding the internal dynamics of the Convention and the way in which this influenced the operations of the 'Convention method' (Crum, 2004b; Giering, 2003; Guérot, 2003; Schönlau, 2004). The Council's directions empowered the Convention's president to decide when he would be ready to 'present its outcome to the European Council'. As a reaction to this presidential prerogative to decide when the debate was supposed to have been concluded, there were demands to extend the Convention's timetable from quite early on. In his opening speech to the Convention, Giscard d'Estaing himself made clear that in his view the Convention should try to meet the tight deadline imposed by the Council, but that he was 'not prepared to sacrifice either the authenticity of our survey of European public opinion or the quality of work of our Convention and the proposals it draws up' (Giscard d'Estaing, 2002c). In fact, Giscard did use his prerogatives tactically, as when, for instance, towards the end of the Convention, he tried to use the time factor by delaying the debate about the crucial institutional questions; for he believed that only under the pressure of the fear of seeing the results of the whole Convention put into jeopardy would the *conventionnels* more readily arrive at an agreement on the text (Crum, 2004b: 3). When interviewed, several *conventionnels* expressed some dismay over the decision to delay the debate over the draft texts, since they were convinced that a longer debate on the institutional questions could have helped to clarify misunderstandings and build a broader support for the compromises which were eventually arrived at (Einem, Fayot, Meyer). In the light of the subsequent disagreements in the intergovernmental conference on some of these questions (notably the size of the Commission, the composition of a double majority, and the extension of qualified majority voting to some key policy areas), it seems possible that the agreements could indeed have been strengthened had there been more time to debate them in the Convention or a dedicated working group (see below).

The timetable arrangements and the role that the president had on such issues set the tone for the rest of the Laeken mandate's specifications on the work of the Convention, which were designed to give the president and the Presidium, appointed by the European Council, a high degree of control over the whole. Under the heading 'working methods', the Laeken text specified:

The Chairman will pave the way for the opening of the Convention's proceedings by drawing conclusions from the public debate. The Presidium will serve to lend impetus and will provide the Convention with an initial working basis.

The Presidium may consult Commission officials and experts of its choice on any technical aspect which it sees fit to look into. It may set up ad hoc working parties.

The Council will be kept informed of the progress of the Convention's proceedings. The Convention Chairman will give an oral progress report at each European Council meeting, thus enabling the Heads of State or Government to give their views at the same time.

(European Council, 2001)

These rules were vague enough to allow for different interpretations, something that put the president on a collision course with the *conventionnels*. In fact, Giscard's first draft of the rules of procedure met with considerable resistance from the Convention plenary, in particular because his proposals curtailed the role of the substitute members (as discussed in the previous chapter), and because they gave to Giscard the prerogative to 'arrange the order in which items are to be taken, determine the length of discussion on each item, decide who is to speak, and apportion and limit the length of each intervention' (CONV 03/02, see also Floridia, 2003). These provisions were later softened (CONV 09/02 of 14 March 2002) under pressure from the Convention floor. The Presidium's revised version allowed 'any member' to *ask* for the inclusion of a new item on the agenda, and gave a *right* to demand new agenda items to 'a significant number of members'. The new rules of procedure gave the right to the *conventionnels* and the Presidium to call experts to be heard by the Convention. Interestingly, the rules contained in document CONV 09/02 were never formally 'approved' but just adopted as a 'procedural memorandum' (Kiljunen, 2004: 40). This memorandum also put the Convention's president in charge of 'the proper conduct of discussions, including by arranging as far as possible that the diversity of the Convention's views is reflected in the debates' (CONV 09/02 Art. 6.7). This provision, together with the general statement that 'the recommendations of the Convention shall be adopted by consensus' (CONV 09/02, Art. 6.4) was the only guideline on how decisions would be reached in the Convention.

This was because the Laeken text had also been rather vague on the crucial question of what kind of result the Convention was to achieve, and how:

> The Convention will consider the various issues. It will draw up a final document which may comprise either different options, indicating the degree of support which they received, or recommendations if consensus is achieved.
>
> Together with the outcome of the national debates on the future of the Union, the final document will prove a starting point for discussion in the Intergovernmental Conference, which will take the ultimate decisions.
>
> (European Council, 2001)

In some ways, this was a weaker formula than that of the (Cologne) mandate for the Charter Convention, where the 'body' had been asked to prepare 'a draft document' and the European Council was then charged to 'propose to the European Parliament and the Commission that, together with the Council, they should solemnly proclaim on the basis of the draft document, a European Charter of Fundamental Rights' (European Council, 1999a). Even though this had been further qualified by the non-decision about the Charter's legal status (as binding or not), it did create the impression, widely shared in the first Convention, that it would propose a draft Charter as a 'take-it-or-leave-it' option for the Council. As mentioned in Chapter 3, the Laeken text aimed to keep the way open for a looser collection of proposals ('options') to be elaborated by the Convention. Yet, once the Convention had been set up, this option was quickly discarded by a large majority of the members. Giscard himself made it clear in his opening statement to the Convention that he wanted it to 'achieve a broad consensus on a single proposal' and this was the only occasion when he was greeted with spontaneous applause during his speech (Norman, 2003: 47). Both Giscard and the large majority of *conventionnels* agreed that only a very widely supported single document would exercise enough political pressure on the European Council to take the Convention's proposal seriously. It followed, as mentioned in the previous chapters, that the *conventionnels* worked 'as if' they were drafting a European constitution (Magnette, 2004a: 212–13).

On the crucial question of decision-making, a comparison with the experience of the Charter Convention is instructive. The explicit reference in the Laeken text to the notion of 'consensus' was probably one of the most important legacies from the earlier Convention. It was a recognition that the method which the Charter Convention's president, Roman Herzog, and his Presidium had in some way 'extracted' from the vague mandate they had received from the European Council, was part of the success of that Convention. The key provision was the one stating that

> when the chairperson, in close concertation with the Vice-Chairpersons, deems that the text of the draft Charter elaborated by the body can eventually be subscribed to by all the parties, it shall be forwarded to the European Council through the normal preparatory procedures.
>
> (European Council, 1999b)

This formula had given rise to a number of discussions in the Charter Convention on the question of whether voting should be used to determine when a consensus had been reached. Roman Herzog was of the opinion that voting would risk entrenching differences and lead to deeper divisions rather than facilitating agreements (Bellamy and Schönlau, 2004a). The curiously under-defined notion of consensus therefore had allowed the Convention to proceed on a delicate balance between majority and unanimous decisions, with the president being the ultimate arbiter. In fact, in the Charter Convention there had been one attempt to take an issue to a vote in the plenary, which had nearly led to a breakdown of debate because a substantial group of *convention-nels* had claimed that votes were 'prohibited' under the Cologne mandate.[1] As Gisela Stuart noted, Giscard himself referred to this incident as a justification for not even contemplating votes in the second Convention (Stuart, 2003: 19). In the plenary debate about the rules of procedure, Giscard explained that

> the Convention was unique and therefore could not abide by the rules of other institutions. It was not a Parliament complete with voting rules. The groups represented were not balanced in terms of democratic legitimacy. It would be impossible to consider the votes of *conventionnels* to be equal.
>
> (Giscard, cited by Kiljunen, 2004: 40)

The debate about the usefulness of votes did resurface at later stages in the process, in particular with regard to the president's own pet project of an elected president for the European Council which was overwhelmingly rejected by the *conventionnels*, but which kept reappearing in the Presidium drafts. In the end this proposal was withdrawn, and even on other occasions (like for example the question of the setting up of a working group on social affairs) the Presidium did bow to overwhelming pressure of an (unspecified) majority of Convention members, which some interpreted as a *de facto* vote (MacCormick, 2004: 3). Nevertheless, and despite continuing criticism of the president's excessive power in 'stating consensus' when he had decided that the debate had run its course (Einem, 2004; interview: Beres, 15 October 2003), the consensus method as such was only seriously questioned by the group of eight *conventionnels* who submitted the minority report to the final proposal (CONV 851/03, Annex) which complained that 'Giscard did not allow democracy and normal voting in the Convention'.

The consensus method thus became the 'established' form of decision-making, even though the interpretation of what consensus meant precisely differed widely amongst the *conventionnels*. One member neatly summarised the attitude towards the consensus formula as a working agreement without which the Convention would not have been successful: 'On one thing, however, there was an agreement: if the Convention ever tried to define "consensus", there would be no consensus as to what "consensus" might be' (Kiljunen, 2004: 41). At the same time it is interesting to note that the Presidium did vote on several occasions (Kiljunen, 2004: 41; interview: Bruton). In fact, Giscard did admit implicitly that the use of majorities might be permissible, on the by now infamous occasion when he invoked the Laeken mandate as stating that candidate country representatives did not have the power to block consensus amongst the old member states. At that time the Presidium was discussing audio-visual policy (an issue of particular importance for France), and it was divided 50/50, with the deciding vote being cast by the Slovenian member Alojz Peterle (who voted against the protectionist French position). Apparently, Giscard turned to the Slovene and told him curtly that his vote 'didn't count' (Kiljunen, 2004: 41).

Overall, however, the consensus method had widespread support in the Convention. At least in the earlier phases of the debates, the search for consensus helped inclusive deliberation, avoiding the entrenchment of positions along predetermined ideological, institutional or national cleavages. Alliances were made and unmade on an issue-by-issue basis, thus contributing to a positive internal dynamic. But the search for consensus was not without problems. As seen, it partly masked the issue of the unequal status of the *conventionnels*. In a context in which the relative weight of each delegation was unclear, the consensus method also provided a way of glossing over the problem of representation in the Convention and, because of the difficulty of defining consensus in precise terms, it was possible for the small group of *conventionnels* who eventually did not agree with the Draft Constitutional Treaty to challenge the legitimacy of the entire Convention process on the basis that consensus was in fact only partial.

Openness and transparency

Apart from the composition of the Convention, its single most innovative feature in the EU context was the openness of its proceedings and its commitment to transparency. The contrast between the successful precedent of the Charter Convention and the bad experience of the Nice summit where weak compromises had been agreed behind closed doors (Ludlow, 2002), served as a point of reference throughout the second Convention process. The provisions for transparency in the Laeken mandate were therefore strengthened. Whereas the Cologne mandate for the Charter Convention had said '*in principle*, hearings held by the Body and documents submitted at such hearings should be public' (European Council, 1999a, emphasis added), the Laeken text stated unequivocally: 'The Convention's discussion and all official documents will be in the public domain' (European Council, 2001). Moreover, the accessibility of the official Convention documents was ensured, as in the previous Convention, through a dedicated website, where documents submitted to the Convention or by the Presidium appeared quite promptly. Most observers agreed that this pledge of the mandate was fulfilled.[2] As for the direct access to the meetings by 'the public' or at least interested members of the public, the larger size of the body, the higher public profile of many *conventionnels* and increased security concerns meant that access to the public gallery in the European Parliament building in Brussels was much more restricted during the Constitutional Convention than during the previous one, and was mainly limited to accredited representatives of either the media or EU institutions. Throughout the Convention process, however, a growing number of people attended the Convention's meetings in the specially designated *salles d'écoute*, where the debates could be followed by video link. While this did not have the same immediacy and atmosphere of being in the debating chamber, it did ensure a degree of access and participation, which was further widened by occasionally making some Convention sessions available through the internet and the Europe-by-satellite service.

Limits to transparency: the Presidium's role

A serious limitation to the spirit of transparency, however, was the internal organisation of the Convention itself. Already in the Charter Convention, crucial debates and the actual drafting of text proposals had been undertaken by the Presidium, whose deliberations were not public. This situation was exacerbated in the second Convention because the larger size of the body as a whole, coupled with the much wider range of issues and divisions within the body, increased the role and importance of the thirteen-member Presidium as the crucial forum where compromises had to be found before the plenary was allowed to debate the issues. Even though the larger Presidium also meant that as a whole it was less coherent than in the Charter case and secrecy was more likely to be broken by individual members of the inner circle, overall the drafting body did work behind closed doors with only the twelve Presidium members, the one invited observer from the candidate countries, the Convention's secretary general, his deputy and the Convention's press officer present. In fact, 'it was only in the final months of the Convention that simultaneous translation was provided for Presidium meetings and we [Presidium members] could be accompanied by an assistant to give legal advice' (Stuart, 2003: 21)

This lack of transparency of the Presidium is clearly the single most serious shortcoming of the Convention method as applied in 2002–3. This fact was further illustrated by the belatedly published and deliberately vague 'minutes' from the Presidium discussions (published on the Convention website as 'secretariat documents' after the end of the Convention, in August 2003). In particular, no information was available on the votes which were taken in the Presidium at various points on important matters of substance – a fact that was severely criticised by the eight authors of the minority report. Even some of those members of the Convention who did support the final outcome, levelled criticism at the composition of the Presidium (which did not reflect the majority of parliamentarians in the plenary) and at the lack of accountability of at least some Presidium members towards the groups they belonged to. This was particularly problematic in the case of the national parliamentarians, where their envoys to the Presidium (Gisela Stuart and John Bruton) were challenged on several occasions for not having faithfully represented the majority view of the national parliament delegation (Einem, 2004: 253). The publication, while the Convention was still on, of more detailed minutes or at least of the results of votes taken in the Presidium would have probably enhanced the legitimacy of the decisions taken by the Presidium itself.

To add to the complexity, and to the detriment of transparency, in the Constitutional Convention the three presidents (Giscard d'Estaing, Amato and Dehaene) formed an additional layer of decision-making, which became important in particular in the final phase of the Convention's work and which operated entirely outside any formal structure. The three presidents met frequently to prepare meetings and, especially in the final phase, to divide the task of sounding out the different components and delegations of the Convention and report back from these meetings. Yet, even the two vice-presidents (Amato and Dehaene) do not seem to have been party to all of Giscard's initiatives. The crucial presentation of the 'skeleton' outline of a Constitutional Treaty which was put to the Presidium in early October 2002 apparently came as a surprise even to the two vice-presidents and seems to have been prepared only by Giscard himself and the Convention's general secretary, Sir John Kerr (Stuart, 2003: 20–1). While the presidential triumvirate played an important role in the final phases of the Convention precisely because of the different styles and political affiliations it covered (and, some would say, the way the two vice-presidents balanced the influence of president Giscard d'Estaing (Duff, 2005:12)), the unclear role of the 'inner Presidium' and the somewhat ambiguous personal relationship between the three presidents did exacerbate the structural problems of transparency within the Presidium.

The working groups

Returning to the organisation of the Convention at large, another core feature of the Convention on the Future of Europe (in contrast to the Charter Convention) was the existence and role of issue-based working groups. This had been envisaged as a possibility also in the Cologne mandate setting up the Charter Convention, but the Herzog Presidium, apparently with support from the Convention, had decided against it in the interest of the coherence of the body as a whole. While the Cologne mandate had given the possibility of creating working groups to the 'body' as a whole, the Laeken mandate unequivocally gave this prerogative to the Presidium. The latter made use of this power by presenting a first cluster of six working groups to the plenary in May 2002 (CONV 52/02 (17 May 2002)). This move clearly indicated the transition from the listening phase to the phase where concrete proposals had to be elaborated (Norman, 2003: 60). A second set of working groups was set up in July to start in September (CONV 206/02 (19 July 2002)) and, after some heated debate, a final working group on 'social Europe' was established in November (CONV 421/02 (22 November 2002)). Interestingly, as far as the internal working methods of the groups were concerned, they followed the consensus idea, but in some cases, unlike the Convention as a whole, indicated in their final reports those issues on which no agreement could be found, listed different options, or specified divergent minority opinions.

Table 5.1   Working groups in the Convention on the Future of Europe

Subject	Mandate	Chair	Final Report
WG I: *Subsidiarity*	30.05.02 Conv. 71/02	I. Mendez de Vigo	23.09.02 Conv. 286/02
WG II: *Inclusion of the Charter*	31.05.02 Conv. 72/02	A. Vitorino	23.10.02 Conv. 360/02
WG III: *Legal personality*	31.05.02 Conv. 73/02	G. Amato	01.10.02 Conv. 311/02
WG IV: *National Parliaments*	30.05.02 Conv. 74/02	G. Stuart	22.10.02 Conv. 353/02
WG V: *Complementary Competences*	31.05.02 Conv. 75/02	H. Christophersen	04.11.02 Conv. 375/1/02 Rev 1
WG VI: *Economic Governance*	30.05.02 Conv. 76/02	K. Hänsch	21.10.02 Conv 357/02
WG VII: *External Action*	10.09.02 Conv. 252/02	J. L. Dehaene	16.12.02 Conv. 459/02
WG VIII: *Defence*	10.09.02 Conv 246/02	M. Barnier	16.12.02 Conv. 459/02
WG IX: *Simplification*	20.09.02 Conv 289/02	G. Amato	20.11.02 Conv. 425/02
WG X: *Freedom, Security & Justice*	12.09.02 Conv. 258/02	J. Bruton	02.12.02 Conv. 426/02
WG XI: *Social Europe*	22.11.02 Conv. 421/02	G. Katiforis	04.02.03 Conv. 516/1/03 Rev 1

From the beginning, there was uneasiness amongst some members that both the working groups and their tasks were decided by the Presidium without consultation. In reaction to the first set of working groups, the delegation of national parliamentarians for example asked the Presidium to submit proposals for the mandates and scope of working groups to the Convention plenary for debate (initiative in the plenary debate 23 May 2002, see Einem, 2004: 45–6). Giscard d' Estaing's response was not to change his own approach, but to put more effort into explaining how and why the working groups had been set up.

The groups had up to thirty members (Norman, 2003: 60), all of them were chaired by a member of the Presidium and their membership was built essentially on the principle of self-selection by the *conventionnels* who could sign up for one or more working groups of their choice. In some cases, the Presidium did invite additional members to ensure a 'balanced composition' of the working groups (interview: Mayer-Landrut, 22 July 2004). Interviews with a number of *conventionnels* show that their choice of working groups was generally based on either personal interest in the issue or some previous expertise on it. There was also some co-ordination within political, national and institutional groupings, so as to guarantee either cross-party or cross-national presence (Kiljunen, 2004: 55). These working groups allowed for a more detailed, and in many cases more frank and more dynamic debate than the plenary, usually on the basis of proposals for final reports drafted by the groups' presidents. Since these presidents all belonged to the Convention Presidium, the working groups further strengthened the steering body as the point of co-ordination of the Convention's work. Significantly, not all meetings of the working groups were open to the public.

The assessment of the working groups and their results varies widely between the different issues treated. Nevertheless, the majority of *conventionnels* interviewed seemed to agree that the working groups were useful and necessary to deepen and to enliven the debates beyond what was possible in the Convention, because the plenary sessions, especially in the earlier phases, were felt to be excessively formal, often consisting in the delivery of pre-prepared statements. In some cases, the working groups produced relatively far-reaching proposals, which eventually formed the basis for consensus within the plenary. Following a categorisation proposed by Peter Norman, the working groups can broadly be divided according to their mandate, into those dealing with 'constitutional issues' (according to Norman the groups on subsidiarity, the status of the Charter of Fundamental Rights, the EU's legal personality, the role of national parliaments, the EU's complementary competences and the simplification of legislative procedures) and those focused on policy areas (i.e. the working groups on economic governance, external action, defence, freedom–security–justice, and social policy) (Norman, 2003: 60–1).

Following this distinction, we may note that the working groups on constitutional issues (which *prima facie* had a more technical remit) were more successful in producing innovative solutions in spite of the initial differences between the participants. This fact highlights the creative potential of the 'Convention method'. For instance, the working group on legal personality, under the leadership of Giuliano Amato, managed to find an agreement on an issue that had seemed intractable in previous rounds of treaty revision. Similarly, the working group on the involvement of the national parliaments in EU policy-making, under the leadership of Gisela Stuart, arrived at a compromise, which a large majority of the Convention considered to be a fair solution to the contrasting aims of guaranteeing subsidiarity and a controlling role for national parliaments on the one hand, and legislative efficiency on the other. In particular the working group on simplification (also chaired by Amato) produced some of the key achievements of the Convention, not least by providing a positive interpretation of the Convention's mandate (Magnette, 2004a: 226–34) even though not all of its proposals survived intergovernmental bargaining at the subsequent IGC.

Among the policy-oriented working groups the results were more mixed. While the working group on the EU's foreign policy (under the chairmanship of Jean-Luc Dehaene), in a generally difficult climate due to the contemporary Iraq crisis, managed to produce a surprisingly coherent vision of the EU as a foreign policy actor, the working group on economic governance (led by Klaus Hänsch) was the one clear failure despite the generally accepted need for a European framework to co-ordinate economic policies. Part of the reason for the failure of this particular working group seems to have been the related, but not equivalent, debate about taxation which was characterised from the beginning by British and Irish intransigence vis-à-vis any form of European tax harmonisation. Under these circumstances, it appears that the group of European socialists reached the conclusion that failure was preferable to a lowest common denominator agreement, and therefore took the tactical decision 'to let this working group fail', even though it was chaired by a fellow PSE member (Einem, 2004: 86–7). Thus the economic governance working group was an example of power-political considerations getting in the way of finding new solutions and thus a decision being trimmed off the agenda (Bellamy and Schönlau, 2004b).

Yet the working groups also provide another interesting illustration of the power relations and dynamics of the Convention. Since early on, and especially after the second wave of working groups had been set up in September 2002, the *conventionnels* of the PSE, in particular Belgian MEP Anne van Lancker, pushed for a general debate and the setting up of a working group on the 'social dimension' of the European Union. This was resisted by the conservative and more Eurosceptic part of the Convention and also, it seems, by Giscard himself who feared a deepening of divisions on ideologically charged social issues. Yet, van Lancker and other PSE members collected forty-five signatures of *conventionnels* in favour of their proposal and Giscard had to agree to set up the eleventh working group in November 2002. This episode demonstrates the strength of the *conventionnels* when they managed to organise themselves in large groups. It also set the prece-dent for the collection of signatures across national and party-political cleav-ages as a means of putting pressure on the Presidium. The working group on social affairs was duly set up under the chairmanship of Giorgios Katiforis, socialist representative of the Greek presidency in the Presidium, and produced a report which was hailed as a success by the PSE, in January 2003. At the same time, no similar concerted effort was made to achieve the creation of a working group specifically on institutional issues, even though some *conventionnels* and commentators were wondering if such a working group would not have facilitated better and quicker consensus decisions on the institutional questions (interview: Kaufmann, 17 September 2003; Kleger, 2004: 80).

Finally, in addition to the working groups, the Convention also saw the creation of another type of sub-body, the so-called 'discussion circles'. Three of these were set up on quite specific issues (the European Court of Justice, the EU's own resources and the EU budget). In contrast to the working groups, membership of the discussion circles was by invitation from the Presidium only and was supposed to be based on expertise and previous experience (interview: Meyer-Landrut, 22 July 2004). The discussion circles had three or four meetings each and produced input for the concrete debate about the respective issues in the final phase of the Convention. As was the case for the working groups, the results of the discussion circles were reported back to the Convention by the Presidium members who chaired them, thus giving additional weight to the Presidium as the forum where conclusions from the debates were distilled into concrete proposals.

The Convention over time

The listening phase

Giscard d'Estaing himself, in the opening speech to the Convention, had set out his 'plan' for the development of the work of the body within the time frame set by the Laeken mandate and a number of external factors (the impending accession of the new member states in May and the European Parliament elections in June 2004; see Schönlau, 2004).

> The first stage of our work will thus be one of open, attentive listening. [. . .] After the listening phase, we shall have to conduct two parallel approaches: First of all we shall have to seek answers to the questions raised in the Laeken Declaration [. . .] At the same time, we shall have to consider carefully the various prescriptions for Europe's Future which others have put forward. [. . .] Once that examination has been completed, the Convention will be able to embark on the third stage of its work: its recom-mendations and indeed, its proposal.
>
> (Giscard d'Estaing, 2002b)

This threefold division was to become the guiding principle of the Convention process, and the Presidium and in particular the president exercised great influence over the style and kind of debate through carefully managing the transition between the phases.

In fact, quite early on (at the end of May 2002) a number of *conventionnels* felt uneasy about the timing of the phases, in particular the length of the first (the listening) phase, because they feared that, in the absence of a concrete agenda for the development of the debates, the Convention could be 'carried along with a kind of "occupational therapy" until November' to then be presented with a ready-made draft by Giscard d'Estaing himself as a 'take it or leave it' option (Einem, 2004: 45). These *conventionnels*, under the leadership of PSE MEP Maria Berger, presented a demand for an early presentation of concrete draft texts as early as 10 July and collected eighteen signatures for this proposal (CONV 181/02). At the time, however, the Presidium did not seem to take notice and the listening phase continued.

Towards a proposal

In fact, the listening phase lasted until Giscard d'Estaing decided to present his own 'skeleton' draft of a structure for the Constitution on 28 October 2002 (CONV 369/02). Yet, even though this initiative came rather too late for many *conventionnels*, and the document was a structure rather than a real draft, the presentation in October was already a success for those *conventionnels* who wanted to go ahead more quickly because, as Peter Norman notes, '[Sir John] Kerr originally wanted to delay production of an outline treaty until the start of 2003' (Norman, 2003: 76). In any case, it marked an important change for the Convention. Until then, the assembly's work had consisted mainly in the presentation, in the plenary, of general statements on European integration and on the questions prepared by the secretariat to get the discussion going, followed by very general debates to allow the *conventionnels* to get to know each other. The president had realised quite soon, however, that these debates were overly static and therefore had introduced the 'blue card scheme' during the 15 April 2002 session of the Convention, whereby five speakers, raising a blue card, would be given one minute each to react to the previous five speakers' three-minute statements. This livened debates up a bit, and through the background documents produced by the Convention's secretariat the discussions became gradually more focused. With the setting up of the working groups (first round) in June and the debates about their reports, and definitely with the presentation of the outline treaty, the Convention moved to the second stage, in which different alternative solutions to the questions set by the Laeken mandate were to be considered.

At the same time, both the European political groupings and the Convention components increasingly tried to develop common positions. Some political groups (notably the European People's Party under the leadership of MEP Elmar Brok and the European Liberals under the guidance of MEP Andrew Duff), as well as several individual *conventionnels* presented complete draft Constitutions at this stage of the Convention (autumn 2002), but these were never debated as such because the Presidium did not include them as items on the agenda (Norman, 2003: 65ff.). The European Commission put forward its own contribution during this phase, though in the shape of two different drafts, and only after Giscard d'Estaing had already set the agenda by putting forward his own view of how the Constitutional Treaty should be drafted, a fact that evidently weakened the impact of the Commission's own proposals (Beach, 2003).

More or less at the same time (October/November 2002), another important development occurred, which clearly changed the internal dynamic and the working methods of the Convention itself. A number of member states 'upgraded' their representation in the Convention by sending their foreign ministers to replace lower profile representatives. Germany started off in late October 2002, nominating Joschka Fischer after the re-election of the Socialist-Green coalition in September. France's Dominique de Villepin followed a couple of weeks later, as did the Greek foreign minister Georgios Papandreou, Latvian foreign minister Sandra Kalniete and Slovenian foreign minister Dimitrij Rupel.

In the eyes of many of the *conventionnels*, the arrival of these political heavyweights changed the atmosphere, raised the stakes in the Convention and for some endangered the very *'esprit de la Convention'* (Dauvergne, 2004: 132). The tendency of the more senior politicians to put in only brief appearances, often followed by cameras, and then to disappear 'to give press-conferences or meet each other, isolated from public scrutiny, in a special guest room of the European Parliament' (Einem, 2004: 117) threatened the spirit of collegiality and equality which had developed over the first nine months of the Convention, not least thanks to the alphabetical seating order that had been adopted in order to discourage partisan and institutional 'clubbing' (Lamassourre, 2004: 49). At the same time, however, the participation of the foreign ministers was also an expression of, and a reason for, the growing profile of the Convention in public perception and among the member states' political establishments. This change coincided with and possibly further increased the pressure on the Presidium to produce concrete draft articles and to launch the crucial debate on those questions which were regarded by many as the most important, and potentially the most difficult ones of the whole Convention process: the future Union's institutional structure. In early December, another initiative of *conventionnels*, this time under the leadership of Hanna Mej-Weggen and Alain Lamassourre (EPP-MEPs) attracted fifty signatures of support for a call on the Presidium to produce a full draft Constitution before the end of February to allow for sufficient time to discuss it in the plenary (Dauvergne, 2004: 131).

Drafting the articles

In response, the Presidium did present the first draft articles on 6 February 2003 but it decided to stick to its original plan of producing draft articles in several instalments. Before the first drafts were presented, however, a first debate about the institutional questions was held on 21 January, during which a joint Franco-German proposal on the institutional issues (CONV 489/03) confirmed the change in atmosphere and working method: this submission was presented not as a contribution from individual Convention members (with or without a certain number of support signatures), but as *the* proposition of 'Germany and France' (Einem, 2004: 113). This marked the transition from the earlier phases in which each member could contribute in a personal capacity and the president had been very free in his summaries of the debates as to what he identified as 'consensus', to the actual negotiating phase where the number and weight of *conventionnels* behind a given proposal started to be increasingly important.

As for the draft articles, the Presidium had decided to start submitting them in three tranches: 'First tranche (Title I, II and III) by end of January for discussion in February; the second (Titles V, VII and IX) by end of February, and the third (Titles IV, VI, VIII and X) by end of March' (Presidium note: 19 December 2002). With this move, the Convention switched to concrete debates about the proposed articles and subsequent written amendments by the *conventionnels*, which meant a very different kind of daily routine for them and their staff. This new procedure, with very short deadlines imposed for amendments (usually between one week and ten days), meant that the Convention closed in on itself to a certain degree. There was now little time for close consultation between the *conventionnels* and outside experts or even their institutions of origin (especially in the case of the national parliamentarians. This new working method also exacerbated the inequalities between *conventionnels* in terms of their staff and logistical support and enhanced in particular the standing of the members of the European Parliament delegation who had access to such facilities on site.

At the same time, this phase (which lasted from February till the end of May) saw an intensification of the work in the political groupings and in the Convention's component groups. Especially the European and, to a lesser degree, the national parliamentarians were becoming increasingly effective in co-ordinating (under pressure) common positions internally, either as political groups or as institutional components. The effectiveness of such co-ordination depended partly on the kind of infrastructures available to the different groups. The European Parliament delegation could rely on a joint multi-national, multi-party secretariat from the Parliament and its political groups, who were used to working together, as were the members of the delegation themselves. As already noted in the previous chapter, this contributed to the common perception of the EP delegation as the most coherent and therefore most influential. The group of representatives of national governments, on the other hand, was increasingly divided by the emerging battlelines over the institutional issues. In particular, the split which had opened earlier (with the presentation of the Franco-German proposal on the institutions) between 'the large' and 'the small' member states became more and more entrenched. A group which called themselves 'like-minded countries' of small and medium size, and which counted at one point eighteen government representatives, tried to build a united front against what they saw as domination by the large member states, exemplified by the intervention of Giscard d'Estaing, through the Presidium's proposals for an elected president of the European Council and for reducing the number of European Commissioners. In many cases these 'like-minded' government representatives tried to get 'their' national parliamentarians on board, but in essence this group remained an initiative of the national governments.

Another division which appeared in this, the third phase of the Convention, was external to the Convention: the war in Iraq had divided Europe and of course impacted upon the work of the Convention, not least on its discussions on the future of the EU's common foreign, security and defence policy. It is one of the great achievements of the Convention method that despite the profound differences among national governments and the deep feelings among many *conventionnels*, dialogue continued and even on the tricky questions of CFSP and ECDP a compromise formula could be found. This must be attributed to the multiple levels of deliberation which were available to the *conventionnels* in various groupings and which allowed for different kinds of compromise to be found on different issues.

These compromises were prepared in a plethora of circles, groups and formal and informal meetings, some with a more stable membership (like the federalist breakfasts organised by the Union of European Federalists or the dinners at the Hilton Hotel organised by Iñigo Mendez de Vigo for an inner circle of 'movers and shakers' in the Convention; see Norman, 2003: 52); others were ad hoc and geared towards grouping support around an individual proposal. In particular, the latter kind produced sometimes surprising results and unexpected alliances, such as the introduction of an element of participatory democracy (the citizens' initiative, DCT Art. I-46.4; TCE Art. I-47.4) due to intense lobbying from an international pressure group for direct democracy, which managed to draw support from a wide range of otherwise unrelated Convention members. Instances such as these also confirmed the informal rule that, despite the established practice of not taking majority decisions, one way to exert pressure on the Presidium became that of collecting signatures among the members. In this, as generally in the rest of the Convention's work, the signatures of substitute *conventionnels* counted 'nearly as much' as those of full members. This may explain why, during this phase (from late May 2003) the Presidium tried once again to limit the role of substitute *conventionnels* by allowing them to speak during debates only once all full members had already spoken (Einem, 2004: 215).

The 'nearly final phase'

The final phase of the Convention's original mandate (in the run-up to the presentation of the results to the Thessalonika summit of 20 June 2003), began with a letter by Giscard d'Estaing to the members of the Convention, dated 8 May (CONV 721/03). Under pressure from the Convention, Giscard d'Estaing had tried to get an extension of the duration of the Convention at the Athens summit of the European Council in April. He had argued for the deliberations to carry on until July or even beyond the summer break; but the heads of states and governments insisted that they wanted the results by 20 June. As a consequence of his failure to get the extension, Giscard proposed to present only a partial draft to the Thessalonika summit, including Parts I, II and IV, while leaving the 340 and more articles of Part III to either the IGC or perhaps to the Convention itself in extra-time. In order at least to finish Parts I, II and IV, in his May letter he asked the *conventionnels* to agree to some changes in the procedures for the remaining period of the Convention. He stressed that the members had to be very flexible, and should plan to be in Brussels at least for three days for each Convention session because

> meetings of the political or component groups, of the working circles may be held in order to identify questions which remain to be resolved and to work out solutions to make it possible to reach a final consensus. The Presidency of the Convention (the Vice-Chairmen and myself) will be involved in consultations and contacts, enabling the Presidium to evaluate progress towards consensus as events unfold.
>
> (CONV. 721/03)

This marked a clear change in the working method: in order to reach consensus (in particular on the controversial issues regarding the institutional questions), the Convention was broken up into its components which were supposed to develop an internal consensus which would then be brokered at the Presidium level. This procedure followed a strategy already adopted in the final phase of the Charter Convention, albeit with one difference. Whereas in the Charter Convention the understanding of the Presidium had been that consensus could be said to have been reached when there was agreement between the four constituent components of the Convention (Schönlau, 2005: 110ff.), Giscard did not clearly state this as the chosen *modus operandi*. Nevertheless it was assumed that the institutionally defined delegations were the appropriate places to assess the extent of consensus or to find the necessary compromises.

In this phase, even the national parliamentarians (who represented the largest group in the Convention) finally managed to overcome some of their internal divisions and to formulate some common concerns, and later on even to agree on some core issues with the European Parliament delegates. This happened despite the strong opposition that many members of the national parliament delegation expressed to the rather muscular way in which a relatively small group of pro-integrationist members from both delegations (Andriukaitis, Dini, Einem, Fayot, Meyer and Kiljunen) pushed for a common position, because of the growing pressure on the Convention to produce an overall result. One member involved directly in the co-ordination group referred to its activity as a *'coup d'état'* (Einem, 2004: 205), but maintained that these pushy methods were probably the only way in which a common position that was likely to be supported by a large majority in the Convention could be agreed (Einem, 2004: 255–6). Thus the final days of the Convention (12–13 June 2003) saw yet another twist in the way in which it functioned. As had already been the case in the Charter Convention, joint meetings between the European Parliament and national parliament delegations took place which reached agreements on lists of so called 'essential points', such as the precise role of the EU foreign minister, the extension of qualified majority voting, etc. These lists had a decisive influence on the final deliberations of the Convention, even though a number of *convention-nels* objected to the way these meetings worked, because they (probably correctly) saw in them an attempt to build a pro-integrationist alliance 'against' the more cautious view prevailing in both the national governments' delegation and the Presidium. It is interesting to note that these highly political meetings of the EP and national parliament delegations were usually open to the public even at this stage in the process, whereas the national government representatives preferred to meet behind closed doors and were much less successful in finding a common position.

The 'final' consensus and extra-time

As a result of the intense bargaining and package dealing of the last few days, a compromise was finally found and consensus reached on Parts I, II and IV of the draft Treaty on a European Constitution in the meeting of 13 June. In a long list of 'obviously pre-arranged contributions of representatives from different groups' (Einem, 2004: 265) the overwhelming majority of *conventionnels* supported the agreement reached. One speaker (Jens-Peter Bonde) voiced his criticism and Giscard d'Estaing clarified that he would communicate collective minority views to the heads of states and governments in Thessalonika as part of his presentation of the Convention's results. The solemn end of this phase of the Convention's work (its original mandate) was marked by the playing of the European anthem at the end of the meeting. Yet, as indicated previously, the Convention was not over yet: it was given the additional task of proposing a set of draft articles concerning the EU's policies, based on and replacing the existing treaties. The compromise reached on this quasi-extension of the Convention's mandate was the formula that the Convention was allowed to make 'technical adjustments' to the existing drafts of Part III. On this basis, the Convention gathered for two further meetings (4–5 July 2003 and 9–10 July 2003). As for the interpretation of what constituted 'technical adjustments', one Convention member quoted the Presidium as having adopted the generous interpretation that 'those questions would be regarded as "technical" on which there was no opposition' (Einem, 2004: 274). Thus, the

Presidium at this stage was confident that it could trust the Convention's self-restraint and did not fear a reopening of all the questions already discussed.

In terms of the working methods, this last phase of the Convention did not introduce any significant change. The *conventionnels* presented about 1600 written amendments to the earlier draft of Part III, which were first discussed in the delegations, mediated at the Presidium level, and eventually presented for approval at the Convention plenary. Yet, during the final Presidium meetings, the earlier fears of the *conventionnels* that the whole process would increasingly resemble the way in which intergovernmental conferences worked, with bargaining and horse-trading between national governments, were partly confirmed. The German and French representatives let the Presidium know that their governments insisted on specific changes to the document on issues of particular importance to their own countries (the use of qualified majority voting in the areas of immigration, and trade of cultural goods, respectively). They apparently threatened to veto the whole of the draft, if they did not get their way. It was in this context, during the Presidium's final meeting, that the already recounted episode of Giscard d'Estaing telling Alojz Peterle that his vote did not count, took place (Norman, 2003: 309–14). This epitomises what was a rather undignified conclusion to the Presidium which ended its otherwise remarkable work by giving in to the demands of the national representatives. This did, however, pave the way for the official conclusion of the Convention, which took place in a triumphant atmosphere the following day.

At the final meeting of the Convention on 10 July 2003, Jens-Peter Bonde was the only member who spoke against the prevailing consensus in support of the draft, even though another seven *conventionnels* had signed the minority report. All other speakers welcomed the result and congratulated the Convention on having jointly achieved a result that few would have believed possible even some weeks earlier. In his concluding speech, Giscard d'Estaing stressed the importance of the Convention experience as a shared 'learning process'. In what many observers and participants in the Convention recognised as another example of shrewd leadership, Giscard lightened up the otherwise solemn spirit of the final gathering by pretending to feed some lettuce leaves to Wui-Kei, a ceramic tortoise with a dragon head that had been presented by members of the youth convention to Giscard, and which during its eighteen-month existence had come to symbolise the slow but steady progress of the Convention.

Conclusion: a new constitutional dialogue?

Ultimately, the Convention's success or failure should be assessed on the basis of its output. Considering the uneasy way in which the intergovernmental conference eventually agreed on a slightly revised text, and the outcomes of the French and Dutch referendums, which, at the moment of writing, leave the Constitution in limbo, it remains to be seen whether one can consider the Convention a success. In any case, judged as a 'preparatory' body, the Convention's impact has been greater than any other example in the history of the EU/EC treaty negotiations. It is also fairly uncontroversial that the process through which the text was produced was both broader and more open than on previous occasions, and that at least for this reason the Convention has set an important precedent for future constitutional discussions.

It is also clear, however, that the Convention was far from perfect by any democratic standard, and that the 'Convention method' fell short of some of the high expectations it had raised – though in truth this may say as much about the unrealistic level of expectations as about the method itself. Yet, the biggest failure of the Convention was clearly to have missed the opportunity for greater public involvement, and for bringing the debate outside its restricted institutional settings. There were also internal problems, as illustrated in this chapter: in particular, the role played by the Presidium, which had too much control over the proceedings, and whose workings lacked transparency; the unequal status of the *conventionnels*, and the ambiguities characterising their accountability; and, finally, the way in which some national governments weakened the integrity of the 'Convention method' by reintroducing low-level bargaining, log-rolling and horse-trading into the process. Part of these failures and weaknesses should perhaps be attributed to the ambiguous role that the Laeken mandate gave to the Convention: neither a fully autonomous decision-making assembly, nor a merely advisory body.

Together with these internal problems, the time constraints imposed on the Convention had an effect on the 'quality' of its output, as has been recognised by both participants and observers. Even so, it is probably true that a certain degree of pressure was necessary in order for the Convention successfully to produce a document on which most of the *conventionnels* agreed. The external pressures that came from enlargement and from the European Parliament elections in June 2004, and the skilful management of the 'internal' pressure created by the way in which the Presidium and in particular the president manipulated the calendar of works, seem to have contributed to a broadly positive result. Yet, it is also apparent that precisely on those issues on which the debate was most rushed and compressed in the last phase of the Convention (i.e. the debate on the institutional arrangements), the consensus reached at the time proved to be fragile and eventually collapsed once the text reached the IGC. Whether further discussion of these issues in the plenary, or the establishment of a specific working group on institutional affairs, would have made things different, is a difficult counter-factual question.

In conclusion, however, it would seem that the 'Convention method' is here to stay, as indeed suggested by the Constitutional Treaty itself (DCT Art. IV-7.2; TCE Art. IV-443), in so far as – when and if it enters into force – it provides for new Conventions to be involved in the process of future amendments to the EU Constitution. But a number of concrete proposals for the improvement of the way in which the 'Convention method' operates have already been advanced. These include, for instance, clear and transparent rules of procedure to be decided *in advance* of any future Convention starting its work; and the election of the Convention chairperson by the body itself as had been the case for the Charter Convention (Arnull, 2003: 574). To these, it could also be added that a working plan and timetable should be discussed at the beginning of the Convention's works, and a clear strategy to engage with the public at large should be developed. Moreover it would be desirable to clarify the role of Convention sub-committees (working groups) and their composition, as well as the mechanisms for registering either dissent or minority opinions. Whatever the eventual fate of the Constitutional Treaty itself, the Convention experiment has contributed to change constitutional politics in the European Union and how its citizens perceive it.

Notes

1. The case occurred under the chairmanship of Iñigo Mendez de Vigo during the plenary debate on 6 June 2000 about proposed compromise amendments. In the event, Roman Herzog did call later on for a 'merely indicative' vote, which resulted in a 19:14 majority in favour of the proposed compromise, which was, however, deemed to be too weak to form the basis for consensus (see Deutscher Bundestag, 2001: 285).
2. But see Chapter 6 for a discussion of the issue of the (non-)translation of these documents.

Part III
The Convention as a Mirror of European Society

Introduction to Part III

If by a constitution it is meant something more than a simple document, organising the institutional skeleton of a state, and determining the basic division of power between its main institutions, a constitution must, in some way, both reflect and shape the society that it is meant to 'constitute', or at least to organise it politically. In spite of its intrinsic ambiguities – which were partly discussed in the previous chapters, and to which we shall return in Part IV – the Convention on the Future of Europe was intended as an ambitious political project meant to address the challenges posed by both the deepening and the widening of the integration process. Part of this ambition, no doubt, was to come to terms with the way in which a very *diverse* European society could be *united* politically. The problem that Part III addresses is precisely the way in which the Convention dealt with some of the diversities and inequalities of European society, and how it reacted to these challenges and gave voice to different people's concerns. To illustrate this, we have chosen some important issues of diversity and social representation, which either the Constitutional Convention had to deal with as part of its proceedings, or it had to solve in order to produce a text that would satisfy the European public. This explains why this part of the book is as concerned with the way in which the Convention worked as with some of the substantive aspects of the constitutional document. So, for instance, in the context of the linguistic diversity that characterises Europe, the Convention needed to operate within a particular language regime, with obvious implications in terms of efficiency, of equal treatment, access and recognition, and ultimately of fairness of the decision-making process. At the same time, the Convention was confronted with the question of linguistic diversity as a substantive issue on which it was asked to lay down general rules and principles for the European Union's day-to-day operations.

Chapter 6 is indeed devoted to the question of what language regime the Convention operated in, how this affected its proceedings (if at all), and whether it tackled the difficult question of multi-lingualism in the EU. Naturally, the language regime adopted by the Convention reflected what was already in operation in the EU and its institutions. But, because of the timescale, the variety of settings through which debate in the Convention took place, and the importance of reaching sustainable agreements, the Convention itself, more perhaps than institutions such as the European Parliament or the Commission, presents an interesting test case for the future development of the EU language regime towards a more restrictive multi-lingualism. Such a development would mainly be driven by considerations of efficiency, which most of the members of the Convention seemed to value greatly in the context in which they were operating. It is more dubious whether a more restrictive multi-lingual regime in the EU might meet other likely requirements such as fairness, and equality in terms of power and recognition. In fact, although the Convention may have been an interesting laboratory for experimenting with deliberation in a multi-lingual context, it failed to produce any general policy, besides reproducing the current status quo.

The reverse seems the case with the gender issue in the Convention, as analysed in Chapter 7. Here the Convention was able to pronounce authoritatively on a number of questions reaffirming the aspirations towards gender equality within European societies. On the more substantive side, the Convention upheld principles of gender equality that are already enshrined in the *acquis communautaire*. Occasionally, it managed to extend the scope of gender equality by pointing at particular areas in which it may need greater efforts for implementation; and more generally it tried to inscribe more firmly the principle of 'equality' as one of the fundamental principles of the EU. But if we turn to its practice, the Convention proved a poor example of gender equality, both in its composition and in its failure to implement the general strategy of gender mainstreaming within its own procedures, something on which the EU has committed itself in all areas of intervention, but not, or so it would seem, when it comes to drafting its own Constitution.

The same discrepancy between declarations of principles and deeds emerges when we come to the participation of civil society organisations and autonomously organised interests in the Convention process. Here there is a strident contrast between the rhetoric of openness to society and the practice of institutional closure. Chapters 8 and 9 address the issue of the participation of civil society organisations and business interests respectively in the works of the Convention. The conclusion that they reach is that, in spite of the institutionalisation of specific moments and places for consultation, social organisations were kept at arm's length throughout the process, and allowed a position of observers rather than participants. Even discounting the fact that most of the organisations that were allowed to participate in the Forum, which was established as a means for 'social dialogue' during the Convention, represented a rather 'domesticated' civil society, the gap between them, and the instances they represented, on the one hand, and the Convention on the other, was still considerable. Such a gap in aspiration was perhaps less evident in the case of business interests, probably because such organisations have greatly contributed to shape the economic agenda of the EU throughout the history of the integration process. However, overall civil society organisations remained at the periphery of the Convention.

The final chapter of Part III moves from the way in which the Convention coped with the challenge of reflecting European society and giving voice to a variety of social interests, to that of how it represented its values. As Chapter 10 illustrates, this was a Janus-faced challenge, since the values of a political community can be interpreted either as the historical product of its cultural past, or as its aspirational civic horizon. Most national societies tend to blend these two perspectives; but for the European Union this is a very difficult feat to achieve, both because the history of its member states is one characterised as much by commonality as by strife between them, and because the common horizon is one on which the peoples of Europe have not yet found full agreement. Indeed, as we have seen in Part I, one of the purposes of the Convention – at least in the intentions of some its participants and promoters – was to provide a kind of ideal cement capable of holding the EU together as a political community. Chapter 10 assesses whether the appeal to common values, which occasionally surfaced in discussions within and outside the Convention, offered a coherent ground for demos- and community-building. In fact, as the chapter concludes, the debate evinced not only a diversity of particular values that people associate with the Europe Union, but also a diversity of visions through which these values are related to the European integration project. This diversity of visions highlights the hybrid nature of the values underlying the Constitution, as this emerged from the work of the Convention, but also, ultimately, the unresolved dilemma of the European project still poised between the benefits of greater unity and the recognition of maintaining and promoting diversity.

6
The Language Regime of the Convention

Chris Longman

This chapter analyses the political and institutional aspects of the 'language regime' of the Convention, and how the challenge of political communication and constitutional deliberation in the context of linguistic diversity was managed. The question of language use (and of the systems in place to facilitate communication) is of crucial importance to the understanding of political relations in a multi-lingual environment because politics is, at its heart, a language-borne process. Language is the medium of political life. Communication, as expression, debate, negotiation, deliberation, exchange and influence, is central to political activity. However, language does not simply have a communicative function in politics, it is also one basic marker of political group identity, and has been the cultural foundation of many nationalist movements (Wright, 2000; Barbour and Carmichael, 2002; Joseph, 2004). Furthermore, the language policy of a particular state or political system (as well as the policies that determine language use, such as education policy) impacts upon the ability of different language communities within that system to participate in the various spheres of social, economic and public life. Thus, language regimes can promote both equality and inequality, and language repertoires give or deny access to power (Mamadouh, 1999).

The operation and success of the Convention greatly depended on the ability of political actors to engage in political communication, and language diversity posed a clear problem in this respect, a problem exacerbated by the different functions that language has within the political domain. Language, as outlined above, is central to politics in terms of being a means of communication, a means of cultural identification, and a means of control, influencing the balance of power between individuals and groups, and it is important to bear this in mind when analysing the language regime and practices of the Convention in order to assess whether trade-offs between functions compromised democratic norms.

The EU challenges the historical assumption of modern politics, as supported by J. S. Mill in one of the core texts of modern liberalism (Mill, 1865: Ch. 16), that a linguistically integrated public sphere (including the political elite) is necessary to provide equality of opportunity, and to provide congruence between these communication, identity and power relations. However, the EU challenges this one polity–one language model by seeking to be a multi-lingual democratic polity, with communication and power being mediated through language services (providing translation and interpretation), and identity constructed through the recognition of diversity.[1] The EU has established a highly ambitious language regime which emphasises its assertion to be much more than just another international organisation (Kraus, 2000). With the development of a more integrated legal system and common political institutions, the increase in cross-border decision-making and a commonality of interests and experiences across countries, it is clear that the EU has developed a definite political dimension, which needs to be sustained by certain forms of democratic legitimacy. By including all member state languages as official and working languages, the EU is laying a claim to legitimacy by making collective decision-making accessible to all its citizens.

The Convention, which was mandated as an open forum for constitutional deliberation, debate and consultation, clearly aimed to enhance this legitimacy by exposing the mechanics of treaty reform (previously an opaque intergovernmental bargaining process) to the scrutiny of citizens, civil society and national parliaments. This greater transparency could only be facilitated by the provision of information and records of proceedings in all the official languages of the Union. Although the Convention was not legally obliged to operate under the EU's 'normal' language regime,[2] from the Laeken Declaration on, it was made clear that a similar multi-lingual regime would operate during the Convention, and that in being supported by an EU secretariat, normal EU working practices would mainly apply. Thus the instrumental communicative imperative would be met, without sacrificing national identifications, indeed enhancing the Union's claim to an identity based on the respect for diversity. Furthermore, power relations, being mediated through translation and interpretation services, would not favour one language group over another.

However, there are clear practical and normative challenges to this type of language regime, which have been increasingly obvious in the EU institutions for more than a decade, and which became apparent during the Convention. The temptation to cut through the Gordian knot of linguistic complexity with the increased use of a restricted repertoire of working languages, or even with a lingua franca such as English is clearly high (Ammon, 1994; Wright, 1999; De Swaan, 2001; Julios, 2002; Phillipson, 2003), thus raising the question of whether there is an insuperable tension between the desire for equality between languages, fairness, respect for cultural diversity, and the avoidance of language disenfranchisement (Ginsburgh and Weber, 2005) on the one hand, and efficiency, cost-cutting, and a desire to establish a communicatively integrated political environment on the other.

The objective of this chapter is to discuss and analyse the tension within the Convention between the needs of communicative efficiency (which tended towards the increased use of a limited number of working languages), and the needs of identity recognition and the avoidance of linguistic marginalisation and disenfranchisement (which tended towards the maintenance of full multi-lingual service provision). The fundamental question is whether the Convention reconciled its drive for an integrated, deliberative forum with its linguistic diversity.

The chapter starts with a brief overview of the different linguistic/communicative contexts that are apparent both in the general workings of the EU and in the specific case of the Convention. The discussion then concentrates on the language regime of the Convention, first as prescribed by the Laeken Declaration and the Rules of Procedure drawn up by the Convention itself, and then as it actually operated, and diverged from the prescribed ideal. The implications of this difference are then explored, and the views of *conventionnels* themselves about the language regime are presented and considered.

Communicative contexts in the Convention

Before moving on to discuss the prescribed and actual language regimes of the Convention, it is necessary to outline the different domains of institutional communication in the EU. It is possible to identify three distinct language contexts: the use of language by officials internally within the various secretariats (what will be referred to as the *'official'* domain); the communications between the EU institutions and citizens (the *'civic'* domain); and the formal and informal interactions between politicians within and between the institutions (the *'political'* domain).

With regard to the first context (use of language within the secretariats), although the EU language regime as outlined in Article 1 of Regulation No. 1, 1958 defines all official languages as being equivalent to working languages, in practice there is a difference between 'working languages' at the political level and 'working languages' at the official/secretariat level.[3] In general, within the EU institutions, the secretariats use English and French as working languages with nearly 90 per cent of all Council and Commission documents being drafted in these two languages.[4] This regime was continued at the Convention where, despite the range of nationalities working in the Secretariat the assumption was made that they would work on the same basis as the institutions: the 'unspoken rule of working in English and French'.[5]

With regard to the second context, the 'civic' domain, Articles 2 to 5 of Regulation 1/58 prescribe the language regime as being one where all official languages are used. Clearly, a polity which legislates and makes decisions that affect the lives of its citizens must provide these laws in a language that is understood in order to be perceived as a legitimate authority. There is thus a highly restricted language regime in the 'official' domain in the EU, but full multi-lingualism in the official languages where relations with citizens and member states are concerned, the 'civic' domain. The Convention, although strictly speaking not bound by the rules of Regulation 1/58, reflected this ideal of full multi-lingualism for its public face, the website, with all official CONV documents being produced in all eleven languages.[6]

The third context is that of communication within the political domain in the EU, for example by MEPs, member state ministers in Council meetings, and within the College of Commissioners. The latter is a different case from the European Parliament and the various Council formations in the Council of Ministers; Commissioners are appointed, not elected, and may therefore be expected to work in languages other than their own.[7]

The situation for MEPs and ministers attending the Council is different, and much more akin to the membership of the Convention. The actors in these contexts are elected politicians who should not be debarred from office nor restricted in their negotiating capacity because of limited linguistic ability outside their own mother-tongue. The political class at the European level may thus expect to be able to work in their own language, and it is *this* meaning of 'working languages' that Article 1, Regulation 1/58 is referring to, rather than the internal language regime of the officials in the various secretariats.[8]

The prescribed linguistic regime of the Convention

The object of this section is to discuss the linguistic regime of the Convention, not what the Convention might have to say about the wider language regime of the EU institutions. In fact, it was not within the remit of the Convention to discuss the latter, and the issue was not discussed formally.[9] The Convention brought together twenty-eight state nationalities, potentially bringing twenty-three recognised official languages (see Table 6.1).[10] However, from the start,

Table 6.1 Official languages of the EU (11), and applicant state languages (12)[*]

EU-15 languages	Applicant state languages
ES – Spanish	BG – Bulgarian
DA – Danish	CS – Czech
DE – German	ET – Estonian
EL – Greek	HU – Hungarian
EN – English	LT – Lithuanian
FI – Finnish	LV – Latvian
FR – French	MT – Maltese
IT – Italian	PL – Polish
NL – Dutch	RO – Romanian
PT – Portuguese	SK – Slovakian
SV – Swedish	SL – Slovenian
	TR – Turkish

[*] Official and applicant languages at the time of the Convention.

as outlined in the Laeken Declaration, the Convention would 'work in the Union's eleven working languages'. Thus although the ten applicant states on track to join the EU in May 2004 (along with the three other applicant states, Romania, Bulgaria and Turkey) were invited to take part in the deliberations, they were not included in the language regime, and thus were not provided with the language resources of translation and interpretation.[11]

The working methods for the Convention, which included stipulations on how the language regime would operate, were first set out in the draft rules of procedure (CONV 3/02), but taking account of suggestions by members of the Convention these methods were updated into the document CONV 9/02. It is interesting to note that a change was made to the language regime between these two documents, in that the first referred to oral reports being made to the European Council, whereas the second document replaced this with a commitment to make summaries and verbatim records of plenary meetings generally available, thus increasing levels of transparency, and providing *conventionnels*, citizens and civil society with a clearer record of proceedings. The full working methods regarding language issues as set out in CONV 9/02 are shown in Table 6.2. It will be seen below that two of these rules were not strictly adhered to, or rather, that the interpretation of these rules was such that a more restricted language regime would operate than was immediately apparent.

The regime was slightly enhanced to reflect the disappointment of some representatives of the applicant states that they could not use their own languages, and a provision was made (CONV 18/02) for members from applicant countries 'to address the Convention in their own language, with translation [sic] (by an interpreter provided by the speaker) into one EU language (and subsequently by the usual interpreters into all eleven languages' so long as 48 hours' notice was given, and provided that the applicant states covered the financial costs themselves. This would only operate one way, from applicant state language into the eleven EU languages, not from EU languages into applicant state languages (see Figure 6.1). The relay language was normally English or French.

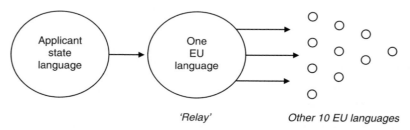

'Relay'   *Other 10 EU languages*

Figure 6.1   Applicant state interpretation scheme for Convention plenary sessions

Table 6.2   The official language regime of the Convention (CONV 9/02)

Article 6
Conduct of meetings
2. The meetings of the Convention shall be held in the eleven languages of the European Union with simultaneous interpretation.

Article 12
Notes and verbatim records of meetings
A summary note shall be circulated to members (full and alternate) and observers of the Convention by the Secretariat after each meeting. A verbatim record of the interventions made during the meeting in their original languages will also be made available.

Article 13
Translation of documents
1. The Secretariat shall provide to the members (full and alternate) and observers of the Convention, in the eleven languages of the Union, the following documents:
>   (i)   documents issued by the Chairman or the Presidium;
>   (ii) written proposals for modification to the final texts from full and alternate members;
>   (iii) summary notes of meetings of the Convention.

2. The Secretariat shall forward to members (full and alternate), and observers of the Convention, and post on the website, in the languages in which they were sent to the Presidium, documents from:
>   (i)   members (full and alternate) of the Convention;
>   (ii) institutions and organs of the Union; and
>   (iii) observers.

3. The Chairman may exceptionally ask for the translation of documents for the Convention other than those listed in paragraph 1.

Many *conventionnels* commented on this, with many feeling that this was unfair. One Polish representative made the point that 'we were too poor to provide translation' (interview: Grabowska, 5 June 2003). Alois Peterle, the candidate countries' representative on the Presidium, made the point that it would have been better if the Laeken Declaration had included candidate country languages from the beginning (interview: Peterle, 4 April 2003).

The discussion above focuses primarily on the political and civic domains, with the regime as it affected how the *conventionnels* were able to communicate with each other, and also how the deliberations would be presented in a transparent way to the world via the CONV documents and the website. As far as the 'official' domain is concerned, the Convention was assisted in its work by language support staff, including a Secretariat, drawn from a variety of European institutions, eleven of whom were drafters.[12] The language support services were provided from a variety of sources, though the majority of the interpretation work (oral/aural) was undertaken by the Joint Interpretation Service of the Commission (SCIC – DG Interpretation) with help from

European Parliament interpreters during plenary sessions, and the translation work (written work) was mostly done by the Translation Service of the Council Secretariat.

The language regime in practice

To summarise the above: all meetings of the Convention were to have interpretation into and out of all eleven then current official languages of the EU; there would be verbatim (untranslated) records of meetings with summaries in the eleven languages provided, and uploaded onto the website; all CONV documents and amendments to final texts would be translated; contributions from *conventionnels*, observers and civil society via the Forum would be published but not translated; and language support would be provided by the language services of the EU.

However, from the beginning it was clear that this prescribed regime would be challenged by financial/budgetary and personnel constraints, time restrictions in terms of providing translations in short time-spans, considerations of social communication (interpretation not being available in more informal settings), and political compromise (politicians not availing themselves of their right to speak their own language in order to reach others more directly, not via a translation and interpretation).

Interpretation

Full simultaneous interpretation in the eleven languages was provided in the plenary sessions. However, the regime adopted in the Presidium was much more restrictive, reflecting the sensitivity felt about the deliberations within the conclave. Interpreters were not encouraged through the first half of the Convention because Giscard preferred to meet in private without collaborators or interpreters, with the consequence that the default languages that were used were French and English. However, one Presidium member, Gisela Stuart, a national parliament representative, German-born but representing the UK, could not speak French. She was provided with a simultaneous 'whispering' interpreter. During the later stages of the Convention, when specific Draft Treaty articles were being discussed, a fuller interpretation service was provided, with English, French, German and Spanish interpreters present. However, in June, when the final stages were being reached the president decided to return to the private meeting format, without interpreters.

The second stage of the Convention was characterised by the working groups. The interpretation of CONV 9/02 was such that it was deemed not to cover the language regimes to be used in the working groups. (The word 'meetings' in the CONV 9/02 document was read as meaning plenary sessions.) The working group language regimes were thus much more restrictive, being limited normally to two or three languages. The eleven groups operated as 'mini-Conventions' on their particular topic, and were composed of 30–35 *conventionnels.* The working methods of each group were determined by the chair of each group, advised by the members of the Secretariat. It was made clear by the Secretariat at the outset of this phase that it would not be possible to ensure a full interpretation regime.[13] English and French were automatically provided, then the formula was read out at the first meeting to the effect that it was hoped that the members would understand why, and that further interpretation would only be provided if absolutely necessary.[14] It was then stressed that in this latter situation it would be easier to offer interpretation *into* that speaker's language rather than *from* his/her language into other languages. Thus, most working groups operated principally in English and French, sometimes with German also being used, and occasionally Spanish or Italian when a member was completely unable to function in the principal working group languages. Most members accepted this regime with good will in a pragmatic way, though there were many complaints from German members, and indeed from the German government. However, the Secretariat took a firm line on this, and sought to enforce the line that interpretation into languages other than English or French would only be done according to real practical need.

Translation

The official documents produced by the Convention (those with the CONV prefix) were translated into all eleven official EU languages. The documents emanating from the working groups, however, were mostly in either French or English or both. As stated above, within the 'official' domain of the Commission and Council secretariats the normal working practice is for drafting to be done in English or French (and very occasionally in German). Consequently the Convention Secretariat, drawn from the Council Secretariat, was simply following normal procedures for EU officials. The consequence of this is that English and French versions of texts were usually made available before those of other languages, when indeed those other languages were catered for. However, great efforts were made by the Convention Secretariat and language services to translate the official CONV documents as swiftly as possible for distribution and inclusion on the Convention website.

Amendments proposed by *conventionnels* were not translated because the sheer number of them outstripped the Secretariat's ability and budgetary allowance to do so. This appears not to satisfy the stipulation in CONV 9/02 Article 13.1.(ii) that, '[t]he Secretariat shall provide to the members (full and alternate) and observers of the Convention, in the eleven languages of the Union, the following documents: written proposals for modification to the final texts from full and alternate members.' The consequence of this was that the majority of amendments to the Treaty drafts were put forward in English and French, the most widely understood languages within the Convention. As an example of this we can look at tabled amendments to three different articles from Part 1 of the Draft Treaty (see Table 6.3).

Table 6.3   Languages in which amendments were tabled*

	Article I-4	Article I-15	Article I-43
	40 proposed amendments	*38 proposed amendments*	*23 proposed amendments*
English	25	24	11
French	8	6	7
German	3	1	3
Italian	3	2	0
Spanish	1	1	0
Danish	1	0	0
Portuguese	0	0	1

* The articles for this illustration were chosen at random from Part I of the Treaty. Numbering changed through the drafting process, and the articles used refer to those in the DCT of July 2004: fundamental freedoms and non-discrimination; CFSP; and enhanced co-operation. Where numbers do not add up exactly, this is because a very small number of amendments are not available on the website, or because amendments were tabled in more than one language (the additional language always being English).
Source: http://european-convention.eu.int/amendemTrait.asp?lang=ES&Content=

Similarly, the contributions sought from outside the Convention (from civil society, the social partners, the business world, non-governmental organisations, academia, etc.) were left in their original languages. This at least did satisfy the stipulations laid out in CONV 9/02 Article 13.2.(iii), but the outcome of this was that the majority of contributions were made in English and French, in order to reach the widest possible audience. To illustrate this, we can look at those contributions sent by socio-economic actors (as categorised on the Convention website). There are 93 contributions, some in more than one language. Sixty-nine are in English, thirty-three in French, twenty-three in German, and five in other languages.[15]

The final output of the Convention, alongside the documents mentioned above, was of course the Draft Constitutional Treaty (DCT). The majority of drafting work on this document had been in French, with some work in English, though projected changes were translated into the other languages in the final stages of the Convention.[16] Because the DCT was to a great extent updating and rationalising previous treaties, there was not the need for a radical overhaul of the language used. Furthermore, there are huge language databases that the EU Secretariat can rely on to provide linguistically accurate versions in different languages. However, there were moments when new concepts emerged with consequent problems. One example was the term *compétences* (in the French), which was a new departure for the EU to include in a treaty. There was debate about whether it should be translated into English as competences or powers. Such subtleties can be intensely political.[17] A further problem was the change of name for the Court of First Instance (which had ceased to be such a court a long while back: the English 'High Court' translated badly into German.

Ziller (2003: 79–85) is highly critical of the translations of the final Draft Treaty, pointing to instances of infelicitous language use, especially in the English version (for example the use of Eurospeak such as 'Council formations' (Article 23 DCT), or the confusion of 'chair' and 'president' in Article 21. However, these criticisms are a little unjust, considering that it was decided that because this was simply a draft which might be altered at the upcoming inter-governmental conference, it would not go through the 'jurist-linguist' process in which specialist lawyer-linguists check the accuracy of the text and translations to ensure legal linguistic coherence. The final text of Article 23 DCT (now Article I-24 TCE) is much more succinct and has been clarified greatly, and Article 21 DCT (I-22 TCE) is consistent in its use of the title 'president'.

Near the completion of the work, Giscard made the pronouncement that the final Draft Constitution would be made available in all official languages *plus* those of the applicant states, which took the Secretariat a little by surprise.[18] Giscard had the right to do this under CONV 9/02 Art. 13, paragraph 3, but the Secretariat had problems in ensuring that sufficient translators of quality were able to do the job, and there was dissatisfaction at the quality of the final printed versions of the DCT.[19]

All languages are equal, but some are more equal than others

The above description of the official bases of the Convention language regime and its subsequent development through practice provides us with the material now to raise certain questions about whether this was the most efficient and equitable system available.

As is common with so many aspects of the workings of the EU, there is a tension between idealism and pragmatism. The language issue is a clear example of such a tension, and the desire to be inclusive and to enable all representatives from (current) member states to speak their own language in all Convention meetings, as set out in CONV 9/02, was clearly overly optimistic. Equally, the desire for all citizens and members of civil society to be fully engaged (which implies that they would be able to communicate with ease with the Convention) was perhaps idealistic when one considers the horizontal stratification of European society into different language communities. There is bound to be a point when the quantity of work and the numbers of professionals needed to service such work, not to mention the financial considerations, reaches a limit. It would not be possible to include provision for all language communities in Europe, including applicant state languages, regional and minority languages, and languages of recent immigrant communities. A line has to be drawn somewhere, for practical and financial reasons. However, the bottom line with the EU language regime more generally (and this could be said of the Convention equally) is that official state languages are provided for, because it is assumed that even though this may not be everyone's mother tongue, each citizen ought to be able to speak a language of such status. Therefore provision should be given, in a polity that seeks democratic legitimacy and the widest possible social acceptance, to facilitate participation in, and comprehension of, political deliberation in a language one understands and can communicate in effectively. The question must be asked with reference to the European Convention whether this was achieved.

There are two obvious points to raise in this respect: one relating to lack of provision for representatives from applicant states; and the other relating to the dominance of English and French in both written and oral communication in the Convention. In both these cases we could refer to a situation of 'language disenfranchisement' (Ginsburgh and Weber, 2005): for applicant state representatives unable to communicate in their own languages (except in extremely restricted circumstances); and for those speakers of languages other than English and French (and even for those speakers of English or French who were not competent in the other language[20]) who were obliged to speak, listen and read in a language other than their own, in a political forum with constitution-making objectives.

The status of applicant state representatives is interesting, in that their standing as non-members of the then current EU configuration was clearly a barrier to their being afforded equal rights as existing member states. However, the Convention was an exercise mandated to explore the means to reform the nature of an enlarged EU in which the acceding states would be full members. Thus the inclusion of these states in the Convention process, but as members who should not prevent consensus being reached, and whose languages would not be represented, may belie a certain arrogance on the part of the current member states who agreed to such a regime in the Laeken Declaration.[21]

However, it is the point about the more general restrictions imposed on members of the Convention that potentially has wider implications. The inequality with which the applicant state representatives were treated was mostly due to the anomalous position of negotiating the future of a polity of which their countries would be full members while still being outside the club, whereas the issue of restrictive language practices through the privileging of English and French is a more general issue, as will be argued below.

The expectation that Convention members should operate in a restricted language regime with little or no support appears to compromise certain tenets of democratic equality regarding political deliberation and the working practices of political representatives: that of equal and simple access to information; that of promoting equality of capacity to evaluate and decide upon matters; and that of the provision of a public forum where facts and opinions can be shared without privileging one set of actors over another. Within the Convention, information provision was linguistically asymmetric, as were the capacities of the members to understand and evaluate the issues.

Furthermore the working group fora certainly privileged English and French native speakers over the rest. This linguistic asymmetry would manifest itself in terms of comprehension difficulties, lack of ability or confidence to participate verbally in debate, as well as the time factor in reading documents and preparing for meetings. The outcome would appear to be that native English and French speakers are potentially more active and influential than non-native speakers of these languages in such a situation.

However, it could be argued that given the practical and financial constraints faced by the Convention Secretariat, in terms of simply not having sufficient staff, nor the financial resources to buy in such capacity of the required calibre, there could be no other option. Furthermore, the linguistic capacity of the *conventionnels* may have been such that few members were seriously disadvantaged or linguistically disenfranchised. Without specific data on the language competence of individual *conventionnels* it is necessary to rely on studies that have been made on subjects not too dissimilar to that in question. Ginsburgh and Weber's analysis of language disenfranchisement which arises if the number of working languages of the EU is reduced, based on figures relating to the linguistic capacity of European citizens in general, suggests that in an English-only environment 45 per cent of the EU population would be disenfranchised, dropping to 30 per cent if French is added, and 19 per cent if German becomes a third language. Thus a predominantly English/French language regime would leave 30 per cent of the population unable to follow or participate in debate (Ginsburgh and Weber, 2005: 281). However, the language repertoires of European elites might be expected to be wider and deeper, a proposal made by Mamadouh and Hofman (2001) in their work on the language constellation in the European Parliament 1989–2004. According to this research, the percentage of MEPs that do not have access to either of these two languages (in terms of conversational skills) declined from 24 per cent in 1992 to 8 per cent in 1998, and then to 4 per cent in 2000. However, a significant number of MEPs are not fluent in one of these languages: 29 per cent in 1993, 14 per cent in 1998, and 10 per cent in 2000 (Mamadouh and Hofman, 2001: 4). It should be remembered that MEPs work in a multi-lingual environment with a history of informal communication in English and French, whereas the majority of the *conventionnels* were representatives of national governments or parliaments, for whom the working environment would be predominantly mono-lingual in the national language. Thus we can tentatively assume that the language disenfranchisement of Convention members faced with a restricted English–French language regime would be greater than 4 per cent (Mamadouh and Hofman's suggestion for the EP) but probably less than 30 per cent (Ginsburgh and Weber's proposal for European citizens in general) given that the European Convention drew its members from an educated elite.

Two points clearly need to be made. First, without specific data this conclusion is highly speculative and imprecise, and second, this type of data is highly problematic in that it relies on self-assessment of language ability by the subjects of such research which might be highly inaccurate. However, despite these caveats, it is credible to propose that many *conventionnels* were challenged in their ability to perform the task for which they were mandated: to deliberate, consider, discuss and to debate the future of Europe.

However, the empirical evidence gathered for this chapter would appear not to support this hypothesis. Although there was some evidence that members felt that their limited communication skills in a foreign language affected their negotiating capacities, and that their lack of proficiency in either English or French, or both, led to problems of time-management in the preparation for meetings when information was not available in their mother-tongue, the majority of interviewees stated that they felt the system had worked well, and that having to work for part of the process in a foreign language did not hamper them to a great extent. Many explicitly referred to the role of English in this respect: 'With English you can normally communicate with all delegates quite well' (interview: Meyer, 17 March 2003); 'We are able to speak with each other mainly in English' (interview: Balasz, 3 March 2003); 'It is completely satisfactory to speak English' (interview: Szájer, 16 May 2003); 'English has become very much the lingua franca . . . in general you get by. In this sense this has become very relaxed' (interview: Einem, 24 April 2003); 'English is the language' (interview: Bruton, 4 July 2003). A highly instrumental view of communication was apparent in many comments. When asked if he always spoke Dutch when possible, Wim Van Eekelen responded, 'No, sometimes English. If I raise a blue card I always speak English, for I don't think for one minute people will focus on Dutch' (interview: 5 June 2003). Goran Lennmarker made a similar point: 'I have made all my interventions in English. I could speak Swedish, but I don't do it. My job is to convince people' (interview: 15 May 2003).[22]

Conclusion: multi-lingual deliberation and cultural translation

Most actors from the official/secretariat and political domains of the Convention appear to have accepted the language regime with good grace and understanding as a pragmatic necessity.[23] Given the high expectations of the Convention apparent from the beginning (as shown by the recurrent comparison with Philadelphia), the relatively short time scale (sixteen months), the range of interests wishing to engage in the process, the number of language communities represented (twenty-eight states with twenty-three official languages), the diversity of constitutional cultures being drawn upon, and the fact that the Convention was running in parallel to the day-to-day running of the EU at a time of great political divergence in Europe (around the issue of the Iraq war), it is surprising that the Convention worked as well as it did. For this to happen, there was clearly a felt need to compromise and not to insist pedantically on absolute equity in all issues. The language regime reflects this pragmatic approach, which understood that to insist on full multi-lingualism of all official languages as working languages in all Convention contexts would have been financially ruinous and practically unfeasible.

However, as Wright (2000: 155–6) points out, language is power: those with mastery are able to be more persuasive; those with less mastery are disadvantaged. Mamadouh (1999: 136) makes a similar point: '[a]n agreement on any working language in any political arena necessarily influences the balance of power between those, individuals and groups, who command the language and those who do not, but also between those with different levels of proficiency.' The paradox here is that the equality achieved by eradicating linguistic difference and constructing a community of communication through the use of an 'international language' at the same time undermines the equality of opportunity for members of such a community who do not have the lingua franca as their mother-tongue. Language, as a political resource, is shared unequally in a forum such as the European Convention, leading to the conclusion that there was something distinctly undemocratic about its workings. However, it is difficult to see alternatives if practical and financial considerations rule out full integral interpretation and translation, and if the political elite are willing to work this way.

Is it possible to draw wider conclusions from the workings of the Convention? There are certainly dangers in trying to extrapolate from the Convention, which was a unique event not bound by the normal institutional rules of the EU, to the functioning of the EU in general. But some tentative inferences may be drawn, especially when considered alongside other evidence concerning the language regime of the EU.[24] The secretariats of the EU will continue to work predominantly in English and French, with English increasingly used in preference to French (especially since the 2004 round of enlargement). The EU will continue to produce all official legal documents in all official languages, and to communicate with citizens in the official language chosen by the citizen, though there will be an increasing amount of information made available (for example on the EU server 'Europa') only in English and French.

Thus far, *plus ça change, plus c'est le même chose*. However, there are further developments in the EU political sphere. It is clear that the provision of translation and interpretation after enlargement to service the needs of political actors within the EU institutions is now a challenge.[25] The Convention has shown that it is apparently acceptable for political actors to work in languages other than their own, and to accept a restricted language regime in certain circumstances with translation and interpretation being provided only according to 'real need'. It is already apparent in the Council that an increasing number of working group meetings at the political level work without interpretation (i.e. using the linguae francae – English and French), and that an intermediate tier is emerging between that of no interpretation and full interpretation, where interpretation is provided on demand with the costs covered by the member state concerned.

A recent Working Document of the Committee of Constitutional Affairs of the European Parliament explores new ways of interpreting the rules of procedure of the EP with regard to language (European Parliament, 2004a). This document notes that 'it is impossible in practice for any of the European institutions to implement unrestrictedly the general principle of full multi-lingualism' (ibid.: 2). The suggestions made appear to echo the pragmatic solutions that emerged in the Convention: full multi-lingualism in plenary sessions, but 'a more differentiated and pragmatic approach should be possible in the case of all Parliament's other bodies', i.e. working groups and committees, with each EP body adopting its own language arrangements (ibid.: 4).[26] The final version of the Rules of Procedure (16th edition, July 2004), clearly shows how this has developed into a more flexible language regime:

> Rule 138. 4. At committee and delegation meetings away from the usual places of work interpretation shall be provided from and into the languages of those members who have confirmed that they will attend the meeting. *These arrangements may exceptionally be made more flexible where the members of the committee or delegation so agree.*
>
> (European Parliament, 2004b, emphasis added)

This more flexible approach, which was apparent in the workings of the Convention, would favour the emergence of a smaller number of working languages within the institutions of the EU. Many *conventionnels* made the point that this was necessary during the Convention, and that it ought to be the model followed by the EU in general.[27] Joszef Oleksey was of the opinion that '[a]t the beginning the Convention should have used all languages. This is the tradition, it is a symbolic thing. But in the future I think we should choose working languages' (interview: 16 May 2003). József Szájer thought that '[i]t would be rather better if the other countries would use also a certain number of limited languages' (interview: 16 May 2003). Frans Timmermans was very clear about where this should lead: 'I think there is only one real solution to the language problem, and that is to retain all the official languages of the member states as official languages of the EU and then to make a step towards working languages, possibly towards one working language which would logically be English . . . Let's be pragmatic' (interview: 4 June 2003).

Thus it may be seen that the language regime which emerged in the Convention may presage the shape of things to come, and, to a degree, a reflection of emerging practices in the wider EU institutional context. Indeed, Pervenche Berès made the controversial and provocative statement that, 'obviously the Convention worked as the avant-guard of the EU, which means it was nicely and smoothly moving to English . . . This doesn't mean that's what I really like, but it is a fact' (interview: 15 October 2003).

However, it should not be implied that this is a clear or desirable route to take. The point was made at the beginning of this chapter that language operates as a medium of communication, identity and power. The instrumental, communicative aspect may favour a subtractive model for a language regime, but the recognition of identity and the promotion of an equitable political environment do not. Furthermore, alongside these strong arguments about symbolic representation and linguistic disenfranchisement, there is a debate about whether language carries cultural assumptions and forms a conceptual filter which may (unintentionally or not) produce political-cultural hegemonies of thought. Language, in this view, is not simply a reflection of reality, but the means by which we constitute reality and make sense of the world (Phillipson, 2003: 108).[28] As Johannes Voggenhuber reflects:

> [t]his touches of course on the language problem in general, but there I think Umberto Eco has indeed found the golden formula: 'the language of Europe is translation'. There you have to see that it is not so much about linguistic translation with generally quite polyglot people, but it is about cultural translations, about the translation of ideas and value systems and language is only a recognition of this achievement. This is of course also to do with the fact that culture of a person or of a country or region or a state themselves can only be transmitted in their respective language, and there are clear hegemonies which are also transmitted by language – cultural and political hegemonies.
>
> (Interview: 9 July 2003)

Thus, although the Convention language regime, which in many respects was restrictive, was accepted with good grace, and even with some enthusiasm, by most *conventionnels*, there are distinct concerns about the implications of accepting the dominance of one or two languages at the elite political level; there are implications for political equity at the elite level, but also implications for how the political processes of the EU are perceived by citizens. As Johannes Voggenhuber says:

> maybe you can make that clear to people . . . not so much to the experts, but to the people, that even just listening to foreign languages reminds you of this core task of Europe, to move towards unity by translating cultures, and to maintain those cultures even in unity – to make that a sensuous reality. And if that stops to be sensuously present then it means that a political class is talking to itself at a virtual level about a Europe which does not exist.
>
> (Interview: 9 July 2003)

Notes

1. In this it offers a sharp point of contrast with international organisations such as the Council of Europe or the UN with their highly restrictive language regimes.
2. The EU language regime was set out in the very first Regulation of the Council of Ministers in 1958, which established a system in which each member state's official

language is also an official and working language of the Community. It has remained fundamentally unaltered since, despite successive enlargements, which have widened membership from six to twenty-seven countries, and from four to twenty-three official and working languages. A language regime designed for a relatively small international entity with limited competences now applies to an extensive polity characterised by intensive interdependence.

3. Article 1, Regulation 1/58 at the time of the Convention (as amended following subsequent enlargements): 'The official languages and the working languages of the institutions of the Community shall be Danish, Dutch, English, Finnish, French, German, Greek, Italian, Portuguese, Spanish and Swedish.'

4. Figures for first drafting of documents in the Council and Commission were as follows in 2001: Council (2001): 59 per cent in English, 28 per cent in French; Commission (2001): 57 per cent in English, 30 per cent in French. English is rapidly becoming the principal drafting language in both institutions. The proportion of English to French has changed radically over the past decade or so. In 1997 the proportion in the Commission was 45.3 per cent English to 40.4 per cent French. In 1986 58 per cent of Commission first drafts were in French (sources: European Commission Translation Service, 1999: 11; Assemblé Nationale Française, 2003: 63).

5. Source: anonymous EU Council Secretariat interviewee.

6. However, as will be discussed below, there were many instances where a more restricted language regime operated (for example, contributions from civil society and amendments were not translated). Also, CONV documents were drafted in either English or French, and thus these language versions appeared on the web before those of other languages. Indeed the Secretariat had to make a delicate decision about whether to hold back the English and French versions and release them at the same time as the others, or whether to send the English or French versions out first and the rest as and when they were ready. The latter option was chosen on the pragmatic assumption that if the English and French versions were issued early most people in the Convention, and indeed in the wider public sphere, would be able to read them.

7. In fact the College has three working languages: English, French and German (McCluskey, 1998); and documents for the weekly Commission meetings 'have always to be available in the three working languages' (ibid.: 6). This is not to say that Commissioners are unable to speak in their own languages, but rather that a restricted regime operates where much reading material (as well as a great deal of oral interaction) is in the three dominant languages, and especially in English and French.

8. Perhaps it would be more appropriate, in order to avoid confusion, to describe the 'working languages' in the context of their use by the officials/secretariats of the EU as 'procedural languages', 'vehicular languages', 'drafting languages' or 'in-house languages'.

9. There were, however, contributions that did try to open the matter of including references to the protection and promotion of linguistic diversity for debate, such as the Europa Diversa contribution, see: http://europa.eu.int/futurum/forum_convention/documents/contrib/acad/0300_c_en.pdf and those from the European Bureau of Lesser-Used Languages (four contributions).

10. Twenty-four if Irish as a Treaty language is included. However, Irish was not considered as an official and working language of the institutions of the Union at the time, and therefore was used to produce a final draft and only one official Convention document (CONV 848/03) on projected changes to Parts III and IV of the DCT. Irish became a full official language of the EU in January 2007. A further

comment should be made here: obviously regional and minority languages were not included in the language regime as they are not given the status of official and working languages of the EU institutions.

11. It should be noted that the terms 'translation' and 'interpretation' are used in very specific ways in the EU: 'translation' refers to written work, and 'interpretation' refers to oral-aural communication.

12. The drafters, or *rédacteurs*, basically prepared all substantive input coming from the Secretariat and going first to the Presidium and then on to the plenary. During the first phase of the Convention the drafters had to draft the background papers and information notes on the various issues on the agenda and to advise, with and for the Secretary General, on tactics and strategy. During the second, working group phase, the drafters became the secretaries for the groups and discussion circles, acting relatively autonomously, helping and advising the chair of each group on working methods (which were the responsibility of each group). Thus mandates were drafted, agendas worked out, and reports of the work of the group drafted and carried through discussion and adoption by each group. During the third phase, work was concentrated on the drafting of the final output, the Draft Constitutional Treaty.

13. The Secretariat had clear instructions from their Secretary General, Sir John Kerr, to this effect.

14. For example, see CONV 164/02, summary of working group II meeting, 25 June 2002, point 4: 'Working languages. It was agreed that, purely as a result of technical constraints, interpreting could only be provided in French and English for working groups. If a group member indicated an imperative need to speak in another language, the Secretariat would explore the practical possibilities.'

15. http://europa.eu.int/futurum/forum_convention/doc_3_402_en.cfm (Convention website, Forum section). We can see here (and with the amendments) the operation of what Philippe Van Parijs refers to as the 'maximin' principle, maximising minimal linguistic competence, i.e. using a criterion of minimal exclusion in order to reach the widest number of people (Van Parijs, 2007).

16. The Chairman of the Convention, Valéry Giscard d'Estaing, was instrumental in keeping the French version to the fore, and was extremely keen that the French version should have a certain stylistic purity. He even suggested sending the final text to the Académie française for revision, 'and to academies in other countries'. The problem was that there are few language academies in other countries to send the draft to (Ziller, 2003: 85).

17. 'Competence' in English also has the connotation of ability, which is somewhat different from having the power or right to do something. Eventually the word 'competence' was opted for. See DCT Part I, Title III, Articles 9–17 (TCE Arts. 11–14).

18. Speaking of the Constitution: 'Il a été établi seulement en trois langues à ce stade des travaux, qui sont l'anglais, le français et l'italien, langues de la présidence. Mais les traductions sont en cours dans toutes les langues de l'Union, y compris les langues des nouveaux membres' (Giscard d'Estaing, 9 July 2003).

19. A point made by more than one anonymous interviewee.

20. For example Gisela Stuart, who was unable to speak French and felt sufficiently aggrieved by the situation to complain about it in her Fabian Society booklet, *The Making of Europe's Constitution* (2003: 21–2): 'It was not unusual for texts to arrive late and only in French. Whenever the President expressed his irritation at my inability to conduct legal negotiations in French, I offered to switch to German. He never took up my suggestion.'

21. On the status of the applicant states and the *conventionnels* representing them, see Chapter 4.

22. For further discussion on the increasing dominance of the English language in European political life see Phillipson (2003) and Longman (2007).
23. The only group of people who appear to have resented the dominance of English and French were some of the German members. Indeed the German government made repeated complaints to the Convention president, but to little avail.
24. Alongside sources discussed below, I should mention that the following is also based on interview data, and other studies such as Phillipson (2003) and the Herbillon report (Assemblé Nationale, 2003).
25. The following EUobserver.com headlines give a flavour of this: 'Translation problems delay crucial EU financial laws' (10 May 2004); 'EU translation service on the brink of collapse' (26 May 2004); 'EU translation problems cost lives, says UK' (28 July 2004); 'EU language bills rocket' (14 January 2005); 'Translation errors in Polish EU Constitution to delay ratification' (20 January 2005).
26. One reason why this issue became so vital to address was that there would be insufficient language service cover for a while after enlargement in all the incoming official languages. There was a procedural problem here in that Rule 139.6 of the EP Rules of Procedure allowed for amendments to be put to the vote *only* after they have been printed and distributed in *all* the official languages. Without this, any member could make a point of order and demand that discussions should be suspended.
27. This would not be to say that full multi-lingualism would disappear. EP plenary sessions, formal Council of Ministers meetings and all communication with citizens and member state governments would still operate under the rule of full multi-lingualism in all official languages.
28. For further discussion of this issue, and the 'linguistic turn' in IR and European studies, see Drulák (2003), and Christiansen et al. (2001), especially the chapters by Marcussen et al., Rosamond and Diez.

7
Gender Equality in the Constitution-Making Process

Emanuela Lombardo

As discussed in Part II, the procedures used for the drafting of the EU's Charter of Fundamental Rights and the Constitutional Treaty have been judged to be more open and democratic than those followed in drafting previous EU treaties. Proceedings were more open to the public, the mode of discussion more deliberative, and feedback was sought from civil society. However, can the two Conventions be deemed open and democratic when analysed from a gender perspective? One source of evidence for their democratic credentials could be the extent to which gender equality has been mainstreamed in the constitution-making process. This includes both the process (the Conventions themselves) and their product (the Constitutional Treaty and the Charter of Fundamental Rights). Though the main focus of the book is on the Constitutional Convention, in this chapter, more than in others, the Charter Convention will be examined closely. This is because of the close connection between issues of gender equality and the rights discourse.

The two Conventions' treatment of gender equality will be analysed by assessing how successful they have been in relation to the gender mainstreaming strategy which was introduced in the EU in the 1990s. The application of such a strategy to the constitution-making process is relevant because mainstreaming requires that a gender equality perspective is incorporated in all policies and at all levels of the policy-making process in the EU. There is no reason to believe, therefore, that the constitution-making process should be an exception to the rule. The analysis takes as its starting point five indicators used to assess whether the gender perspective has effectively been incorporated in policy and institutions. These indicators are: a shift towards a broader concept of gender equality; the incorporation of a gender perspective into the mainstream; equal representation of women; the prioritisation of gender objectives and gender-sensitive issues such as social policy; and a shift in institutional and organisational culture that should affect policy process, mechanisms and actors. After a brief overview of current EU legislation in the area of gender equality and mainstreaming, the chapter attempts to assess the work of the Convention on the Future of Europe in relation to the five indicators of gender mainstreaming. It concludes that the positive results of maintaining the existing EU *acquis* on gender equality and incorporating the Charter into the Constitution, to which gender advocates actively contributed, are partly offset by a limited mainstreaming of gender in the process and outcome of the Constitutional Convention.[1]

Gender equality and mainstreaming in the European Union

When the first Convention started its work on the Charter in 1999, the *acquis communautaire* already included both hard and soft measures in the area of equality and non-discrimination at work. The main provision is Article 141 TEU (directly effective) on the 'principle of equal pay for male and female workers for equal work or work of equal value'. It encourages the Council to 'adopt measures to ensure the application of the principle of equal opportunities and equal treatment of men and women in matters of employment and occupation' (141.3) and allows member states to introduce positive actions, defined as 'specific advantages in order to make it easier for the under-represented sex to pursue a vocational activity or to prevent or compensate for disadvantages in professional careers' (141.4). The aim of these measures is that of 'ensuring full equality in practice between men and women in working life'.

The Amsterdam Treaty of 1997 introduced Article 13, which allows the Council to take action 'to combat discrimination based on sex, racial or ethnic origin, religion or belief, disability, age or sexual orientation'. The Article, however, has no direct effect (unlike the non-discrimination clause on ground of nationality included in Article 6) and requires unanimity in the Council and consultation of the European Parliament for measures to be adopted (again unlike Article 6 that allows for co-decision and qualified majority voting in the Council). Binding provisions also include a series of directives[2] on equal pay, equal treatment at work and as regards access to and supply of goods and services, and social security.

At the time when their deliberations began respectively in 1999 for drafting the EU Charter and in 2002 for forging a European Constitutional Treaty, both Conventions could draw on an existing body of legislation, practices and structures aimed at the promotion of gender mainstreaming. The Treaty of Amsterdam recognised a prominent role for gender mainstreaming by introducing a new Article 2 ToA establishing the promotion of equality between men and women as a task of the Community, and a new Article 3.2 ToA stating that in all its activities 'the Community shall aim to eliminate inequalities, and to promote equality, between men and women'. Gender mainstreaming was also reflected in the Third, Fourth and Fifth Commission's Action Programmes for Equal Opportunities between women and men (1991–5, 1996–2000 and 2001–5).

Soft legislation on gender mainstreaming includes, among other documents, a Commission Communication 96/67 on 'Incorporating equal opportunities for women and men into all Community policies and activities', stating that a gender mainstreaming approach 'involves not restricting efforts to promote equality to the implementation of specific measures to help women, but mobilizing all general policies and measures specifically for the purpose of achieving equality by actively and openly taking into account at the planning stage their possible effects on the respective situation of men and women (gender perspective)'. The dictates of the relatively new and more proactive strategy of gender equality, enshrined through both hard and soft EU legislation in the course of the 1990s, seemed difficult to ignore in a constitution-making process. Gender mainstreaming requires in fact 'the (re)organisation, improvement, development and evaluation of policy processes, so that a gender equality perspective is incorporated in all policies at all levels and at all stages, by the actors normally involved in policy-making' (Council of Europe, 1998: 15).

Indicators of gender mainstreaming

The definition of gender mainstreaming by the Council of Europe and a number of reflective studies (Jahan, 1995; Verloo, 1999; Hafner-Burton and Pollack, 2000; Beveridge et al., 2000; Shaw, 2000; Lombardo and Meier, 2006) provide us with a set of indicators of application of gender mainstreaming in the policy process. These will serve as reference points for exploring how it has been applied in the Constitutional Convention.

First, *a broader concept of gender equality*. This includes not only formal legal equality but also equality *de facto*. The latter requires the adoption of a whole range of different strategies, from equal opportunities to positive actions, with a view to achieving substantive equality. It requires a 'gender perspective and not a focus limited to women's issues' (Council of Europe, 1998: 169). This means, for example, that changes in men's lifestyles are necessary as the role of one sex significantly affects the opportunities and lifestyles of the other. This broader concept implies the adoption of a more holistic approach to gender policy, which explicitly targets patriarchy by tackling the multiple interconnected causes which create an unequal relation between the sexes to the disadvantage of women in the areas of family, paid work, politics, sexuality, culture and male violence (Walby, 1990). The translation of this approach to policy-making would require the extension of EU gender legislation to cover with binding provisions all areas not only within but also beyond the labour market.

Second, *incorporation of a gender perspective into the mainstream*. Reference to gender issues and considerations regarding the extent to which a given provision could affect women and men in different ways (and how this could be limited) should be found in all policy areas. Moreover, to be able to claim that a more 'agenda-setting' approach has been employed, there must be evidence that the mainstream political agenda has been reoriented by rethinking and rearticulating policy ends and means from a gender perspective (Jahan, 1995).

Third, *women's representation in decision-making.* Gender mainstreaming requires an equal representation of women and men in decision-making bodies and processes. A growing number of EU provisions support a gender balance in the participation of women and men in the decision-making process and in committees and expert groups of the Commission, recommending that the participation of women should be at least of 40 per cent (Commission, 2000a).

Fourth, *prioritising gender equality objectives and policies of special relevance for women* (e.g. social policy), with the aim of achieving substantive equality. There should be evidence that gender equality objectives and policies that are of special concern for women have been given relevance in the EU among competing objectives (in terms of financial and human resources, type of measures with respect for example to binding/non-binding legislation, direct effect, voting systems required to take decisions, i.e. unanimity and European Parliament consultation vs. QMV and EP co-decision).

Fifth, *a shift in institutional and organisational cultures.* This change involves three aspects: (a) policy process; (b) policy mechanisms; (c) policy actors.

(a) A shift in *policy process* means that the latter 'is reorganised so that the actors usually involved take a gender perspective into account, and gender equality as a goal is reached' (Council of Europe, 1998: 166). As the Council of Europe group of experts on mainstreaming clarifies, this can mean that 'the policy process is reorganised so that ordinary actors know how to incorporate a gender perspective' or that gender expertise is included 'as a normal requirement for policy-makers' (Council of Europe, 1998: 165).

(b) A shift in *policy mechanisms* involves three elements. One, the adoption of new approaches to policy-making that would emphasise horizontal co-operation on gender issues across all policy areas, levels and departments. Two, the use of appropriate policy tools and techniques that would integrate the gender variable in all policies, monitor and evaluate the latter from a gender equality perspective (for example, gender impact assessment, an analysis *ex ante* of the consequences that a given policy could have on gender in order to reorient or moderate the proposed measure if it results that this would negatively affect gender equality). And three, the opening of new (and reinforcing of existing) channels of consultation and co-operation with civil society actors.

(c) The range of *policy actors* participating in the policy-making process should be broadened to include, apart from ordinary policy-makers and public administrators, gender policy experts and civil society actors (NGOs, interest groups, associations, social movements and representatives of workers and employers).

To verify the extent to which gender equality has been mainstreamed in the agenda of the Convention, some or all of the five indicators of a gender mainstreaming approach described above must be observed.

A broader concept of gender equality

The Charter of Fundamental Rights includes equality as a Union value and refers to equality between women and men and non-discrimination on grounds of sex respectively in Article II-83 and II-81.1,[3] while it also mentions the sharing of work and family responsibilities in Article II-93. In the same way as it opens opportunities for a broader concept of gender equality, the ambiguous framing of Article II-83 also raises doubts concerning the scope of equality provided by the Charter. Its first paragraph states: 'equality between women and men must be ensured *in all areas, including employment, work and pay'*. The extension of gender equality to all areas represents progress compared to an *acquis* mainly centred on equality at work. However, the added clause 'including employment, work and pay' reorients the application of equality to the usual labour-related areas of EU gender policy.

The way in which judges will interpret the Article will be the determining factor in clarifying the scope of the provision and in redefining the extension of the concept of gender equality in the Charter. In the best of cases the interpretation of Article II-83 would apply the concept of gender equality not only to the area of employment but also to family, politics, sexuality, culture and violence, which are all the areas of patriarchy in which we encounter gender discrimination (Walby, 1990). This would be a considerable shift towards a broader concept of equality and as a result towards a more serious consideration of gender mainstreaming. It is possible, though, that the principle of equality included in the Charter will apply to the areas that are specified in Article II-83 (employment, work and pay) rather than to 'all areas' that are not specified in the text.

Article II-83's mismatch with the *acquis* also reveals some of the limits of the Charter's concept of equality. Unlike Article 141 EC on equal pay, Article II-83 CFR is not directly effective, it is a 'general statement of intent' rather than a 'rights conferring measure' (León et al., 2003: 13) and does not include any positive obligation to promote gender equality as do Articles 2 and 3.2 EC (McCrudden, 2003). Reference to positive actions included in Article II-83 falls short of the *acquis* in two senses. First, the Charter treats positive measures as a derogation from the principle of equality rather than as means to achieve substantive equality, as Article 141 EC prescribes in its first sentence: 'With a view to ensuring *full equality in practice* between men and women in working life . . .'. Second, while Article 141 EC allows for positive actions even *'to prevent or compensate* for disadvantages in professional careers', Article II-83 limits the possibility of adopting positive actions to situations in which one sex is under-represented and not as a 'preventive or compensatory mechanism even when no under-representation of one sex is evident' (León et al., 2003: 13). McCrudden (2003) believes that even Article II-83 on the reconciliation of family and professional life fails to match the *acquis* represented by Directive 76/207 on equal treatment at work and Directive 92/85 on pregnant workers and Directive 96/34 on parental leave and the ECJ case law on the matter. He argues that Article II-83 CFR, 'refers only to paid maternity leave, rather than paid parental or paternity leave' (McCrudden, 2003: 7). Further reference to gender equality can be found in Article II-81.1 CFR that prohibits discrimination on a wide number of grounds among which is sex. The list of types of discrimination prohibited in the Charter is wider than that of Article 13 TEU (Article III-124 TCE), as it includes sex, race, colour, ethnic or social origin, genetic features, language, religion or belief, political or any other opinion, membership of a national minority, property, birth, disability, age or sexual orientation. Despite this progress, decisions based on Article II-81.1 CFR are subject to unanimity (rather than QMV) in Council and consultation (rather than co-decision) of the European Parliament, which means that agreement on a given proposal is more difficult to achieve and that the Parliament has a weaker role in the decision-making process.

As concerns the articulation of a broader concept of gender equality, the Constitutional Convention performed worse than the Charter Convention, also considering that, by the time the Constitutional Convention started its work, a considerable amount of EU soft legislation, mechanisms and infrastructures to apply gender mainstreaming had been produced. From the presentation of the first sixteen Articles of the Draft Constitutional Treaty in October 2002 it appeared that the concept of gender equality of the Constitutional Convention was not so broad as to include equality among the values of the Union as expressed in Article 2 TCE. After months of intense lobbying on the part of a great number of *conventionnels* (among whom were female members and alternates Lone Dybkjaer, Sylvia-Yvonne Kaufmann, Pervenche Berès and Anne van Lancker), actors of civil society, the EP Committee on Women's Rights, and gender experts, 'equality' (but not between women and men) was added to the values of the European Union in one of the very last drafts of the Constitutional Treaty (CONV 797/03) in June 2003.[4] The fact that the value of equality had to be fought for instead of being taken for granted shows that the Constitutional Convention had embraced a remarkably limited concept of gender equality.

Gender advocacy coalitions,[5] active during the process of the Constitutional Convention, agreed on proposals for strengthening the legal basis on gender equality that often coincided with the final report of the Working Group on Social Europe.[6] These included equality between women and men as a value and an objective of the Union, 'gender equality' added to the list of policies of shared competence between the Union and the member states in the first part of the Treaty, and the creation of a separate Title covering gender equality in the third part of the Constitution. In addition to these demands, Jean Monnet Professors at a Conference on 'Gender Equality and the New European Union' organised by Commission DG Education in March 2003[7] also proposed an Article on ensuring maternity and paternity protection and the reconciling of family and work, and recommended adding the phrase 'combating violence and trafficking in persons' both to the objectives of the Union and to the Policies (Part III of the Constitution). The European Women's Lobby also demanded gender parity in institutions. The petition to create a separate Article on 'non-discrimination on grounds of gender (or sex)' to recognise that women suffer multiple discrimination due to their sex *and* other reasons, remained unanswered. The Convention only responded to these demands by integrating the Charter within the Treaty, referring to 'equality' and 'non-discrimination' among the values of the Union in Article I-2, and 'equality between women and men' among the objectives of the Union in Article I-3. A reference to combating trafficking in persons (but not violence) was included in part III of the Treaty, reproducing existing EU provisions.

The *acquis communautaire* on gender equality was preserved as it is in the Constitutional Treaty, with the addition of Article III-118, a non-discrimination clause on several grounds that applies to the policies of the third part of the Constitution. This is a positive inclusion, although it differs from the main demands of gender advocates in favour of a non-discrimination clause on grounds of sex. Moreover, the phrasing is vague, as it does not require commitment on the part of member states or a strong prohibition, as shown by the use of the verb '*shall aim to* combat discrimination' instead of '*shall prohibit*'. The means for taking action against discrimination are those laid down in Article 13 TEU (Article III-124 TCE), without any improvement in the procedures of decision-making. Finally, Article 141 EC on equal pay for equal work has been reproduced as it is in Article III-214 of the Constitution and Article 3.2 on gender mainstreaming is now part of the clauses of general application as Article III-116. This means that mainstreaming will cover all policy areas of part III of the Constitution including Common Foreign and Security Policy and Justice and Home Affairs. A new general clause III-115 claims that in the policies included in section III, the EU will take into account the objectives of the Union (equality and non-discrimination among them).

In sum, the *acquis* is safe but the concept of gender equality has not been broadened so as to cover other policies beyond employment. Nor has the legal basis of gender policy been strengthened, and neither has the strategy of gender mainstreaming. The inclusion of a general clause of non-discrimination shows a shift in the concept of equality towards an emphasis on non-discrimination policies, with developments that are currently difficult to foresee, also due to the weak legal instruments provided to decide on measures and to claim rights.

The incorporation of a gender perspective

To satisfy this requirement we should encounter not only a reference to gender mainstreaming like Article 3.2 TEU (Article III-116 TCE), but also the application of a gender perspective to all areas and a gender sensitive reorientation of the political agenda. Both the Charter and the Constitution contain relevant omissions at least in the areas of violence, asylum, sharing of work and family responsibilities, health, culture and education, budgeting, and security and defence policy.

Violence against women has not been explicitly addressed in the Constitution. Article II-64 of the Charter prohibits 'torture, inhuman or degrading treatment or punishment'. However, the adoption of a gender perspective on violence would also have specified that female genital mutilation, rape, or domestic violence are forms of 'inhuman or degrading treatment or punishment'. The only reference to gender violence is a declaration (Declaration 13 on Article III-116 in the Final Act) on the Union's aim to combat 'all kinds of domestic violence', introduced in the June 2004 IGC at the request of the newly elected Spanish socialist government. Despite the possible positive developments of the declaration, particularly when read together with Article III-269.3 on family law with cross-border implications, the measure is not legally binding.

Provisions against trafficking have received a more explicit treatment by both Conventions. Article II-65.3 CFR prohibits trafficking in human beings and the explanations provided in the Constitution clarify that the Article will be used to combat trafficking in women and children. In the section on judicial co-operation on criminal matters of the Constitution, Article III-271 (Article 17 TEU) allows the introduction of rules for combating the traffic 'of human beings and sexual exploitation of women and children'. Similar is the text of Article III-267 TCE, in the section on 'Policies on border checks, asylum and immigration'. No analogous progressive treatment was provided to grant the right of asylum to women who seek to escape from gender-specific forms of persecution imposed by law, religion or social norms. Moreover, while the Draft Constitutional Treaty (CONV 848/03) had included a new Article III-46 in the section on 'Capital and payments' that established that in order to fight 'trafficking in human beings' a European law may define measures with regard to capital movements and payments such as 'freezing of funds, financial assets or economic gains' held or owned by natural and legal persons and groups, the final text in its Article III-160 has deleted any reference to it, limiting the provision only to the fight against terrorism.

The sharing of work and family responsibilities between the sexes has been addressed in the Charter (Article II-93.2) but not in the Constitution. It is true that once the Constitution has incorporated the Charter there would be no need for replicating provisions. However, the inclusion of a measure on the reconciliation of family and work in a section such as 'Free movement of workers' could promote changes in the organisation of work required to allow the equal involvement of women and men in family and labour responsibilities. A gendered approach to freedom of movement of persons would require a consideration of the conditions that would enable both women and men to move freely and to enjoy social protection autonomously. Since women are more often than men marginalised as paid workers (or are more likely to choose part-time jobs that are more compatible with family responsibilities), in a system like the EU based on employment-related social protection they are the most likely to suffer (Hantrais, 1995).

A gender perspective is also absent in policies such as health, culture and education where the Union can take 'coordinating, supplementary or supporting action', but which are mainly of national competence. The EWL had asked in its contribution to the Charter Convention to maintain reproductive health services at an affordable price for women, considering maternity as a matter of social concern. Article II-95 of the Charter and the part of the Constitution on Public Health omit any reference to reproductive rights. In the chapters on culture (Article III-280) and education (Article III-282) of the Constitution, no reference is made to measures for combating cultural gender stereotypes and for promoting gender equality and non-discrimination at all educational levels and in cultural production.

Finance is a policy area where the integration of a gender perspective could have a substantive impact on women's conditions. Gender budgeting has been introduced in the guidelines of the European Structural Funds 2000–6 together with a review of the gender dimensions of tax/benefit systems in EU countries. Gender budgeting aims to produce a budget in which gender has been 'mainstreamed' by analysing public expenditure and methods of raising public revenue from a gender perspective, identifying the implications for women as compared to men (Elson, 2003). In 'The multiannual financial framework' and 'The Union's annual budget' of the Constitution there is no reference to gender budgeting or gender equality considerations.

Finally, a gender perspective has not been incorporated into the 'Common Foreign and Security Policy' and 'Common Security and Defence Policy' of the Constitution. UN General Secretary Kofi Annan has recognised women's crucial role in conflict resolution and their fundamental contribution to the consolidation of international peace and security.[8] However, claims Annan, without strengthening women's participation in negotiations and decision-making, their peace-keeping potential is lost. To this aim, the UN Security Council has unanimously adopted Resolution 1325 on 'Women, peace and security' that establishes the need to protect women in armed conflicts and their central role in conflict-prevention, peace construction and peace-keeping. No similar provision has been included in the European Constitution.

With the exception of trafficking, and, only in a marginal way also the sharing of family and work responsibilities, all other areas of the Constitutional Treaty considered do not show any consistent integration of a gender perspective. Nevertheless, the text includes formal provisions on gender mainstreaming. The Convention thus appears to have been committed to promoting gender mainstreaming, but not ready to put it into practice in the context of its own constitution-making process.

Women's representation in decision-making

Perhaps this lack of attention to gender mainstreaming should not surprise us if we consider the composition of the Convention. Expectations that women would be better represented in the more open and democratic process of both Conventions were soon dashed. The percentage of female representatives in the Convention that drafted the Charter was 16 per cent. The criticisms of gender campaigners regarding the under-representation of women in the Charter Convention did not affect selection procedures of the subsequent Constitutional Convention: in February 2003 only 17.14 per cent (18/105) of the body that drafted the document which could become the future European Constitution were women. If we break this figure down it can be seen that women comprised only 20 per cent of the representatives of the heads of states or governments of the member states (3/15), 10 per cent (3/30) of the representatives of national parliaments, 0 per cent (0/2) of the representatives of the European Commission, 31.25 per cent (5/16) of the representatives of the European Parliament, 30.77 per cent (4/13) of the representatives of the governments of the accession countries, and 11.54 per cent (3/26) of the representatives of the national parliaments of accession countries. None of the female representatives in the Constitutional Convention occupied a leading position as president or vice-president. Only two out of the twelve members of the Presidium were women, and only one of them, Gisela Stuart, chaired one of the eleven working groups. These figures do not remotely approach the 40 per cent recommended by Commission Decision 2000/407. Commenting on this low degree of female representativeness in the Constitutional Convention, President Giscard d'Estaing (2002a) wrote: 'Elles compensent cette situation d'inferiorité numérique par la forte personalité de beaucoup d'entre elles' [sic].[9]

Not only had the existing EU provisions recommending a gender balance in decision-making almost no effect on mechanisms of selection of representatives of the two Conventions, but even member states that have a relatively good record of women's representatives in their national parliaments sent a much lower female representation to the Constitutional Convention. Denmark, which has a female parliamentary representation of 38 per cent, did not send any women members and only two women alternates from the EP; Germany, with 32.2 per cent of women in Parliament, sent 16.6 per cent of female members to the Convention; also the Netherlands, Sweden and Finland, that respectively have 34 per cent, 45 per cent and 36 per cent of female MPs, reduced their female representatives in the Convention to 25 per cent, 33.3 per cent and 25 per cent respectively. However, some member states and candidate countries (Latvia, Bulgaria, Poland, Slovakia, the Czech Republic, Cyprus and Romania) sent a higher percentage of women to the Convention than their national parliaments (León et al., 2003). Women are slightly more represented among alternates than among members in all groups, that is in total 20 per cent of female alternates and 17.14 per cent of women members in February 2003. These scant results reveal that one of the greatest obstacles that gender mainstreaming must face is the fact that the decision-making process, be it deliberative or based on traditional methods of negotiating, takes place in an environment in which power mechanisms are not gender neutral.

Prioritising gender equality objectives and policies

The inclusion of provisions on gender equality and non-discrimination in the Charter and in the Constitution indicates that gender objectives have been integrated to a degree in both constitution-making processes. Social policy provisions were included in Chapter III on equality and Chapter IV on solidarity of the Charter, and the Constitution maintains social measures contained in the *acquis*. In spite of their inclusion, however, the type of guarantees that have been granted to gender equality provisions is not very strong. Article II-83 CFR on equality between women and men has no direct effect and is merely a programmatic measure (León et al., 2003). The establishment of equality as an objective and a value of the Union, as well as the general mainstreaming clause III-116 are important as they communicate a sense of positive obligation to promote gender equality in all EU policy areas and structures. The guarantees of Article III-214 (141 EC) on equal pay are also strong since the Article is directly effective. Article III-118, the general anti-discrimination clause, may affect all policy areas but has weak means to implement measures.

The struggle over the inclusion of the value of equality during the process of the Constitutional Convention reveals that gender was not especially prioritised. A statement by one of the Presidium members, Klaus Hänsch, at a special meeting of the EP Committee of Women's Rights on 2 October 2002, exemplifies this state of affairs: 'The battle is not so much to put more in, but to maintain what exists' (European Parliament, 2002a). Mr Hänsch was concerned about the fact that debates on EU competences and the principle of subsidiarity could weaken the existing *acquis* on gender equality with the argument that, as gender policy was sufficiently developed in the member states there would be no need to include it in the European Constitution. Whether the risk of losing existing equality rights in the Constitution was real or not, the fact that equality was added to the values of the Union in one of the last drafts (CONV 797/03) speaks volumes regarding the consideration of gender as a priority for the Constitutional Convention.

The treatment of social policy in the process of the Constitutional Convention is also indicative of the priorities of the Presidium and its president on issues of special relevance for women. As more extensively argued in Chapter 8, the establishment of the working group on Social Europe encountered some resistance on the part of the Presidium, particularly the president. It was not created from the beginning together with the other working groups, and when, after intense lobbying and protesting, it was finally formed, its deliberations were not taken into account in the first sixteen articles of the Draft Constitutional Treaty issued by the Presidium (CONV 528/03). Although some of the measures proposed by the working group on Social Europe were finally included in the Treaty (in a watered-down version), the attitude maintained by the Presidium towards equality and social issues during the process is indicative of the fact that social issues and actors concerned with them such as women were *de facto* marginalised, rather than prioritised, in the discourse of the Convention.

A shift in institutional and organisational culture

The fifth requirement of gender mainstreaming is a shift in institutional and organisational culture that should be observed in three aspects of EU constitution-making: policy process, mechanisms and actors.

Policy process

The reorganisation of a policy process so that actors take a gender perspective into account can mean that 'the policy process is reorganised so that ordinary actors know how to incorporate a gender perspective' or that gender expertise is included 'as a normal requirement for policy-makers' (Council of Europe, 1998: 165).

The President of the Committee on Women's Rights of the European Parliament, Karamanou, in a letter addressed to the President of the Convention, Giscard, and distributed to all *conventionnels* in June 2002, made the following proposals for reorganising the policy process 'to compensate for the under-representation of women amongst the *conventionnels* and to aim at an outcome of the Convention that reflects the aspirations of societies composed of active and concerned women as well as men':

- In each of the working groups currently created, one person should be specifically mandated to incorporate a gender perspective into the issues under consideration.
- A working group on gender issues should be created and presidencies of the working groups should be equally distributed between women and men.
- Gender expertise should be ensured in the secretariat of the Convention.
- *Conventionnels* should also be encouraged to call on existing gender expertise (in the Committee on Women's Rights and Equal Opportunities, in the European Commission, in academic institutions and NGOs).
- A group of experts could monitor the work of the Convention from a gender perspective (European Parliament, 2002a).

None of these proposals was taken on board. Only one woman, Gisela Stuart, led one of the eleven working groups. Giscard's reply to Karamanou's letter avoided answering the proposals and instead addressed a general, degendered appeal to the role of citizens' 'vigilance' over the work of the Convention (European Parliament, 2002b, 2003). In spite of the efforts of gender advocates, the Convention did not bring evidence of a shift towards a reorganisation of the policy process so that institutional actors could take a gender perspective into account.

Policy mechanisms

Evidence of a shift in policy mechanisms should be sought in the use both of horizontal co-operation on gender issues across policy areas and of tools for integrating a gender perspective and then monitoring and evaluating its integration in the policy process. Horizontal co-operation was relatively easy in the Conventions due, on the one hand, to the fact that these bodies had sufficiently defined tasks to perform (more precise in the first than in the second Convention) within a limited time-span, and on the other hand, to the method of deliberation, based on the need to achieve consensus and a certain autonomy enjoyed by the members, that facilitated internal communication and debate. The Constitutional Convention created eleven working groups on different issues, the results of whose deliberations were then discussed in plenary sessions. An analysis of the final reports of the working groups[10] (none of which concerned gender equality, as the Committee on Women's Rights had recommended) reveals that gender was not a transversal issue across the groups. Gender equality was debated only by the working group on Social Europe, the 'Cinderella' of all working groups of the Convention, as Shaw has described it (2003b). Rather than a horizontal approach to gender equality, there was a policy-specific approach limited to the social sector. With regard to the instruments for integrating, monitoring and evaluating gender in all areas, the Convention did not adopt any of the methods proposed by the EP Committee on Women's Rights to ensure gender expertise in the work of the Convention and to evaluate its results from a gender perspective.

Policy actors

The process of the Charter Convention set a precedent in the opening of channels of consultation with civil society that was repeated in the Constitutional Convention. Actors from civil society could send their contributions to the debate via the internet and both Conventions organised hearings with representative organisations of civil society. The Constitution includes Article I-47 (IGC 87/2/04 REV 2) on the 'Principle of participatory democracy' which introduces the concept of civil dialogue into the Treaty, although not with the conditions demanded by organisations of civil society. However, it is not clear that this change has occurred to comply with gender mainstreaming, as it is part of the moves towards better governance that the Union is making to open the policy-making process to a wider range of actors (Commission, 1998, 2000b, 2001).

Civil society groups in both Conventions were active on gender. In the Constitutional Convention, gender equality was a transversal issue across civil society organisations: during the hearings of 24–25 June 2002 five contact groups out of eight addressed gender equality issues in their demands to the plenary of the Convention (CONV 112/02, 120/02 and 167/02).[11] Opening the EU institutional process to civil society actors can reinforce debates on gender equality also within the European institutions. However, gender equality could become a priority for civil society but not for EU institutional actors. Not only has civil society no decision-making power in the policy process but also the role that the Convention accorded to civil society was of a 'passive' rather than an 'active' nature (Closa, 2003), with little capacity to influence process and outcomes, as will be further discussed in the next chapter. Rather then being mainstreamed into the political agenda, gender equality could run the risk of becoming a marginalised issue in the hands of equally marginalised actors. Moreover, the few women's groups who were actively engaged in the Convention process were European-based organisations, more familiar with the EU institutional context and language.

Conclusion: achievements and limits of the Convention

The Convention experiment succeeded in maintaining the existing *acquis communautaire* on gender equality, adding 'equality' to the values of the Union, and incorporating the Charter into the Constitutional Treaty. This was to a great extent the result of the activism of gender advocacy coalitions throughout the constitutional debates. However, the Convention failed to effectively mainstream gender into its own policy-making process. The attempt to achieve a shift towards a broader concept of gender equality during the process produced limited results concerning the covering of policies beyond the area of employment and the strengthening of the legal basis on equality. The incorporation of a gender perspective into the political agenda of the two Conventions partially occurred for the issues of trafficking (less for violence) and sharing of work and family tasks, but not for health, culture and education, budgeting, and security and defence policy. The representation of women has been far from the 40 per cent recommended by the Commission, with 16 per cent of female representatives in the Charter Convention and 17.14 per cent in the Constitutional Convention. Furthermore, there is no evidence that gender equality and social policies have been prioritised in the process over other policy issues. Finally, the gender advocates' demands for a more gender-sensitive process and mechanisms went unmet. Even though the Convention process was more open than the traditional IGC method to specialised gender policy actors, it gave them little influence.

One of the reasons for explaining the limited integration of a gender equality perspective in the constitution-making process could be the low number of female members of the Convention: '17 women out of 105 *conventionnels* is a small number to make your voices heard', argued Agnès Hubert.[12] Although not all women speak for gender equality, it was difficult for the few female members who did so to raise gender equality issues and to have a receptive audience on these matters, considering that *conventionnels* had only two or three minutes to speak on the basis of an agenda that was decided by the predominantly male Presidium.

Another hypothesis is that in the contested process of 'norm-setting' that took place in the Convention (Elgström, 2000), the goal of gender equality had to give way to other priorities. Rather than being framed as an explicit opposition to the goal of gender equality, the discourse of the Convention privileged institutional reform (i.e. the Convention's mandate) over more substantive issues, such as equality. Moreover, the priority given to debates on EU competence and the principle of subsidiarity promoted the perception that gender equality provisions could be limited in the constitutional text (with the argument that gender equality is a national competence), as Hänsch's concern suggested. Finally, the Presidium and particularly President Giscard d'Estaing were extremely influential in steering debates towards the prioritising of issues other than gender equality.

In spite of the limited results achieved, the Convention represented an opportunity for both building alliances between institutional and non-governmental actors in support of equality (something that proved effective in the final inclusion of the latter among the Union values), and for raising public awareness on the still problematic question of the incorporation of a gender perspective in the EU policy-making process.

Notes

1. Since the purpose of this chapter is to assess the extent to which gender has been mainstreamed in the EU constitutional process, the position of individual female *conventionnels* on specific constitutional questions is not analysed here, in spite of its relevance.
2. EU gender directives cover the fields of equal pay (Directive 75/117/EEC); equal treatment at work (Directive 76/207 EEC on equal treatment in employment-related areas and its most recent version Directive 2002/73/EC, Directive 97/80 EC on the burden of proof, Directive 96/34/EC on the framework agreement on parental leave, Directive 92/85/EEC on health and safety of pregnant workers, women workers who have recently given birth and women who are breast-feeding); equal treatment in social security (Directive 79/7/EEC on statutory social security and Directive 86/378/EEC that extends the principle of equal treatment also to private or occupational social security schemes, amended by Directive 96/97/EC); equal treatment as regards access to and supply of goods and services (Directive 2004/113/EC); and the recast Directive 2006/54/EC on the implementation of the principle of equal opportunities and equal treatment of men and women in matters of employment and occupation, and equal pay. Two directives cover multiple discriminations occurring in employment and occupation by prohibiting discrimination on the grounds of race or ethnic origin (Directive 2000/43/EC) and discrimination based on religion or belief, disability, age or sexual orientation (Directive 2000/78/EC). EU 'soft' legislation on gender equality includes a wide range

of provisions (Recommendations, Decisions, Communications, Programmes, etc.) in areas that extend also beyond employment, as is the case for women's political participation.

3. All references to the Articles of the Charter of Fundamental Rights are to the text incorporated in the Treaty for a Constitution of Europe (TCE) approved by the IGC. The Article numbers of the TCE in part II correspond to those in the Draft Constitutional Treaty adopted by the Convention (DCT).

4. The text approved by the IGC on 25 June 2004 (IGC 86/04) mentions 'equality' as a value and then states that 'These values are common to member states in a society in which pluralism, non-discrimination, tolerance, justice, solidarity, and equality between women and men prevail.' The second sentence, which makes reference to gender equality, is vaguer than the first. It merely mentions a list of general principles that member states supposedly share, but that have a less binding nature than values (particularly as values are criteria that candidate countries need to respect).

5. Gender coalitions included the EP Committee on Women's Rights, *conventionnels* (the Working Group on Social Europe and EP female representatives such as Anne Van Lancker, Sylvia-Yvonne Kaufmann, and the alternates Lone Dybkjaer and Pervenche Berès), academics, and civil society organisations such as European Women's Lobby (EWL), European Women Lawyers Association (EWLA), Association of Women of Southern Europe (AFEM), and Women of Europe Citizens Network (RCE).

6. See http://register.consilium.eu.int/pdf/en/03/cv00/CV00516-re01en03.pdf

7. See http://www.europa.eu.int/comm/education/ajm/equality/index.html

8. Message of Secretary General Kofi Annan on International Women's Day, 8 March 2001 http://www.un.org/News/Press/docs/2001/sgsm7726.doc.htm

9. Giscard d'Estaing (2002a).

10. For a discussion of the working groups, see Chapter 5.

11. Contact groups are umbrella organisations grouping similar associations that were in charge of making contact with members of the Convention and that, according to the Convention, had to represent 'major sectors of interest'. Each contact group selected representatives who had to speak during the hearings.

12. Agnès Hubert was at the time liaison person in the Secretariat of the EP Committee on Women's Rights on secondment from the Commission.

8
The Participation of Civil Society

Emanuela Lombardo

One of the favourite terms in the public language of the Constitutional Convention was 'civil society'. References abound to the need to listen to citizens' views (CONV 14/02, 25 March 2002), to the importance of establishing 'a genuine dialogue . . . with civil society' (CONV 7/02, 11 March 2002), and to the intention of using civil society's contributions 'as input into the debate' (Laeken Declaration). The aim of this chapter is to explore the extent to which these promising claims were put into practice in the deliberative process of the Convention in order to assess whether there was a substantive shift on the part of the Union towards the creation of a more democratic and pluralistic European public sphere.

The concept of civil society employed in the EU context commonly refers to civil society organisations, i.e. NGOs and advocacy groups. This is a more limited concept than that used by scholars, which includes a wider and more articulated social space where issues are raised and debated and political demands are addressed to decision-makers (Cohen and Arato, 1992, 1995; Dryzeck, 2000; Habermas, 1992b; Walzer, 1995; Young, 2000). This chapter refers to the notion of civil society as it is employed in the EU, by focusing in particular on the role of social NGOs in the Convention, while the place of economic interests is discussed in Chapter 9.

The Convention's discourse on civil society is analysed in relation to the substantive issues on Social Europe that were of particular concern to the participants in the Forum, which was the place assigned for the 'voice' of civil society to be heard, something made clear at Laeken:

> In order for the debate to be broadly based and involve all citizens, a Forum will be opened for organisations representing civil society (the social partners, the business world, non-governmental organisations, academia, etc.). It will take the form of a structured network of organisations receiving regular information on the Convention's proceedings. Their contributions will serve as input into the debate. Such organisations may

153

be heard or consulted on specific topics in accordance with arrangements to be established by the Presidium.

(Laeken Declaration)

The extent to which dominant frames[1] in the Convention's discourse operate to include or to marginalise civil society's perspectives, issues and actors will enable us to observe the distance existing between words and deeds on the part of the Convention. An analysis of the proceedings of consultation with civil society, the main demands of civil society, and the outcome of Convention deliberations may help to verify how successful the Convention was in reaching civil society, engaging in a real dialogue with it, and giving proper representation to its demands.

The chapter is divided in two parts. The first reflects on the Convention's discourse concerning civil society and the second explores the experience of the Forum. The argument developed is that the Convention's emphasis on civil society was a rhetorical device to gain legitimacy rather than a genuine move towards a more pluralistic EU democracy capable of complementing representative democracy through mechanisms of active participation of citizens and social actors in the policy-making process.

The discourse on civil society: dominant attitudes and frames

The first stage of the Convention's workings, that is the listening phase, placed from its beginnings a special emphasis on the need to *hear the voices* of civil society. The president, Giscard d'Estaing, opened the first substantive debate of the Convention claiming that 'the citizens of Europe felt that their voice was not being heard on the future of Europe and that the first phase of the Convention should therefore be a listening phase' (CONV 14/02: 1).[2] Convention members stressed not only the aspect of listening but also the need 'to take account of citizens' expectations and give citizens a greater say in and fuller scrutiny of European decision-making' (CONV 14/02: 4). In other introductory debates the members of the Convention welcomed it as a 'unique opportunity to bring European construction closer to the citizen' by establishing 'a genuine dialogue' with civil society, and leaving the listening activities of the Forum open throughout the whole of the Convention's proceedings (CONV 7/02: 3).[3]

Although it is often referred to as a 'dialogue', the relationship with civil society can better be described as a process of 'hearing' and 'consultation' (Laeken Declaration; CONV 14/02; CONV 167/02). This is because in none of the Convention documents is there any mention of feedback activity from the Convention to civil society organisations and any reference to how far contributions have affected specific issues, general orientation of the Convention, not to mention the Constitutional Treaty. Moreover, there is a risk that this consultation may be a one-way process from civil society to the Convention and the EU at large and not vice versa. Convention documents make clear that, in order to have people's support, the Convention must benefit from civil society's contributions (CONV 8/02: 4). The Convention's expectation of benefiting from the consultation of civil society was asserted during the plenary session devoted to civil society, in which Mr Dehaene, vice-chairman, stated that the 'dialogue with civil society' had been 'highly enriching, above all for the Convention' (CONV 167/02: 14).

One can raise a question about the extent to which this 'dialogue' has been enriching for actors from civil society as well. In so far as there is no mention of the type of impact that such contributions have had on the Convention and the feedback that organisations will receive from it, doubts may be expressed concerning the genuine character of the Convention's interest in civil society. To a question concerning the type of interaction maintained with the Convention, a member of civil society who participated in the Forum significantly answered that: 'Interaction with the Convention is proof positive of the existence of black holes. You send something but nothing ever comes out. No answer to any letters. No acknowledgement of receipt. Nothing.'[4]

Thus, a first general attitude of the Convention towards civil society that can be detected is that of 'listening without committing to an answer'. What was described as an attempt at 'genuine dialogue' was instead a rather 'banal exercise of freedom of expression', as De Schutter defined a similar experience in the process of the Charter (De Schutter, 2001: 169). There was not a clear commitment on the part of the Convention to stating how and to what extent contributions from civil society groups would be taken into account in the deliberations and in the Constitutional text.

With respect to dominant frames, the neo-liberal mindset of the EU operated as a tacitly accepted broad setting for discourses taking place in the Convention, by supporting a general assumption about what was 'natural' and 'important' to be discussed in the Convention. This means that issues and perspectives that accepted the existing neo-liberal trend were prioritised, while social issues that challenged this model were marginalised and actors defending them were constrained to adopt 'realistic' (that is within the dominant neo-liberal paradigm) standpoints to participate in the debate.

Furthermore, the fact that Convention discourse was more institutionally driven limited wider debates about the nature of the EU project and marginalised actors willing to discuss more substantive questions about the type of polity that is being aimed at. In a speech for the opening of the academic year at the College of Europe, in Bruges (2 October 2002), Giscard said that institutional matters would be discussed at the end, as 'institutional arguments must not drive our debate on the basic questions: rather our answers to these basic questions about competences and means of action of the Union will dictate our eventual institutional prescriptions' (Giscard d'Estaing, 2002b: 17). This claim was contradicted on several occasions in which the president of the Convention steered the discussion towards more institutional questions. The debate on social policy is exemplary.

The discussion on Social Europe represented an opportunity to raise fundamental issues concerning the nature of the European project that is planned for the future and the unquestioned neo-liberal focus that has characterised the EU integration process in the past few decades. The opening of a debate on Social Europe, proposed by a number of members of the Convention[5] and the Social Platform of European NGOs, was justified as follows:

> The numerous statements and contributions of *members of the Convention* within the plenary meetings of the Convention, the various statements of representatives of *civil society*, the conclusions of the *Youth convention*, and the results of the *Eurobarometer* reflecting the expectations of the European citizens (the fight against unemployment, poverty and social exclusion has highest priority) show *the need and the necessity to establish a social Europe*.
>
> (CONV 300/02: 3)

The plenary meeting on Social Europe took place on 7–8 November 2002 (CONV 400/02: 6).[6] On several occasions the president of the Convention acted to steer the debate towards more institutional and less contentious issues and away from substantive discussions on the nature of the EU project that aimed at revitalising the European social model and at questioning the existing neo-liberal approach. The questions prepared by the Presidium for members of the Convention to structure the debate on social issues were entirely focused on possible institutional amendments to EU social and economic policy and left little space for a more general discussion on the need for a European social model, that, although highly controversial, had been the main reason for requiring a plenary.[7]

A merely institutional focus on social issues would marginalise or exclude discussions on issues such as the current challenges posed by economic globalisation to social policies, the dismantlement of European welfare states, increasing (long- and short-term) unemployment, the changing nature of work with fixed jobs disappearing together with social protection, flexibility, precarious and temporary jobs, ageing population, inequality, poverty, social exclusion, and so on. These and similar issues were raised by representatives of civil society in the June 2002 hearing and in the European Social Forum in Florence in November 2002 that coincided with the Convention debate on Social Europe on 7–8 November.

The establishment of a working group on social issues also encountered some resistance on the part of the Presidium, particularly from the president. Although Giscard noted at the end of the debate on Social Europe that there was a considerable support for the creation of such a group, he 'was distinctly less enthusiastic about the idea'. After campaigns by Ms Anne Van Lancker, Ms Sylvia-Yvonne Kaufmann, Mr Johannes Voggenhuber and the other members who had proposed the debate on Social Europe, support in favour of a working group on social policy from a considerable number of delegates, and with backing from the EPP, the largest political family, Presidium members Klaus Hänsch and Giuliano Amato acknowledged the calls for the setting up of a new group. 'We've got the message,' said Mr Hänsch, while Mr Amato admitted that the 'demand seems to be widely supported' (EUobserver, 8 November 2002).

The Working Group on Social Policy of the Convention was finally created, indeed representing a victory of civil society and of those *conventionnels* subscribing to a more proactive view of Social Europe, though the period of time to discuss and deliberate on many contentious social issues was far more limited than for the rest of the working groups (only five meetings to discuss a seven-point mandate). The dispute over the creation of a working group on social policy significantly highlighted the Presidium's and its president's attitude towards social issues as one of attempting to silence or marginalise contentious issues that would question the tacitly assumed neo-liberal mindset of the EU. This attempt revealed a certain lack of concern not only for the will of members of the Convention, but also for representatives of civil society and European citizens who attached a great significance to social issues. A member of the ILGA (International Lesbian and Gay Association), one of the NGOs that participated in the Forum, claimed: 'Initially none of the Working Groups dealt with social issues explicitly. This was very disappointing from our perspective, but indicative of the position of social issues in the EU in general.'[8]

In effect, the largest group of civil society organisations, classified in the Forum website as 'other, civil society, NGOs and schools of thought (O)', attached great importance to the working group on Social Europe. Although the latter did not have sufficient time to take direct advice from civil society, due to its late creation, individual members seemed to have listened to and taken into account civil society's contributions (Shaw, 2003b). This emerges from the Final Report that the working group produced (CONV 516/1/03). The working group treated the question of Social Europe as a fundamental piece in the EU constitutional framework, and not just a question of policy content (Shaw, 2003b) by reaffirming the role of 'social objectives as equivalent, not subordinate to, economic objectives', as 'forming an integral part of the spirit in which the European Union was conceived and of the direction in which it develops' (CONV 516/1/03: 8). This statement, and the whole report, expresses a project of Social Europe that is understandable by, and in line with, most civil society and in general citizens' concerns, giving a direction and a name to the Union whose future is being discussed.

In spite of the wide support that welcomed the report in the plenary session of 7 February, the draft of the first sixteen articles of the Constitutional Treaty issued by the Presidium at the end of January explicitly admits that results of the discussions of the working group on Social Europe had not been taken into account in writing the preliminary document. The precedent set by the draft sixteen articles is not irrelevant, as Shaw points out, considering that 'even though these draft articles are only "suggestions", as

Giscard has reminded us, they still represent an unfortunate reference point' (Shaw, 2003b: 3). This is effectively confirmed by the amendments to the Draft which did not include a large number of points covered in the Social Report and ignored by the Presidium's preliminary Treaty. Beside the fact that the Convention was missing an opportunity to construct a 'strong Europe' by aiming for a 'social Europe' (Shaw, 2003b), it also missed the opportunity to give representation to civil society's main concerns, concerns shared by the working group on Social Europe. As one participant to the Forum claimed: 'We were very disappointed to see that the Social Europe report was to a very limited extent taken into account.'[9] The Convention's emphasis on the relevance of civil society appears to be a rhetorical device to gain legitimacy rather than a genuine attempt to abandon the EU elitist attitude towards the citizen.

Civil society in action: a structured dialogue?

As we have seen, the Laeken Declaration sets the basis for the establishment of a Forum consisting of a network of civil society organisations whose contributions are explicitly described as providing 'input' into the Convention's debate and whose character is consultative. Consultation through the Forum was characterised by a distinctive openness in the process of participation. A user-friendly website was created for the Forum, in which contributions were attached and updated, hearings with civil society organisations were organised in June 2002, culminating in a public debate on the plenary session of the Convention on 24–25 June; national debates with civil society were run in the member states; and regular contacts were kept between civil society and Mr Dehaene, the Presidium vice-president in charge of relations between the Convention and civil society groups.

No further requirement was asked for participating in the Forum than to send a written contribution to the Convention, to be submitted in a pre-defined format, which would then be posted on the Forum's website. This gave rise to a multiplication of inputs and meant that the number of participants to the Forum grew constantly from around 200 groups in September 2002 to over 500 organisations in March 2003. This certainly contributed to the publicity of the Convention process, at least among the organised civil society, and enabled a great number of actors to express their views on the future of Europe. However, it also implied a number of problems which had already emerged in the previous consultation that accompanied the drafting of the Charter. Moreover, the formal openness of the process did not necessarily mean that no substantive selection was actually made. In fact, a number of more or less invisible obstacles were apparent in the selection of participants to the Forum and, in particular, to the hearings of 24–25 June 2002.[10]

The Forum repeated some of the mistakes of the Charter consultation, revealing once more that a wide open consultation process does not necessarily equal effective participation. It has been suggested in fact that other requirements are necessary to achieve the latter. As one commentator observed, 'the more open the consultation process, the less the right to be "heard" may in fact impose on the institution addressed an obligation to answer' (De Schutter, 2001: 169).

De Schutter (2001) questioned whether the EU institutions should actively structure existing organisations (at the same time encouraging the emergence of new groups) or whether they should not intervene in the process at all. With respect to the latter, he warned of the risk that leaving civil society as it exists, without any structuring of the network, may favour the better-organised, better-informed and better-situated and resourceful groups and exclude organisations that do not enjoy the same benefits despite their representativeness or their competence on the matter. De Schutter's proposal is therefore to structure civil society's network according to a number of criteria of representation defined by ECOSOC (ECOSOC, 2001: point 3.4.1., p. 6), and to organise the consultation process by identifying the questions of general interest on which organisations of civil society could contribute (e.g. gender equality, environment). For each area of concern, fora with the most representative organisations should be established and consulted both at an early stage of the legislative proposals and in the process of policy evaluation.

A structured organisation of civil society participating in the EU policy-making process would ensure what the Commission has defined as a right 'to receive appropriate feedback on how their contributions and opinions have affected the eventual policy-decision, thereby making the relationship a real dialogue' (Commission, 2000b: n.5, p. 10). It is argued that this dialogue would only be manageable with a selection of participant organisations. The merit of this procedure is that it would force the EU institutions to commit to a more genuine dialogue with civil society and would control the more informal lobbying that might benefit more powerful groups. After the experience of the two Conventions which saw considerable participation but without any feedback on how civil society had affected the process, suggestions similar to the ones recommended by De Schutter have multiplied among civil society organisations.

Treaty articles on participatory democracy

The preliminary Draft Treaty included in Title VI, 'The Democratic Life of the Union', an explicit reference to participatory democracy, particularly in its Article 34 but also in Article 36 (CONV 369/02).[11] A later version of the Treaty mentions the 'Principle of participatory democracy' in its Article I-46 (CONV 724/03), while Article I-45 deals with representative democracy. Article I-46 also adds a third paragraph on the Commission's task to maintain 'broad consultations with parties concerned' (as proposed in the *White Paper on Governance*). The final version of the Constitutional Treaty renumbers the

Article on the principle of representative democracy as Article I-46 and the Article on the principle of participatory democracy as I-47 and adds to the latter a fourth paragraph, which states that 'Not less than one million citizens who are nationals of a significant number of Member States may take the initiative of inviting the Commission, within the framework of its powers, to submit any appropriate proposal on matters where citizens consider that a legal act of the Union is required for the purpose of implementing this Constitution' (IGC 87/2/04 REV 2). Although the feasibility of this Europe-wide collection of signatures is yet to be seen, this provision introduces the right for citizens to propose legislation to the Commission. Moreover, it could have positive developments towards the promotion of a European public sphere as it could favour the creation of broad alliances among civil society organisations, giving at the same time more relevance to national grass-root groups rather than European ones. However, as Schmitter points out, the provision still grants citizens limited possibilities of influence, as it does not even include the possibility of proposing a referendum.[12]

The first paragraph of Article I-47, 'The Institutions shall, by appropriate means, give citizens and representative associations the opportunity to make known and publicly exchange their views in all areas of Union action' (IGC 87/2/04 REV 2), raises several doubts among civil society organisations. The first concern refers to the means that will be used: a Forum only based on the internet may create social disparities due to the unequal distribution of internet access both within the EU members and between old and new members.[13] Doubts are also raised with regard to the criteria for defining a 'representative' organisation and the extent to which it will be possible to participate in the process of decision-making in the preliminary stages of initiatives when the term used is the Union 'action'.

The second paragraph of Article I-47 is positive in that it recognises the role of civil dialogue in the Treaty. However, it was criticised by civil society organisations for not including any reference to a 'structured' civil dialogue nor to any feedback from the EU to input from civil society. The text states that 'the Union institutions shall maintain an open, transparent and regular dialogue with representative associations and civil society' (IGC 87/2/04 REV 2). The issue of participatory democracy, and Article I-47, was discussed by the Convention during the plenary of 24–25 April 2003, but no consistent changes were made to the existing text, in spite of civil society criticisms. The Civil Society Contact Group[14] declared its dissatisfaction with the treatment of participatory democracy in the Draft Treaty for the restriction of appropriate means for consultation to the internet, the absence of a reference to a structured dialogue, and the emphasis on the social partners as representative associations, together with regions and local authorities, while civil society is added without specifying what is meant by this broad concept.[15]

A recognition and promotion of the role of the social partners at the EU level is included in Article I-47 DCT (I-48 TCE), specifying a respect for their autonomy and a consideration of the diversity of national systems. NGOs fear that their role does not enjoy an equal recognition to that of the social partners and feel that the Convention has made meagre efforts to promote their participation in the decision-making process. During the April plenary that discussed the Articles on participatory democracy, NGOs' suggestions to Convention members were unanimous in demanding that the Treaty should include a reference to structured civil dialogue. However, while some Convention members defended this point, the Presidium did not take on board these demands by including them in the text.

In spite of its popularity among NGOs, a more structured consultation process raises at least four types of problems. The first is the 'domestication' of civil society through its inclusion in the institutional process (Armstrong, 2002). By reinforcing institutional ties with state authorities, civil society organisations run the risk of losing their independence and the challenge they represent for institutional actors.

The second is the dominance of private over public interests, a problem that concerns participatory versus representative democracy in general, as NGOs represent particular interests and they are not accountable to the people as elected representatives are.

The third problem has to do with possible criticisms of the EU institutions for selecting among civil society organisations those which are supposedly the most representative ones, but whose selection criteria have not been open to public deliberation, a decision that could be easily judged as undemocratic.

The fourth is that the Convention seeks to fit the 'fluid' and articulated nature of civil society into a structured network of organisations, the Forum, which has the privilege to be informed about Convention proceedings. Scholars argue that this 'instrumental' character affected the relationship of the Convention with civil society in a way that was not respectful of the 'fluid nature of the latter' (Closa, 2003: 16). Both the filter of civil society's contributions through a Forum and the 'highly structured' public hearing in the plenary of June 2002 are described as 'inimical' to the 'chaotic premise' of an 'open-ended initiation' that would be most advisable during the listening phase of the Convention (Shaw, 2002: 11). There seems to be a trade-off between the achievement of an extremely structured and well-organised public hearing and the generation of a genuine exchange of views between *conventionnels* and civil society participants. As the words of a participant from the academic contact group make clear, there was 'no excitement and no real interplay between the Convention and the civil society representatives'.[16]

That said, given that a considerable number of NGOs and the ECOSOC (1999, 2000, 2001) supported a more structured dialogue, the Convention should have taken their views on how to establish a more participatory democracy into more serious account, if it intended to turn the rhetoric of listening to civil society into reality. Besides, most NGOs are aware of the risks of institutionalisation and attach relevance to how the civil dialogue should be institutionalised. They deem it important not to consider interest representation to be solely in the hands of the Economic and Social Committee, but rather in 'the broader realm of civil society as represented by NGOs, as well as trade unions and employers' representation'.[17] They have different views on whether the process should be open to all civil society groups or whether there should be a selection of organisations (representation via umbrella organisations as in the case of contact groups or the Social Platform), but they do warn about the risk of including only Brussels-based groups.[18] They are in favour of a regular consultation of civil society and through clearly structured channels rather than occasional meetings with the EU institutions, and they propose several modes of selecting representative organisations.[19] Above all, they want to see the results of this dialogue with EU institutions, that should not just be an 'alibi, as the current [Convention] consultation is'.[20]

The Forum's representativeness

Whatever the future development of the consultation process and its selection procedures, even openness of participation does not guarantee that any supposedly 'undemocratic' selection does not *de facto* occur. A number of hidden obstacles operated to select participants to the Forum and above all to the hearings of the plenary session of the Convention in June 2002. The most evident obstacle was that the Forum was open only to those with internet access, thus excluding a rather high number of 'web-illiterate' European citizens.

Problems of representativeness emerge from the analysis of the organisations that contributed to the Forum. The more than 500 organisations of civil society which participated in the debate on the future of Europe were divided in the Forum website into four thematic categories: political or public authority (P); socio-economic (S); academic and think-tank (A); other, civil society, NGOs and schools of thought (O). The great majority of associations were of a European level. This was a second obstacle, as there was a 'natural' selection that favoured organisations based in Brussels which were thus better-informed, better-situated and more acquainted with the EU institutional arena.

Some nationalities were better represented than others, with German and French in the lead, while other nationalities were practically non-existent, as in the case of Portuguese groups. There were very few associations from Greece, the Netherlands and the former applicant countries. A possible explanation for the very limited number of associations from the former candidate countries could be the fact that the Forum was available to those who speak an official language of the EU, which may have discouraged the participation of people from candidate countries (internet questionnaire: Krzeczunowicz).[21] Moreover, although in the category described as 'other' there was a high number of social NGOs, some social concerns such as those of immigrants and asylum seekers were not explicitly represented. This raises the question of whether the weakest groups of European civil society received a proper representation in the Convention that drafted the intended future European Constitution.

As for organisations grouped under the academic and think-tank category, they appear to represent a rather conventional and institutional sector of the European cultural world. The more alternative and radical cultural, artistic and political voices were missing from the Forum. Thus, the dominant frame traced in the discourse of the Convention, described as a tendency to privilege a traditional institutional perspective, is a fifth hidden obstacle that can exclude from the debate a great number of actors, discourses and issues which are more unconventional and not institutionally focused, operating a selection among existing organisations of civil society.

A sixth hidden obstacle can be identified in the selection of the contact groups. The Convention left this process to the organisational capability of the participants, thus biasing the process to the advantage of the better-organised groups and promoting informal networking that presupposes a prior knowledge of the EU institutional environment. On 24–25 June 2002 a plenary session of the Convention was 'devoted to civil society' (CONV 48/02). Previous meetings of the different groups took place between 10 and 18 June 2002 (CONV 120/2, 19 June 2002; CONV 79/2, 31 May 2002; CONV 85/02). These were aimed at: discussing preliminary issues; establishing contact groups (umbrella organisations grouping similar associations) in charge of making contact with *conventionnels* and which, according to the Convention, had to represent 'major sectors of interest'; and selecting representatives of civil society who had to speak during the plenary. The Presidium left the success of contacts to the ability of civil society to organise itself into contact groups. This procedure had the effect of favouring the most active groups, rather than those with a higher profile, and of promoting informal consultation with members of the Convention (Closa, 2003: 16), that greatly depended on the previously existing network of a given organisation and on its familiarity with the Brussels institutional world (which inevitably favoured European-based associations over national ones).

The system to decide who was to speak at the hearings consisted of a process of 'self-selection among participants of the working group meetings'. Ms Claire Godin from *Equilibres et Populations*, and spokesperson for the Development sector, expressed some satisfaction about the consultation of civil society during the June plenary, although she also added: 'mais j'aurais préféré qu'un membre de la convention dirige un peu plus le choix des représentants du groupe de contact. A l'inverse, les gens se sont plus ou moins *auto-désignés*'.[22] Mr Krzeczunowicz, from the Polish NGO Office in Brussels, described the consultation process as

a farce from an organisational point of view. Just a few weeks to prepare position papers, consult these with members, and then a rather strange system to decide on who is to speak. I spoke at the session on 24 June, but that was not because the Polish NGO Office in Brussels is an especially important NGO, but rather because there was a sense that there had to be someone from the candidate countries and I happen to be based in Brussels. So it was being at the right place at the right time, not the importance of the message or of the organisations.

(Internet questionnaire: Krzeczunowicz)

Participants from civil society have complained about a number of issues concerning the way in which hearings occurred. Physical space was insufficient to house all the groups present in the debates. Presentation time was reduced to five minutes for speakers of the seven groups and three minutes for the academia and think-tank sector, due to the higher number of speakers designated to take the floor on the days of the plenary. Each group of representatives of civil society had in fact been assigned a total of twenty-five to thirty minutes to be divided among the various speakers during the plenary session. Time for the contact groups to discuss their topics was also highly limited (for example, the contact group 'Culture' had one day to discuss art, heritage, church and religions, education and minority languages), with the further restriction of having to limit their comments to institutional aspects. These problems limited the potential exchange of ideas that could have taken place between civil society groups and members of the Convention, leading some commentators to argue that hearings of civil society served merely as an 'alibi' for the Convention, having a window-dressing rather than a substantive function (Cassen, 2002).

'Radical' issues from a 'domesticated' civil society

In spite of criticisms about the limits of time, space and representativeness of civil society that characterised the hearing procedures, during the Convention's plenary session of 24–25 June 2002 speakers of each sector designated during previous meetings were able to make their voices heard on different topics. Issues discussed in the course of this meeting reflect a selection of some of the concerns of European citizens. Most of them have little to do both with institutional questions and with the neo-liberal focus adopted by the EU in the last decades. Though very few representatives may be considered as expressing radical approaches, as they generally represent middle-class moderate views, their demands are closer to some kind of social-democratic project of European society. Their concerns focus on substantive issues such as participatory democracy, gender equality and non-discrimination, social rights and services of general interest, respect for the environment and human rights, education and cultural values, 'true subsidiarity', dialogue with civil society, and eradication of poverty. Their discursive frames are based on the language of human rights, citizenship and democracy.

The plenary session of 24–25 June included reports by the Economic and Social Committee, the Committee of the Regions and Social Partners, reports from representatives of civil society whose organisations were divided into contact groups, and reports on the national debates taking place in the different member states and to which one member of the Convention from each country represented was invited to refer (CONV 48/02). The eight contact groups created to represent the views of civil society organisations that participated in the Forum included the following sectors: social, environment, academia and think tanks, citizens and institutions, regional and local authorities, human rights, development, and cultural (CONV 167/02). Two demands were common to all contact groups: the first refers to the introduction in the Treaty of a legal basis for a regular dialogue with civil society (including a right to be consulted at an early stage in the framing of EU legislation); the second concerns an extension of the scope of the Charter and the incorporation of the latter in the Treaty, as well as the EU accession to the European Convention on Human Rights. As for the remaining issues, each group concentrated on a different range, according to the specific matters that most affected them.

As Jo Shaw points out, 'there appears to be considerable dissonance between the immediate concerns of the majority of civil society groups concerned especially with the interests of vulnerable or minority groups, or with environmental protection, and the rather institutionally-oriented and legal category focused manner in which the Convention's work has been structured' (Shaw, 2002: 24–5). The institutional frame of the Convention's discourse derives, according to Shaw, more from the Convention's own internal interests than from a receptive listening to civil society's concerns. The only institutional references that occur more frequently in the words of civil society representatives have to do with provisions that could ensure a better empowerment for the citizen, such as extending qualified majority voting and the Parliament co-decision powers, incorporating the Charter and extending its scope, institutionalising civil dialogue, recognising the role of local, regional authorities and social partners, electing the president of the Commission through the European Parliament, and giving more powers to the Commission rather than to the Council as the latter is considered as not democratically answerable to any elected European assembly.

It has been argued that the voices that were heard in the June plenary were those of a domesticated civil society whose speakers were selected from among Commission-funded organisations that some commentators described as 'the usual suspects' saying the usual things (Closa, 2003: 16; Scott, 2002). It was a clean and refined civil society that the Convention was prepared to listen to for the few minutes that were accorded to them. Indeed it was an extremely different congregation of people from the one that met in Florence at the European Social Forum in the first week of November 2002 to debate alternative solutions for the complex questions posed by our globalised world.

Rather than sending a delegation to Florence to listen to the concerns and perspectives of the more 'fluid' and 'less sanitised' civil society, *conventionnels* felt more comfortable interacting with a pre-packaged civil society that would pose less problems for the European project, whatever that is, that the Convention was drawing up. One participant to the Forum argued that the Convention should have been a little more daring and should have invited some speakers from important organisations who may have been more con- troversial. The result of the 'cowardly' attitude demonstrated by the Convention, was, instead, that the 24–25 June meeting was, according to one participant 'very polite, very proper, very boring'. To which he added, 'There is nothing wrong with the first two (although journalists were unhappy about it, with their stilted view of NGOs), but the boring bit was a shame. In effect, as some Eurosceptic Convention members rightly pointed out, it was Brussels talking to Brussels' (internet questionnaire: Krzeczunowicz).

In spite of the moderate character of the 'domesticated' civil society that spoke at the plenary, the 'dissonance' of their voices from the Convention's agenda is noticeable. Civil society sent a clear message to the Convention by drawing a vision of Europe which was more citizenship-oriented than market- oriented, more open to listening to people's concerns and more willing to maintain the European social model. In this respect, civil society was more in agreement with the conclusions of the working group on Social Europe, the 'Cinderella' of all working groups of the Convention, as Shaw described it (2003b).[23] The story of the 'affinity' between civil society and the working group on Social Europe might be said to have ended with two Cinderellas, because, as participants feared, the results of the consultation were not really taken on board by the Convention.[24]

Conclusion: a one-way dialogue?

The process of consultation of civil society in the Convention's debate on the future of Europe has had its undeniable positive elements. The openness of the procedure has ensured a great participation of organisations that have sent their inputs via the Forum. Despite the numerous criticisms about the excessive or insufficient structuring of the Forum and hearings, the more or less domesticated character of the civil society consulted, and the various hidden obstacles that limited groups' representativeness and steered the debate towards more institutional issues, civil society has put forward its own proj- ect for Europe. This goes in the direction of revitalising the European social model, defending the interests of vulnerable or minority groups, protecting the environment and promoting a more participatory democracy. In this respect, civil society could have taught a lesson to a Convention which was in effect closed within its internal institutionally oriented debates and unable to propose a clear and coherent project of a political Europe that went beyond the tacit acceptance of the EU neo-liberal frame.

There were interactions and exchanges of ideas with members of the Convention at a personal level (internet questionnaire: Spiliotopoulos), depending on whether there were active Convention members who were happy to meet citizens (internet questionnaire: Godin), or where there was a culture of consultation at a national level (internet questionnaire: Krzeczunowicz). However, there was no official feedback from the Convention as such. It seems that, unless there was action by individual members of the Convention, there was no contact between the Convention and NGOs outside the Brussels ring road (internet questionnaire: Krzeczunowicz; Hardt). Civil society at large was not successfully reached by the Convention, as shown by the fact that the overwhelming majority of civil society at a national and regional level knew very little about the activities of the Convention and was involved in a very limited way (internet questionnaire: Hardt). Something did not work in the involvement of the wider civil society, with the result that the most successful aspect of the 'participation' of civil society was the fact that debates and meetings were held in public. Organised civil society acted as an audience to the discussions with a few representatives occasionally playing as extras on the stage of the Convention.

An analysis of the consultation process confirms the impression expressed by many of the participants that in the Forum civil society groups were accorded what Carlos Closa defines as a 'passive' role. Such a passive role frames civil society groups as 'receivers of information' and as an 'audience' for the Convention, securing publicity, and supposedly more legitimacy, for the Convention's proceedings, but denies them the capacity to influence either the process or the outcome of the Convention itself (Closa, 2003: 15–16). According a more 'active' role would have meant treating civil society groups as real actors in a dialogue through which their input was taken seriously. In no document of the Convention does one find a mention of how civil society's contributions were used, nor is there any reference to the eventual feedback that contributors would receive on the part of the Convention. The passive role for civil society is another consequence of the attitude identified in the discourse of the Convention as 'listening without committing to an answer'. This attitude reveals, as Jo Shaw states, that 'there remains a gap between the types of moves that the Convention has made towards receptiveness, including the Forum, the Hearing of Civil Society, and the Youth Convention of July 2002, and the creation of a genuine public sphere' (Shaw, 2002: 25).

Notes

1. Frame analysis is a method developed by social movement theory (Snow and Benford, 1988, 1992) which enables us to identify dominant frames operating both explicitly and implicitly in the discourse of the Convention and that are driving it to select and focus attention on certain discourses and actors while at the same time ignoring or marginalising others (see also Triandafyllidou and Fotiou, 1998). A policy frame is 'an organising principle that transforms fragmentary

or incidental information into a structured and meaningful policy problem, in which a solution is implicitly or explicitly enclosed' (Verloo, 2005: 20).

2. 25 March 2002. Note on the plenary meeting, 21 and 22 March 2002.
3. 11 March 2002. Note on the inaugural meeting, 28 February 2002.
4. Pawel Krzeczunowicz, Polish NGO Office in Brussels, internet questionnaire, April 2003.
5. Ms Anne Van Lancker, Mr Johannes Voggenhuber, Ms Sylvia-Yvonne Kaufmann and other members of the Convention demanded that a debate on the issue of a Social Europe be put on the agenda of the Convention.
6. 13 November 2002. 'Summary report of the plenary session 7–8 November'.
7. 'From Presidium to Convention: Questionnaire for the debate on Social issues. The working group on economic governance has agreed that the issue whether to introduce additional economic and social objectives and competences should be the subject of a plenary debate of the Convention. The following questions refer to this recommendation: they might be addressed in the debate on Social Europe on 7 November which has been arranged at the request of certain members of the Convention.
    (1) What extent should social policy be considered to be part of the Union's overall objectives? How should this be reflected in the constitutional treaty?
    (2) How, if at all, should the current Treaty provisions on social issues be amended? Should the existing areas of competence be extended? If so, to which new areas? Should other provisions, such as those on the internal market or competition be amended in order to enhance social policies?
    (3) Should the current provisions for the involvement of the social partners be amended?' (CONV 374/02: 2. 29 October 2002).
8. Birgit Hardt, internet questionnaire, April 2003.
9. Sophia Spiliotopoulos, vice-president of AFEM (Association des Femmes de l'Europe Méridionale), president of EWLA (European Women Lawyers Association). Internet questionnaire, June 2003.
10. The obstacles are discussed below.
11. The focus of Article 36 is on the 'Transparency of the proceedings of the Union's institutions'. It affirms that 'In order to promote good governance and ensure participation of civil society, the Union institutions shall conduct their work as openly as possible', that the Parliament shall meet in public and the Council too, but only when it is discussing a legislative proposal, and finally it guarantees access to EU documents for all Union citizens (CONV 650/03).
12. Philippe Schmitter, Keynote Address, ECPR Second Pan-European Conference on EU Politics, Bologna, 24–26 June 2004.
13. According to Eurostat May 2003, the level of internet access in the households of the fifteen EU members was 40.4 per cent in 2002 (36.1 per cent in 2001), with the highest levels in the Netherlands (65.5 per cent), Sweden (64.2 per cent) and Denmark (64.5 per cent) and the lowest levels in Greece (9.2 per cent), Spain (29.5 per cent), Portugal (30.8 per cent), Italy (35.4 per cent) and France (35.5 per cent). The remaining EU members are slightly over the EU average, while the new members are below it: Czezh Republic, 11 per cent in 2001; Estonia, 9.8 per cent in 2001; Hungary, 2.6 per cent in 2000; Lithuania, 3.2 per cent in 2001; Latvia, 2.3 per cent in 2001; Poland, 7.7 per cent in 2001; Slovenia, 24 per cent in 2001; Cyprus, 20 per cent in 2001; Malta, 11.2 per cent in 2000; while no data exist on Slovakia.
14. Members of the Civil Society Contact Group are the platforms/sector groups of the four large NGO families – environmental (Green 8), social (Social Platform), developmental (Concorde) and human rights – plus the ETUC.

15. Nicolas J. Beger, act4europe campaign co-ordinator, Secretariat of the Civil Society Contact Group (internet questionnaire, May 2003, and 'Act4Europe Fax campaign on Participatory Democracy', www.act4europe.org).
16. Crossick (2002).
17. Birgit Hardt, ILGA (International Lesbian and Gay Association) Europe, internet questionnaire, April 2003.
18. Claire Godin, Chargée de mission Politique, Equilibres et Populations, 205, boulevard Saint Germain, 75007 Paris, internet questionnaire, April 2003.
19. See Forum website at http://europa.eu.int/futurum/Forum_convention/organlist_en.htm#list
20. Sophia Spiliotopoulos, vice-president of AFEM (Association des Femmes de l'Europe Méridionale), president of EWLA (European Women Lawyers Association), internet questionnaire, June 2003.
21. See Chapter 6 for further discussion of this issue.
22. '. . . but I would have preferred a member of the Convention to direct the choice of contact group representatives a little more. However, these people more or less selected themselves.' Claire Godin, Chargée de mission Politique, Equilibres et Populations, 205, boulevard Saint Germain, 75007 Paris, internet questionnaire, April 2003.
23. This reference to 'Cinderella' was due to its later creation, the obstacles posed to it, the short time it had to meet and deliberate, and the fact that, as the Convention explicitly admitted, its deliberations were not taken into account in the preparation of the draft Articles 1-16 of the constitutional text that was presented at the end of January (CONV 528/03).
24. Nicolas J. Beger, act4europe campaign co-ordinator, Secretariat of the Civil Society Contact Group, internet questionnaire, May 2003.

9
The Contribution of Business Interests

Nieves Pérez-Solórzano Borragán

The EU's liberal agenda embodied in its search for prosperity and global competitiveness explains the important role played by business interests in the history of European integration. Early explanations of the integration process identified the role of organised interests in transferring loyalties from the nation-state to a supranational set of institutions acquiring an increasing number of competences (Haas, 1958: 11–12). The single market programme was driven by business, which enhanced the EU's output legitimacy through its provision of specialised expertise (Bouwen, 2006: 283). The opportunity to engage in treaty reform that the Convention process offered was therefore welcomed by business organisations, which sought an active presence in the debates. During the Convention process, business interests participated as observers, and as already discussed in the previous chapter, the Forum website was set up to allow organised interests to keep track of the Convention's proceedings and to provide input into the debate, clearly reflecting the Convention's official attempt to consult beyond its own membership. Furthermore, the European Economic and Social Committee (EESC) participated as an observer and it was proactive in organising meetings with civil society, which were attended by Presidium members.[1]

Whereas citizens' associations' involvement has been dealt with in Chapter 8, this chapter is concerned with the socio-economic actors, including employers' organisations, professional organisations and chambers of commerce.

The main purpose of this chapter is therefore to investigate the challenges and opportunities that the Convention offered business interests by assessing their preferences, strategies and engagement in the deliberative process. Specifically, this chapter will assess the participation of business interests in the light of their generally agreed centrality to the formative years of the integration process and through the normative lens of the discourse on participatory democracy and EU governance. It is here argued, in line with the analysis developed in Part II of this book, that the Convention experiment displays the traditional dynamics of constitution-making processes: organised interests are consulted at the drafting stage but they do not intervene in the decision-making process (i.e. the IGC). Moreover, this new phase of constitutionalisation has prompted business interests to define their priorities beyond narrow policy issues and to engage in the wider debate on participation and EU governance. The Convention became the framework for the articulation of business interests and their vision of the future of the EU.

The chapter is divided into three sections. The first section briefly sets the background to the debate on EU governance and business interest representation. The second section outlines the actual Convention experience by presenting the point of access available to business interests, their policy priorities, discourses and agendas, as well as their own assessment of the Convention experience. The concluding section reflects on the lessons learned from the Convention, while incorporating a number of tentative reflections on the future challenges and opportunities for business interests.

Business interests and EU governance

Lobbying as a means of influencing the formulation and implementation of European policies has a long tradition. After the creation of the European Economic Community in 1957 it became evident that supranational decisions were inevitable, and that therefore, interest groups would need to engage in lobbying activities at the EC level in order to influence the shape and direction of large-scale policy outcomes. Europe-wide pressure groups were created and their strategies incorporated all levels of the EC policy-making process. The literature on EU interest representation identifies the existence of a 'European model of interest intermediation', which 'has both transformed national policy-making systems and fundamentally changed the roster of actors who constitute the power elites in Europe' (Mazey and Richardson, 2001: 220). Kohler-Koch (1994: 177) argues that:

> Whenever regulatory competences are shifted onto the EC-level, the heterogeneous national arenas will lose their importance and be substituted by a far more homogeneous set-up which then will develop its own 'logic of influence'. At the same time it could be assumed that growing economic interdependence and the increasing harmonisation of legal frameworks will ensure that the 'logic of membership' will also develop similar characteristics.

Drawing on empirical data and public policy analysis, Mazey and Richardson (2001: 218–33) distinguish four factors explaining the growth in the number of organised interests active in Brussels, namely, the Commission's constituency mobilisation strategy, the interest groups' risk avoidance approach, their preference for Euro-level solutions, and the development of opportunity structures. The EU's system of multi-level bargaining confronts interest groups with a tremendous challenge: the 'target structure' is fragmented.

The main problem 'is not the shortage but the over-supply of potential routes to power' (Van Schlenden, 1994: 11). The EU reveals a scenario where power is fragmented and public decision-making bodies are integrated into shifting networks of joint decision-making, characterised by uncertain agendas and unstable procedural rules. Mazey and Richardson (2001: 218) maintain that this uncertainty provokes 'promiscuous' lobbying activity amongst policy actors. Thus interest groups exploit and sometimes create new opportunity structures, which they believe will maximise their ability to influence public policy to their advantage.

In the context of the democratic deficit debate, the EU has emphasised the importance of rendering policies and decision-making processes more accessible and open to civil society and the wider European public, to ensure their quality, relevance and effectiveness. Particularly the European Commission's *White Paper on European Governance* develops the emergence of the 'good governance' agenda in European public policy- and decision-making. New modes of governance, based on networking among stakeholders and a stronger articulation of the interests and stakes of citizens and consumers in the policy process, have been proposed along with traditional modes of government, based on hierarchical, state-led decision-making processes.

The literature on interest representation has reflected this discursive turn and acknowledged the role of interest groups as an additional source of legitimacy in the EU beyond the traditional output democracy paradigm which regards the EP as the ultimate democratic institution and the democratic nature of the EU as being based on its ability to produce more efficient, transparent and accountable policies. Dehousse (2003: 151) regards the work of organised interests at the EU level as a means towards promoting more consultation and openness, which might improve public awareness and contribute to the emergence of a pan-European public sphere. In this context, recent debate on the role of organised interests at the EU level identifies functional participation (as opposed to territorial representation) as the normative lens to understand interest groups' contribution to the legitimacy of the European project (Smismans, 2004a: 70–9). In his analysis of the UEAPME case,[2] Smismans reflects on the Court of First Instance's ruling that, in the context of the social dialogue, the role of the social partners can assure 'the participation of the people' and thus the respect of the principle of democracy on which the Union is founded. In other words, for the CFI in this particular case, the sovereignty of the people as a whole is not based on general direct elections (territorial democracy), but rather, as Smismans maintains, in a more functional democracy, which requires that 'the democratic legitimisation of the social dialogue procedure resides neither in the Council nor in the Commission but in the participation of the social partners, and *solely* in their participation' (2004a: 348).

Traditionally, the business sector has dominated institutionalised functional participation at the EU level through its participation in the European social dialogue and the European Economic and Social Committee, and 'remains the best mobilised of all outside interests' (Greenwood, 2002: 22). However, business interests do not monopolise the consultation process since from the point of view of the European Parliament and particularly of the European Commission, pursuing an exclusive policy towards interest groups would limit the robustness and workability of policy proposals and curtail their legitimacy: 'the Commission recognises that relying on producer groups for advice, however technical and accurate it might be, is a risky business in terms of legitimacy' (Mazey and Richardson, 2001: 228–9).

Recent literature on the subject of business interest representation repositions the debate, highlighting the legitimating role of business organisations through their participation in EU policy-making. Bouwen's logic of access explains the access of business interests to the three main players in the EU legislative process as the result of the exchange of access goods between business interests and the EU institutions. Business interests provide expert knowledge, information about the European Encompassing Sectoral Interest (IEESI), and information about the Domestic Encompassing Sectoral Interest (IDESI). According to Bouwen (2006: 280–5), it is possible to identify a relationship between access goods and input/output democracy. 'Access goods provide input legitimacy to the EU institutions because they serve as a source of information about the domestic encompassing and representative interests' (Bouwen, 2006: 283), while expert knowledge provides output legitimacy to the EU institutions by providing them with the necessary expertise to deal with their problems efficiently.

Business input in the Convention experiment

At the outset of the Convention, the general perception amongst stakeholders was that despite the creation of the Forum and the contact groups (see Chapter 8), informal lobbying in the corridors was still the most effective way to get results, while the hearings with civil society involved mainly the Brussels establishment and were only conducive to producing a few ideas (Berger, 2004: 8; ECAS, 2005: 11).

Following the Laeken mandate, the Convention offered organised interests the possibility of expressing opinions and providing suggestions on wide-ranging issues regarding European integration. This new phase of constitutionalisation has prompted business interests to define their priorities beyond narrow policy issues and to engage in the wider debate of participation and EU governance. Arguably, this is a trend initiated by the debates on the EU's democratic deficit and the need to involve the citizens and the public interest. The European Commission's *White Paper on European Governance* placed the good governance agenda on European public policy at the core of the debates about the EU. Business interests have had to engage in a discourse traditionally dominated by civil society and thus compete for new agendas by addressing wider governance issues (see Smismans, 2003, 2004b).

The implications of Treaty reform are essential for business interests as they define the overall political environment and the specific sectoral environments in which European business operates.[3] Consequently, the main leading multi-sectoral business organisations in Europe, namely the AmCham (American Chamber of Commerce), the ERT (European Round Table of Industrialists), EUROCHAMBRES (Association of European Chambers of Commerce and Industry), EUROCOMMERCE (European Federation of Retailing and Distribution), UEAPME (European Association of Craft, Small and Medium-Sized Enterprises) and UNICE[4] (Union of Industrial Employers' Confederations of Europe) made their views known, before and during the Convention, on both institutional and policy issues.

The leading business organisations' participation in the Convention was characterised by their strong support for the process as a means to further enhance European integration. Business interests were represented in the Convention proceedings by the then president of UNICE,[5] George Jacobs, who participated as an observer contributing to plenary sessions and working groups.[6] The social partners had asked for such a status to be conferred upon them in their common statement on the Laeken Declaration (Social Partners, 2001). Throughout the proceedings, business organisations offered a cohesive front, while presenting joint opinions with the trade unions on issues regarding the issue of social dialogue.[7] This reflects a shift between patterns of successful collusion and competition among varying interests already detected by the literature on interest representation (Wallace and Young, 1997). The key business priorities featured general principles of EU governance, social dialogue and the role of social partners, simplification of decision-making procedures and ensuring growth and competitiveness. The general outline of these positions is briefly reviewed in the rest of this section.

General principles of EU governance

According to business organisations, liberty, democracy, respect for human rights, diversity, fundamental freedoms, rule of law and social cohesion should remain the basis for further European integration. The principle of participatory democracy is regarded as a keystone of European integration. Its implementation, according to business interests, should incorporate increased consultation to bring Europe closer to its citizens and business. EUROCHAMBRES maintained that citizens and businesses should be better informed about European policy objectives and the processes by which these policies are decided. To this end EUROCHAMBRES (2002: 11) proposed a more convincing communication policy based on information distribution networks in the form of partnerships.

To improve the quality of consultation UNICE (2002: 4) advocated the adoption of a comprehensive code that would set out clear guidelines for the definition of core stakeholders and their representativeness, and the purpose, content, methodology and time frame of the consultation. The criteria should assess each organisation's representativeness, internal accountability, independency and expertise.[8] These are very exclusive criteria, which would secure business' status as partners in the consultation process, while marginalising other organisations with less resources and expertise.

The EU Committee of the American Chamber of Commerce (AmCham, 2003b: 2) supported UNICE's proposal and suggested that the Constitution should incorporate a 'Transparency and Consultation' chapter to ensure a non-discriminatory and general right of participation of all relevant stakeholders (AmCham, 2003a: 3). Moreover, building on the US experience, AmCham called for a clear and common framework binding all institutions to a common transparency code similar to the Administrative Procedures Act in the US[9] (AmCham, 2003a: 16).

Social dialogue and the role of social partners

The interaction between civil society and organised business interests was also part of business' strategy to improve participation and bring the EU closer to its citizens. Both UNICE and EUROCOMMERCE supported a flexible relationship with civil society whenever possible but without jeopardising social dialogue. According to the business organisations, social dialogue should remain the privilege of employer and employee federations with limited access for other organised civil society players. UNICE called for a distinction between social dialogue and consultation of civil society, while strongly opposing any changes to the social dialogue procedures of Articles 137 and 138 of the EC Treaty:

> [S]ocial dialogue at European level is a clearly structured and autonomous process involving the social partners. In the framework of the Treaty's social chapter, the social partners have a responsibility for political decision-making which cannot be extended to other areas or other players in civil society.
>
> (UNICE, 2002: 5)

EUROCOMMERCE expressed a similar view and explained the disadvantages of an arbitrary inclusion of other actors in the process of social dialogue:

> Opening the debate to everybody would jeopardise the relevance of the response to be taken, as it dilutes the debate and considerably increases its length as well as the complexity to reach a common position.
>
> (EUROCOMMERCE, 2002: 5)

Unsurprisingly, EUROCHAMBRES, which has a secondary status as a social partner, raised the need for further inclusion of the chambers of commerce in the consultation process because they

> are the only organisations that are able to illustrate concretely the principle of proximity as a result of their regional implantation, are the only organisations that carry out horizontal actions in support of the economic development of their region.
>
> (EUROCHAMBRES, 2002: 3)

Simplification of decision-making and allocation of competences

'Business are [sic] keen to operate in a legal environment that is characterised by certainty' (AmCham, 2003a: 2), hence the Convention was regarded by business as an excellent opportunity for the EU to clarify values and objectives, general competences, decision-making procedures and division of power, with the aim of creating rapid, predictable, transparent decision-making procedures that guarantee democratic participation. In the view of the ERT (2002: 2), a growing lack of 'unity of purpose' at EU level and slow decision-making in areas crucial to business negatively affect the competitiveness of companies operating in Europe.

Business organisations called for the simplification of the Treaties into one single text containing the rights and obligations imposed on all EU citizens and on the Community institutions and thus increasing legal certainty. The incorporation of the Charter of Fundamental Rights into the Constitution was welcomed by business organisations as a means to make those rights and freedoms more visible to the citizens, while expressing their opposition to the text becoming legally binding since it would contain elements which fall outside the remit of EU competences (AmCham, 2003a: 5; UNICE, 2002: 1).

To clarify the allocation of competences, business suggested that the EU should focus on those core tasks that could be best resolved at Community level while observing the principles of subsidiarity and proportionality. Specifically, UNICE (2002: 2) proposed the creation of an independent body entrusted with the task of reviewing the observance of the subsidiarity principle. Along a similar line of argument, the ERT (2002: 6) suggested the definition of an independent subsidiarity test to be applied 'quickly and early in the decision-making process'. UNICE (2002: 3) highlighted the dual nature of the subsidiarity principle. Subsidiarity has a vertical (territorial) and a horizontal (functional) dimension. Hence, it should not be assessed only in the context of the distribution of competences amongst levels of government, but also in the context of the distribution of competences amongst actors with specific expertise. AmCham called for the principle of subsidiarity to be subject to review by national parliaments and to appropriate judicial review explaining the justification for Community action and the choice of legal basis. Moreover, it suggested linking the justification for any Community action to the result of an impact assessment and prior consultation of the stakeholders affected (AmCham, 2003a: 10). At the same time it called for the incorporation of an independent and quantifiable Business Impact Assessment to the application of the proportionality principle (AmCham, 2003a: 3).

Regarding the Union's institutional architecture, business interests supported an independent and strong Commission able to retain exclusive right of initiative for legal proposals while reinforcing its role in monitoring the implementation of EU legislation. Additionally, the Commission should implement more effective and transparent administrative procedures that ensure preservation of the rights of companies (UNICE, 2002: 5). Business organisations proposed a more efficient distribution of competences between the European Council and the Council of Ministers and an extension of qualified majority voting (QMV) to all areas relevant to cross-border business in Europe as well as to external economic relations of the Union. According to UNICE, 'qualified majority voting should be the rule', while unanimity should only be reserved to social policy matters and new policy initiatives in the field of taxation (UNICE, 2002: 5).

Regarding the European Parliament, the ERT (2002: 6) maintained that 'the EP's own complicated decision-making procedures should be simplified and made more transparent'. UNICE (2002: 6) called for the EP to acquire full budgetary rights and responsibilities alongside the Council. While acknowledging the role of the European Economic and Social Committee (EESC) as the forum for civil dialogue, UNICE (2002: 6) expected a clear distinction between civil dialogue and social dialogue, the latter being an autonomous process between the social partners, and one which takes place outside the EESC.

Ensuring growth and competitiveness

Many of the measures suggested above were clearly aimed at securing a business-friendly environment by furthering economic growth. In the view of business organisations, the EU should deliver such an environment in order to allow companies to compete and adapt to the increasing challenges of globalisation (UNICE, 2002: 1). These would be achieved by: strengthening European competitiveness, including adaptability to structural change and improvement of employment prospects; strengthening Europe's economies and full realisation of EMU's potential; ensuring that enlargement does not distort the internal market; and strengthening Europe's role on the international stage (UNICE, 2002: 1).

In this context business organisations called for a lighter regulatory framework and a better use of self- and co-regulation. Thus streamlining and simplification of legislation should be included in the operating process of the EU. For this purpose UNICE (2002: 3) suggested the creation of specific mechanisms to better assess the impact of regulation, namely an independent institution that would examine 'the need for EU regulation, its economic impact, and its added value to the functioning of the internal market'. All business associations coincided in proposing mechanisms to test Community regulation before it comes into force. EUROCHAMBRES (2002: 10) offered specific guidelines to be followed: 'to analyse the socio-economic consequences of its application; to identify who is targeted and to what extent; to assess the effects of this proposal on national laws'.

To streamline and simplify legislation EUROCOMMERCE and UNICE proposed a clarification of the hierarchy and applicability of Community instruments. The former asked for a further extension of the open method of co-ordination, while the latter proposed the division of these instruments into three categories: legislative and quasi-legislative instruments; nonlegislative instruments; and sui generis instruments. UNICE recommended:

> A greater role for other types of instruments between representative stakeholders, on specific topics [. . .] self-regulation and codes of conducts should also find more recognition as possible instruments to reach EU objectives, instead of systematic legislation. Business is keen to assume its responsibilities in this context. This would alleviate the legislative tasks of the EU and would democratise the rule-making exercise.
>
> (UNICE, 2002: 4)

Business interests supported giving the EU a legal personality in order to enhance the global dimension in the framing of EU policy in the area of external economic relations while allowing the EU to speak with one voice (UNICE, 2002: 6).

Assessing the outcome from a business perspective

Business interests made a very positive assessment of their Convention experience. In their view, the final outcome provided:

> a good basis to allow further integration of Europe and for business to develop and prosper in the EU [. . .] The draft treaty that is on the table should allow the EU to be more transparent, more competitive and closer to its citizens.
>
> (UNICE, 2003)

This positive outlook, however, is not widely shared by other stakeholders involved in the process. For the groups representing civil society, the Convention took too cautious an approach to civil society participation, thus its contribution was demoted to the Futurum website (Pérez-Solórzano Borragán, 2005: 18–19). ECAS (2003) suggests that the Forum was used as a substitute for real dialogue. Or as Closa argues, the Convention only 'marginally' improved accountability because its steering organs had a 'preeminent position' giving them a 'significant capacity to bias debates and even final results' (Closa, 2003: 21).

The most positive outcome derived from business organisations' participation in the Convention process was the official recognition of the nature and role of social partners and social dialogue, and the protection of its specific character limiting the extension of partner status to other stakeholders.

Hence Article I-48 on 'social partners and autonomous social dialogue' reads:

> The Union recognises and promotes the role of the social partners at its level, taking into account the diversity of national systems. It shall facilitate dialogue between the social partners, respecting their autonomy.
>
> The Tripartite Social Summit for Growth and Employment shall contribute to social dialogue.
>
> (TCE)

The text reflects the spirit of Jacobs's address to the Convention on 4 April 2003: 'the social partners have a responsibility for political decision-making which cannot be extended to other areas or other players in civil society'. Articles III-211 and 212 ensured that the implementation of the social dialogue procedure remained unchanged.

Article I-47 on 'the principle of participatory democracy' could be regarded as a mixed blessing for business organisations. The article reads:

> 1. The institutions shall, by appropriate means, give citizens and representative associations the opportunity to make known and publicly exchange their views in all areas of Union action.
> 2. The institutions shall maintain an open, transparent and regular dialogue with representative associations and civil society.
> 3. The Commission shall carry out broad consultations with parties concerned in order to ensure that the Union's actions are coherent and transparent.
> 4. Not less than one million citizens who are nationals of a significant number of Member States may take the initiative of inviting the Commission, within the framework of its powers, to submit any appropriate proposal on matters where citizens consider that a legal act of the Union is required for the purpose of implementing the Constitution. European laws shall determine the provisions for the procedures and conditions required for such a citizens' initiative, including the minimum number of Member States from which such citizens must come. (TCE)

On the one hand, it consolidates the principle of participatory democracy, delineating the terms of reference for the interaction between stakeholders and the European Union, while incorporating measures for further citizen participation and good governance and, crucially, not interfering in the established social dialogue process. On the other hand, Article I-47 carries the risk of creating an opposition between representative associations and civil society by establishing a clear separation between them. UNICE tabled an amendment on those exact grounds so that the paragraph could be reworded as follows: 'The Union Institutions shall maintain an open, transparent and regular *dialogue with civil society*.' Rather, as feared by UNICE, paragraph 2 reads: 'The institutions shall maintain an open, transparent and regular *dialogue with representative associations and civil society*.'

As Smismans rightly argues (2004b: 133), the terminology is confusing since the concept of representative associations appears to be in opposition to that of civil society. Tracing the origins of the debate Smismans finds that these representative associations are those which do not come under the civil society heading (employers' associations, trade unions, regional and local authorities). UNICE's concerns in this regard reflect the unwillingness of the business sector to see a meaningful civil dialogue developing that would leave 'representative associations' out of the process. In other words, while social partners are fiercely protective of the social dialogue process, they oppose the emergence of a similar procedure under the label 'civil dialogue' that would preclude their involvement.

It is no coincidence, therefore, that in his address to the Convention on 24 June 2002, Mr Jacobs stated that 'companies are also an important part of civil society'. Article I-47, while offering business organisations the chance to contribute to a more open and accessible EU, also challenges any role for them as a bridge with civil society. The EU Committee of the American Chamber of Commerce expressed concern about the wording and endorsed UNICE's proposed amendment, explaining that:

> The balancing of all interest is crucial in order to allow business and consumer/citizens to fully benefit from that internal market. The EU Committee believes that consumers, citizens and industry need to create a platform for the understanding of each other's interests and concerns. The opposition of representative organizations to (instead of the inclusion in) the concept of civil society, is considered as being unhelpful in creating such a platform.
>
> (AmCham, 2003b: 1)

Article I-47 fails to outline the terms of reference for the Commission's consultations, which may allow for minimalist interpretations. While stakeholders would welcome an early and wide consultation with the Commission, Jean-Luc Dehaene maintains that the Constitution does not include detailed provisions to ensure flexibility and effectiveness. In his view, while participatory democracy should be enshrined in the Constitution, practical arrangements should be established through regulatory and legislative procedures (Dehaene, 2003: 14). Moreover, while the right to suggest policy initiatives to the Commission is enshrined in the text, clearly not all items in the EU agenda lend themselves to this approach (ECAS, 2004: 3). More crucially, the Commission is the main actor in this procedure and the decision whether to pursue the legislative initiative or not (if invited to by one million citizens) is entirely at its own discretion. As Smismans (2004b: 137) maintains, 'it is doubtful whether [the article]. . . will be able to give the citizens' initiative a minimum of compulsory flavour'.

At the same time, one million signatures collected from a significant number of countries must show that there is a genuine European policy issue, which would be of relevance to European citizens across countries. Clearly, the citizens' initiative will be more practical for single-issue causes, while this requirement will affect the choice of issues and the way in which they are presented (ECAS, 2004: 7). In this context it can be argued that, despite their heterogeneity and narrow specialisation, business organisations are better placed than civil society organisations to galvanise individual support across the board. Typically horizontal, cross-sectoral interests, business organisations can maximise their narrow specialisation, high membership densities and low collective action problems (Greenwood, 2007: 50) to mobilise their national constituencies along regulatory issues that require a high degree of expertise and professionalisation. In other words, as Bouwen argues, 'the specialisation of national and European associations in providing encompassing access goods guarantees that they will be able to contribute to both the input and output legitimacy of the EU policy-making process' (Bouwen, 2006: 285). The implementation of Article I-47 also raises questions about the actual packaging of the citizens' initiative: How should it be worded? What kind of amendments should the Commission be able to make? Could the Commission refuse citizens' initiatives? The vagueness of the Article may work in favour of further professionalisation of interest representation in the EU, while at the same time bridging the gap between expertise and citizens' involvement. Civil society and business organisations will need to develop an expertise in signature gathering across the EU by making the policy initiative appealing enough to the relevant constituencies across the board, while packaging the same policy issues with the professional and expert content traditionally welcomed by the European Commission. One could argue that politically sensitive issues would be the best candidates for this kind of action, but the fact that the European Parliament (which incidentally has experience in assessing citizens' petitions) is not involved in the process may limit their suitability. In this context Smismans (2004b: 137) ponders whether this citizens' initiative will add much to the existing right to petition the EP. Overall, ECAS's assessment would seem to be correct, that the citizens' initiative may be rarely used as a method behind legislative initiative and that it will be applicable only 'in such areas where there is a rare link between concerns shared by large numbers of people and the EU's capacity to legislate' (ECAS, 2004: 8).

Regarding the rest of the text, business organisations regard the inclusion of a specific reference to European competitiveness and free and undistorted competition in Article I-3 on the 'Union's objectives' as a reflection of their success in shaping the Convention outcome. The element was not included in the initial draft version of the Article, which prompted an amendment by Jacobs and a letter to Giscard d'Estaing on 28 May 2003 *insisting* 'on the importance of ensuring that such a reference is reintroduced in the Treaty'. At the same time Jacobs drew attention in his letter to the legitimacy of his claim on the basis of UNICE's constituency: 'Companies in Europe do not understand why this reference has been taken out of the revised draft [. . .] The justifications for the amended version do not evidence any request to withdraw this reference' (Jacobs, 2003).

The final versions of Article 3 paragraphs 2, 3 and 4 now read:

> 2. The Union shall offer its citizens an area of freedom, security and justice without internal frontiers, and an internal market where *competition is free and undistorted*.
> 3. The Union shall work for the sustainable development of Europe based on balanced economic growth and price stability, a *highly competitive* social market economy, aiming at full employment and social progress, and a high level of protection and improvement of the quality of the environment. It shall promote scientific and technological advance.
> 4. In its relations with the wider world, the Union shall uphold and promote its values and interests. It shall contribute to peace, security, the sustainable development of the Earth, solidarity and mutual respect among peoples, *free* and fair *trade*.
>
> (TCE [all emphases added])

Business organisations pushed their liberal agenda as far as EU economic governance is concerned. However, their assessment of their actual input in shaping the text of the Article may be exaggerated, since the principles of free competition, competitiveness and free trade would have been included anyway following the tone of recent discourses on economic governance, particularly in view of the Lisbon agenda. Moreover, the more liberal principles coexist in the Article with principles of social market economy, employment creation and sustainable development which clearly dilute the principles incorporated in the business interests' agenda. Finally, UNICE's reference to its membership base as part of the arguments put forward to the president of the Convention reflects the usual approach undertaken by the employers' association in reasserting the strength of its wide membership and thus its representativeness, very much in line with the criteria for the consultation code discussed earlier in this chapter.

As mentioned above, other business priorities are included in the final text such as the Union's legal personality (Article I-7). Business also welcomed the incorporation of the Charter of Fundamental Rights into the Constitution, and the increased direct access of individuals to the European Court of Justice.

However, they did voice a clear warning against 'an unwarranted and unjustified extension of the Union's competence in the social policy area' (AmCham, 2003a: 5). Concerns regarding transparency were partially addressed by Article I-50 on 'transparency of the proceedings of Union institutions, bodies, offices and agencies', yet a common procedure is clearly absent: according to paragraph 4, 'each institution, body, office or agency shall determine in its own rules of procedure specific provisions regarding access to its documents'.

Business welcomed the precise structure of Article I-11 on *Fundamental Principles*, clearly distinguishing the concepts of conferral, subsidiarity and proportionality. The *Protocol on the Application of the Principles of Subsidiarity and Proportionality* incorporates national parliaments into the procedure and calls upon the Commission to 'consult widely' and to give reasons for the non-consultation in the case of exceptional circumstances (Article 2). On institutional matters, the Commission's right of initiative is confirmed by Article I-26, paragraph 2. Article I-23, paragraph 3 confirms QMV as the decision-making procedure in the Council. Regarding the category of competences, the spirit of UNICE's amendment in favour of the member states' co-ordination of their economic policies at EU level is incorporated in Article I-12, paragraph 3, while the proposed amendment calling for energy and public health not to become shared competences was ignored.

Yet, there are some issues of concern for business. The incorporation of the Charter of Fundamental Rights means a strengthening of the Union's social objectives which might affect future Union legislation and its judicial interpretation in the long run (Crossick and Allio, 2003: 2). Some of the liberal ideas proposed by European business organisations were not taken on board by either the Convention or the subsequent IGC. Crucially, the amendment to Article I-38, *Principles common to the Union's legal acts*, in support of self-regulation and co-regulation, was not incorporated into the final text either. Finally, some of the most interesting proposals tabled by business to increase consultation have been disregarded as well. Specifically these were: the creation of an independent body entrusted with the task of reviewing the observance of the subsidiarity principle; the development of the functional dimension of subsidiarity to involve actors other than EU institutions in achieving the objectives of a proposed EU action; the establishment of specific criteria to assess the representativeness of organisations; and common guidelines for the implementation of the transparency principle across institutions.

Conclusion: a view from the periphery

The business organisations' experience of the Convention process has been a very revealing exercise for a number of reasons. Firstly, some of business' general objectives were reflected by the text that was eventually approved. These included, for instance, the formal recognition and promotion of the role of the social partners at EU level; a more precise definition of the principle of participatory democracy, and that of allocation of competences; and the more active involvement of the national parliaments, so as to make a better assessment of the application of the principles of subsidiarity and proportionality. Other issues of interest to organised business that made it into the Constitutional Treaty included: the simplification of existing treaties and procedures; the conferment of legal personality to the EU; the expansion of the use of QMV to enhance efficiency; and the consolidation of the role of the European Parliament, and of the Commission's right of policy initiative. Although it is true that most of these objectives were also part of the overall agenda of the member states and that, with perhaps the exception of the social dialogue issue, they would have appeared in the final text regardless of business involvement in the Convention, this coincidence of interests should not detract from the fact that business interests have contributed to shape the context in which the Convention operated. But, overall, the Convention focused primarily on institutional design, a priority that does not feature heavily on the agendas of business organisations. Business organisations did not exercise a crucial influence in the Convention debates, though they were able to benefit from the main players' debates and preferences. Moreover, the final text confirms the status quo as far as the basic framework for EU governance is concerned, with a few additions such as the expansion of QMV, the strengthening of the Commission's right of initiative, and the clarification of the allocation of competences. Business has nothing to worry about from these cautious developments, but the absence in the final draft of the most innovative suggestions put forward by business organisations suggests that their influence was limited. One cannot conclude, however, that business organisations do not count anymore; they do indeed, but it is obvious that in an essentially politically driven EU, business prefers to focus on issues of economic governance which are closer to its most immediate interests and concerns.

While it is undeniable that the Convention offered a unique opportunity for organised interests to advocate their concerns and to engage in a process that was previously inaccessible to them, the Convention experiment – as also discussed in Chapter 8 with specific reference to civil society, and more generally in a number of chapters of Parts II and III – reveals a clear gap between the rhetorical discourse on participation and its implementation. In the context of the Convention, civil society and participation became rhetorical devices to gain legitimacy rather than a genuine move towards a more pluralistic EU democracy capable of including mechanisms of active participation of citizens and social actors in the policy-making process that would complement and enrich representative democracy. Thus the engagement of organised interests in the Convention experiment should not be exaggerated. The fact remains that they only acted as observers and were at the margins in many of the crucial debates in the Convention and subsequently in the IGC. One may wonder whether the actual debates and the final text would have changed much if the stakeholders had not been present as observers.

Business' overall positive assessment of the experiment should be considered within the context illustrated by Crum's observation that 'initiatives to reach out to wider society have taken a rather perfunctory character and have failed to reach much beyond the established European political in-crowd' (Crum, 2002). And yet, if Articles I-46 and I-47 are saved from the present constitutional débâcle, and the differentiation between civil dialogue and social dialogue is put into practice, one result of the Convention would be for business interests to see their functional legitimacy enhanced.

Notes

1. Civil society, according to the *White Paper on European Governance*: '[i]ncludes the following: trade unions and employers' organisations (social partners); nongovernmental organisations; professional associations; charities; grass-roots organisations; organisations that involve citizens in local and municipal life with a particular contribution from churches and religious communities' (Commission, 2001).
2. Case T-135/96 *UEAPME v Council* [1998] ECR II-2338.
3. For a more detailed account of the impact of the Convention on business interests see Pérez-Solórzano Borragán (2004).
4. Since January 2007, UNICE has changed its name to BUSINESSEUROPE (The Confederation of European Business). As the material in this chapter refers to events before this date, the old acronym will be used throughout.
5. UNICE was the only association granted observer status, thus being directly involved in the discussions of the relevant working groups and being invited to participate in plenary sessions. This clearly explains the wealth of position papers and other documents produced by UNICE in comparison to other business organisations, and the more detailed suggestions for policy-making and policy areas provided by the employers' organisation.
6. Jacobs addressed the Convention on five occasions: 4 April 2002, 24 June 2002, 6 February 2003, 17 March 2003 and 15 May 2003.
7. This reflects the co-ordinating impact of the social dialogue procedure, already evident in the Joint Contribution by the Social Partners to the Laeken European Council (Social Partners, 2001).
8. Specifically, the criteria outlined by UNICE sought to determine whether the organisations would be: composed of members mandated to act at a European level; representative in a majority of member states; representative of collective interests; composed of member organisations that are considered representative at the national level; capable of justifying their actions to their members; composed of members who join voluntarily at national and European level; independent of the public authorities; based on a well-resourced consultation structure; able to guarantee a certain degree of expertise.
9. This Act sets specific guidelines for publication of proposed rules in the Federal Register, deadlines for public comments, public hearings, written explanations and official responses to public comments.

10
The Debate on European Values

Chris Longman

Since Maastricht at least, the European Union has suffered from a legitimacy crisis, due to the fact that integration through ad hoc calculations of national advantage and the assumption of a permissive consensus have not been perceived as sufficient to justify and legitimise the EU to its citizens. Consequently, at the turn of the millennium a revitalisation of the European project was deemed to be necessary. Although some believe this to be a false problem (Moravcsik, 2005a), many strategies to tackle the problem have been suggested, some based on greater democratic engagement on the part of the EU citizens, others on the strengthening of the legal and/or political institutions at a European level, and yet others focused on the identity-creation and demos-formation of the European project (Chryssochoou, 2000). The Convention experiment, and more generally the attempt to give the EU a proper constitutional text, could be seen as connecting to each of these strategies. This chapter is particularly interested in the way in which such an attempt is linked to the latter, and how the Convention dealt with the wider debate about European values.

Indeed, it is often argued that, in order for a sense of shared political belonging in the EU to develop, there needs to be a framework of shared values – a 'public philosophy', a language of values through which the integration process is perceived, and conflicts can be addressed and resolved (Olsen, 2004). One of the problems for the search for such a public philosophy, however, is that there are different ways of conceiving values, and different ways in which values can be seen to provide both political cohesion and legitimacy for a polity. In the following analysis we shall refer to three ideal-type visions of the EU, each of which develops separate conceptions of what 'European' values are, and what kind of legitimacy they offer to the European integration process.

These three ideal-type visions can be referred to as a 'Europe of nation-states', a 'communitarian Europe' and a 'cosmopolitan Europe'.[1] The first model perceives the EU as an instrument for resolving member state problems, and is associated with an intergovernmentalist theoretical perspective on European integration (Moravcsik, 1998). From this view, values and principles are a by-product of intergovernmental negotiations. There is a clear absence of a transnational demos in this perspective. Rather, there is a community of different demoi, of distinct political communities; the EU being characterised by deep national diversities and being legitimated both instrumentally by the outputs of its decision-making (Majone, 1996, 2000) and normatively through the conditional aggregation of discrete constitutional settlements which are based on distinct national value systems. Distinctly *European* values are therefore unnecessary.

The second model, of an identity-based community, requires the existence or construction of a distinct European people and a European identity. It presupposes a shared sense of belonging (or wanting to belong), based on the perceived commonality of European values, and has at its core the notions of territorial, social and generational solidarity. 'In this view, the legitimacy of the constitution is based on the traditions and common values of the community as an ethical community' (Olsen, 2004: 78). As such, this model presupposes historical patterns of European culture which may be mobilised as European 'core values' to provide a legitimising normative teleology for the Union.

The third model is based on more cosmopolitan conceptions of values, and the role of *universal* rights. From this more liberal perspective the fundamental issue is that of equal respect for individuals and the search for impartial principles. The normative basis of this view rests on a combination of individualism, universality and generality, and the empirical justification of such a position rests on the thesis that social, cultural, economic and political processes over the last few decades have transformed individuals' identifications and allegiances, and that a new 'post-national' orientation exists in twenty-first-century Europe. Such a post-national, rights-based European Union would have at its heart a constitution that emphasises shared rights as principal values.

In the rest of this chapter, the focus of our analysis will be on what kind of vision of Europe has emerged – if indeed one single vision has emerged – from the debate about values in and around the Constitutional Convention.

Background to the values debate

As a starting point to our discussion of the 'values debate', a working definition of values is offered, as standards that people have about what is good and bad, i.e. abstract standards of goodness, moral principles or ideals. Core values shape societies and their norms by providing approved principles which steer action and the articulation of norms. Values may be social, cultural, religious, political, economic or legal/rights-based, and indeed within any set of values there may well be contradictory tensions, such as between those that stress the rights of individuals, which may clash with those that stress community and solidarity, or those that place emphasis on freedom of expression, which may conflict with those which seek to protect the sensitivities of specific groups within society.[2]

The obvious question to be raised in the context of this chapter is whether there is any consensus on what European values might be, and whether such values are specifically European or more universal. Academic discussion can be divided into those attempts to explore or critique a *historical development* of common European identity (Hay, 1957; Wilson and van der Dussen, 1995; Delanty, 1995; Heffernan, 1998; Rietbergen, 1998; Pagden, 2002), and those that produce and explore *contemporary* data such as the European Values Study.[3] However, in neither of these modes of study is there consensus about essential and particular 'European' values. Indeed, in reading the vast litera-ture on the history of the idea of Europe, and the contemporary studies on European identity one is reminded of the point made by Ludwig Wittgenstein, that in 'spinning a thread we twist fibre on fibre. And the strength of the thread does not reside in the fact that some fibre runs through its whole length, but in the overlapping of many fibres' (Wittgenstein, 1967: 32e).

It is this multiplicity of historical legacies that makes up the current con-cept of 'Europe' and its perceived values, and it is from an array of conceptions of 'Europe' and European values that the Convention needed to construct a coherent and meaningful set of principles that would legitimise the European integration project, and guide the actions of European politicians and pol-icies, and, potentially, the behaviour of its citizens.

In this, the task of the Convention was indeed great. This may be illustrated by the fact that at the same time as the Convention was meeting, a high-level Reflection Group was initiated by the then Commission President, Romano Prodi, to explore 'The Spiritual and Cultural Dimension of Europe', and to 'reflect on those values that are particularly relevant to the continuing process of European unification' (Biedenkopf et al., 2004: 3). The conclusion of this study was that '[t]here is no essence of Europe, no fixed list of European values' (Biedenkopf et al., 2004: 12).

It is worth at this point making a distinction between, on the one hand, an attempt to find a coherent set of European values that have grown organi-cally through European history, a romantic projection of European historical continuity onto the present political needs of the European Union; and, on the other, a rather different attempt to provide a more rationalistic, political construct of civic values to which European politicians and citizens could aspire (Wæver, 1993: 209). It will become clear in the following analysis of the 'val-ues debate', that the tensions inherent in the historical style of argument were indeed highly problematic, and that in essence the values that eventu-ally predominated were of the more aspirational variety.

Values and the Charter Convention

It is not being implied here that the values debate which occurred in the Constitutional Convention was the first time that an attempt had been made to elucidate values that could legitimise and guide the EC/EU.[4] There have been EC/EU pronouncements on European values before. The 1973 Declaration on European Identity from the Copenhagen European Summit of 14/15 December,[5] for instance, referred to values, 'which give the European identity its originality and its own dynamism'. Five features were outlined within the document: cultural diversity within the framework of a common European civilisation; attachment to common values (without stating what these values might be); increasing convergence in Europe to attitudes to life; awareness of having specific interests in common; and the determination to construct a United Europe. Yet the only time when an open debate of a constitutional nature took place on the values underlying the European project was at the Charter Convention in 2000 (Schönlau, 2003). It is here that the foundations were laid for the subsequent Constitutional Convention debates on values.

The Convention was the product of the Cologne European Council in June 1999, which stated that the '[p]rotection of fundamental rights is a founding principle of the Union and an indispensable prerequisite for her legitimacy'.[6] While, as Schönlau points out, 'it was probably not the intention of the heads of state and government at their Cologne meeting to launch a general debate about Europe's value foundation, it soon became clear that an attempt to increase the Union's legitimacy by drafting a catalogue of fundamental rights would inevitably touch on the values which are supposed to justify the rights in question' (Schönlau, 2003: 114). The formulation of values in the preamble to the Charter is of particular interest because it anticipates the debates in the later Constitutional Convention, discussions which focused on the scope, purpose and normative foundations of the EU. For instance, the second paragraph of the Charter preamble underwent a change in the 14 September 2000 draft (CONVENT 47), when the notion of 'religious heritage' appeared alongside Europe's cultural and humanist legacy in order to give substance to the vague formulation of 'common values' mentioned in the first sentence. This reference to religion caused an uproar in the Convention, pitting Christian Democrats against Social Democrats/Greens, and politicising the issue of values to a high degree. It was only with the substitution of the word 'religious' with 'spiritual' that a compromise was reached. It is especially interesting that the most heated debates in both the Charter Convention and Constitutional Convention, as well as in subsequent IGC discussion and the debates surrounding the subsequent Buttiglione affair and Turkish accession, focused on religion.

The Constitutional Convention: a debate unfolds

The Laeken European Council Declaration of December 2001 which set out the mandate for the Convention made some explicit points about European values, characterising Europe as 'the continent of humane values', of 'liberty, solidarity and above all diversity'.[7] Furthermore, Laeken tells us that '[t]he European Union's one boundary is democracy and human rights', and that the Union is 'only open to countries which uphold basic values such as free elections, respect for minorities and respect for the rule of law'. With reference to the EU's position in the world, Laeken makes the claim that the Union is '[a] power seeking to set globalisation within a moral framework'. In highlighting the reforms needed in the EU, the document states that the EU derives its legitimacy from the democratic values it projects, and sets as one of the tasks for the Convention to explore 'the values which the Union cherishes'. Thus the mandate for the Convention was clear from the start. The constitutional future of the EU should be founded on a discussion and exploration of the fundamental values which underpin the legitimacy and raison d'être of the Union itself.

The Convention's exploration of values may be divided into three key contexts: (i) the drafting of, and debate surrounding, Article 2, which explicitly states the Union's values;[8] (ii) the drafting of the preamble, the debates about which attempted to provide a historically based moral foundation for the Constitution;[9] and (iii) the incorporation of the Charter of Fundamental Rights into the Constitution, and especially the preamble to the Charter which sets out the fundamental values upon which the Charter is based.

The above three contexts should not been seen as exclusive, however. There are other aspects of the Constitution and associated debates that are relevant to the discussion of values, especially those connected with Article 3, the objectives of the Union, as well as articles that deal with fundamental freedoms, democracy and participation and respect for national identities. These will be dealt with briefly in the analysis below, but the main emphasis will be on the three contexts outlined above.

The Union's values (Article 2)

From the start, this was an Article whose title specifically refers to 'Union' values, not 'European' values, more widely understood. However, when the first draft of Article 2 was presented to plenary in February 2003 (CONV 528/03), attached to it was a very interesting 'explanatory note' which gives the reasoning behind the drafting of the articles; the notes from Article 2 are highly pertinent:

> This Article concentrates on the essentials – a short list of fundamental European values. Further justification for this is that a manifest risk of serious breach of one of those values by a Member State would be sufficient to initiate the procedure for alerting and sanctioning the Member State . . . This Article can thus only contain a hard core of values meeting two criteria at once: on the one hand, they must be so fundamental that they lie at the very heart of a peaceful society practicing tolerance, justice and solidarity; on the other hand, they must have a clear non-controversial legal basis so that the Member States can discern the obligations resulting therefrom which are subject to sanction. That does not, of course, prevent the Constitution from mentioning additional, more detailed elements

which are part of the Union's 'ethic' in other places, such as, for instance, in the Preamble, in Article 3 on the general objectives of the Union, in the Charter of Fundamental Rights . . . in Title VI on 'The democratic life of the Union' and in the provisions enshrining the specific objectives of the various policies.

(CONV 528/03, pp. 11–12)

Thus the claim is being made that this should be a list of 'fundamental *European* values', not specifically Union values. This is symptomatic of the confusion of 'Europe' and the 'EU' which is endemic in both popular and elite level discourse. The other obvious example of this is the fact that the Treaty itself was eventually and strangely entitled 'A Treaty establishing a Constitution for *Europe*'. There is then the claim that these values lie at the heart of any peaceful society. Thus a more universalistic claim is being made. This confusion about whether the values are basic to the EU, or to Europe more generally, or are supposed to be more universal in their conception remains throughout the many debates and different drafts that followed. Leaving this aside for the moment, the other point to raise here is that these values are supposed to be 'essential', 'fundamental', a 'hard core'. So what, then, are these values as set out in the first draft?

The Union is founded on the values of respect for human dignity, liberty, democracy, the rule of law and respect for human rights, values which are common to the Member States. Its aim is a society at peace, through the practice of tolerance, justice and solidarity.

(CONV 528/03, p. 2)

The suggested amendments and the debate which followed later in the month raised questions about the definition and content of the values mentioned, and secondly raised the issue of a reference to religion. With regard to the content, there were many complaints that equality was not mentioned, nor respect for pluralism or diversity. Giscard defended the omission of equality on the grounds that there was a close relationship between the values listed and potential sanctions against member states which were in breach of these principles, and that 'equality' did not have a water-tight legal definition.[10] However, by the time the next draft appeared in June, the missing values had emerged:

The Union is founded on the values of respect for human dignity, liberty, democracy, *equality*, the rule of law and respect for human rights. These values are common to the Member States in a society of *pluralism*, tolerance, justice, solidarity and *non-discrimination*.

(CONV 797/03, p. 2) (emphasis added)

This formula did not change with the publication of the final draft Treaty at the end of the Convention period. However, the IGC developed the list of values even further, being much more explicit about the rights of persons belonging to minorities and equality between men and women.[11] So what justification was given within the context of the Convention for including values in the Constitution? The explanatory notes in CONV 528/03 give three reasons: they enshrine what makes the peoples of Europe feel part of the same Union; they provide criteria to judge whether applicant states are worthy of accession; and they provide criteria for suspension or sanctioning of member states in breach of these values.[12]

The debate which surfaced regarding religion certainly did not appear to satisfy the first of the above justifications. It was a highly charged and divisive debate, just as it had been in the Charter Convention previously (see above). There were many interventions which asked for a reference to God, Christianity or to Judaeo-Christian roots to be included.[13] Olsen (2004) analyses the arguments that ensued. He characterises the approach of those who argued for the inclusion of a reference to Christian values as (Euro-)communitarian: European values cannot be understood without reference to Europe's religious tradition; religion has been a beneficial social force in Europe, especially as a force against violence and oppression; a lack of recognition would alienate from the EU those with religious affiliations; and lastly the (rather dubious) claim that the separation of church and state is a Christian principle (Olsen, 2004: 85–6). Some interventions were crudely exclusionary. For example, Peter Skaarup (a Danish Parliament representative) thought that the Constitution ought to mention Christendom because that would prevent Turkey, as a state with a predominantly Muslim population, from joining the EU.[14]

Ranged against this view were more liberal arguments: for example, how God was not responsible for the flowering of liberal democracy, so should not appear in the Constitution (Duff); how the values were designed as guidance for sanctions against member states, and thus religious references might compromise the secular nature of European public institutions making these decisions (Paciotti); how, more generally, reference to the past, such as the Christian tradition, would simply show Europe's history to 'look like a river of blood' (Paciotti again); and how reference to God would divide believers and non-believers (Kaufmann). As Olsen (2004: 86–8) makes clear, the liberal-cosmopolitan arguments sought to stress the importance of Union neutrality regarding religion, and how such an explicit reference to a Christian heritage would endanger the principle of equal treatment, as well as the instrumental worry of how the inclusion of God could alienate non-believers. For liberal-cosmopolitans, religion (whatever denomination or faith) would be protected through the Charter of Fundamental Rights, to be included in the Constitution, which guarantees freedom of thought, conscience and religion.[15]

The argument about the status of Christianity with regard to the Union's values may be seen as illustrative of the models presented earlier in this chapter, with religious Euro-communitarians emphasising perceptions of common heritage and identity, with Christian values providing the foundations for the development of subsequent fundamental European values, and more liberal-cosmopolitan arguments stressing the Union's need to be neutral, to promote equal respect for individuals, and to search for impartial principles. The final result was that no reference was made in Article 2 to either religion in general, or Christianity in particular. Although this appears to be a clear victory for the liberal-cosmopolitan perspective, this is not entirely accurate because the values debate with its associated religious discussion was transferred to the debates and drafting of the preamble, which will be discussed below.[16]

Before moving on to discuss the preamble, it is worth lingering a while on Article 3, which as a list of objectives is highly value-laden.[17] However, the explanatory note with the first draft provided the rationale behind this distinction between 'values' and 'objectives':

> The philosophy of this Article is to set out the general objectives justifying the very existence of the Union and its action for its citizens in a more cross-sectoral fashion and not to list the specific objectives pursued by the various policies of the Union ... The fundamental difference between this Article and Article 2 therefore needs to be emphasized: while Article 2 enshrines the basic values which make the peoples of Europe feel part of the same 'union', Article 3 sets out the main aims justifying the creation of the Union for the exercise of certain powers in common at European level.
>
> (CONV 528/03, p. 12)

The debate about the Union's objectives was less acrimonious than that on its values, with elements that satisfied most political and philosophical perspectives. There are references to solidarity and cohesion to satisfy the communitarians, and nothing illiberal to frighten the more cosmopolitan-minded. The result of the debates was that the list of objectives grew somewhat, with more emphasis given to diversity (respect for linguistic diversity being added) and to the protection and promotion of Europe's cultural heritage. The only item to be lost was the extra-terrestrial commitment to the 'discovery of space'.

The preamble to the Constitutional Treaty

The values debate moved from Articles 2 and 3 to the preamble rather late in the Convention process, the first draft being in May 2003 (CONV 722/03). This draft is very interesting for many reasons. First, it includes a motto, quoting Thucydides on democracy, defining power as being in the hands of the whole people. Given the perceived 'democratic deficit' that the Union suffers from, this appeared to beg embarrassing questions. The motto was removed during the IGC, and is absent in the final Treaty. Second, the first paragraph has a highly Euro-centric and arrogant flavour, claiming that 'Europe is a continent that has brought forth civilisation'.[18] This paragraph was also dropped in the final Treaty. Third, the next paragraph of the first draft provides an outline of the historical legacy of this 'civilisation' which provides a justification and explanation for the rights and laws enjoyed in Europe today. This, as discussed below, was the focus of much debate. Fourth, included in this outline is a reference to Europe's 'religious inheritance', which would be bound to reopen the debates that occurred around the drafting of Article 2, and from the previous Charter Convention. Fifth, there is a very notable absence of the words 'European Union' in all the draft preambles produced by the Convention. In the substantive paragraphs of the first draft there are five mentions of 'Europe' in general. It is only with the very last version, the final post-IGC Treaty, that a paragraph was added which referred explicitly to the EU.[19]

Thus, the first draft may be characterised as being highly Euro-communitarian, emphasising European uniqueness and common historical roots, and implying an equivalence between 'Europe' and 'the EU'. Although there is a passing reference to a state-centrist vision of Europe/EU ('remaining proud of their own national identities and histories', and the word 'peoples' in the plural) there appears immediately afterwards the contentious Euro-communitarian claim that the 'peoples of Europe are determined to transcend their ancient divisions, and, united in an ever-closer fashion, to forge a common destiny'. This clearly begs the question whether the citizens of Europe are really buying into the European integration project with the enthusiasm implied here, or whether this sense of destiny is more the belief system of a self-selecting Euro-elite.[20] This issue will be assessed below.

The reactions in the Convention to the first draft preamble focused principally on the paragraph dealing with Europe's historical legacy. Many *conventionnels* saw this as the opportunity to make explicit reference to a Christian or Judaeo-Christian heritage. Interestingly, the first draft does mention the 'religious' inheritance of Europe, despite the fact that during the Charter Convention in 2000 the debate had led to the replacement of the word 'religious' by the more neutral 'spiritual'. However, this was still insufficient for many in the Convention, and the debate was ignited again, with Christians arguing that 'it would be a falsification of history not to mention Christianity alongside Greece, Rome and the Enlightenment' (Olsen, 2004: 88). The debate on religion even awakened much wider media interest across Europe, pushing the Convention into the public consciousness in a way that few of the other debates had achieved.[21] The eventual compromise was to retain the reference to religious inheritance without specifying Christianity, but also removing references to Greece, Rome and the Enlightenment.[22]

The fact that these historical references to Europe in terms of heritage and legacy were so problematic should alert us to the wider implications of trying to legitimise a present project through reference to specific past episodes, movements, epochs or developments. As Delanty (1995: 1) rightly points out, every age reinvents the idea of Europe in the mirror of its own identity, and that 'what we call Europe is, in fact, a historically fabricated reality of ever-changing forms and dynamics' (ibid.: 3). In stressing the historical basis for 'European' values such as equality of persons, freedom, respect for reason and law, peace, justice and solidarity, the authors of the preamble seemed to be selectively blind to Europe's seemingly interminable history of religious and nationalistic wars, Crusades against 'infidels', the Holocaust and genocides, and susceptibility to authoritarian political 'solutions' which have resulted in such obnoxious systems as Nazism, fascism and Soviet-style communism. The list of values the Convention proclaimed as 'core' European values have developed in spite of, or in reaction to, most of European history. They should be seen as such, rather than in the partial, essentialist and teleological fashion that emerged during much of the drafting and debating process of the Convention.[23]

Once the Convention had finished its work, the text of the draft Treaty was left in the hands of the Italian, then Irish presidencies of the EU to steer through the IGC. Once again the issue of Europe's Christian heritage arose,[24] but the final version of the Treaty preamble resisted calls for more explicit references to religious heritage, and indeed the final preamble does not emphasise historical references except in the most general terms (see Appendix, Table A1). However, there was one vital expression added during the IGC drafting stage which draws attention to the negative historical legacy: 'reunited Europe' becomes, 'Europe, reunited after bitter experiences'. This could refer to most of European history, or to more specific twentieth-century World War and Cold War divisions. Furthermore, as stated above, in the IGC version, reference is made to the development of European integration through the Treaties and the *acquis*, thus situating the more general aspirations of the preamble and the Constitution within the framework of post-war political integration in Europe.

The overall ethic of the preamble is thus communitarian in its Convention form, with liberal-cosmopolitan features, whilst in its final post-IGC form it retains a communitarian character, though stripped of most of the references to historical patterns of European culture which were suggested as European 'core values' to provide a legitimising normative teleology for the Union.

The preamble to the Charter of Fundamental Rights

Before moving on to a general analysis of the drafts, texts and debates associated with the writing of the TCE, it is worth remembering that the first major open discussion on the values that underpin the European project occurred during the Charter Convention of 2000, as discussed near the beginning of this chapter. At the start of the Charter is a preamble, and during the later Constitutional Convention of 2002–3 (where it was agreed early on that the Charter would form a part of the Constitution itself) there was discussion about whether the Charter preamble should be a part of the final text, whether it should be the preamble for the entire Constitutional text, or whether it should be left out altogether because a new preamble was to be written and so two preambles might be considered strange.

The discussions of the working group tasked to look into the status of the Charter within the framework of the Constitution suggested the following:

> A number of speakers stressed that the preamble to the Charter, which was an essential part of it, had been drafted in such a way that, besides fundamental rights, it more generally encompassed the values and foundations of the Union. In the opinion of these members, the preamble could therefore be used (possibly with additions) as the preamble to a new basic treaty.
> (CONV 203/02: 5)

The final report of the working group simply suggested that the preamble should be retained, without saying where:

> The Group considers the Charter Preamble as a crucial element of the overall consensus on the Charter reached by the previous Convention. The Group therefore recommends that this element should in any event be preserved in the future Constitutional Treaty framework. The Group also recalls that the Charter Preamble comprises language on the fundamental nature of the Union going well beyond the area of fundamental rights.
> (CONV 354/02 A III.2)

What is clear from these quotes is that the Charter preamble gives an account of the foundational values of the Union, which are to be considered alongside values expressed in the overall Constitutional Treaty preamble and Article 2. The Charter preamble provides a good example of compromise between (or synthesis of) a Euro-communitarian vision ('ever-closer union', 'common values'), a state-centrist perspective ('respecting the diversity of the cultures and traditions of the peoples of Europe as well as the national identities of the Member States', 'the principle of subsidiarity'), and a liberal-cosmopolitan view ('the Union is founded on indivisible universal values', 'it places the individual at the heart of its activities', '[e]njoyment of these rights entails responsibilities and duties with regard to other persons, to the human community and to future generations').

The outcome of the Convention (and the subsequent IGC did not change this) was that the Constitutional Treaty not only has a general preamble, but also a preamble at the start of Part II, the Charter of Fundamental Rights, both of which give clear values discourses of a Euro-communitarian/liberal-cosmopolitan fusion.

After the Convention

Once the Convention had finished its work, and had presented its draft Treaty to the Italian presidency to take forward to the subsequent intergovernmental conference, it was the job of member state governments to negotiate any changes. Most issues on the IGC agenda were minor, second-order issues dealing with tidying up the draft Constitutional text. The main sticking points were over institutional/procedural aspects, such as the number of votes in the Council, where Poland and Spain dug their heels in and refused to accept proposed changes to the status quo of the Nice Treaty. However, as mentioned above, the issue of religion rumbled on in the background. The failure of the Italian presidency to reach agreement on the Treaty by December 2003 was not attributable to values issues though. Despite various governments wishing to introduce a reference to Christianity, it was the institutional matters (as well as poor presidency skills exhibited by Silvio Berlusconi) that were crucial to the failure to agree at this stage. It took a more focused Irish presidency and a change in government in Madrid to break the log-jam, and the final Treaty establishing a Constitution for Europe (with the various changes discussed above, such as those in the Constitution preamble) was signed on 29 October 2004.

However, while the arrangements were being made for the signing of the Constitution, a row broke out. Rocco Buttiglione, prospective justice and home affairs commissioner, with strong Catholic beliefs, made his anti-gay views known, which were deemed by many to be inappropriate for a Commissioner with responsibility for civil liberties. During his hearing with the EP, Buttiglione said that he considered homosexuality a sin, and that marriage was intended 'to allow women to have children and to have [the] protection of a male'. After the storm that followed (which overshadowed the signing of the Constitutional Treaty), Buttiglione was withdrawn by the Italian government as its nominee, but the row simmered on with Buttiglione, a friend of Pope John Paul II, starting a campaign to form a European 'theocon' movement for those who believe traditional Christian values should be part of public life in Europe, partly inspired by the role of the Christian vote in US politics.[25] Railing against 'creeping totalitarianism' and 'religious discrimination', Buttiglione reignited a debate about religion and Christian values in Europe and brought the tension between religious Euro-communitarianism and more secular, liberal-cosmopolitan, visions once more to the forefront of public debate.

A second development which echoes the above is the debate about the accession to the EU of Turkey, with a predominantly Muslim population, albeit with a secular constitution. Although there are many reasons why Turkish accession may be problematic (its human rights record, its large population which would make it one of the largest member states, its sensitive geographical and geo-political situation, its huge agricultural sector), it is the fact that it is an overwhelmingly Muslim country that has sparked off most public debate, especially in France, where the Turkish issue played a part in derailing the ratification of the Constitutional Treaty in the French referendum of May 2005 while provoking an unprecedented change to the French constitution in view of future EU enlargements.[26]

Both the Buttiglione affair and the ongoing debates about Turkish suitability for EU membership show the contested nature of what Europe is, and what values lie at the heart of any project that seeks to unite the continent politically. Thus, the debates which surfaced in the Constitutional Convention, and the compromises that have been made to provide a normative foundation for the Constitution of the EU, reflect wider debates about membership, allegiance, belonging and identity in European society.

European values in the Constitution: which values, whose vision?

As argued in Part II, the Charter Convention and the Laeken Declaration ushered in a new style of treaty negotiation which put other actors apart from national governments centre-stage in the treaty reform process, allowing the emergence of a more emboldened Euro-vision which is delineated in the preamble, Articles 1–3 and the Charter preamble. The preamble, which started in a very Euro-communitarian fashion, was toned down, but was still a bold statement of pan-European aspiration. The vision, which in the first draft outlined a teleological explanation for 'Europe', became more aspirational and less historically determined, as well as being finally connected to the EU in the final TCE. As for Article 1 (the establishment of the Union), the first sentence refers to 'the will of the citizens and states' as co-constituents, which marks a significant move away from the TEU, for example, where Article A of the Treaty refers to 'high contracting parties', and 'relations between the Member States and between their peoples'. The first Convention draft of Articles 1–16 is interesting in this respect. Although the Constitution, according to this first draft of Article 1, 'reflects the will of the peoples and states of Europe', which suggests a more (nation) state-based position, EU competences will be administered 'on a federal basis', which gives a more Euro-communitarian political emphasis. However, as usual with Union documents, the f-word was swiftly expunged and the less specific phrase 'community basis' inserted. By the end of the Convention, the Draft Constitutional Treaty had changed again, this time to reflect the will of 'the *citizens* and states of Europe' as co-constituents of the Constitution, thus neatly reflecting the hybrid polity that most commentators agree that the EU has become.[27]

Article 2, listing the values of the Union, has a definite liberal-cosmopolitan flavour, with a little non-religious communitarianism added ('solidarity' and the mention of 'a society' in which member states are situated). However, the rationale behind presenting these values is not only the communitarian-oriented desire to make citizens feel part of the same Union, but also the more pragmatic and instrumental need to provide criteria by which member states or candidate states can be judged as to their worthiness for membership.[28] Article 3, although ostensibly about the Union's objectives, has a highly value-laden content, and again, a hybrid liberal-cosmopolitan and

Euro-communitarian ethic dominates. However, it is interesting to note that the solidarity clause (Article 3.3) does not promote solidarity among peoples or citizens, but among member states.

The Charter of Fundamental Rights (Part II of the Constitution) offers a model of rights that is more liberal-cosmopolitan than communitarian- or state-based. However, the preamble to the Charter clearly justifies its existence by synthesising the three models to produce another hybrid.

From this brief analysis of the constitutionalisation process since the Laeken Declaration, and of the attempt to provide a legitimation ethic based on a common conception of values as a foundation for the Constitution, can it be said that there has been a transformation in values discourse within the context of treaty reform? Has there been a move away from a more state-centred justification for the EU, towards a more complex hybrid system of values that combines elements of the three models discussed at the beginning of this chapter? It would appear so, but the question then arises of whether this subtle transformation is justified in terms of *whose* values are being promoted and projected onto the European project.

This question may be sub-divided into two distinct queries: For whom were these institutionalised/constitutionalised values written? And, by whom were they written? As far as the first question is concerned, a state-centrist vision would suggest that any common EU values are shared because the states which make up the EU have similar historical backgrounds of nation-building and democratisation, and that the source of legitimacy of the EU rests on common acceptance between distinct member states (as nation-states) of legitimising sovereignty residing in each constituent national community, which share basic principles of democratic governance, human rights and free market capitalism. A Euro-communitarian approach would emphasise the people, rather than the peoples of Europe, and stress the importance of values shared amongst citizens of the European Union. The Constitution and the values it seeks to reflect and project in this view are the shared values of Europeans. The third perspective, that of a rights-based community, would also emphasise the importance of the citizen, with each individual of the political community benefiting from the post-national promotion of cosmopolitan values.

The Constitution, as discussed in the paragraph above on the preamble and Article 1, is supposed to reflect the values and aspirations of the citizens and states of Europe. We can assume that because all twenty-five member state governments were engaged in the negotiation process, and signed the Treaty in October 2004 that the states were well-informed and represented. But what about the citizens? Are they truly 'resolved to transcend their former divisions and, united ever more closely, to forge a common destiny' (TCE preamble)? Were the citizens of the EU aware and content that this exercise was being done 'on behalf of the citizens and states of Europe' (TCE preamble)? On whose authority were the people who agreed the text speaking? This relates to the second question, *who* the writers and framers of these values were. How representative and accountable were the members of the Convention? By what right did they pronounce on issues of fundamental values and aspirations of Europeans?[29]

Gisela Stuart, the British Parliament representative, who was also on the Presidium, claimed that the Convention brought together a 'self-appointed elite', that 'those who were directly accountable to their electorate . . . were in a minority', while the MEPs 'spoke for the institution of the European Parliament, not for the people who elected them' (Stuart, 2003: 17–19). This is perhaps an extreme view, but it does point to a rather difficult problem which was also raised by a group of eight Convention members who tabled the 'minority opinion' (CONV 851/03 Annex), concerning the lack of representation of a particular view on European integration. According to the signatories of the minority report, the 'Convention had no Members from that half of the population, which rejected the Maastricht Treaty in France or the Nice Treaty in Ireland' and 'not one single Eurosceptic or Eurorealist person was allowed to observe or participate in the work in the Presidium, nor any of its assisting secretariats' (ibid.: 22). Given that EU membership is viewed with a certain ambivalence by a large proportion of the EU population (as evidenced by successive Eurobarometer polls, referendum results, and low turnouts at European elections), this is an important criticism to bear in mind. The Constitution may thus be viewed as either a step too far, as the articulation of a set of values that are not shared in reality by the citizens of the EU, or as a document which aims to construct such a community of values, which is as much *aspirational* as it is an attempt to reflect actual commonalities within the diverse cultures of Europe. However, this may be considered a little harsh. The Convention was in many ways more representative and open than the closed IGC method which was the normal method of treaty reform, and the Convention itself was a preparatory body which would produce a document that would be debated and changed in an IGC, then put to all national parliaments or peoples in referendums to accept or not. Thus an in-built realism about what could be said or not was built into the process, and Convention members would have been aware of this all along.[30]

Conclusion: values, for what kind of polity?

The negotiation of fundamental values will always be an interesting site of contestation. This is certainly true of the public discussion of 'European' or EU values in the last five years. However, it is perhaps also true to say that the actual discussions and debates tell us as much about the issue as the final list of values in Article 2 and the sonorous proclamations in the preamble. It is pertinent to note that apart from the debates about a Christian heritage for Europe, and a reference to God in the text itself, the values debate was not overly contentious. The agreed values were mostly ones that any early twenty-first-century Western democratic polity could sign up to, which begs the question of how specifically *European* these values are. The arguments about European heritage, which resulted in specific references to historical epochs or movements being removed from the preamble, show how difficult it is to agree on the core historical sources of the values being projected and promoted. Without these specific historic references, the preamble read much more like a statement of contemporary political aspiration, which is perhaps what it should be.

This is not to argue that the values and aspirations set out in those parts of the EU Constitution which stress foundational principles and objectives are the best result that could be expected. There are reasons to be concerned about the negotiation, expression, justification and objective of these values and aspirations.

The first concern (discussed above) relates to whether they are the products of a process driven by elites who have lost contact with the citizens in whose name they are negotiating. Do the values and aspirations delivered in the Constitution reflect wider truths about commonality of Europe, European culture and values, and Europeans? Or do they reflect the narrower concerns of a Europeanised 'mainstream voice' of the political elite? It could be argued that this does not matter so much; political identities are often elite-driven, and eventually populations come to share the views of the elites who drive projects forward, as can be seen with nationalist movements across the world. However, the EU starts from a very difficult position. The Europeanised elite is not forging an identity in the same way as homogenising nation-state builders in the nineteenth and earlier twentieth centuries who wished to create unity by overcoming or destroying diversity, nor are they attempting to construct an identity in contrast to a hated or feared Other. (For many people the Europeanised elite actually represents the Other.) For this elite to write a constitution 'on behalf of the citizens of Europe' may appear very presumptuous to say the least.

A further worry relates to the use of such expressions as 'the citizens of Europe'. The appropriation of the idea of Europe to stand for the European Union is troubling, especially as it is given such prominence through the actual title of the 'Treaty establishing a Constitution for Europe'. The preamble hardly mentions the EU (as mentioned above, a reference was only added at a very late stage during the IGC), and the very first sentence of Article 1 states that the Constitution reflects 'the will of the citizens and states of Europe', not of the European Union. The confusion of Europe and European values, on the one hand, and the EU and the values that this polity rests upon and aspires to uphold on the other, ought not to be confused. It is offensive to those who are European but not part of the Union, and it fails to differentiate between Europe as a cultural construct and the European Union as a political construct. This confusion is amply demonstrated by the debates surrounding the use of European cultural heritage in the preamble to justify and legitimate the current EU political project.

In pointing out this merging of concepts, Europe and EU, we return to a theme that has emerged in this chapter: that of hybridity. It has been suggested that the essential value system that provides a foundational justification for the EU is a hybrid of nation-state-based, Euro-communitarian and liberal-cosmopolitan values. Hybridity is, however, a relatively neutral term. If we were to want to put a more positive spin on this we might want to talk of a synthesis; if we wished to be more negative we could point to compromise. If all three ideals have been included in the Constitution, the architects could hope that there is something for everyone to buy into. In seeking consensus and compromise, the Convention and then the IGC have produced a document that appears to offer something for everyone to identify with. However, as the French referendum campaign, with opposition to the Constitution coming from widely different ideological angles, has shown, there is also something for everyone to dislike. The kind of Europe or European Union that has emerged from the values debate in the Constitutional Convention is one characterised by hybridity, something that highlights the value of European diversity as well as the perils of its unreconciled divisions.

Notes

1. These three ideal-types are based loosely on those proposed by Eriksen and Fossum (2004) and developed by Closa (2004a).
2. A good example of this latter conflict may be seen in the debate surrounding the publication of cartoons in the Danish newspaper *Jyllands Posten* depicting the Islamic prophet Mohammed, which greatly upset the sensitivities of Muslims in Europe and across the world in the winter of 2005–6.
3. The EVS is a network of social and political scientists who carry out pan-European surveys to explore whether Europeans share a homogeneous and enduring set of values, whether values are changing, and what the implications are for European unity. There have been three waves of surveys: a more limited one in 1981; a wider pan-European survey in 1990; and the latest in 1999–2000 in 32 countries across Europe, with 40 000 respondents answering more than 300 questions. For further details, see: http://www.europeanvalues.nl/index2.htm
4. Indeed the Treaty of Rome in 1957, alongside the determination to promote an ever closer union among the peoples of Europe, committed the EEC to social progress, solidarity, the preservation of peace and liberty amongst other intentions (see preamble TEC: http://europa.eu.int/eur-lex/lex/en/treaties/dat/12002E/pdf/12002E_EN.pdf). And the Treaty of Maastricht 1992 confirmed the EU's commitment to liberty, democracy and respect for human rights and fundamental freedoms and the rule of law, as well as social rights, solidarity, social progress, sustainable development, peace and security (preamble and Art. 6 TEU: http://europa.eu.int/eur-lex/lex/en/treaties/dat/12002M/pdf/12002M_EN.pdf). However, because the negotiation of these treaties was a matter of intergovernmental bargaining behind closed doors, we do not have access to the explicit debates such as those that are in the public domain from the Convention. Furthermore, there are no articles within these treaties that explicitly state what the values of the EC/EU are.

5. 'Declaration on European Identity', *Bulletin of the European Communities*, No. 12, December 1973, pp. 118–22.
6. European Council: 'Decision on Drawing up a Charter of Fundamental Rights of the European Union', Annex IV to Conclusions, 4 June 1999: http://db.consilium. eu.int/df/intro.asp?lang=en
7. Interestingly, 'diversity' is defined in the Declaration as 'meaning respect for others' languages, cultures and traditions'. Diversity is thus not a statement of fact (there are diverse cultures in Europe), but a norm (diversity as respect).
8. See Appendix, Table A2 for the text of Articles I-1 to I-3.
9. See Appendix, Table A1 for different versions of the preamble as it developed.
10. CONV 601/03, p. 4.
11. See Appendix, Table A2 for a comparison of Articles 1–3 between the DCT and the TCE.
12. It is interesting to note the difference between the first and latter two reasons. The first has normative implications of belonging/political identity, whereas the latter two are more pragmatic, instrumental reasons.
13. For an exhaustive list of proposed amendments to Article 2, see CONV 574/03, pp. 17–23.
14. Plenary session, 27 February 2003.
15. See Article II-70 in the final TCE.
16. The decision not to include a religious reference in Article 2 was taken by the Presidium, though its president, Giscard, 'was keen to have a reference to Europe's religious identity written into a preamble' (*The Independent*, 6 February 2003).
17. See Appendix, Table A2 for Article 3 in full in both the DCT and TCE.
18. The lack of a qualifying adjective or the indefinite article ('a civilisation') implies, in the English version, that Europeans were responsible for the development of civilisation in general, in every global context.
19. See Appendix, Table A1 for a paragraph-by-paragraph development of the preamble through four drafts, from first draft to final Treaty.
20. See Shore (2000) for a critical socio-anthropological analysis of the Euro-elite and European integration as a cultural project.
21. Very interesting academic debate was also stirred up. See, for example, J. H. H.Weiler's (2003b) arguments for references to Christianity to be included in the Constitution and Menéndez's response (2004).
22. See second draft CONV 797/03 (in Appendix, Table A1).
23. For an interesting discussion on the role of history and forgetting in constructing a European identity, see Varouxakis (2000). From a social constructivist perspective what was happening in the Convention was that in the attempt to construct or reinforce conceptions of European identity, certain aspects of European history were selected and mobilised, which would hopefully be accepted as the dominant 'story' of Europe, becoming 'locked into' public consciousness of what 'Europe'/'the EU' is, and creating a legitimising political identity. However, in arguing that distinct aspects of European history were essential to our understanding of what Europe is today, the consensus appears to have been that although there are essential core characteristics, the Convention as a body could not agree on what they should be due to fundamental political, philosophical and religious cleavages within the body. It could be argued that the general feeling amongst those who wanted references to the legacy of European history was essentialist in spirit, but that the process of identity construction apparent in the process can be explained from a social constructivist perspective.

24. See the *International Herald Tribune*, 13 November 2003 for an account of the debate during the Italian presidency, and *International Herald Tribune*, 26 May 2004 for that during the Irish presidency.
25. See article in *The Guardian*, 8 November 2004, 'Buttiglione to campaign for Christian Europe', http://www.guardian.co.uk/international/story/0,,1345729, 00.html
26. The Flash Eurobarometer (The European Constitution: Post-referendum Survey in France) gives details: 6 per cent of those who voted 'no' did so because they wanted to keep Turkey out of the EU. See: http://europa.eu.int/comm/public_opinion/flash/fl171_en.pdf
27. Article 1.2 does, however, reiterate the basic EU criterion for membership, i.e. membership is only open to states.
28. Incidentally, this new check list has moved the goal posts for future accessions.
29. For a further discussion on the composition of the Convention and the representativeness of the *conventionnels*, see Chapter 4.
30. Clearly, the fact that the Constitution was rejected in both the French and the Dutch referendums, shows that many citizens were not convinced by the vision of the future EU and its fundamental values that was encapsulated in the Constitutional Treaty.

Part IV
The Convention and its Aftermath

Introduction to Part IV

The final part of this book looks at the developments after the Convention. So far, we have discussed how the Convention itself operated and how it came to produce a draft document that reflected both political pressures and some of the interests of European society. This discussion has highlighted some of the innovative features that the Convention experiment has brought to constitution-making in the EU, while analysing the various claims to greater democratic legitimacy advanced on behalf of the 'Convention method' when compared to previous, more intergovernmental, treaty-making procedures.

The Convention did not have the final word on the Constitutional text; this remained with the national governments and with either the national electorates or national parliaments. The Convention therefore does not bear direct responsibility for what has happened afterwards, and particularly for the stalling of the ratification process. Nonetheless, the legitimacy of the Convention experiment and its effectiveness need also to be judged by the way in which the draft Constitutional text fared after the Convention. In truth, at the time of writing, the picture is still a very confused one. From a more formal perspective, the majority of member states have approved the Constitutional Treaty, and only two openly rejected it in popular referendums, while a few have decided to wait for clarification on what the way forward is likely to be. But, the fact that final ratification is dependent on each member state ratifying it – as is typical of international treaty making – means that in effect the ratification process has so far failed. In this respect, the European Constitution can, to all intents and purposes, be declared dead, in spite of some new attempts to revitalise it.

And yet, as should be clear from the first three parts of this book, this is neither the whole of the story nor the end of it. The two final chapters of this book are therefore an attempt – though a preliminary one – to assess the immediate impact of the Convention and of its work, when judged from either a legal or a political perspective. Chapter 11 engages with the significance of the Constitutional Convention from the point of view of its effects on the 'living law' of the European Union. It suggests that, on the whole, there are two ways in which the Convention has contributed to the EU's 'living constitution'. First, by acting as the focal point of a European symbolism that may indeed strengthen, as many tend to believe, the constitutionalisation process of the Union. From this perspective, however, the chapter highlights one of the main limitations of the Convention, already raised in the course of this book, namely its fundamental ambiguity between a technical exercise in legal and institutional 'simplification' and an ambitious 'new beginning' of a more radical political integration. The second main effect of the Convention on the 'living law' of the EU is the way in which the work of the Convention has resonated in the more ordinary process of EU legislation and legal development, interacting with the EU consolidated 'constitution' on a number of important issues (from citizenship to access to justice), but also providing some (indirect) opportunity for further development and consolidation, even though the Constitution itself has not yet been ratified. Here, the analysis returns to the problem of the relationship between 'constitutional moment' and 'constitutional process' already discussed in Chapter 2, suggesting that, certainly from a legal perspective, it is not always clear where constitution-making and constitutional debates take place, and that the 'living law' may not always look like that 'mapped' by documentary constitutions as they are drawn by constitutional conventions.

The concluding chapter briefly charts the progress of the Draft Constitutional Treaty (eventually the Treaty establishing a Constitution for Europe) from the final phase of the Convention to the IGC and finally to the turbulent, and still unresolved, phase of national ratification. It discusses some of the political dynamics and the issues at the centre of both the IGC, and of the ratification debates in France and the Netherlands, which have produced a decisive, though highly ambiguous and partly inconclusive, defeat of the Constitutional Treaty project. This discussion is important because it highlights the still unresolved problem of the nature of the EU and how its decision-making mechanisms, even at the constitutional level, tend to oscillate between supranational and intergovernmental directions. As is evident from the current discussions initiated by Angela Merkel, and the emerging compromise of a 'mini' Treaty with no need for popular referendums (suggesting a return to the old ways of the IGC), the Convention experiment has not yet opened up an entirely new phase in EU constitutional politics.

The final sections of Chapter 12 engage with the reasons for the Convention's failure to have a greater constitutional impact, and with some of the counterfactuals that may help to explain why the Constitutional Treaty was rejected in France and the Netherlands. Such a discussion is not only important to assess the effect of the Convention, but also its long-term significance for the integration process. By putting the Convention experiment in a broader political context, the concluding chapter advances the hypothesis that there is more to the present crisis than the question of whether Europe needs a 'documentary' constitution. What is at stake is what European citizens and European peoples think Europe means to them and to their lives.

11
The Convention and the 'Living Law' of the European Union

Miriam Aziz

As the concluding chapter will argue in more detail, in spite of the great amount of work and effort put in by all those involved in the Constitutional Convention, the constitutional text they produced has not (or at least not yet) become the hoped-for Constitution of Europe. Should we therefore conclude that such an elaborate exercise in constitution-making was pointless? Even if the present Constitutional Treaty is never ratified, there are at least two reasons for believing that the Convention experiment was not in vain. The first relates to the role that symbolism plays in the process of constitutionalisation, a role that should not be overstated any more than it should be understated. In the case of the Constitutional Convention it is difficult to assess the impact of symbolism because it was never clear whether the Convention experiment was meant to generate the political will for a full constitutionalisation of the European Union, or merely as a way of reforming the *acquis communautaire*. The second reason for not writing off the whole experiment concerns the 'spill-over' effect of constitutionalisation produced by the very happening of the Convention, and the way in which there has been a reciprocal influence between the Convention process and the Community method, affecting the 'living law' of the existing Treaties and of the *acquis communautaire*. This is, for instance, the case with regard to EU citizenship, which has arguably evolved in the context of the free movement legislation, in a rather complex relationship with the 'constitutional moment' inspired by the Convention experiment. This chapter discusses the way in which the Convention has either affected or failed to affect the 'living law' of the European Union. It does so from a more legal perspective and by developing some of the arguments about the EU Constitution as a 'moment' and as 'process', which were discussed in Chapter 2 from a more political perspective. The aim of this chapter is therefore to assess the Convention's legacy on EU law, regardless of whether the Constitutional Treaty comes into effect or not.

Between symbolism and reform

Symbols are representative of the values espoused by a particular community at a particular time. This is nowhere more so than in the case of constitution-making, in which the members of a community and its representatives, through a collective covenant, seek to (re)affirm the principles, aims and objectives upon which their joint enterprise is based. Such a covenant is one in which the members of a community seek to assert their shared identity, that is to say, a common sense of the characteristics that all those belonging to the 'people' seem to share. The assertion of a common identity can take the form of either 'We, the People. . .', as in the Constitution of the United States, or 'We are the People. . .' ('Wir sind das Volk. . .'), as proclaimed by the people of the former German Democratic Republic in the run-up to German unification. As also discussed in Chapter 10, the role of values as part of this search for a common identity is central because, in their aspirational sense, values contribute to generate a certain commonality, and, by extension, they create the perception people have of being engaged in a joint enterprise. Conversely, values are also generated *by* the community as reflections and refractions of a common sense of belonging.

A constitutional moment, such as the Convention experiment appeared to be, provided the opportunity for both debating and deliberating about the sense of common belonging amongst the peoples of Europe. It also made it possible to discuss whether references to religious beliefs or to values such as peace, equality and the respect for cultural diversity should be considered part of that shared sense of belonging and inscribed in the constitutional text. The Convention as a constitutional moment gave the opportunity to scholars of European integration to observe, consider and evaluate the role of values as part of the process of constitutionalisation of the Union.

In general, the process of adopting a constitution can be considered a method for mobilising a community (Habermas, 2001). In the absence of a European demos (Grimm, 1995: 282), the Convention seemed to function as a catalyst for the generation of a political community, through a process of deliberation in which the 'learning and the alteration of preferences' were promoted (Eriksen and Fossum, 2000b) and common values formed. A number of European politicians expressed views reinforcing such an interpretation of the Convention's function. One delegate to the Convention characterised it as an opportunity to 'think about the whole of Europe'.[1] Pat Cox, the then president of the European Parliament, spoke of the Convention as a revolutionary and decisive phase of democracy in Europe. Romano Prodi, who was the head of the Commission, regarded the Convention as the moment when the European peoples were trying to define the reasons for being together, acknowledging, on the world stage, their responsibility for the promotion of peace and development, and on the internal stage, their willingness to defend a balanced society, capable of reconciling economic development with social solidarity, liberty with security, thus making Europe a model for others to imitate.

In partial contrast, other politicians and delegates to the Convention interpreted it as having a narrower scope. At the very beginning of the Convention's deliberations, Giscard d'Estaing stated, for instance, that the EU's decision-making machinery had 'become more complex to the point of being unintelligible'. In this way he conveyed the impression to the general public that the mandate of the Convention was to be interpreted mainly as that of introducing institutional reforms. In many of his public utterances he made other references to the 'sclerotic EU decision-making process', suggesting that the Convention needed to come up with 'fundamental reforms'. Whilst admitting that the constitution-making process needed to transmit a strong sense of belonging to the EU (though not in opposition to national identity), and that it needed to involve Europe's youth, Giscrard emphasised the role of the Constitutional Treaty in modernising the institutions.[2] José Maria Aznar's opening remarks to the Convention took a somewhat similar line, when, speaking as the then Spanish prime minister, he described the main function of the Convention as that of completing the reforms of the EU institutions, which had partly failed at Amsterdam and Nice. There were also pleas within the Convention to proceed with caution and modesty, since some delegates worried that too much was being attempted, too quickly and indiscriminately. With reference also to the EU in general, less is more, they argued,[3] a position that was to re-emerge later in the ratification phase, and that profoundly divided some political parties in Europe, particularly the French socialists.

In short, the Convention seemed to mean different things to different people, straying dangerously towards trying to be all things to all people. Part of the reason for the different messages was that they were addressed to different audiences and, ultimately, to different electorates. In that sense, the Convention was an accurate reflection of the way in which European politics is segmented into different constituencies which do not always operate within the same public space or frame of political discourse. This difference of audiences and messages produced very different rhetorics: one preoccupied with the reform of the Treaties and of the institutional architecture of the Union – which could be called the 'reform Convention'; the other, as already suggested, of a more symbolic nature, aimed at bolstering the Union's democratic legitimacy, and at gaining (or manufacturing) the consent of the European citizens, on the basis of the adherence to the values upon which the Union is supposedly founded.

Academic commentators sought to categorise the aim of the Convention differently, thus avoiding the simple dualism between 'reform' and 'symbolism'. Thus, for example, Paul Craig distinguishes between two critical issues in the work of the Convention: the content of the reform agenda on the one hand, and the reform process on the other (Craig, 2003). Neil Walker, for his part, distinguishes four basic constitutional functions that can be attributed to the Constitutional Treaty: providing a structural design for the EU; constituting its authority; development of an episteme; and mobilisation of the community (Walker, 2005). The latter function can be linked with the emphasis of the Laeken Declaration to gain the consent of the governed. This recommendation, which was variously interpreted as either the duty to provide information or the need to persuade people and ultimately gain their support, evolved into a language of political mobilisation, a language which was increasingly spoken during the IGC and in its aftermath, as became apparent during the process of nomination of the new college of European Commissioners in August 2004. Indeed, Barroso, the newly appointed President of the Commission, framed the duty of the new college in terms of both mobilising Europe and remedying the communication deficit, by claiming to 'plaider la cause de l'Europe' in order to combat both Euroscepticism and *l'euro-apathie*.[4]

But on the whole, the two main aims of the Convention often overlapped, reflecting the ambivalence already implicit in the Convention's mandate. This is clear from the reading of the text of the Constitutional Treaty as this was progressively drafted and finally approved by the IGC. In talking about the issue of democratic legitimacy, Gisela Stuart, one of the members of the Presidium, for instance, writes about the need to 'make sure that the people agree with the direction their political leaders are taking them' (Stuart, 2003: 6). The key words here are the idea of 'agreeing with the direction'. Such a formulation makes one wonder whether the European Constitution is a political declaration or whether it is a legal document. Arguably, it is both. Indeed, the process of its adoption (if it is eventually ratified in its current or in some modified form), and of its mediation, reception and implementation will necessarily take place through both political and legal conversations. Both conversations will have to reflect and deal with the two underlying aims here outlined, of reforming the *acquis* and of providing a symbolic basis for Europe.

The Convention's internal divisions and its unresolved ambiguities

The divergence between the 'reform' and the 'symbolic' Convention is evident, for instance, in the way in which the issue of simplification, which was one of the main objectives of the Convention, was dealt with. As well as being embedded in the technicalities of reform, simplification was a politically contentious issue, for it related to the Treaty texts and the Treaty architecture as a whole. The aim of simplification was to make the political and administrative process within the EU more transparent, so that the citizen could more easily understand it, and hence identify its problems, thus being able both to criticise and to control the process. All this implied a number of complex tasks such as that of codification (to give legal value to the new document), merging texts (merging two Treaties and codifying successive amendments), and restructuring the texts (to bring constitutional provisions to the fore), while abandoning the pillar structure, providing more detailed procedures and instruments, and a common and consistent terminology, so 'making the system more "readable" for the citizen and the practitioner' (De Witte, 2002: 96). This in itself was part of a more general trend towards simplifying legal instruments, as is exemplified by the proposed directive on free movement rights, the aim of which was to replace most of the present secondary legislation on free movement, that applies to both workers and the self-employed. According to the Council's common position reached in December 2003, the nine directives on the free movement of Union citizens currently in force shall be replaced by a single directive on the right of citizens of the Union and their family members to move and reside freely within the territory of the member states, based on Articles 12, 18, 40, 44 and 52 EC.

A further example of overlap of the two main aims of the Convention is found in the working group on economic governance, where references to social justice were sparing. The mandate of the group was three-fold: monetary policy, economic policy and institutional issues. Those members of the group who favoured inclusion in the Draft Constitutional Treaty of references to full employment, to social and regional cohesion, and to a better balance between competition and public services in a social market economy, were less persuasive than those who favoured the importance of the inclusion of a reference to sustainable growth and competitiveness. Some wished to separate, for example, employment from social policy.[5] Others argued that economic policies should include not only monetary policy, but also fiscal and social policies (including education, health care, pensions and employment), even envisaging the necessity of setting minimum levels of benefits and services and benchmark tax tariffs at the Community level and the convergence of welfare policies.[6]

Generally speaking, it was felt that most 'social issues', such as social dialogue, ought to be discussed by the Convention as a whole. The main bone of contention was not, as one might have expected, the issue of social justice, but that of whether the Open Method of Co-ordination (OMC) should be inserted into the Draft Constitutional Treaty.[7] The evaluative criteria regarding the constitutionalisation of OMC shifted interchangeably from one goal to the other as part of the different types of conversations going on during different phases of the constitutional moment, with the emphasis moving away from detailed reform to trying to produce a symbolic consent. As stated by the outgoing president of the European Parliament, 'We've now adopted the constitutional treaty politically; the time starts now to explain it to the public, to sell it and to ratify it.'[8] In effect, there were repeated attempts to separate technical issues from issues requiring further political debate, which created tensions in the aftermath of the adoption of the Constitutional Treaty during the battles for ratification.

A further case in point was the working group on the Charter chaired by Antonio Vitorino. The mandate of this group stressed the need to avoid the 'major political questions' such as incorporating the Charter or acceding to the ECHR. According to Vitorino, these should be left to political debates in the plenary sessions 'on the assumption that these two questions will meet with a positive political response' (Norman, 2003: 86). The implicit understanding amongst members of the Presidium to leave the *acquis communautaire* untouched, or at least to treat it deferentially, suggests, as also discussed in Chapter 5, that the *dirigisme* at work was partly due to the tight timetable with which the Convention was saddled, but also because it was harnessed for the purposes of limiting or at least containing debate which could prove to be too contentious (Stuart, 2003: 6; Kokott and Rüth, 2004: 1319). The way in which the 'explanations' relating to parts of the *acquis* furnished by the Presidium were introduced reveals a tendency towards diplomacy, whilst also constraining dissent. Thus, for example, the updated explanations relating to the Charter of Fundamental Rights of 9 July 2003 stated from the outset that, 'although they [these explanations] do not as such have the status of law, they are a valuable tool of interpretation intended to clarify the provisions of the Charter' (CONV 828/03).[9] Whereas it was agreed from the outset that the substance of the Charter would not be altered, adjustments were made to Articles 51 and 52, which is the reason why the Presidium asked Working Group II to prepare a report on the Charter. However, the explanatory note covers the entire Charter and does not merely address Articles 51 and 52. The message to member states was that the Charter would not extend the Union's competences or powers. Thus, the Convention's proposals would not, as Jack Straw put it in remarks addressed to the House of Commons, 'alter the fundamental constitutional balance between the Union's institutions and the member nation states'.[10]

The issue of 'taboo' subjects had already arisen prior to Nice in the context of taxation, the environment, social justice and matters pertaining to the second and to the third pillars. As regards timing, one must remember that not only was time at a premium but also, unlike in the case of the IGC, the Convention was mandated to come up with a text, and not simply, as in the case of the *travaux préparatoires* of Nice, to indicate and propose a host of options for reform. Notwithstanding this, the tactical advantages of forcing the pace must not be underestimated, and neither should the tactic of agenda setting in a time-limited context. Other previous examples of tight chronology, arguably bulldozing potential for dissent by member states, can be seen in the Commission's timetable for the completion of the internal market, and the brinkmanship of negotiating institutional reform prior to the Nice summit in 2000.

There were underlying tensions and signs of dissent in the final reports of the working parties, where reference was often made to what 'some felt', instead of talking of majorities versus minorities. Of course, at times dissent was vociferous, as reported by the press and the media.[11] But dissent was neither effective nor far-reaching, leading one to wonder just how this can be squared with the attempts to foster open debate in the name of democratic legitimacy. Time to express one's opinions in the Convention was extremely limited, each delegate being allowed interventions of no more than two or three minutes.

There was, however, a diversity of approaches to constitutionalism as a whole. This diversity reflected national and professional views regarding constitutionalism and the idea of a constitution as a political and/or legal document and as a political and/or legal process. The absence of a common terminology to describe it is notable. This leads one to wonder to what extent legal and political elites sometimes spoke at cross purposes. There was also a diversity of political ideologies. Members of the Convention, such as the MEPs, national parliamentarians, government representatives, political caucuses such as the European People's Party, the Socialists, the Liberal Party and so on, vehemently differed on the model of liberalism upon which the European project ought to be based. Thus, for example, the working group on economic governance illustrates the divergence between the neo-liberal Anglo-Saxon approach and those who espoused an approach which supported greater integration of economic policy regarding the euro. Indeed, this was reported as being one of the first major impasses of the Convention.

In the past, the divergences and inherent ambiguities of the debate concerning the European integration project have been addressed within the context of a discussion of legitimacy. The problem has been seen in terms of the need for wider participation: 'A more open and wider process of consultation and information, even one which reveals the divisions over the nature and direction of European integration today, needs to take place, instead of one which is confined to self-selecting groups and elites.'[12] The key phrase for the purposes of our analysis is 'even one which reveals the divisions'. It is precisely this that has been mostly neglected, also because the question of the divisions of views and values is a moving target – nonetheless, this is a question that needs to be taken seriously as part of the analysis of the process of constitutionalisation. In the Convention, as we have seen, the major difference of opinion was between those who wanted the Constitutional Convention to limit its role to reforming the *acquis communautaire*, and those who wanted it to mobilise the consent of the European citizens around a set of shared values. In the event, such a divergence ended up by creating a fundamental ambiguity over the function of the Convention itself.

Simplification and the constitutional debate: the case of EU citizenship

Whether as part of the reform process or of the construction of consent, the main aim of the Convention as indicated by the Laeken Declaration was, ideally speaking, an exercise in simplification, thereby reducing the state of alienation of the EU citizen *vis-à-vis* the Union. In this respect the Convention arguably mystified more than it simplified by either saying too little (about practical, day-to-day implications for the citizen concerning the adoption of a European Constitution) or too much (as in the case of the plethora of legal instruments proposed as part of the simplification exercise) or nothing whatsoever (as on questions of access to justice for EU citizens, standing requirements, legal aid and so on) (Constantinesco, 2004: 223).

Reminding EU citizens that they are rights bearers is one thing. Translating such a status in real terms is quite another, particularly as the more rights instruments are available, the more confusion there is. Indeed, in the Constitutional Treaty there is a plethora of rights instruments, which makes its rights architecture somewhat unclear. The relative silence concerning access to justice is regrettable as substantial reform of the judicial system of the Union is arguably part and parcel of the EU's constitutionalisation process (Alonso Garcia, 2002: 507). The rules on *locus standi* or standing for direct actions before the European Court of Justice and the Court of First Instance are deficient. There are no provisions regarding legal aid, and the extent and degree of justiciability of the rights contained in the Constitutional Treaty are unclear. Whereas the European Court of Justice was represented in some of the meetings of the Convention, national judges were not involved. This omission is worrying, particularly as it is these judges who will be responsible for the implementation of the Treaty if and when it is adopted, just as they are already partly responsible, alongside member state public officials, for the recognition and implementation of the *acquis communautaire*. Here also, the Convention omitted to address the need for legal measures regarding implementation or monitoring at great length, despite the reference to 'effective and better implementation of Union objectives and priorities' in the Laeken Declaration (Lenaerts and Desomer, 2003: 114); something that is in keeping with the tradition of procedural issues evolving on an ad hoc default basis, as in the case of European administrative law (Cassese, 2003: 104), as opposed to constitutional design (Gnes, 2001: 524). Thus, questions such as the extent to which the Constitution constructs the citizen or whether the Convention was a testament to the emergence of a European people or demos, whilst not meaningless, must be approached with caution. In fact, the citizens' presence in and around the Convention was one characterised by absence, except for the players in the Brussels lobbying circuit. Furthermore, as more extensively discussed in Chapters 5, 8 and 9, the lack of information about the constitution-making process within and outside the Convention proceedings left much to be desired in terms of transparency and, by extension, accountability. One needs only to be reminded of the Convention's Futurum website, which, particularly towards the end of the Convention, was flooded with too much information, something that made its usefulness questionable. The role and influence of the Presidium in shaping the proceedings, as also discussed in Part II, was probably too great and it still remains to be clarified. For instance, at times, the Presidium proposed innovative measures on which it refused to comment. Other times, it included amendments proposed by delegates with neither discussion nor justification.[13] Thus, the absence of the citizen, the relative lack of information, and the power of the Presidium in shaping and moulding the agenda suggests that arguably the Convention's contribution to citizens' empowerment was limited.

This may become clearer when looking at the issue of free movement, which goes to the heart of EU citizenship, and on which there was a great deal of activity outside the Convention, namely by the European Commission and the Council as well as the Court of Justice. It is difficult to say whether these institutions were inspired by the Convention. It is, however, clear that as part of the intricate work of reform undertaken by the Convention, little attention was paid to the minutiae of citizenship rights such as free movement and in particular, the implications *inter alia* for social security, pensions and health care. It is arguable that other EU and national institutions have greater capacity (financial, informational, organisational and institutional resources) to do this. Indeed, this is particularly so in the case of the European Commission, the European Parliament and the Court of Justice (Oliver and Roth, 2004: 407) which have, to some extent, pioneered the process of addressing the minutiae of EU citizenship. These institutional actors command resources which bear little or no comparison with the Convention in addressing the detail of the citizenship provisions. More importantly, they benefit from experience and time. Their respective experience was not, however, consolidated. Indeed, their contribution to the Convention was severely limited not least by the agenda, the framing and maintenance of which was greatly influence by the Presidium. One is reminded of the Presidium's habit of providing a commentary to the skeleton drafts of the Constitution, and the way in which it would, for example, remain silent about many new innovative provisions of considerable importance. The early warning mechanism which was incorporated in the new text of the subsidiarity protocol is a case in point. Accordingly, before the adoption of legislation, the Commission must send proposals to national parliaments for a subsidiarity and proportionality 'audit' in order to check whether the Union is better placed to achieve the policy in question. The innovation introduced by the European Constitution regarding the early warning mechanism is that it allows national parliaments six weeks to consider Commission legislative proposals. Indeed, if one-third of national parliaments object to a proposal, the Commission is obliged to review it. It is arguably not a very strong mechanism in legal terms, but it does contain considerable political weight and thereby worthy of inclusion in the Presidium's commentary.

From the examples above, it may be evident that the Convention was given neither the time nor a sufficiently broad mandate to address issues which, though they might not strike the ordinary citizens as being of immediate relevance to them, are crucial to the realisation of EU citizenship. Arguably, these are issues on which it was thought that the status quo is sufficient. However, the opportunity to create an effective communicative interface amongst institutional and extra-institutional actors at the national and supranational level regarding EU citizenship was lost, something which is regrettable.

Looking at the issue of EU citizenship, one may wonder whether the EU's 'constitutional moment' failed to promote a proper constitutional debate. If indeed it failed to do so, one may wonder where else the 'real' European constitutional debate does take place. Looking at the Convention ex-post, one may suggest that, at least from a legal perspective, the law maintains a pivotal role as part of the European integration process, and that on some crucial issues such as citizenship the 'living law' of the EU was only partly affected by the Convention.

Spill-over effects

Central protagonists of the real constitutional debate in the EU are undoubtedly the judges and in particular, the European Court of Justice. The European Court of Justice has been a driving force of the European integration process (Stein, 1981; Burley and Mattli, 1993; Poiares Maduro, 1998; Stone Sweet, 2000). It has also been assisted by lawyers and national judges who have contributed to the development of the legal integration process according to their means, and to serve the ends dictated by their case load. This has created a type of 'spill-over', the dynamics of which have fed back into the wider political environment (Stone Sweet and Brunell, 1998: 64).

The European Court of Justice, for instance, has had a key role on the evolution of EU citizenship. In some policy areas, many of the decisions the Court has taken have been far-reaching, as in the case of cross-border access to social security, health care and education (Van Der Mei, 2002). The implications for member states, EU citizens and denizens are considerable, though at times rather confusing, since the free movement provisions, as already discussed in the previous section, are highly complex. Anyone who is familiar with the free movement provisions will testify to the maze of provisions which are highly detailed and cumbersome to navigate, particularly in the context of cross-border access to welfare. Not only is it impossible for the citizen to understand what their rights are, it is also difficult for national public authorities to grasp the extent of the duties which arise as a consequence of the free movement provisions. It is also difficult for lawyers and judges who have to deal with the provisions. Errors can be costly to particular individuals, who stand to lose out on social welfare provisions and pensions. Moreover, public authorities can be sanctioned for failure of implementation or faulty implementation of the *acquis de l'Union*.

The citizens as well as legal and administrative elites are all too often faced with a labyrinth of legal minutiae, which are often both contradictory and uncertain. Indeed, an exercise in simplification would have been worthwhile.

The Convention omitted many of these issues, something which is regrettable not least because it could have included them as part of its detailed reform work, as well as being seen to bridge the gap between the citizen and the Union, in both symbolic and substantive terms, very much in keeping with the spirit of the Laeken Declaration. Whereas EU competence as regards free movement is widely defined, given that it is framed under the aegis of the internal market, many of the consequences which arise from free movement, such as the impact on social welfare systems of the member states (concerning, for example, access to social security, health care, education), are such that they were addressed in more modest terms by the Convention, so to respect the sensitivities of the member states. Moreover, there appears to have been an understanding amongst the *conventionnels*, arguably generated by the Presidium, that the *acquis communautaire* should not be tampered with, though accounts of this tend to vary (Stuart, 2003). It is certainly the case, however, that the *acquis* was treated with deference.

As previously noted, the free movement provisions are key components of EU citizenship, something which has been recognised by the ECJ. Furthermore, the European Commission championed their simplification throughout the duration of the Convention. For its part, the Constitutional Treaty contains provisions in Parts I, II and III, which act as a restatement of the general right to free movement for EU citizens.[14] If the Constitution ever enters into force, the wording of Article 18 (1) EC will be restated within a dimension which emphasises the fundamental rights character and the direct effect of the right of free movement. Generally speaking, the Constitution does little to alter the status quo regarding the free movement provisions. Even the authorisations to enact secondary law, such as European laws or framework laws regarding *inter alia* passports, identity cards, residence permits and social security or social protection may only be adopted on the basis of unanimity in the Council after having consulted the European Parliament (Article III-9).

The innovations that were discussed in very general terms in the Convention have, however, been implemented through the 'ordinary' means of the community method by the Commission (Scheuing, 2003: 744). The Convention, to some extent, created a catalyst for the generation of secondary legislation in an area that has traditionally been highly contested. This was not a simple coincidence, since it was in May 2001 that the Commission adopted a proposal for a comprehensive new directive designed to streamline the existing provisions for the right of free movement of Union citizens.[15] This proposal had already been announced in 1993 and was eventually submitted to the Council in July 2001, with the Commission amending the proposal in April 2003 in pursuance of the first reading of the European Parliament. The Council finally adopted a common position in December 2003.[16] In effect, the Council proposes to replace the nine directives on the free movement of Union citizens by a single directive, which contains a number of innovative measures. In particular, if a Union citizen has resided legally and continuously for five years in the host member state, he or she shall have the right of permanent residence. The proposal covers citizens as well as their family members which includes registered partners (if the host member state regards registered partnerships as being equivalent to marriage). The Council also drew inspiration from the ECJ's decision in *Grzelczyk* in stating that Union citizens and their family members shall have the right of residence as long as they do not represent an unreasonable burden on the social assistance system of the host member state.

The potential impact of this kind of legislation on national legal and administrative cultures is considerable and constitutes a significant challenge to member state sovereignty. One is reminded of the transfer of asylum policy to the first pillar subsequent to the Treaty revisions introduced at Amsterdam, which substantially Europeanised member state competences regarding immigration to the extent that asylum policy was included under the aegis of free movement (Monar, 1998; Hailbronner and Thiery, 1998; Marschang, 1998; Guild, 1995). The realisation that there is an impact of free movement of citizens on national regulations concerning immigration as well as naturalisation laws was more gradual. In the case of Germany, for example, many commentators have only recently started to realise the extent to which the Foreigners Law or *Ausländergesetz* has been Europeanised. This area has traditionally been a source of conflict, particularly regarding regulations concerning spouses of EU citizens who are third country nationals (Alber, 2004: 313). The *Ausländergesetz* emphatically denies rights of residence to this category of individuals. EU policy concerning third country nationals is, however, less coherent, providing room for interpretation, and giving rise to new tensions between EC and national laws.[17] The Convention could arguably have clarified matters pertaining to the practice of citizenship in connection with the free movement provisions. It chose not to go into too much detail, possibly because of the likelihood of conflict between member states which might not have been reconcilable or might have created difficulties in reaching consensus on other issues.

As we can see, although the Commission was marginalised in the Convention experiment, it maintained its role as one of the key players in the constitutionalisation process. Much of the legislation that was pushed through via the community method throughout the duration of the Convention had some spill-over effects. Another interesting example is the coexisting policy development of pan-European research initiatives as part of the European Research Area (ERA) funded by the European Commission's 6th Framework programme, which was framed by the twin objectives of employment and competitiveness in the EU.[18] Prior to the amendments to the constitutional text introduced at the Naples summit by the Frattini draft, Article III-146 concerning technological research and development included a reference to encouraging the Union to become more competitive at 'international level', which was arguably framed in intergovernmental terms. The Frattini draft dropped this reference to the development of international co-operation altogether, and placed the Article on the 'firmer' footing of the community method, by making references to the internal market. This was 'firmer' ground, to the extent that the closer policy initiatives are to the achievement of the internal market, the more extensive EU competence is framed and by extension the less need there is to obtain unanimous approval of research programmes funded by the Union. For its part, the Article refers to the circulation of researchers, scientific knowledge and technology and the competitiveness of industry.[19] Moreover, the Frattini draft contains references to the necessity of implementing measures for the European Research Area, which were not included in the original draft Treaty but are almost verbatim from the European Commission's policy and legislative documents, which came to the fore in the context of the moratorium on stem cell research.[20]

The constitutional debate surrounding the European Constitution must therefore be understood holistically, that is to say in the wider context of both the community method and the intergovernmental process. Not only does it surface at the level of the 'top down' community method, but it also arises in an altogether more nuanced manner through implementation, since this is vital for ensuring that rights and duties contained in the *acquis de l'Union* do not become insignificant, something which would undermine the rule of law and by extension erode the trust of the citizens towards the law. How else, it might be argued, might the gap between the citizen and the Union be bridged than through ensuring effective implementation of the *acquis*? Such a more nuanced and holistic approach to EU constitutionalism, which gives due prominence to the effective implementation of the *acquis*, has clear ramifications for the future of the European Constitution to the extent that it goes some way towards ensuring that it does not become a 'paper tiger'. Whereas echoes of these sentiments are visible in the Laeken Declaration, they seemed to disappear from the main deliberations of the Convention, except implicitly in some of the rare discussions concerning access to justice, to which it is interesting to turn in order to see another aspect of the way in which the 'constitutional moment' of the Convention and the European 'living law' interacted (or failed to interact).

Access to justice and the Convention's limits

Strictly speaking, debates concerning access to justice in the EU are a rarity. There are few references to it in the Treaties; moreover, it is not the foremost consideration of either national or supranational policy-makers. Little time was accorded to justice during the Convention, which is a curious omission given that it is a central component of the relationship between the citizen, the EU and the public authorities of the member states. Discussions concerning access to justice have tended to frame the issue too narrowly and superficially, both in the context of scholarship and also at the coal-face of policy-making and implementation. The community of legal scholars concerned with European integration have largely focused on remedies and sanctions in a framework in which socio-political considerations and constraints posed by the 'living law' are mostly absent (Szyszczak, 1996; Biondi, 2000; Chalmers, 1997: 167). The tensions posed by access to justice have, more often than not, been framed in the quantitative terms of the excessive case load of the ECJ.

Access to justice should be distinguished along the following lines: first, how a plaintiff has access to a court; secondly, the interaction with the actual phase of judicial deliberation; and thirdly, the consequences of the judgement (implementation, monitoring, compliance, enforcement mechanisms). Each of these phases is dependent on resources (financial, informational), capacity (institutional, personal) and co-operation (of public authority officials, legal, political and business elites). They each contribute, in their own way, and according to their own constraints, to generating trust, that is to say, to produce compliance on the part of the citizens towards the law, in this specific case to the *acquis de l'Union*. Let us consider each of these issues in turn within the European context.

The European Court of Justice has contributed to the development of access to justice through its decisions concerning the preliminary reference procedure (Article 234 EC), infringement proceedings (Article 226 EC) and administrative adjudication (action for annulment according to Article 230 (4) EC) and failure to act under Article 232 (3) EC. The difficulties associated with these provisions have tended to focus on standing or *locus standi*, which the ECJ has tended to construe narrowly and, at times, inconsistently (Arnull, 2000). The inconsistencies have tended to arise in circumstances where individuals, whilst not being addressees, were nonetheless affected by a given EC act. They were, however, precluded from challenging the act under Article 230 (4) EC, because they did not satisfy the so-called *Plaumann* test.[21] The introduction of the principle of effective judicial protection was developed under the aegis of an opinion by Advocate General Jacobs in his opinion in *UPA*,[22] and it was this that was drawn upon by the members of the Convention in drafting a number of provisions of the European Constitution.

Once the admissibility criteria have been fulfilled the second issue arises, namely, the judicial proceedings of the European Court of Justice, which favour actors who are at ease with the context in which it operates, that is to say, a juridical environment which is multi-national, multi-lingual and multi-'jurisdictional'. It is a culturally diverse legal sphere. It is one in which the working language is French, there are no dissenting opinions, and the judgements reflect the rich tapestry of juridical rules, principles, customs and etiquette drawn from the diverse legal traditions of the member states. Indeed, it is a melting pot of legal reasoning (Mancini and Keeling, 1995). Generally speaking, lawyers who are able to navigate the expansive and complex body of European Community law by force of habit are few – though that is likely to change given that EC law is now a compulsory part of legal education in most EU member states, either in its own right, or as a component of a variety of subjects, such as Employment, Commercial, Environment, Constitutional and Administrative Law. However, mere knowledge of the *acquis* is not enough, it must be mastered in practice. Working knowledge of the *acquis* gained by the rough and tumble of legal practice which includes submissions to the European Court of Justice is possessed by few legal practitioners. Indeed, in the United Kingdom, most 'European Work' is referred to specialist law firms in London, who in turn refer the cases to a handful of barristers' chambers. This is also true in other member states. In Italy, for example, it has been noted that the closer the administrative tribunals were to Rome, the more recourse was made to the EC Treaties and in particular to the preliminary reference procedure (Gnes, 2001). Several empirical investigations exist concerning the preliminary reference procedure (Stone Sweet et al., 1998). There is no doubt that further investigations of this kind are needed, particularly regarding the legal instances across the entire legal spectrum (that is to say, across the multi-levels of courts and tribunals) and not just the higher courts, particularly in view of the consequences of the *Köbler* decision of the European Court of Justice.[23] Accordingly, lower national courts enter into the fray of adjudication concerning damage caused to individuals by infringements of Community law which includes assessing alleged infringements of their own highest national courts. Future research agendas must also take into account the need to monitor the practices in the new member states. The data which has been compiled so far reveals that access to justice by EU citizens is a question of 'hit or miss', that is to say, much depends on whether their legal representative is conscious of the European dimension of the legal complaint, or indeed is able to 'create' a European legal dimension as part of innovative legal reasoning.

As regards the third issue, namely, implementation, it has generally been addressed in an ad hoc manner by a plethora of institutional actors in a variety of policy spheres. Most models of implementation of the *acquis* have focused on compliance, the monitoring of which has tended to be affected rather sporadically, emphasising specific policy areas, such as the internal market, EU environment policy (Levy, 2000; Jordan, 1999: 69), competition law, anti-discrimination, and fundamental rights. Implementation of the *acquis* is rendered complex by the disaggregation of sites of legal, political and administrative authority across national, supranational and international lines, which arises as a consequence of implementation of EU policy. We are faced by a multi-level 'network of interrelationships' existing between the different instruments and actors (McCrudden, 2000: 499) particularly in the case of comitology (Joerges and Vos, 1999; Dehousse, 2003: 135) and in the role that European agencies play in the European administrative space (Chiti, 2000). Not only is the system opaque but it lacks accountability, the implications of which are mainly two-fold. First, its credentials concerning democratic legitimacy are questionable. Secondly, a system which is opaque and lacks accountability is one which is unable to provide legal certainty. In order for rights, duties, interests and obligations to be relied upon, their content and their articulation must be clear and transparent, that is to say, capable of being understood and of being enforced, an issue which has been addressed primarily by the European Court of Justice.

The principle of effectiveness has been recognised as a general principle of Community law by the Court of Justice (Tridimas, 1999).[24] It is also referred to in the Treaty (Article 226 of the TEU) and has been incorporated in the Constitutional Treaty, notably in Articles I-28 (1) and II-47. We know little about what actually happens in practice given that we do not have the means to monitor this effectively. Substantive issues concerning effective implementation were not at the forefront of the concerns addressed by the delegates of the Convention, nor were they central to the deliberations during the intergovernmental conference. For their part, legal scholars have omitted to address the issue in detail. It has been the European Court of Justice which has championed the cause, albeit more by implication, as part of its decisions on *inter alia* state liability and infringement proceedings, than directly. By contrast, the importance of monitoring has been recognised in certain policy areas such as the enlargement process, anti-discrimination, competition law and fundamental rights. It is difficult, however, to evaluate the data properly, given the different mechanisms of implementation, monitoring and enforcement which exist in a variety of legal and administrative fora across regional, national, supranational and international lines. Furthermore, whereas the data gathered may be indicative, it is by no means conclusive about the general trends concerning implementation of the *acquis*, a legacy which the European Constitution will have to come to terms with, if it is eventually ratified.

Access to justice *per se* was not addressed by the Convention in great detail, apart from the incorporation of a right to an effective remedy contained in Article II-47, which refers to 'effective access to justice'. However, there were other issues that were relevant to access to justice, namely, simplification, the incorporation of the EU's Charter of Fundamental Rights, and the possibility of extending the jurisdiction of the European Court of Justice. Moreover, the recalibration and reconfiguration which the European Constitution will engender between the sources of rights and duties also impacts upon those actors whose duty it is to interpret and implement constitutions, namely, judges who in this context are key actors to the extent that they are 'duty bound' to enforce Community law, under the aegis of Article 10 EC. This has been taken up in Article I-5 (Relations between the Union and the Member States) of the Constitutional Treaty, which formulates the 'duty' in terms of the respect of the national identity of the member states, of the principle of loyal co-operation and mutual respect, and of member states' duty to guarantee the fulfilment of those obligations flowing from the Constitution, or resulting from the acts of the institutions of the Union (Temple Lang, 1997, 1998, 2001). There is no explicit mention of a 'duty' to enforce Community law, nor does this appear in the subsequent Article dealing with the primacy of Union law. However, it can be deduced and derived from the case law of the European Court of Justice such as, for example, the duty to protect Community fundamental rights in the sphere of Community law and the duty to refer questions concerning validity of Community law to the European Court of Justice.

More fundamentally, from the point of view of the work of the Convention, there are three key dimensions of access to justice in the EU that one should consider, namely: clarity, consistency and coherence. The key to clarity is the simplification not only of the Treaties, but more generally, of the *acquis* as a whole. Consistency refers to the interpretation, development and recognition of the *acquis* by institutional actors, notably by the European Court of Justice and by the national legal and administrative authorities. Coherence refers to the acknowledgement of the multi-dimensional and levels across which the rights of citizens are recognised. The importance of institutional balance, in particular the development of a matrix of courts which is able to deal with the plethora of judicial decisions, must not be overlooked. This was, to some extent, already recognised by the Treaty of Nice with its introduction of *inter alia* judicial panels, even though some have argued that this does not go far enough (Ziller and Lotarski, 2003: 67). Indeed, the impact of EU citizenship is particularly pronounced in connection to member states' administrative authorities, which for their part, may not always have sufficient capacity (informational, resources, personnel) to reconcile the tricky relationship between the EU citizen, the Union and those national institutions which are responsible for recognising and implementing European rights, duties and obligations. In addressing the issue of simplification the Convention implicitly touched on important aspects of access to justice, but without, however, tackling the issue directly. From this perspective, its influence on the EU 'living law' remains limited.

Conclusion: the role of elites

As has already been argued, judges of both the European Court of Justice and national courts have been key actors in the European integration and constitutionalisation process. The 'creation' of the EU citizen as a rights holder evolved prior to the Maastricht Treaty EU citizenship provisions, albeit on an ad hoc basis. The European Court of Justice has been pivotal in 'constructing' the identity of the citizen as a rights holder, resorting, at times, to 'dressing up' legal rights as either fundamental or human rights (Nic Shuibhne, 2002: 179). From this perspective, it could be maintained that the impact of the Constitutional Convention on EU citizenship has been minimal, at best purely or merely symbolic. As this chapter has tried to argue, however, symbolism is revelatory. Both the Convention and the Constitutional Treaty have rendered the rights dimension of EU citizenship more visible. Yet, just as symbolism can reveal, it can also conceal. In this case, what was revealed – or consolidated – was the identity of the citizens as rights holders. But the Convention experiment was less decisive on the mechanisms by which these rights holders could 'realise' their own identity, and in particular, on the intermediation that legal and administrative elites offer for the defence of citizens' rights.

It is clear that given the role of national administrations in the recognition and protection of rights arising from the *acquis de l'Union*, a recalibration and reconfiguration of elites' duties entails a certain degree of reconditioning, or 'social mobilisation' (Inglewood, 1990). It is difficult to predict how national elites will respond to a European Constitution. Are we seeing the emergence of cross-European elites and the emergence of a common way of looking at constitutions, constitutionalism and constitution-making? It is difficult to say. What is clear is that there are split loyalties, not only to the state but also to legal disciplines. Much depends on how national elites perceive the challenge posed by European law to their own national legal systems. The supremacy debate in the European integration process was revealing of tendencies that presumably will arise in relation to the European Constitution (Slaughter et al., 1998), as has already been demonstrated during the halted ratification process. Rights were central to the supremacy debate, and indeed, the primacy clause of the Constitutional Treaty does little to address the heated debates amongst jurists in the Union (Craig, 2003; Dougan, 2003). Echoes of these debates surfaced during both the Convention and the not yet concluded ratification phase in those member states where the supremacy debates were most contested.

The 'living law' generated by the Constitutional Treaty is reliant – and arguably overly reliant – on elites operating in the realm of national and supranational bureaucracies, who exercise their competence (and arguably also their incompetence) in a variety of spheres (the law, politics, commerce). This gives rise to professional profiles amongst the elites, which are of a particular nature. That is to say that there is a certain kind of legal, political and business elite who know how to 'play the system'. The question is whether their influence is excessive and if so, what can be done in order to constrain and contain their domination. After all, as is repeatedly stressed in EC competition law, it is not a dominant position in itself that is questionable, but its possible abuse. A constitutional framework which maintains an institutional balance is one which arguably provides 'checks and balances' for dominant positions to be constrained. In other words, the role of institutional and indeed extra-institutional balance is crucial. Indeed, the importance of institutional balance must be stressed in connection with EU citizenship provisions. However, the significance of the institutional balance must not be overestimated just as constitutionalism must not be overburdened with expectations which it may not be able to satisfy. The events following the

Convention show not only how European constitutionalism played back to politicians, but that the Constitution was mainly an elite political project. Moreover, many actors, such as economic actors, though key to the process of European integration, have repeatedly undercut the European constitutional framework, since they have a limited interest in it. In this sense the Convention was never the exclusive place for the 'real' constitutional debate. Locating the 'real constitutional debate' is a bit like abandoning guide books in search of the 'real' country. The 'real' country of the European Constitution is the one that will eventually emerge from the 'living law' of the European Union.

Notes

1. These were the opening remarks of Danuta Hübner, then Minister for European Affairs and the Polish government representative, at a conference on 'Enlargement and the European Constitutional Process' at the European Centre Natolin on 31 January 2003.
2. Giscard d'Estaing's opinions were reported by the European press; see in particular: *Financial Times*, 1 March 2002, p. 1; *The Independent*, 25 February 2002, p. 10; *Il Manifesto*, 1 March 2002, p. 5; *Il Sole 24 Ore*, 1 March 2002, p. 5; *Le Monde*, 1 March 2002, p. 3; and *Le Monde*, 1 March 2002, p. 1. In response to a question by Andrew Duff during a meeting of the Convention on 24 May 2002, Giscard d'Estaing said: 'il faudra un texte nouveau avec une architecture nouvelle et une réécriture des articles clés', reported on the Convention's website on the plenary sessions: http://european-convention.eu.int
3. See an open letter by David Heathcoat-Amory, the Earl of Stockton and Richard Spring to the President of the Convention, 'Doing Less and Doing it Better: A Debate on Substance and Direction': CONV 592/03: 'Whatever our different views may be on the practicalities, we deserve at least a debate on what Europe should do less of, in order to do it better.'
4. Reported in *Le Monde*, 3 August 2004, p. 2.
5. See, for example, the contribution by Katiforis at WD007 WG VI at pp. 52 et seq.
6. See contribution by Follini at WG VI 3 rev at pp. 13 et seq.
7. See generally WD 015 – WG VI Coordination of National Policies: the open method of coordination.
8. Reported by BBC Online on 19 June 2004.
9. CONV 828/03. The explanations were provided to the Presidium by Working Group II.
10. On this, see 'EU Treaty: A Great Prize for Britain', edited transcript of a debate in the House of Commons by the Foreign Secretary, Jack Straw, 11 June 2003.
11. See, for instance, *Le Monde* of 31 October 2002.
12. This is from a document of the Reflection Group, mainly composed of representatives of the member states, which was established by the Corfu European Council of June 1994 to prepare for the IGC: see Bull EC 6-1994, I.25, p. 375.
13. This was, to some extent, accepted by the Presidium: see CONV 770/03.
14. In Part I, EU citizenship is referred to in conjunction to the right of free movement. Article I-8 (2) (a) provides that citizens of the Union shall have the 'right to move and reside freely within the territory of the Member States', which is reproduced verbatim in Article II-45 of the European Constitution. In Part II, the

Charter of Fundamental Rights guarantees the right of free movement of EU citizens. In Part III, competences are established to enact secondary law concerning the policies and the functioning of the Union. See Article III-9.

15. See the Commission Proposal of 23 May 2001 for a European Parliament and Council Directive on the right of citizens of the Union and their family members to move and reside freely within the territory of the Member States: COM/2001/257 final – COD 2001/0111, OJ EC 2001 C270, 150.

16. See Common Position (EC) No. 6/2004 adopted by the Council on 5 December 2003: OJ EC 2004 C 54 E, 12.

17. See Case C-370/90 *R v. Immigration Appeal Tribunal and Surinder Singh, ex parte Secretary of State for the Home Department* [1992] 3 CMLR 358.

18. To which the Sixth Framework Programme, 2002–6 was committed to developing. See Decision 1513/2002/EC OJ 2002 L 232/1.

19. Thus: 'The Union shall aim to strengthen its scientific and technological bases, with the aim of achieving a European research area in which researchers, scientific knowledge and technology circulate freely, and encourage it to become more competitive, including in its industry, while promoting all the research activities deemed necessary by virtue of other Chapters of the Constitution': CIG 52/03 ADD 1.

20. See Article III-149 (4): CIG 52/03 ADD 1.

21. Which provides that non-addressees are only regarded as being individually concerned by an EC act if they are affected by it by reason of certain attributes peculiar to them, or by reason of a factual situation which differentiates them from all other persons and distinguishes them individually in the same way as an addressee. See Case C-25/62 *Plaumann v Commission* [1963] ECR 95, 107.

22. Opinion of 21 March 2002, Case C-50/00 P *UPA* [2002] ECR I-6677, para. 36.

23. Case C-224/01 *Köbler v. Austria*.

24. See, for example, *Brasserie du Pêcheur v. Germany and the Queen v. Secretary of State for Transport, ex parte Factortame Ltd.* Joined Cases C-46 and 48/93 [1996] ECR I-1029, para. 95. Although in earlier cases, the Court referred to the 'effectiveness of Community law' rather than the principle of effectiveness. See, for example, *Amministrazione delle Finanzo dello Stato v. Simmenthal* Case C-106/77 [1978] ECR 629, paras. 18, 20. 22-3; *Factortame and Others* Case C-213/89 [1990] ECR I-2433, para. 21.

12
Conclusion: From the Convention to the Referendums and Beyond

Justus Schönlau and Dario Castiglione

In this concluding chapter, we focus our attention on the Convention's political impact. This can be assessed, first and foremost, on the basis of what has become of the Draft Constitutional Treaty prepared by the Convention. But, as argued in other parts of this book, there is more to the Convention experiment and to the whole debate surrounding it than the mere approval of a 'documentary' constitution. A proper assessment of the Convention can only be done within the broader context of the ongoing process of constitution-making in the EU.

Part of such an assessment has already been conducted in the previous chapters. In Part I we provided the normative context within which to judge the Convention, and we did so by emphasising both the tension and the interplay that there is between some specific defining 'moments' of constitution-making and the more processual way in which constitutional arrangements are established and developed. The same theme has been explored, but from a more legal perspective, in Chapter 11, where it was suggested that, although trailing behind the development of the EU 'living law' on a number of important issues to do with citizenship, the works of the Convention offered a point of reference for both EU legislation and judicial activity.

The chapters in Parts II and III have offered a more sustained assessment of the workings of the Convention, exploring the ways in which the Convention experiment represents a new turn in EU constitutional politics. This is partly as the result of a redefinition of representation in the EU constitution-making process, in so far as the Convention provides an institutionally more differentiated membership than the IGC. But it is also an effect of the greater openness in the working methods that the Convention was meant to have, both in terms of greater transparency and greater inclusion. These virtues of the Convention experiment are not, however, unmitigated. As our analysis has shown, the workings of the Convention have been characterised by a fundamental ambiguity of purpose, and by half-fulfilled promises. The Presidium, and the role that this (and particularly its president) has played throughout the proceedings, has often been pointed out as either the manifestation or the cause of the Convention's limits in giving a new direction to constitution-making in the EU. In many occasions, the Presidium acted as the practical reminder that the Convention worked under the shadow, so to speak, of the IGC, whose responsibility it was ultimately to approve the text of the Constitutional Treaty before it was put to ratification.

In this respect, it is useful to remember that, although the Convention contributed to a shift towards a more supranational direction in constitution-making, the overall process was still finely balanced between this and the intergovernmental method. The political impact of the Convention experiment needs therefore to be judged from different perspectives, taking into account both its more narrow function as a 'drafting body' for the IGC, but also its more 'democratic' functions as expression of more general European public opinion.

In this chapter, we analyse the Convention's achievements from three different perspectives. First, we enquire about the Convention's impact as a drafting body, by looking at how the draft agreed upon by the Convention was received by the IGC. In doing so, we concentrate on the institutional issues, which turned out to be at the centre of the final phase of the Convention. The Convention itself only managed to reach unstable compromises on these issues, so that they were partly renegotiated by the IGC, in some cases reversing the Convention's agreements, in spite of the fact that these had been reached through a supposedly more democratic and transparent process. Secondly, we look at the ratification process, and particularly at the reasons for the defeats of the Constitutional Treaty in France and the Netherlands. In this respect, we ask the question of whether the way in which the Convention worked was in some way relevant to the negative result of these referendums, and therefore what, if anything, could have been done to prevent such an outcome. Finally, we consider the general significance of the Convention experiment in relation to the process of European constitutionalisation and to the current phase of political integration.

The return of intergovernmental politics?

The institutional conundrum

As already suggested, the uneasy transition from the Convention to the IGC phase was dominated by persistent disagreements on institutional issues. We therefore start from a general appraisal of the institutional question, and of how it was framed as part of the Convention experiment. The basic institutional structure of the EU is normally represented as a 'triangle' consisting of the European Commission, the Council of Ministers and the European Parliament (Höreth, 2004). Although this structure has remained basically unchanged since it was adopted at the time of founding the European Communities, it has required a continuous readjustment, to maintain a certain inter-institutional balance of power, which has repeatedly been 'disturbed', partly due to the proliferation of 'lesser' institutions and the creation of new decision-making practices at the margins of this core structure, but also by successive enlargements. Some of the tinkering has taken place in the evolutionary development of the EU, mostly driven by the combined dynamics of deepening and widening. The main rationale behind institutional adaptation has usually been couched in terms of efficiency and effectiveness, but increasingly and especially since the 1990s, issues of legitimacy have been invoked to argue for improvements both in the delivery of policy output and in the organisation of popular input (Schönlau, 2005). The question of getting the institutional design 'right' has thus become one of the core challenges for the continued existence and development of the European project.

It is no surprise, therefore, that amongst the more than sixty questions listed by the Laeken Declaration (European Council, 2001) as the basis for the work of the Convention, there were a significant number concerning the reform of the EU's basic institutional structure, including the three central ones on which the Union's internal balance of power mostly depends: the weighting of national votes under qualified majority voting (QMV) in the European Council; the scope of QMV (also known as the 'national veto' issue); and the size and composition of the European Commission. Besides their obvious institutional importance, in the course of the debate, these three questions acquired an increased symbolic relevance, for they became the test case for issues of national sovereignty and of relative power within the European Union.

Indeed, QMV came to epitomise the very challenge to national sovereignty contained in the idea of European integration itself, while issues such as the weighting of votes, the use of a double majority system, and the size and composition of the Commission became the touchstone for the relationship between large and small states in the Union. In this way, issues of institutional efficiency and fairness became overloaded with issues of power and national pride.

These were not, however, the only institutional issues that the Convention had to confront. Under the broad headings of 'bringing the institutions closer to the citizens' and making the Union (institutionally) better able to shoulder its 'global responsibilities', the Laeken Declaration also contained a number of other questions with strong institutional implications, such as the role of the European Commission, how its president should be elected, the functioning of the co-decision procedure, the way in which the European Parliament is elected, the composition and functioning of the Council of Ministers, the issue of the rotating presidency, and the prospect for new institutions (such as a third chamber). In fact, as some of the chapters in Part III also indicate, a widespread perception was that issues of institutional design dominated the Convention. This was perhaps the product of the fact that they seemed to be more controversial, and also more widely reported by the media. In truth, on the institutional side the Convention was hardly innovative, nor did it suggest anything remotely radical. If anything, some of the policy-related innovations (mainly in Part III), for example in the area of justice and home affairs, and issues of 'simplification', were more so (Magnette, 2004b). Yet, it is true that institutional reforms offered the occasion for discussions of general significance on decision-making in the EU, and on the nature and scope of integration.

From the Convention to the IGC

The symbolic significance of the institutional debates may explain why the Presidium of the Convention, and in particular its president, Giscard d'Estaing, handled these issues rather cautiously during the Convention. Through his power over the agenda and the internal organisation of the Convention (see Chapter 5), Giscard tried to put a lid on the debate regarding the more controversial institutional questions. On the one hand, he refused to give in to demands from several members of the Convention to set up a working group on institutions. His argument was that institutional questions should not be treated in isolation, but should represent a sort of 'horizontal' issue to be debated by the whole Convention in plenary sessions. On the other hand, he deliberately delayed the discussion on these issues by postponing the submission of proposals concerning them until late in the process (Norman, 2003: 135). Indeed, it could be argued that Giscard would have waited even longer, had it not been for the submission of a joint Franco-German proposal in January 2003 (CONV 489/03), which included important suggestions on the Commission president, majority voting in the Council, the co-decision procedure, and the creation of a European foreign minister (Emmanuoulidis, 2004: 4). This fact reinforces the perception that, whether by accident or by intention, on some important issues the Convention preferred to wait for the member states to make the first move.

In any case, the appearance of these and other proposals in January 2003 initiated an intense debate, which became somewhat divisive as the result of what came to be regarded as Giscard's personal 'coup' on the institutional issues, when, without prior notification, he unveiled his own draft articles on the institutions to the other members of the Presidium, while at the same time leaking them to a number of journalists. As Peter Norman reports, '(the P)raesidium members were flabbergasted and furious' (Norman, 2003: 223), both in view of the breach of collegiality, and for what they considered the 'unbalanced' nature of Giscard's proposals, which made the European Council the 'highest authority of the Union', endowed it with an elected president to represent the EU on the world stage, and proposed that it should report annually to a 700-strong 'congress' consisting of one-third members of the European Parliament and two-thirds members of national parliaments. The new EU foreign minister proposed in the document would be responsible to the European Council and to its president, and be rather detached from the Commission. Giscard's proposal seemed also radically inclined towards the large member states on a number of other issues, such as the replacement of QMV with a double majority system, with a high population threshold, or the drastic reduction of the size of the Commission to 'a president, two vice-presidents and up to ten members' (Giscard's draft articles 14–19, as quoted in Norman, 2003: Annex A, 343–9).

Nevertheless, the Presidium managed to tone down Giscard's proposal before this was put to the Convention. Its members worked hard, and apparently in good faith, to find substantive agreement on a common solution on the future EU's institutions. They partly succeeded, even though the eventual proposal was presented to the Convention's plenary with a covering note stating that the Presidium itself was divided on whether or not to maintain the Nice agreement on three core issues – i.e. 'representation of the European Parliament, the definition of a qualified majority and the composition of the Commission' (CONV 691/03, quoted in Norman, 2003: 230). Such a division within the Presidium, and more generally within the plenary, carried on throughout the final phase of the Convention and beyond, as the institutional provisions continued to be the key battle-ground in the final weeks of its work. After the Athens summit on 16 April 2003, and the presentation of the draft Articles a week later, it became clear that a number of member states as well as many *conventionnels* remained unconvinced by the proposals. In particular, the division between large and small member states became more marked. In late March, a group of *conventionnels* (mainly government representatives) from sixteen small member states had already signed a submission to the Convention (CONV 646/03), arguing for 'one Commissioner per member state' and 'against a long term elected president of the European Council'. The size of the European Parliament, which the proposal fixed at 700, also came in for criticism from smaller member states. The cleavage between small and big states therefore become an important element in the debate about institutions, marking the end of the Convention and the passage to the IGC phase.

This also affected the style of debate and negotiations, which shifted markedly, as discussed in Chapter 5, towards a series of increasingly frantic cycles of debate and compromise involving different constituent caucuses and political groups within the Convention. Inevitably, a less deliberative and consensus-searching style prevailed, with different groups trying to strike more traditional 'bargains' and 'compromises' in order to arrive at some agreement. A number of important changes to the draft were thus introduced without these being subjected to intense and detailed debate in the plenary meetings.

In the end, an agreement was found on an institutional package which provided for a fifteen-member Commission with a second tier of 'junior Commissioners' (to come into effect in 2009, DCT, Art. I-25); a system of double majority based on 'a majority of Member States, representing at least three fifths of the population of the Union' (DCT, Art. I-24.1); an elected 'Chair' of the European Council (DCT, Art. I-21) with a limited mandate to organise the European Council's work and represent the EU abroad (without

usurping the competences of the foreign minister); and a significant extension of QMV in the area of justice and home affairs. The final draft text set the
maximum number of MEPs at 736 (a mere technical adjustment of the formula in the Nice Treaty of 732), and the minimum number per country at
four (two less than under Nice).

After three further weeks of discussion following the Thessaloniki summit,
the Convention officially handed over a draft text to the European Council
at a meeting in Rome on 18 July 2003. The handover was accompanied by
a declaration, which claimed amongst the Convention's achievements that
of providing Europe with stable, democratic and effective institutions:

- the European Parliament becomes the Union's main legislature. It will
  enact laws together with the Council. European legislation will be the
  product of agreement between citizens' elected representatives and States;
- the Council will have a face and a measure of durability; its President will
  organise Member States' work and will be able to plan ahead;
- the Commission, organised so as to fulfil its European role, will act as a
  driving force and the main executive. It will embody the common
  European interest.[1]

The text also called for the Italian presidency 'to conduct the IGC at the
highest political level, so as to bring it to completion . . . in December 2003',
something that tallied with the wish of the Italian prime minister, Silvio
Berlusconi, to use the signing of the Constitutional Treaty as a prestigious
testimonial for what he hoped was going to be a triumphal European presidency. To all intents and purposes, this rather showbiz view of the IGC
proved to be hopelessly unrealistic. The very reception of the DCT by the
governments of the member states was rather lukewarm. Many saw the
document merely as 'a good basis' for discussion, but without feeling bound
to respect the 'integrity' of the text as prepared by the Convention (Ludlow,
2003). In fact, the main lines of divisions between small/medium and large
states, which had come to dominate the last phase of the Convention,
re-emerged almost immediately as the main fault-line along which the member states divided during the IGC phase. So, from the outset, battle lines were
drawn over the composition of the Commission (small versus big states),
and over the double majority principle (Spain and Poland, on the one hand,
and the rest, mainly France and Germany, on the other).

The Intergovernmental Conference – I

From the beginning, the problem of timing was an issue with the IGC. When
the whole process had originally been discussed, some heads of governments,
especially the British prime minister, Tony Blair, had argued for a 'cooling
off' period after the Convention. As we have seen, this was not in the perceived
interest of the Italian presidency, due to Silvio Berlusconi's own ambitions,

but it did not find much support from other member states either. In the event, the IGC was officially opened on 4 October 2003, to allow for the accession referendums in the new member states to take place before the IGC itself started. It was, however, given a tight six-week schedule, in the hope that it could complete its work by the mid-December summit.

In the view of some, the use of the time-pressure factor was a deliberate attempt to prevent reopening the debate on the compromises reached in the Convention, particularly on some of the sensitive institutional issues. Because of the shortage of time, the IGC would end up concentrating on a small number of core issues, leaving the Convention draft almost unchanged. Thinking as much, the Italian presidency circulated a questionnaire asking the member states to make suggestions on what issues should be debated at the IGC, but at the same time urging them to exercise restraint in their requests. This advice, however, went largely unheeded, so that the IGC opened with a considerable list of issues on which member states wanted to reopen discussion. Moreover, because of the Italian presidency's decision to run most of the conference at the highest political level, with meetings of the foreign ministers and the heads of states and governments, there was no possibility of weeding out some of these issues from the agenda through preparatory meetings either at the level of COREPER, or of government representatives (Ludlow, 2004a).

In spite of the large number of issues submitted by member states for further discussion, the focus of attention was inevitably on the three central institutional questions, with the one on QMV in particular seemingly the most difficult to solve. Indeed, both the Spanish and the Polish governments made it clear that they were unwilling to accept a change to the Nice formula. The cleavage between 'large' and 'small' member states was also evident, with Austria and the Czech Republic, together with Finland and Estonia, and with the support of other small member states, insisting that the principle of 'one Commissioner per country' should be reinstated as part of the final text of the Constitutional Treaty. Similarly, the issue of small countries' minimum representation in the EP (from four to six seats) resurfaced in the discussion as the result of pressure from Cyprus, Malta and Luxembourg. These, and the question of the extension of QMV, which was resisted by the British government because of its concern to keep taxation as an exclusively national issue, proved to be the main stumbling blocks for the IGC. Moreover, it soon became apparent that the Italian prime minister, Berlusconi, lacked the necessary diplomatic skills (and political clout) to broach an agreement on such controversial issues in such a short time (Ludlow, 2004a: 7).

In spite of all this, the IGC, particularly through the meetings of the foreign ministers, made some speedy progress on the other issues on the table, so that by early December 2003 most of them had been resolved. On the institutional agenda, agreement had been reached on the fact that there would be no Legislative Council, that there should be a system of rotating team-presidencies for the different Council formations rather than elected longer-term ones, that the newly created European public prosecutor would have responsibility for investigating 'crimes affecting the financial interests of the Union' (TCE Art. III-274) rather than 'serious crime having a cross-border dimension, as well as crimes affecting the interests of the Union' (DCT Art. III-175), and that there would be an 'emergency break' for one national parliament in applying the 'simplified' move from unanimity to qualified majority decision-making (TCE Art. IV-444.3).

Yet the core institutional questions remained undecided and little discussed, until the Brussels meeting of the heads of states and governments in mid-December 2003. In these conditions, there was little chance for them to be agreed at the meeting itself, not just because of the previously mentioned problems of leadership from the Italian presidency, but also because, as it may be argued with the benefit of hindsight, some key member states, notably France and Germany, may have had no strong interest in reaching an early agreement (Ludlow, 2004a). Even though it was not inconceivable that some form of compromise might be reached on the most vexed questions, the respective positions became more rigid at the summit, on the one hand because the defence of the Nice formula had acquired a symbolic importance for Spain and Poland, and on the other hand because the German chancellor Gerhard Schröder and France's president Jacques Chirac sensed that 'the balance of power within the Union was moving so decisively in France's and Germany's favour that they stood to gain from a prolongation of the conference' (Ludlow, 2004a: 14). The latter was perhaps due to the weakening of the front of the small member states, to the UK distancing itself from the Spanish and Polish position, and finally to the approaching negotiations on the EU's budget for the years 2006–13, which would indubitably shift power towards the larger countries. In the end, the Brussels summit failed, and it was left to the Irish presidency to pick up the pieces of the constitutional debate.

The Intergovernmental Conference – II

The IGC's 'second round' took place under changed political circumstances. By the end of the Irish presidency, the political climate in the EU inspired greater optimism. This was due to many causes, not least a reduction of the internal divisions over the war in Iraq, and in part to the official accession of the ten new member states on 1 May 2004, which was widely celebrated across Europe. The European elections held in June the same year and the prospect of a new Commission (and a new Commission president to replace Romano Prodi) were also seen as signs of a fresh start. Thus, it seemed that the circumstances were more propitious for the IGC to reach an agreement on a revised constitutional text (and subsequently move to the ratification phase), and to deal with pressing policy issues, such as the revival of the Lisbon agenda and the need cut a deal on the next financial perspective (2007–13). All this made France and Germany more amenable to an agreement, even though this required some concessions on their part (Ludlow, 2004b: 8).

There was, finally, the not inconsequential fact of the change of government in Spain, which *de facto* weakened the front in support of the Nice formula on QMV. Although the new Spanish prime minister, Rodrigo Zapatero, claimed that Spain was still committed to defend the Nice formula, he was much keener than his predecessor on ending the relative isolation in which Spain had found itself during the last months of the IGC. This left the Polish government, weakened by a lingering domestic political crisis, even more isolated.

The changed political conditions, as much as changes in leadership style and in member states' attitudes, contributed to the IGC's successful conclusion in June 2004. From the very beginning, the Irish presidency had tried to limit the number of issues to be debated by drawing up a list of twenty or so questions that were still open (Emmanoulidis, 2004: 6). The prime minister, Bertie Ahern, had also arranged a series of bi-lateral meetings with other heads of governments, in order to agree on a number of 'focal points' on which to concentrate the negotiations at the foreign minister level. In this way, some progress was made, though the most sensitive questions were once more left for the concluding summit, to be held in Brussels in mid-June 2004. The latter was opened with a short document of the Irish presidency, divided into an institutional and a non-institutional section (Document CIG 82/04, 16 June 2004). This separation was significant because it allowed for the disentanglement of some issues and thus a more focused discussion.

Because of the intervening changes, it was possible for Bertie Ahern to start the discussion on the institutional agenda from the position that '(t)he principle of a double majority appeared now to be acceptable to everybody' (Ludlow, 2004a: 10). The only remaining issue was therefore to find a formula that would embody this principle without humiliating Spain and Poland, who had opposed the very idea of a population threshold in QMV throughout the previous phase of the IGC. This led to some intense haggling over the exact percentage figures of states and population on which to construct the double majority system. But more than a technical debate, informed by the likely scenarios that might follow from the use of different percentages, this was a debate about perceptions, since the central question was that of saving face. In the end, the presidency's proposal of a 55 per cent threshold for member states, and 65 per cent of the population was adopted, though it was further qualified by several 'safeguards' biased in favour of smaller member states. These were spelled out in a declaration annexed to the Treaty (Declaration 5 on Article I-25), setting a late starting date for the new system (1 November 2009), and allowing sizeable minorities who reach three-quarters of the thresholds the right to refer the issues involved to the Council in order to find some negotiated solutions. This formula, based on a similar mechanism known as the 'Ionnina compromise', which was established in 1996 and hardly ever used, can be considered an 'ugly compromise' (Bellamy and Schönlau, 2004b), in so far as it complicates decision-making unnecessarily, making it also more rigid, but it seemed to be the only way to avoid gridlock.

Having found a solution to the double majority issue, it became easier to tackle the other institutional problems still under contention. On the composition of the Commission, the decision was to delay considerably (until 2014) the application of a new system, while departing from the less than convincing proposal that had emerged from the Convention. The solution adopted – instead of the fifteen-member Commission, plus a number of 'junior' Commissioners to 'represent' the other member states – was that of limiting the number of Commissioners to two-thirds of that of the member states (after 2014), mitigated by the reiteration in a special declaration (Declaration 6 on Article I-26) of the principle that the Commission should strive to take all member states' concerns (and their geographical balance) into account. The IGC also included an 'exit option', according to which the European Council, by unanimous vote, can change the constitutional provision on the Commission's composition. The compromise reached on this issue, therefore, strikes an uneasy balance between the supranational view that the Commission is not meant to represent individual countries, and the intergovernmental balance of power logic, which is reasserted by giving the European Council the right to change the constitutional text of its own accord.

Finally, on the extension of QMV, an issue on which Britain had drawn its 'red lines', threatening the use of its veto power over the whole draft treaty, the IGC proposed the introduction of an 'emergency brake' on a number of issues under QMV, such as criminal law (Arts. III-270/III-271) and social security provisions (Art. III-136.2). The 'emergency brake' gives a member state the prerogative to refer the matter back to the European Council, and, if no agreement is found, for the country to be given an opt-out. In this, as in the case of the Commission's composition, the solution proposed by the IGC, when compared with that of the Convention, reinforces the 'intergovernmental method' against the 'community method' by *de facto* strengthening the powers of the European Council.

The Treaty establishing a Constitution for Europe

On 18 June 2004, the IGC thus concluded its work. The Draft Constitutional Treaty prepared by the Convention, and now amended by the intergovernmental conference, acquired the more definite status of the 'Treaty establishing a Constitution for Europe', and as such was eventually signed by the heads of states and governments and foreign ministers in a meeting held in Rome on 29 October. Naturally, the constitutional phase was not yet completed, for the Treaty needed to be put to national ratification in all member states. But a first assessment of the Convention's work can be made at this stage. Did the Convention make a difference as the preparatory phase for the new Treaty? How much did it influence the IGC, since the latter was not, in theory, bound to follow the draft proposed by the former? The fact that the

IGC made only limited changes to the draft text in the end testifies that the Convention did exert some influence. Giscard d'Estaing famously calculated that out of the 14 800 words of the Convention draft, 13 500 were left unchanged (quoted in Ludlow, 2004b: 20). Admittedly, Giscard must have referred to Part I of the Constitution only, since the entire text is much longer. Yet, in its substance, the observation seems correct, for the bulk of the original text did not change.

Nevertheless, if one looks at the more controversial questions on the institutional structure of the EU, the observation appears to be less convincing. As we have seen, although the Convention prepared the ground for some important changes to the EU's structure, pointing towards a more supranational direction, it singularly failed to provide a text that would satisfy all member states on such matters. As Ludlow (2004a: 3) says, the 'Convention did not and could not provide conclusive answers to any of the three issues [double majority, extension of QMV and size of the Commission]'. It thus left these questions of primary political importance to the IGC. Moreover, for all the talk of openness and deliberation associated with the 'Convention method', the IGC itself managed to arrive at a general agreement over the key institutional questions by more traditional bargaining methods (Bellamy and Schönlau, 2004a), described by *The Economist* as 'arm-twisting, obfuscation and opt-outs' (26 June 2004, p. 3).

In a sense, all this was probably inevitable. The Convention's mandate, as discussed in Part II of this book, was mainly that of a drafting body, without the power or the necessary legitimacy to impose a text on the IGC, where the ultimate power of decision-making resided. The Convention on the Future of Europe was neither a proper Constitutional Convention nor a Constitutional Assembly (as we suggested in Chapter 2). Yet, for all intents and purposes, the Convention was more than a mere technical body appointed to draft the text. Its composition was both wide and politically representative. Its methods of work were both public and open to a certain influence. As such, the Convention could pretend to some popular legitimacy, which put it in the position to force some issues onto the IGC's agenda, though not enough to force a decision on them. Its ambiguous nature, between that of a technical and a political body, reflects the ambiguity of the constitutional process as discussed in the previous chapter, between the task that the Constitution had been given to simplify the EU's legal and political structure, and that of providing a more symbolic basis for the Union.

So, the answer to our first question on the relationship between the Convention and the IGC, and how much influence the former exercised on the decisions of the latter, is a mixed one. Both in terms of methods and substance, the Convention played at best an auxiliary role to the IGC and to the 'intergovernmental method'. But its very existence, and the way in which it was composed and in which it worked, testify that the Convention experiment has contributed to a marked shift towards a more supranational way of conceiving the constitution-making process in the European Union.

The ratification test

The politics of referendums

The second test of the efficacy of the Convention experiment concerns the way in which it affected, if at all, the ratification process. Since one of the reasons for setting up the Convention was to enhance mobilisation as part of the process of European constitution-making, its influence on the ratification process is an important indicator.

There was, of course, no direct link between the Convention and ratification, both because, as we have seen, the text prepared by the Convention had to pass through the IGC, and because the ratification process was organised on a country-by-country basis, reinforcing the intergovernmental method of the IGC process. There were calls, during the period of the Convention, for the Constitutional Treaty to be put to a European-wide referendum, or at least to hold national referendums within the space of a few days, if not on the very same day. These were rejected out of hand by the representatives of many national governments as politically unfeasible and legally dubious. We shall return to this point, but this lack of a direct link between the Convention and the ratification phase does not exclude some influence of the former over the latter. In order to assess such influence, we need first to analyse the ratification process as it took place, even though this has not yet been completed at the time of writing, due to the well-known difficulties created by the negative results in France and the Netherlands.

As had been the case with the ratification of previous treaties – and in keeping with a still predominant international law view of national sovereignty and the treaty-making process in the EU – it was left to individual member states to decide the appropriate way in which each country should ratify the Constitutional Treaty. In the past, the majority of member states had chosen to do this through a parliamentary procedure, although this was not an option for both Ireland and Denmark, who are required by their own constitutional arrangements to go through a popular referendum for the ratification of international treaties that have direct internal effect. However, it soon became apparent that this time a considerable number of other countries wished to go for the referendum option.[2]

One of the first national leaders to indicate such a preference was Luxembourg's prime minister, Jean-Claude Juncker, in early 2003 on the basis of the argument that the Constitutional Treaty had a 'sovereign dimension', which necessitated a popular vote. Juncker's declaration was followed in October of that year by that of the then Czech prime minister, Vladimir Spidla, who also announced his intention to hold an early referendum on the Constitutional Treaty. In the Czech case, however, the situation was rather confused, since this option required an amendment to the Czech Constitution, which needed the support of all main political parties. But, in the situation of uncertainty characterising Czech politics of the time, it was difficult to see how such a consensus could be achieved in the short term. The situation was further complicated by the fact that Czech president, Vaclav Klaus, was at the time the only head of state in the EU who had expressed a clear opposition to the Constitutional Treaty in disagreement with the Czech government and large parts of his own party.

The Polish case was similarly complex. The referendum option was originally raised by then prime minister, Leszek Miller, in late 2003, arguably 'in the first instance as a threat vis-à-vis the representatives of Germany and France in the IGC' (Maurer, 2005: 50), to strengthen the Polish government's hand in its bargaining on QMV. Once this issue was agreed at the IGC during 2004, the possibility of holding a referendum became an empty threat, but by then it was too late for the Polish government to withdraw its proposal without losing face. Moreover, a gap seemed to have emerged between the general public, whose support for the Constitution seemed to be increasing, at least according to opinion polls, and the political establishment, which had become decidedly more Euro-sceptic during the last few years and in particular after the European Parliament elections of 2004. There was also the added complication that, in order to be valid, a referendum required a high turnout (50 per cent of those having a right to vote), which would not be easy to achieve. In order to obviate this problem, the government had planned to hold the referendum at the same time as the first round of presidential elections in autumn 2005, though eventually everything was put on hold after the Brussels summit of June 2005, when a 'period of reflection' was declared in response to the Dutch and French 'no' votes.

Both Portugal, under its then prime minister José-Manuel Barroso, and Spain had also pledged to hold referendums. But whereas the Portuguese one was put on hold after the negative results of the French and Dutch referendums, in Spain the referendum took place in February 2005, making Spain the first country to have a popular vote on the Constitutional Treaty. The use of the referendum there was supported by both the Aznar government, when it was still in power, and the opposition. The change of government in March 2004, and the more conciliatory position that Spain had taken on QMV during the second stage of the IGC, changed the political meaning of the referendum in Spain. The new prime minister, Rodriguez-Zapatero, hoped to use it to establish his pro-European credentials, in opposition to the more ambiguous role played by his predecessor. So, for Spain, there was little point to stage its referendum close to the ratification deadline, whereas an early date seemed more appropriate (Sorroza and Torreblanca, 2005).

While in all previous instances, it was the prerogative of the governments of the day to call for referendums to ratify the Constitutional Treaty, in the Netherlands this was the result of a surprise move by three MPs from the lower House, who managed to have Parliament force the referendum onto the government (Toonen et al., 2005). Indeed, this was a rather unorthodox instrument in Dutch politics, since the only previous plebiscite had been held in 1798, and furthermore 'The Temporary Referendum Act' had entered into force on 1 January 2001 and expired in January 2005, with no referendum organised in the interim period. Indeed, the use of the referendum to decide on the Constitutional Treaty was entirely ad hoc. All this may perhaps explain the somewhat 'detached' attitude that the Dutch government took in the run-up to the referendum in June 2005, thus contributing to what all observers describe as a lacklustre campaign for the 'yes' vote (Toonen et al., 2005).

Yet, in the event, the biggest surprise in terms of a pledge to use a referendum (instead of the parliamentary procedure) for the ratification of the Constitutional Treaty came from the UK, where Prime Minister Tony Blair, who had earlier rejected similar calls from the Conservative Party, decided to call a referendum on the EU Constitution in April 2004. The move was probably intended to remove the European question from discussion during the national elections of 2005; the referendum date was to be announced soon after the UK presidency (scheduled for the second half of that year), which would make the UK one of the last member states to ratify it. This would at a stroke reduce the electoral relevance of what the Labour government felt to be a difficult issue, and also, perhaps, offer it the opportunity of using the UK presidency to build consensus for the referendum. But, whether this was calculated or not, it also put intense pressure on the French president and the French government to follow suit and have a ratification referendum in France.

In fact, Jacques Chirac was already under considerable political pressure from many sides, including from the Convention president Giscard d'Estaing; as a consequence, he found it politically difficult to refuse to call a referendum, once the British government declared that it was going down that route. Accordingly, during his 14 July speech in 2004, Chirac announced that the French electorate would also have its say on the Constitutional Treaty. His hope, presumably, was that the issue of the European Constitution would split his political opponents, particularly the socialist party. In itself, this calculation was correct, though Chirac failed to appreciate the difficulties ahead, and how these would impact on his own position both in France and Europe.

It may be evident from this account that the decision to use the referendum as the ratification instrument – though almost invariably justified by appeals to the need to involve the national electorate in such an important decision and improve the democratic credentials of the EU – was often related to issues of internal politics and expediency. The more traditional ratification process, through parliamentary approval, was less troublesome, but offered very few opportunities for mobilisation, and consequently was politically 'neutral', from the perspective of party politics and national governments' internal fortunes. Also regarding the mobilisation of a European-wide public opinion, ratifications through parliaments were a non-starter. The very different national procedures for the parliamentary route made it extremely difficult to have all member states ratifying the Constitution within a very short period, as it had been suggested during the Convention by a group of 97 *conventionnels*, who had proposed to hold all the referendums simultaneously. Since such a decision was regarded as a political impossibility, the European Parliament adopted a resolution calling at least for a 'coordinated approach to the time-tabling of national ratification procedures' and suggested that 'the period from 5 to 8 May [2005] might be chosen as a suitable period for holding the planned referendum on the Constitution in the Member States, as this period would be of symbolic value, both for peace on our continent and for European integration' (Resolution B6-0067/2004, adopted 14 October 2004). Yet, the intergovernmental conference had already given a very different signal, more in line with the individual member states' intention to decide on the timing of their ratification according to national criteria, by including in TCE Art. IV-447 the target date for completed ratification in all member states as that of 1 November 2006 (i.e. two years after the signing of the Constitution). This left member states a relatively long period in which to complete ratification, giving them the opportunity to play with time, and hence try to manipulate the ratification process to their own advantage, and according to their 'internal' agenda. Moreover, by adding declaration 30 to the final text, stating that 'if two years after the signature of the Treaty. . . four fifths of the Member States have ratified it and one or more Member States have encountered difficulties in proceeding with ratification, the matter will be referred to the European Council', the IGC clearly indicated that it was theoretically possible to extend the ratification process beyond the stated deadline of the end of 2006.

The first countries to ratify the Constitutional Treaty were Lithuania and Hungary in November and December 2004, respectively. They did so by large majorities in their Parliaments. Significantly, these were countries in which there was very little public debate on the Constitutional Treaty, due also to the attempt to rush ratification through Parliament. The same was true of most of the other countries which used parliamentary votes to ratify the Constitutional Treaty, at least until the French and Dutch referendums took place.

In Spain, however, a degree of public debate and mobilisation was inevitable, due to the decision to hold a referendum. Although the electoral commission in Spain had ruled that the government had to remain strictly neutral in the referendum campaign (and withdraw its slogan 'The First with Europe', since this seemed to assume a 'yes' vote), a substantial information campaign was launched in the run-up to the February referendum. More than five million copies of the Constitutional Treaty were distributed and national and international celebrities were recruited to inform the public through the use of the mass media. Despite such efforts the turnout for the referendum was low (42.32 per cent) – the lowest in any national vote since Spain's return to democracy. Furthermore, the level of (self-declared) knowledge of the Spanish public about the EU Constitution remained virtually unchanged, with more than 85 per cent of Spaniards admitting that they knew 'very little or nothing' about the Constitution (Sorroza and Torreblanca, 2005: 5). The public opposition to the Constitutional Treaty was rather muted and reduced to a few parties on the extreme left, and some regionalist or nationalist parties (in particular in Catalonia and the Basque Country). The debate within the main parties was non-existent, and even though a few prominent foreign politicians, notably Jacques Chirac and Gerhard Schröder, went to Spain to campaign in favour of the 'yes' vote, there was never the sense that this was part of a genuine European debate.

A popular 'no'

The decision to adopt the ratification procedure used for past treaties, which left both the methods and timing of the process to the member states, and was subject to the rigid legal condition of unanimous approval, clearly reflected a strong will, on the part of the national governments, to keep the constitutional moment within the boundaries of the intergovernmental method. Arguably, it also reflected a certain political caution on the part of national governments, who were supported in this by the Commission. Indeed, both the Council and the Commission hoped to be able to stage-manage the process, so as to produce a momentum in favour of the Constitution. If this was part of the intention, however, the effect of the Spanish referendum contributed little to it, having no effect on the public opinions of those countries, like France and the Netherlands, who were preparing to vote in the following months. From the end of 2004 onwards, opinion polls in France showed a gradual erosion of popular support for the Constitutional Treaty. Whereas in September 2004, 64 per cent of those who declared to have 'decided' how to vote said they would vote 'yes', by January 2005 support had dropped to 59 per cent (IPSOS poll figures, quoted in Maurer, 2005: 29). President Chirac and his government came under increasing pressure to bring forward the referendum, originally expected for July 2005, so preventing the anti-Constitution campaign from gaining further momentum. Accordingly, the date was set for 29 May 2005, though this did nothing to halt the slump in popular support. By mid-March the opinion polls started showing a majority for the 'no' option (52 per cent against 48 per cent, see Maurer, 2005: 29), a trend that continued virtually unabated until the actual vote, which saw the 'no' prevail by 54.87 per cent against 45.13 per cent who voted 'yes'.

Although the Dutch no-campaign had a momentum of its own, the immediate proximity of the French rejection of the Treaty (four days earlier) clearly provided it with a powerful boost. It probably contributed both to a high turn-out (62.8 per cent, higher than the one for the 2004 European elections), and to a larger majority against the Treaty than anticipated (61.6 per cent 'no', 38.4 per cent 'yes'). Although the result of the referendum was legally non-binding according to the Dutch referendum law, the government had pledged that it would consider itself politically bound to the result if the turn-out was higher than 30 per cent. In the circumstances, the government was left with no alternative but to acknowledge defeat and withdrew the legislation for the formal ratification in Parliament.

The reasons for the rejection of the Constitutional Treaty in both France and the Netherlands are complex and cannot be fully analysed in the context of this book. A few things can, however, be said before we turn to a general assessment of the impact of the Convention process on the ratification phase. In the first place, it would appear that the rigid rule requiring the unanimity of all member states, combined with the 'national' dimension of the ratification process, tend to produce ambiguous results; for this produces a mixture of European and national politics that is confusing, and which plebiscites cannot unravel. Indeed, the rejection of the Constitutional Treaty in France and the Netherlands is something of a puzzle, if one considers the persistent support that the idea of a Constitution has in the public opinions of these countries, as consistently shown by opinion polls both before and *after* the referendums. The latest available data show an increase in support for the Constitution across Europe, and particularly in France and the Netherlands, where those in favour are respectively 56 per cent and 59 per cent (Eurobarometer 66: Autumn 2006; see also Toonen et al., 2005). This may suggest that perhaps the results of both referendums, though decisive in political terms, did not fully reflect the overall preferences of the two electorates. Part of the reason for this paradox is to be found in the way in which referendums work, leaving no space for more nuanced, or mid-way positions. In the French case, for instance, it was quite clear that the 'no' campaign was deeply divided on whether they were rejecting *this* Constitution at *this* particular time, or whether they wished to reject *any* European Constitution. The Dutch case may be less easy to characterise, in that general support for Europe and the idea of a European Constitution do not seem to translate into a declared willingness to vote in favour of the Constitution, if this were put again to a popular vote. This may reflect not so much an opposition to the Constitution in itself, but to its symbolic connotation. On the one hand, the Dutch electorate seems to be preoccupied by the fact that the proclamation of the Constitution, more than its content, may sanction a further erosion of national sovereignty. On the other, there seems to be a more general preoccupation with the way in which further integration in the EU may weaken the position of small states *vis-à-vis* big ones. In this sense, the Dutch 'no' would seem to express a rejection of the substantive compromises from which the Constitutional Treaty emerged, rather than a principled rejection of an EU Constitution.

The above considerations undermine an interpretation of the 'no' to the Constitutional Treaty as the expression of popular scepticism towards further political integration. But there is a second line of interpretation that it is worth considering. This is founded on the suggestion that the 'no' to the Constitutional Treaty was not so much about the Treaty itself, but about other political issues or popular grievances, so that in rejecting it, the French and Dutch electorates were giving a signal to their governments and political elites, rather than expressing a considered opinion on the Constitutional Treaty, or about the consequences of either approving or rejecting it. This observation, which echoes similar discussions about the Danish rejection of Maastricht and the Irish rejection of Nice (both of which were reversed in subsequent referendums), takes three different forms. The first is to suggest that issues of 'internal' politics unduly dominated the campaigns, and that the electorate was using the referendum as a form of protest, in order to send a message to either the government or the political class in general concerning matters that were, however, largely unrelated to the question of the Constitution. Thus in France, the vote is interpreted as expressing strong opposition to the Chirac government, but also discontent with the main opposition party, in a state of general dissatisfaction with the economic and social situation. In the Netherlands, the main 'internal' context is seen as dominated by issues of immigration and racial and religious tensions, following in particular the murder of film-maker Theo van Gogh, in the autumn of 2004. Indeed, opponents to the Constitutional Treaty, particularly those on the political right, tried to establish a link between the Constitution and Turkey's membership of the EU, thus bringing into the discussion the contentious issue of Muslim immigration.

There is some truth in this way of interpreting the 'no' votes; after all, as we have indicated, many national governments (or for that matter, opposition parties) were all too happy to use referendums to their political advantage. So, it would be rather disingenuous to suggest that the electorates were wrong in voting as they did, because wrongly motivated, without applying the same argument to the way in which national governments, or interest groups, use European politics for internal purposes. Besides, this argument seems to advance a rather elitist view of popular plebiscites, implying that the electorates were incapable of seeing the consequences of their vote and therefore acted irrationally. In truth, this may well be the case, but the argument tends to prove too much, undermining popular consultations at large.

The second form that the argument takes is that the general public are not in a position to appreciate the complexities and intricacies of the constitutional text, and that they were therefore swayed in their judgement by misleading simplifications. This argument has a variant, applying to those in France, in particular, who presented their position as a 'constructive no', motivating their rejection of the Constitutional Treaty with a demand for renegotiation of the Treaty, so as to strengthen its social dimension. The 'constructive no' is criticised as both unrealistic and disingenuous, given the fact that the constitutional text was the product of protracted and complex discussions at a European level. This criticism has a kernel of truth, particularly in so far as it challenges the view that a 'no' vote had no costs. Besides, it rightly emphasises how the campaign for a 'constructive no' was in fact abdicating its political responsibility by proposing no alternative as to how it would be possible to achieve the objective of a more 'social' constitution. However, the general argument against popular involvement in the ratification process fails to convince for very similar reasons to those already mentioned with regard to the first one, since it implies a strongly elitist conception of politics and further suggests that the function of the ratification processes was simply to rubber stamp what had already been decided at the Convention and the IGC, given the complexity of unravelling compromises negotiated at supranational and intergovernmental levels.

The third and final version of the interpretation of the 'no' as an answer to a different question is more interesting, since it is more sanguine with regard to the legitimacy of democratic input into constitutional politics, and points to the important relationship between institutional and policy issues in constitutional matters. This version accepts that the vote reflected widespread legitimate concerns with issues of European relevance, but denies that these had anything particular to do with the Constitutional Treaty. So, for instance, in France the debate focused on issues such as the Bolkestein directive for a single market in services, or the effect of enlargement on the internal labour market, or, as in the Netherlands, the consequences of extending EU membership to Turkey. Also, in the Netherlands the 'no' campaign tried to use to its advantage the lingering uneasiness in Dutch public opinion about the level of the exchange rate at which the guilder had entered the euro (Crum, 2005). In a technical sense, this argument is correct in emphasising how the approval of the Constitution had no direct relevance to any of these questions, and that therefore dissatisfaction with EU substantive policy was not to be addressed by a rejection the Constitution. If anything, it could be argued that in some cases the reverse could hold true. However, this final argument undercuts the significance of the Constitution itself by suggesting that it had no relevance to the things that people identified with the European project. As we shall see in the concluding section of this chapter, there is something to say on the relationship between the Convention experiment and the future of the European project. For the moment, we can draw our conclusions on the impact (or lack thereof) that the Convention had on the ratification process.

A period of reflection

Whatever the reasons for the popular rejection of the Constitutional Treaty in France and the Netherlands, this put the ratification process into jeopardy. In the immediate aftermath, the question was what those countries which had not yet ratified the Constitutional Treaty should do. In June 2005, both the acting president of the European Union, Luxembourg prime minister Juncker, and Commission president Barroso stated the public intention of the EU institutions for the process of ratification to continue as planned. A 'period of reflection' was called to assess the situation. In practical terms, the period of reflection (called originally for one year and later extended for a further two years) has been nothing more than a way of covering up the stalemate. The only initiative taken by the Commission has been a rather vague proposal from the communication Commissioner, Margot Wallstrom, for a 'plan D' – where 'D' is meant to stand for dialogue, debate and democracy. In the meantime, most of the countries where ratification was planned through the parliamentary route have gone through the motions and ratified the Constitutional Treaty – even though, as in the case of Germany, the process has not formally concluded, because of a pending challenge to the EU Constitution before the German Constitutional Court, which for the moment prevents the German president from putting his signature to the Treaty. However, of greater political significance is the fact that in all those countries, apart from Luxembourg,[3] where ratification was meant to take place through national referendums, the plebiscites have been put on hold until some solution is found.

From a purely formal perspective, it should be noted that with the accession of Romania and Bulgaria on 1 January 2007, both of whom had previously ratified the Constitutional Treaty, the significant threshold of two-thirds has been passed (if one includes Germany and Slovakia as having formally ratified the Constitutional Treaty). From a more political perspective, as the results of the most recent Eurobarometer (66: Autumn 2006) show, the majority of European public opinion, even in the countries that voted 'no' at the referendums, is in favour of a Constitution. These facts have kept the constitutional debate alive beyond the Brussels circle. In January 2007, representatives of eighteen countries who have already ratified the Treaty, plus two others who seemed willing to do so (Portugal and Ireland), met in Madrid at the invitation of Spain and Luxembourg, in order to argue the case against ditching the Constitution or for substituting it with some more 'technical' treaty. This has become known as the 'Constitution Plus', which stands to signify that, if anything, what is thought to be needed is a strengthened constitutional text in order to meet some of the concerns expressed by the French public during the referendum debate. On the other hand, another part of European public opinion is still firmly opposed to the Constitution as the symbol of what is seen as a bureaucratic and centralising tendency in the EU.

The way out of such a political impasse is unclear. At the beginning of its presidency of the European Council in the first half of 2007, Germany announced its intention to put the constitutional debate back on the agenda. This more or less implied the conclusion of the 'reflection period', and there is some evidence that there is general consensus that some kind of decision should be reached by the end of 2007. At the moment, a compromise solution seems to be emerging, suggesting a return to the old ways of the IGC, which would approve a 'mini' treaty comprising the main institutional proposals contained in the Constitutional Treaty, but which would not require ratification through national referendums in most of the member states.[4] Something along these lines emerged behind the scenes of the Berlin

Declaration, which suggests as an aim that of 'placing the European Union on a renewed common basis before the European Parliament elections in 2009'. Although this solution may satisfy those who want a constitution to address the institutional problems created by a greatly enlarged Europe, it would ultimately represent a new swing of the pendulum back to a more intergovernmental Europe. This is clearly underscored by the way in which the text of the Berlin Declaration was agreed, behind closed doors, and with one-to-one negotiations between the Council presidency and individual member states. This would of course be a rather paradoxical outcome for the Convention moment.

All this shows that the ratification crisis can only be solved politically. However, in the present 'constitutional' structure of the EU, political solutions are subject to rather complex legal constraints (Shaw, 2004; De Witte 2004a; Ziller, 2006), which make it difficult for any solution that is not unanimously accepted by all member states to be adopted. From the perspective of this book, whose focus is on the Convention moment, the particular way in which the EU institutions will address the ratification crisis is of little relative importance. The question we are more directly concerned with is what the crisis tells us about the Convention experiment and about the constitutional moment this was meant to embody, and whether things could have been different. In the first place, the ratification crisis testifies to the extreme difficulty of seeking popular approval at a national level for complex products of European compromises such as the EU treaties. This was not different in the case of the Constitutional Treaty, and although the experiment of the Convention was intended to enhance the democratic legitimacy of the treaty-making process, this remained ultimately in the hands of national governments, and subject to the piecemeal ratification by the member states. From this point of view, the Convention experiment did not change the treaty-making process in such a way to make a difference at a ratification level.

Could the Convention have done things differently? Short of imposing a different ratification process – something on which, as we have seen, only half-hearted attempts were made – the Convention could have influenced the ratification process in two other ways. One would have been to encourage the development of a European-wide debate, and a more distinctive form of citizens' participation in European affairs. As many of the chapters in this book illustrate, in spite of the more diffuse representation of voices and the greater openness of proceedings that characterised the 'Convention method', this did not translate into a much higher level of citizens' participation, mobilisation or awareness. Citizens' participation and representation in the Convention were highly indirect. The selection process was a low-key affair, conducted entirely by and within the normal governmental and representative institutions. Little was done concretely to address either the low level of public interest shown during the Convention, or the fitful way in which the press and the media covered its proceedings. Some of the initiatives organised to give it public visibility were fairly perfunctory, as was the case with the Youth Convention, while the attempt to involve citizens more directly through the participation of civil society organisations was largely symbolic and not thought out properly.

It was significant that, while the Convention was still in session, denunciations were made at the Social Forum organised in Florence (in 2003) of the aloofness of the Convention process from the debate about Europe and its geo-political place in a globalised world – an issue that the Social Forum's participants regarded as of true concern for the peoples of Europe, as indeed some of the national debates during the ratification process later confirmed. In this situation, the only formal role assigned to citizens as part of the process – and this only in some member states – was that of sanctioning the constitutional text through referendums. But, as we have seen, the incapacity of generating a European-wide debate and a more widespread level of participation during the preparatory phase of the Constitution made it inevitable that the ratification battle would be fought on a national terrain.

The second level at which the Convention could have made a difference for the ratification phase was in deciding whether there was any other way in which to pose the constitutional questions to the peoples (and/or parliaments) of Europe, besides presenting them with a single text, thus putting them in the unenviable position of either accepting the Constitutional text wholesale or rejecting it. This made it impossible to develop a genuine debate beyond the crude 'take-it-or-leave-it' option. It also failed to generate a proper understanding of the contents of the Consitutional Treaty and what precisely it was meant to do. In view of the lack of clear forms of *ex ante* legitimation, such as a directly or indirectly elected Convention, the issue of debate and mobilisation during the ratification phase became indeed a crucial issue. In this sense it might have been preferable for the Convention to come up with alternative texts to submit to the IGC, with the understanding that they would eventually be put to the people and/or parliaments for ratification. This may have also forced the argument that the ratification process could not be conducted exclusively on national lines, so to avoid a stalemate, with different countries choosing different options. It would also have been possible to have a European-wide consultative referendum in the first instance, so as to gauge the real opinions of the European public and prepare the ground for formal ratification. This and other options could have been explored instead of opting for a single text to put to the vote. Indeed, there was nothing in the Laeken mandate that suggested that the Convention should have produced a single text. The decision to arrive at a single draft was partly the consequence of the willingness, shared by many of the *conventionnels*, to force the hand of the IGC in order to avoid the danger that the governments could cherry-pick from different proposals and settle for a low level compromise, which would have devalued the work of the Convention and possibly the entire process. Nonetheless, with hindsight, this might have been a gamble worth taking from the Convention's perspective. By attempting to foreclose the IGC's options, instead, the Convention ended up by curtailing the possibility of a true political debate amongst the European citizens.

Conclusions: a constitutional crisis or a crisis of Europe?

The main message that comes from the ratification crisis is that neither was proper citizen participation facilitated nor was public debate fully encouraged. Whatever popular participation and public debate eventually emerged, they were rather the effect of growing opposition to the Constitutional Treaty than a positive campaign on the merits of the Constitution. Low levels of popular mobilisation and lack of debate are often explained as the consequence of a lack of salience of institutional and constitutional issues in the lives of European citizens. This argument often complements the one we mentioned in the previous section, according to which the French and Dutch electorates voted more on issues of policy than on the Treaty. Indeed, it could be argued that it is precisely the momentous nature of the policy decisions taken by the EU and its member states over the past few years that precipitated the present round of constitution-building. Enlargement and monetary union were substantive policy decisions with considerable constitutional implications, though they were treated as part of 'normal' politics with no real public discussion encouraged. In those instances where public debate surfaced at the national level, as in the British case about the euro, it was more from the presence of a strong opposition rather than from a genuine desire to engage in a well-informed public debate.

It is therefore hardly surprising, and certainly not unexpected, that once a popular debate emerged over the Constitutional Treaty as part of the ratification process, this would tend to focus as much on the main policy changes that have shaped the EU since Maastricht as on the Constitution itself. For this reason, one should look at the Convention moment in a broader historic-political context. The more immediate and most obvious aspect of such a context is given by the process of enlargement, which, in spite of being protracted through time, and conceived as the preserve of the European political elites, has become a dominating political issue, posing numerous political and institutional challenges to the European Union and its current member states (from agriculture to redistribution policies across countries, from minority rights to internal migrations and border control). But also, perhaps less obviously, part of the political context for the constitutional debate has been determined by monetary unification. Although this has been presented as the natural completion of the single market, it can be construed as the beginning of a more ambitious integration process, involving fiscal and other macro-economic decision-making processes that may need more careful co-ordination, greater flexibility and responsiveness in order to be managed in relation to the economic cycle. The need for a different institutional setting for economic management at the European level has become the more apparent during the years of slow economic development that have characterised most of the EU countries in recent years.

A second context within which to see the emergence of the constitutional agenda is the social question. This had become more evident since the late 1990s, during the period when there was a return of social-democratic parties to government in many European countries after a long phase of neo-liberal governments and policies. Although the season of third-way-governments (most of them in ideological and electoral retreat as soon as they were elected) was short, and although there was no concerted attempt to move towards a more 'social Europe', it nonetheless contributed to the shift of popular perception from a market-based to a more welfare- and rights-based vision of Europe. So far, this shift of emphasis has produced no real shift in policies, but the relevance of such a theme during the ratification debate cannot be easily dismissed. How Europe will deal with the social dimension as economic integration progresses and internal mobility increases, is a question with profound constitutional ramifications.

The political context within which to place the constitutional moment would not be complete, however, without mentioning the international context, and how this has recently been literally shattered by the dramatic events of 9/11, the emergence of the global threat attributed to so-called 'fundamentalist Muslim terrorism', and the transformation of the geo-political context following the American-led invasion of Iraq. These events have dramatically changed the context in which the EU operates, but also the way in which Europeans see themselves both 'externally' and 'internally', as they face new risks and challenges, requiring co-ordinated action, and discover new divisions and new commonalities amongst themselves.

By considering the Convention moment as one of the expressions of the EU coming to terms with the changes and challenges posed by transformed political contexts, one can also see how the 'ratification crisis' is perhaps nothing else but the expression of a larger crisis presently affecting the European project in the eyes of its peoples: a crisis of perspectives and of legitimacy, and one to which a Constitution may only be a very partial answer, but one that the Convention and its aftermath have perhaps been expedient in manifesting. The extent of such a crisis can also be seen in the apparent difficulties that the Council found in agreeing on a text (the Berlin Declaration) in celebration of the fiftieth anniversary of the Treaty of Rome in March 2007. Although this was meant to be a mainly rhetorical exercise, it became evident that any statement about the past achievements and the future aims of the EU was open to contestation: a clear sign that the increasing powers and functions of the EU need more definite support from European citizens, though it remains unclear what the nature and the extent of such support would have to be in order to legitimate the next stages of integration.

The way in which the Convention experiment contributed to bring to the fore the legitimacy crisis that started at Maastricht is perhaps one more reason for looking at it as an important moment. It is the moment when European citizens and European peoples have become more conscious of the increasingly important role that the EU may play in their future lives. Indeed, this is something upon which, according to the Berlin Declaration, Europe is united. As the Declaration states: 'For we know, Europe is our common future'. But whether this really reflects a consolidated view of the European citizens is still an open question. This is the real political question that the 'Convention moment', which started with the Laeken Declaration and has arguably concluded with the Berlin Declaration, has put on the European agenda.

Notes

1. Rome Declaration – V. Giscard d'Estaing, Chairman of the European Convention (18 July 2003), available at: http://european-convention.eu.int/docs/Treaty/Rome_EN.pdf. This document is not to be confused with the later IGC 'Declaration of Rome' of 6 October 2003 (CIG 3/03), available at: http://www.consilium.europa.eu/igcpdf/en/03/cg00/cg00003.en03.pdf
2. The following reconstruction is indebted to Nasser Hussain (2004: 3–4).
3. In the event, Luxembourg voted in favour of the Constitutional Treaty by a comfortable, though not overwhelming, margin of 56 per cent against 43 per cent.
4. Even a 'mini-treaty', containing just the essential institutional changes, would probably require referendums in Ireland and Denmark because of their constitutional arrangements.

Appendices

Table A1: The development of the Preamble

First Draft of the Preamble from the Convention CONV 722/03 May 2003	Second Draft of Preamble from the Convention CONV 797/03 June 2003	Final Convention Preamble in the Draft Constitutional Treaty CONV 850/03 July 2003	Final Preamble from the Treaty establishing a Constitution for Europe CIG 87/1/04 REV 1 October 2004
Our Constitution is called a democracy because power is in the hands not of a minority but of the whole people.	*Our Constitution is called a democracy because power is in the hands not of a minority but of the greatest number.*	*Our Constitution is called a democracy because power is in the hands not of a minority but of the greatest number.*	(no motto)
Thucydides II, 37	*Thucydides II, 37*	*Thucydides II, 37*	
Conscious that Europe is a continent that has brought forth civilisation; that its inhabitants, arriving in successive waves since the first ages of mankind, have gradually developed the values underlying humanism: equality of persons, freedom, respect for reason,	Conscious that Europe is a continent that has brought forth civilisation; that its inhabitants, arriving in successive waves since the first ages of mankind, have gradually developed the values underlying humanism: equality of persons, freedom, respect for reason,	Conscious that Europe is a continent that has brought forth civilisation; that its inhabitants, arriving in successive waves from earliest times, have gradually developed the values underlying humanism: equality of persons, freedom, respect for reason,	(paragraph removed)
Drawing inspiration from the cultural, religious and humanist inheritance of Europe, which, nourished first by the civilisations of Greece	Drawing inspiration from the cultural, religious and humanist inheritance of Europe, which, always present in its heritage, has embedded	Drawing inspiration from the cultural, religious and humanist inheritance of Europe, the values of which, still present in its heritage,	Drawing inspiration from the cultural, religious and humanist inheritance of Europe, from which have developed the universal values *(Continued)*

Table A1: Continued

First Draft of the Preamble from the Convention CONV 722/03 May 2003	Second Draft of Preamble from the Convention CONV 797/03 June 2003	Final Convention Preamble in the Draft Constitutional Treaty CONV 850/03 July 2003	Final Preamble from the Treaty establishing a Constitution for Europe CIG 87/1/04 REV 1 October 2004
and Rome, characterised by spiritual impulse always present in its heritage and later by the philosophical currents of the Enlightenment, has embedded within the life of society its perception of the central role of the human person and his inviolable and inalienable rights, and of respect for law,	within the life of society its perception of the central role of the human person and his inviolable and inalienable rights, and of respect for law,	have embedded within the life of society the central role of the human person and his or her inviolable and inalienable rights, and respect for law,	of the inviolable and inalienable rights of the human person, freedom, democracy, equality and the rule of law,
Believing that reunited Europe intends to continue along this path of civilisation, progress and prosperity, for the good of all its inhabitants, including the weakest and most deprived; that it wishes to remain a continent open to culture, learning, and social progress; and that it wishes to deepen the democratic nature of its public life, and to strive	Believing that reunited Europe intends to continue along this path of civilisation, progress and prosperity, for the good of all its inhabitants, including the weakest and most deprived; that it wishes to remain a continent open to culture, learning, and social progress; and that it wishes to deepen the democratic and transparent nature of its public life, and to	Believing that reunited Europe intends to continue along the path of civilisation, progress and prosperity, for the good of all its inhabitants, including the weakest and most deprived; that it wishes to remain a continent open to culture, learning and social progress; and that it wishes to deepen the democratic and transparent nature of its public life, and to	Believing that Europe, reunited after bitter experiences, intends to continue along the path of civilisation, progress and prosperity, for the good of all its inhabitants, including the weakest and most deprived; that it wishes to remain a continent open to culture, learning and social progress; and that it wishes to deepen the democratic and transparent

for peace, justice and solidarity throughout the world,	strive for peace, justice and solidarity throughout the world,	strive for peace, justice and solidarity throughout the world,	nature of its public life, and to strive for peace, justice and solidarity throughout the world,
Convinced that, while remaining proud of their own national identities and history, the peoples of Europe are determined to transcend their ancient divisions, and, united in an ever closer fashion, to forge a common destiny,	Convinced that, while remaining proud of their own national identities and history, the peoples of Europe are determined to transcend their ancient divisions, and, united ever more closely, to forge a common destiny,	Convinced that, while remaining proud of their own national identities and history, the peoples of Europe are determined to transcend their ancient divisions and, united ever more closely, to forge a common destiny,	Convinced that, while remaining proud of their own national identities and history, the peoples of Europe are determined to transcend their former divisions and, united ever more closely, to forge a common destiny,
Convinced that, thus 'united in its diversity', Europe offers them the best chance of pursuing, with due regard for the rights of each individual and for their responsibilities towards future generations and the Earth, the great venture which makes of it a special area of human hope,	Convinced that, thus 'united in its diversity', Europe offers them the best chance of pursuing, with due regard for the rights of each individual and in awareness of their responsibilities towards future generations and the Earth, the great venture which makes of it a special area of human hope,	Convinced that, thus 'united in its diversity', Europe offers them the best chance of pursuing, with due regard for the rights of each individual and in awareness of their responsibilities towards future generations and the Earth, the great venture which makes of it a special area of human hope,	Convinced that, thus 'united in diversity', Europe offers them the best chance of pursuing, with due regard for the rights of each individual and in awareness of their responsibilities towards future generations and the Earth, the great venture which makes of it a special area of human hope,
			Determined to continue the work accomplished within the framework of the treaties establishing the European

(Continued)

Table A1: Continued

First Draft of the Preamble from the Convention CONV 722/03 May 2003	Second Draft of Preamble from the Convention CONV 797/03 June 2003	Final Convention Preamble in the Draft Constitutional Treaty CONV 850/03 July 2003	Final Preamble from the Treaty establishing a Constitution for Europe CIG 87/1/04 REV 1 October 2004
			Communities and the Treaty on European Union, by ensuring the continuity of the Community acquis,
Grateful to the members of the European Convention for having prepared this Constitution on behalf of the citizens and States of Europe,	Grateful to the members of the European Convention for having prepared this Constitution on behalf of the citizens and States of Europe,	Grateful to the members of the European Convention for having prepared this Constitution on behalf of the citizens and States of Europe,	Grateful to the members of the European Convention for having prepared the draft of this Constitution on behalf of the citizens and States of Europe,

Table A2: Articles I-1 to I-3 – DCT and TCE compared

Draft Constitutional Treaty CONV 850/03 July 2003	Final (post-IGC) Treaty establishing a Constitution for Europe CIG 87/1/04 REV 1 October 2004
Article 1: Establishment of the Union	*Article I-1: Establishment of the Union*
1. Reflecting the will of the citizens and States of Europe to build a common future, this Constitution establishes the European Union, on which the Member States confer competences to attain objectives they have in common. The Union shall coordinate the policies by which the Member States aim to achieve these objectives, and shall exercise in the Community way the competences they confer on it.	1. Reflecting the will of the citizens and States of Europe to build a common future, this Constitution establishes the European Union, on which the Member States confer competences to attain objectives they have in common. The Union shall coordinate the policies by which the Member States aim to achieve these objectives, and shall exercise on a Community basis the competences they confer on it.
2. The Union shall be open to all European States which respect its values and are committed to promoting them together.	2. The Union shall be open to all European States which respect its values and are committed to promoting them together.
Article 2: The Union's values	*Article I-2: The Union's values*
The Union is founded on the values of respect for human dignity, liberty, democracy, equality, the rule of law and respect for human rights. These values are common to the Member States in a society of pluralism, tolerance, justice, solidarity and non-discrimination.	The Union is founded on the values of respect for human dignity, freedom, democracy, equality, the rule of law and respect for human rights, including the rights of persons belonging to minorities. These values are common to the Member States in a society in which pluralism, non-discrimination, tolerance, justice, solidarity and equality between women and men prevail.
	(Continued)

Table A2: Continued

Draft Constitutional Treaty CONV 850/03 July 2003	Final (post-IGC) Treaty establishing a Constitution for Europe CIG 87/1/04 REV 1 October 2004
Article 3: The Union's objectives	*Article I-3: The Union's objectives*
1. The Union's aim is to promote peace, its values and the well-being of its peoples.	1. The Union's aim is to promote peace, its values and the well-being of its peoples.
2. The Union shall offer its citizens an area of freedom, security and justice without internal frontiers, and a single market where competition is free and undistorted.	2. The Union shall offer its citizens an area of freedom, security and justice without internal frontiers, and an internal market where competition is free and undistorted.
3. The Union shall work for the sustainable development of Europe based on balanced economic growth, a social market economy, highly competitive and aiming at full employment and social progress, and with a high level of protection and improvement of the quality of the environment.	3. The Union shall work for the sustainable development of Europe based on balanced economic growth and price stability, a highly competitive social market economy, aiming at full employment and social progress, and a high level of protection and improvement of the quality of the environment.
It shall promote scientific and technological advance. It shall combat social exclusion and discrimination, and shall promote	It shall promote scientific and technological advance. It shall combat social exclusion and discrimination, and shall promote

social justice and protection, equality between women and men, solidarity between generations and protection of children's rights.

It shall promote economic, social and territorial cohesion, and solidarity among Member States.

The Union shall respect its rich cultural and linguistic diversity, and shall ensure that Europe's cultural heritage is safeguarded and enhanced.

4. In its relations with the wider world, the Union shall uphold and promote its values and interests. It shall contribute to peace, security, the sustainable development of the Earth, solidarity and mutual respect among peoples, free and fair trade, eradication of poverty and protection of human rights and in particular children's rights, as well as to the strict observance and development of international law, including respect for the principles of the United Nations Charter.

5. These objectives shall be pursued by appropriate means, depending on the extent to which the relevant competences are attributed to the Union in the Constitution.

social justice and protection, equality between women and men, solidarity between generations and protection of the rights of the child.

It shall promote economic, social and territorial cohesion, and solidarity among Member States.

It shall respect its rich cultural and linguistic diversity, and shall ensure that Europe's cultural heritage is safeguarded and enhanced.

4. In its relations with the wider world, the Union shall uphold and promote its values and interests. It shall contribute to peace, security, the sustainable development of the Earth, solidarity and mutual respect among peoples, free and fair trade, eradication of poverty and the protection of human rights, in particular the rights of the child, as well as to the strict observance and the development of international law, including respect for the principles of the United Nations Charter.

5. The Union shall pursue its objectives by appropriate means commensurate with the competences which are conferred upon it in the Constitution.

References

Legal cases

Case 29/69 *Stauder v. City of Ulm* [1969] ECR 419 et al.
Case C-224/01 *Köbler v. Austria* [2004] 2 WLR 976.
Case C-336-96 *Gilly* [1998] ECR I-2793.
Case C-208/00 *Theresa Emmott* [1991] ECR I-4269.
Case C-453/00, *Kühne & Heitz NV v. Productschap voor Pluimvee en Eieren*.
Case C-370/90 *R v. Immigration Appeal Tribunal and Surinder Singh, ex parte Secretary of State for the Home Department* [1992] 3 CMLR 358.
Case C-25/62 *Plaumann v Commission* [1963] ECR 95, 107.
Case C-50/00 P *UPA* [2002] ECR I-6677.
Case C-365/97 *Commission v. Italy* [1999] ECR I-7773.
Joined Cases C-46 and 48/93 *Brasserie du Pêcheur v. Germany and the Queen v. Secretary of State for Transport, ex parte Factortame Ltd.* [1996] ECR I-1029.
Case C-106/77 *Amministrazione delle Finanzo dello Stato v. Simmenthal* [1978] ECR 629, paras. 18, 20. 22–3.
Case C-213/89 *Factortame and Others* [1990] ECR I-2433.
Case C-60/90 and C-9/90 *Francovich and Others* [1991] ECR I-5357.
Case C-48/65 *Lütticke v. Commission (First Lütticke Case)* [1966] ECR 19.
Case C-237/87 *Star Fruit* [1989] ECR 301.
Case C-5/88 *Wachauf v. Bundesamt für Ernährung und Forstwirtschaft* [1989] ECR 2609.
Case C-60/00 *Mary Carpenter v. Secretary of State for the Home Department* [2002] ECR I-6279.
Case C-314/85 *Foto-Frost v. Hauptzollamt Lübeck-Ost* [1987] ECR 4199.
Case C-465/93 *Atlanta Fruchthandelsgesellschaft mbH v. Bundesamt für Ernährung und Forstwirtschaft* [1995] ECR I-3761.
Case T-135/96 *UEAPME v. Council* [1998] ECR II-2338.

EU Treaties, Charters, Declarations and European Commission documents

Charter of Fundamental Rights of the European Union. *OJ* 2000/C 364/01, 18 December 2000.
Commission (1996) Communication on 'Incorporating equal opportunities for women and men into all Community policies and activities', COM (1996) 67 final.
Commission (1998) Communication of the Commission 'Promoting the role of voluntary organisations and foundations in Europe', COM (1997) 241 final, *OJ C 95*, 30 March 1998.
Commission (2000a) 'Commission Decision of 19 June 2000 relating to gender balance within the committees and expert groups established by it', COM 2000/407, *OJ* L 154, 27 June 2000.
Commission (2000b) Commission discussion paper 'The Commission and Non-governmental organisations: Building a Stronger Partnership', presented by President R. Prodi and Vice-President N. Kinnock, COM (2000)11 final, 18 January 2000.

Commission (2001) *The White Paper on European Governance*, COM (2001) 428 final, 25 July 2001.

EU Committee of the American Chamber of Commerce in Belgium (AmCham) (2003a) Position Paper on the Work of the Convention on the Future of Europe, 3 March (Brussels).

EU Committee of the American Chamber of Commerce in Belgium (AmCham) (2003b) Accompanying Letter to the American Chamber of Commerce in Belgium's Position Paper on the Work of the Convention on the Future of Europe, 23 April (Brussels).

EUoberver 8 November 2002, 'Convention demands more social Europe debate'. http://www.Euobserver.com

EUobserver, 14 January 2003, 'Convention to reject minimum wage'. http://www.Euobserver.com

EUobserver, 11 February 2003, 'Convention social debate mixes constitutional with political'. http://www.Euobserver.com

EUROCHAMBRES (2002) *European Convention on the Future of Europe. Contribution of Eurochambres* (Brussels).

EUROCOMMERCE (2002) *How to Improve the Social Dialogue at the European Level in the Framework of the Convention's Works on the Adaptation of the Institutional Rules to the Future of the European Union*, April (Brussels).

European Commission Translation Service (1999) *A Multilingual Community at Work* (Luxembourg: Office for Official Publications of the European Communities).

European Communities (1975) Leo Tindemans, 'Report to the European Council on European Union', EC Bulletin Supplement 1/76.

European Communities (1985) Ad Hoc Committee for Institutional Affairs: Report to the European Council, Brussels, 29/30 March 1985, 'Dooge Report'.

European Communities (1995) Report of the Reflection Group to the European Council on the IGC (Messina, 2 June 1995–Brussels, 5 December 1995), 'Westendorp Report'.

European Convention (18 July 2003) *Draft Treaty establishing a Constitution for Europe*, Luxembourg, OOPEC.

European Council (1996) 'Council Recommendation 96/694 on the balanced participation of women and men in the decision-making process', *OJ* (1996) L 319/11.

European Council (1999a) Presidency Conclusions of the European Council Meeting at Cologne, 3/4 June 1999, Annex IV, 'The Cologne Mandate'.

European Council (1999b) Presidency Conclusions of the European Council Meeting at Tampere, 15/16 October 1999, Annex.

European Council (2001) Presidency Conclusions of the European Council Meeting at Laeken, 14/15 December 2001, Annex I, 'The Laeken Declaration'.

European Parliament: Resolution on the draft Treaty establishing the European Union *OJ C 77*, 19 March 1984, rapporteur Altiero Spinelli.

European Parliament, Committee on Women's Rights and Equal Opportunities (2002a) 'Highlights of debate', and 'Letter of Anna Karamanou, President of Committee on Women's Rights of the European Parliament, to Valéry Giscard d'Estaing, President of the European Convention', 3 June, *Le fil d'Arianne* No. 1, Gender Equality Newsletter.

European Parliament, Committee on Women's Rights and Equal Opportunities (2002b) 'Message of the President Valéry Giscard d'Estaing for the meeting of the Women's Convention', 2 October, *Le fil d'Arianne* No. 2, Gender Equality Newsletter.

European Parliament, Committee on Women's Rights and Equal Opportunities (2003) 'Letter of President Valéry Giscard d'Estaing to Anna Karamanou', 20 December, *Le fil d'Arianne* No. 3, Annex 1, Gender Equality Newsletter.

European Parliament (2004a) Committee of Constitutional Affairs. *Working Document on precautionary measures for the application of general arrangements on multilingualism provided for in Rules 117 and 139 of the Rules of Procedure (2003/2227(REG))* rapporteur: Gianfranco Dell'Alba. http://www.europarl.eu.int/meetdocs/committees/afco/2004 0119/513315EN.pdf

European Parliament (2004b) *European Parliament Rules of Procedure (16th Edition) July 2004.* http://www2.europarl.eu.int/omk/sipade2?PUBREF=-//EP//TEXT+RULES-EP+ 20040720+RULE-138+DOC+XML+V0//EN&HNAV=Y

European Union (2001) Declaration 23 on the Future of the Union, Annex to the Treaty of Nice.

European Union (2005) *Treaty establishing a Constitution for Europe*, Luxembourg, OOPEC. 'Treaty establishing a Constitution for Europe'. IGC 87/2/04 REV 2, Brussels, 29 October 2004.

CONV Documents from the 2002–3 Convention on the Future of Europe

'Draft Articles 1 to 16 of the Constitutional Treaty'. CONV 528/03, 6 February 2003. http://register.consilium.eu.int/pdf/en/03/cv00/cv00528en03.pdf

'Draft Constitution, Volume II'. CONV 848/03, 9 July 2003. http://european-convention.eu.int/docs/Treaty/cv00848.en03.pdf

'Draft Treaty establishing a Constitution for Europe'. CONV 820/03, 20 June 2003. http://european-convention.eu.int/docs/Treaty/cv00820.en03.pdf

'Draft Treaty establishing a Constitution for Europe'. CONV 850/03, 18 July 2003. http://european-convention.eu.int/docs/Treaty/cv00850.en03.pdf

'Text of part I and part II of the Constitution'. CONV 797/03 REV 1, 12 June 2003. http://register.consilium.eu.int/pdf/en/03/cv00/cv00797-re01en03.pdf

European Convention 'Composition of the Working Group on Social Europe'. CONV 445/1/02 REV 1, 13 December 2002. http://register.consilium.eu.int/pdf/en/02/ cv00/00445-r1en2.pdf

European Convention 'Contact Groups (civil society)'. CONV 120/2, 19 June 2002. http://register.consilium.eu.int/pdf/en/02/cv00/00120en2.pdf

European Convention 'Digest of contributions to the Forum'. CONV 112/02, 17 June 2002. http://register.consilium.eu.int/pdf/en/02/cv00/00112en2.pdf

European Convention 'Draft Articles 1 to 16 of the Constitutional Treaty'. CONV 528/03, 6 February 2003. http://register.consilium.eu.int/pdf/en/03/cv00/ cv00528en03.pdf

European Convention 'Draft Treaty establishing a Constitution for Europe'. CONV 820/03, 20 June 2003. http://european-convention.eu.int/docs/Treaty/cv00820.en03.pdf

European Convention 'Final report of Working Group XI on Social Europe'. CONV 516/1/03, 30 January 2003. http://register.consilium.eu.int/pdf/en/03/cv00/ cv00516en03.pdf

European Convention 'Follow-up to inaugural session of the Convention'. CONV 8/02, 8 March 2002. http://register.consilium.eu.int/pdf/en/02/cv00/00008en2.pdf

European Convention 'List of contributions to the Forum'. CONV 112/02 ADD1, 19 June 2002. http://register.consilium.eu.int/pdf/en/02/cv00/00112-a1en2.pdf

European Convention 'Motions to the Presidium according to Article 2 and Article 15 of the Working Methods'. CONV 300/02, 26 September 2002. http://register. consilium.eu.int/pdf/en/02/cv00/00300en2.pdf

European Convention 'National debate on the future of Europe: Italy'. CONV 110/02, 18 June 2002. http://register.consilium.eu.int/pdf/en/02/cv00/00110en2.pdf

European Convention 'Note on the inaugural meeting 28 February 2002, Brussels'. CONV 7/02, 11 March 2002. http://register.consilium.eu.int/pdf/en/02/cv00/00007 en2.pdf

European Convention 'Note on the Plenary meeting Brussels 21 and 22 March 2002', CONV 14/02, 25 March 2002. http://register.consilium.eu.int/pdf/en/02/cv00/00014 en2.pdf

European Convention 'Note on the plenary session Brussels 24 and 25 June 2002'. CONV 167/02, 4 July 2002. http://register.consilium.eu.int/pdf/en/02/cv00/00167 en2.pdf

European Convention 'Preliminary Draft Constitutional Treaty'. CONV 369/02, 28 October 2002. http://european-convention.eu.int/docs/sessPlen/00369.en2.pdf

European Convention 'Preparations for plenary session devoted to civil society'. CONV 79/2, 31 May 2002. http://register.consilium.eu.int/pdf/en/02/cv00/00079 en2.pdf

European Convention 'Preparations for plenary session devoted to civil society'. CONV 85/02, 7 June 2002. http://register.consilium.eu.int/pdf/en/02/cv00/00085 en2.pdf

European Convention 'Questionnaire for the debate on social Europe'. CONV 374/02, 29 October 2002. http://register.consilium.eu.int/pdf/en/02/cv00/00374en2.pdf

European Convention 'Summary report of the plenary session Brussels 7 and 8 November 2002'. CONV 400/02, 13 November 2002. http://register.consilium.eu. int/pdf/en/02/cv00/00400en2.pdf

European Convention 'Text of part I and part II of the Constitution'. CONV 797/03 REV 1, 12 June 2003. http://register.consilium.eu.int/pdf/en/03/cv00/cv00797-re01 en03.pdf

European Convention 'The Convention and civil society'. CONV 48/02, 13 March 2002. http://register.consilium.eu.int/pdf/en/02/cv00/00048en2.pdf

European Convention 'The democratic life of the Union'. CONV 650/03, 2 April 2003. http://register.consilium.eu.int/pdf/en/03/cv00/cv00650en03.pdf

European Convention. 'Contact Groups (civil society)'. CONV 120/2, 19 June 2002. http://register.consilium.eu.int/pdf/en/02/cv00/00120en2.pdf

European Convention. 'Digest of contributions to the forum'. CONV 112/02, 17 June 2002. http://register.consilium.eu.int/pdf/en/02/cv00/00112en2.pdf

European Convention. 'List of contributions to the forum'. CONV 112/02 ADD1, 19 June 2002. http://register.consilium.eu.int/pdf/en/02/cv00/00112-a1en2.pdf

European Convention. 'Note on the plenary session Brussels 24 and 25 June 2002'. CONV 167/02, 4 July 2002. http://register.consilium.eu.int/pdf/en/02/cv00/00167 en2.pdf

European Convention. 'Preliminary Draft Constitutional Treaty'. CONV 369/02, 28 October 2002. http://european-convention.eu.int/docs/sessPlen/00369.en2.pdf

European Convention. 'Draft Constitution. Volume I. Revised Text of Part One'. CONV 724/03, 26 May 2003. http://register.consilium.eu.int/pdf/en/03/cv00/cv00724 en03.pdf

Bibliography

Ackerman, B. (1991) *We the People. Foundations* (Cambridge, Mass.: Harvard University Press).

Ackerman, B. (1992) *The Future of the Liberal Revolution* (New Haven and London: Yale University Press).

Alber, S. (2004) 'Gewitterwolken über dem Ausländergesetz', *Die Öffentliche Verwaltung* 57 (313).

Alonso Garcia, R. (2002) 'The General Provisions of the Charter of Fundamental Rights', *European Law Journal* 8 (492).

Amato, G. (2003) 'Prefazione', in J. Ziller, *La nuova costituzione europea* (Bologna: Il Mulino).

Ammon, U. (1994) 'The Present Dominance of English in Europe with an Outlook on Possible Solutions to the European Language Problems', *Sociolinguistica* 8.

Annan, K. (2001) 'Message of Secretary-General Kofi Annan on International Women's Day', 8 March 2001. http://www.un.org/News/Press/docs/2001/sgsm7726.doc.htm

Arato, A. (2000) 'Forms of Constitution Making and Theories of Democracy', in *Civil Society, Constitution, and Legitimacy* (Lanham: Rowman and Littlefield), pp. 229–56.

Armstrong, K. A. (2002) 'Rediscovering Civil Society: the European Union and the White Paper on Governance', *European Law Journal* 8 (1) March: 102–32.

Arnull, A. (2000) 'Private Applicants and the Action for Annulment Since Cordorniu', *Common Market Law Review* 7 (51).

Arnull, A. (2003) 'The Future of the Convention Method', Editorial in *European Law Review* 28: 573–4.

Assemblé Nationale (2003) *Rapport d'information sur la diversité linguistique dans l'Union européenne*, Herbillon Report, 11 June 2003. http://www.assemblee-nationale.fr/12/pdf/europe/rap-info/i0902.pdf

Aziz, M. (2004) *The Impact of European Rights on National Legal Cultures* (Oxford: Hart Publishing).

Aziz, M. (2005) 'The Value of Implementation', in M. Aziz and S. Millns (eds), *Values in the European Constitution* (Dartmouth: Ashgate).

Azoulay, L. (2002) 'The Judge and the Community's Administrative Governance', in C. Joerges and R. Dehousse (eds), *Good Governance in Europe's Integrated Market* (Oxford: Oxford University Press).

Bapuly, B. (2003) 'The Application of EC Law in Austria', IWE Working Paper No. 39, June (Österreichische Akademie der Wisschaften Forschungsstelle für Institutionellen Wandel und Europäische Integration).

Barbour, S. and Carmichael, C. (eds) (2002) *Language and Nationalism in Europe* (Oxford: Oxford University Press).

Beach, D. (2003) 'Towards a New Method of Constitutional Bargaining? The Role and Impact of EU Institutions in the IGC and Convention Method Treaty Reform', Federal Trust Constitution online paper, April, www.fedtrust.co.uk

Beetham, D. and Lord, C. (1998) *Legitimacy and the European Union* (London: Longman).

Beger, N. (2004) 'Participatory Democracy: Organised Civil Society and the "New" Dialogue' (London: Federal Trust and UACES conference 'Towards a European Constitution').

Bellamy, R. (1999) *Liberalism and Pluralism: Towards a Politics of Compromise* (London: Routledge).

Bellamy, R. (2001) 'The "Right to Have Rights": Citizenship Practice and the Political Constitution of the EU', in R. Bellamy and A. Warleigh (eds), *Citizenship and Governance in the European Union* (London: Continuum).

Bellamy, R. (2003) 'Sovereignty, Post-Sovereignty and Pre-Sovereignty: Reconceptualising the State, Rights and Democracy in the EU', in N. Walker (ed.), *Sovereignty in Transition* (Oxford: Hart), pp. 167–89.

Bellamy, R. (2004) 'Which Constitution for What Kind of Europe? Three Models of European Constitutionalism', paper presented at the CIDEL Workshop 'Constitution-making and Democratic Legitimacy in the EU', London, 12–13 November.

Bellamy, R. and Castiglione D. (1996) *The Constitution in Transformation* (Oxford: Blackwell).

Bellamy, R. and Castiglione, D. (1997) 'Constitutionalism and Democracy – Political Theory and the American Constitution', *British Journal of Political Science* 27: 595–618.

Bellamy, R. and Castiglione, D. (1998) 'The Normative Challenge of a European Polity: Cosmopolitan and Communitarian Models Compared, Criticised and Combined', in A. Føllesdal and P. Koslowski (eds), *Democracy and the EU* (Berlin: Springer Verlag).

Bellamy, R. and Castiglione, D. (2000) 'The Uses of Democracy: Reflections on the European Democratic Deficit', in E. O. Eriksen and J. O. Fossum (eds), *Democracy in the European Union: Integration through Deliberation?* (London: Routledge).

Bellamy, R. and Castiglione, D. (2002) 'Beyond Community and Rights: European Citizenship and the Virtues of Participation', *Quaderni Fiorentini* 31 (1): 349–80.

Bellamy, R. and Castiglione, D. (2003) 'Legitimizing the Euro-"Polity" and its "Regime": the Normative Turn in EU Studies', *European Journal of Political Theory*, 2 (1): 1–34.

Bellamy, R. and Schönlau, J. (2004a) 'The Normality of Constitutional Politics – An Analysis of the Drafting of the EU Charter of Fundamental Rights', *Constellations* 11 (3): 412–33.

Bellamy, R. and Schönlau, J. (2004b) 'The Good, the Bad and the Ugly: the Need for Constitutional Compromise and the Drafting of the EU Constitution', in L. Dobson and A. Føllesdal (eds), *Political Theory and the European Constitution* (London: Routledge).

Bellamy, R. and Warleigh, A. (1998) 'From an Ethics of Integration to an Ethics of Participation: Citizenship and the Future of the European Union', *Millennium: Journal of International Studies* 27 (3): 447–70.

Beveridge, F., Nott, S. and Stephen, K. (2000) 'Mainstreaming and Engendering of Policy-making: a Means to an End?', *Journal of European Public Policy, Special Issue: Women, Power and Public Policy in Europe*, guest ed. Sonia Mazey, 7 (3): 385–405.

Biedenkopf, K., Geremek, B. and Michalski, K. (2004) 'The Spiritual and Cultural Dimension of Europe: Concluding Remarks' (Vienna, Brussels: Institute for Human Sciences), available at: http://www.iwm.at/publ/rep-fin.pdf

Biondi, A. (2000) 'Effectiveness Versus Efficiency: Recent Developments on Judicial Protection in EC Law', *European Public Law* 6.

Bonde, J.-P. et al. (2003) 'Alternative Report – The Europe of Democracies', Published as Annex II of 'Report of the Presidency of the Convention to the President of the European Council', CONV 851/03 (18 July 2003).

Bouwen, P. (2006) 'Business Interest Representation', in S. Smismans (ed.), *Civil Society and Legitimate European Governance* (Cheltenham and Northampton: Edward Elgar), pp. 277–96.

Brown, T. (2004) 'Conventional Wisdom – What Have We Learned from the Convention Experience?', Federal Trust Constitution online paper No. 11. www.fedtrust.co.uk

Brunn, Gerhard (2005) 'Die Europäische Einigung von 1945 bis heute', *Bundeszentrale für politische Bildung*, Bonn.

Burley, A.-M. and Mattli, W. (1993) 'Europe before the Court: a Political Theory of Legal Integration', *International Organization* 47 (41).

Cangelosi, R. (2004) 'Le Conferenze Intergovernative e il Ruolo dell'Italia: Dall'Atto Unico alla Conclusione della CIG del 2003', in S. L. Rossi (ed.), *Il Progetto di Trattato-Costituzione: Verso una Nuovo Architettura dell'Unione Europea* (Milan: Giuffrè).

Cassen, B. (2002) 'Una convenzionale Convenzione europea', *Le monde diplomatique. Il Manifesto*, 4 July.

Cassese, S. (2003) *Lo Spazio Giuridico Globale* (Roma: Laterza).

Castiglione, D. (1995) 'Contracts and Constitutions', in R. Bellamy, V. Bufacchi and D. Castiglione (eds), *Democracy and Constitutional Culture in the Union of Europe* (London: Lothian Foundation Press), pp. 59–79.

Castiglione, D. (1996) 'The Political Theory of the Constitution', in R. Bellamy and D. Castiglione (eds), *The Constitution in Transformation* (Oxford: Blackwell).

Castiglione, D. (2000) 'Public Reason, Private Citizenship', in M. Passerin D'Entreves and U. Vogel (eds), *Public and Private: Legal, Political and Philosophical Perspectives* (London: Routledge), pp. 28–50.

Castiglione, D. (2004) 'Reflections on Europe's Constitutional Future', *Constellations* 11 (3): 393–411.

Castiglione, D. and Schönlau, J. (2006) 'Constitutional Politics', in K. E. Jørgensen, M. A. Pollack and Ben Rosamond (eds), *Handbook of European Politics* (London: Sage).

Cederman, L.-E. (ed.) (2001) *Constructing Europe's Identity: the External Dimension* (London: Lynne Rienner).

Chalmers, D. (1997) 'Judicial Preferences and the Community Legal Order', *Modern Law Review* 60 (164).

Chiti, E. and Franchini, C. (2003) *L'integrazione amministrativa europea* (Bologna: Il Mulino).

Chiti, M. P. (1999) *Diritto Amminstrativo Europeo* (Milan: Dott. A. Giuffrè).

Chiti, M. P. (2000) 'The Emergence of a Community Administration: the Case of European Agencies', *Common Market Law Review* 37 (309).

Christiansen, T. (2002) 'The Role of Supranational Actors in EU Treaty Reform', *Journal of European Public Policy* 9.

Christiansen, T., Jørgensen, K.-E. and Wiener, A. (2001) *The Social Construction of Europe* (London: Sage).

Christodoulidis, E. (2003) 'Constitutional Irresolution: Law and the Framing of Civil Society', *European Law Journal* 9 (4): 401–32.

Chryssochoou, D. (1998) *Democracy in the European Union* (London: Tauris Academic Studies).

Chryssochoou, D. (2000) 'Meta-Theory and the Study of the European Union: Capturing the Normative Turn', *European Integration* 22: 123–44.

Chryssochoou, D. (2001) *Theorizing European Integration* (London: Sage).

Chryssochoou, D. (2003) 'EU Democracy and the Democratic Deficit', in M. Cini (ed.), *European Union Politics* (Oxford: Oxford University Press).

Closa, C. (2003) 'Improving EU Constitutional Politics? A Preliminary Assessment of the Convention', *Constitutionalism Web-Papers*, ConWEB No. 1/2003,Queens University Belfast, http://les1.man.ac.uk/conweb

Closa, C. (2004a) 'Deliberative Constitutional Politics and the EU Value-Based Constitution', in C. Closa and J. E. Fossum (eds), *Deliberative Constitutional Politics in the EU* (Oslo: ARENA report No. 5).

Closa, C. (2004b) 'The Convention Method and the Transformation of EU Constitutional Politics', in E. O. Eriksen, J. E. Fossum and A. J. Menendez (eds), *Developing a Constitution for Europe* (London: Routledge).

Closa, C. and Fossum, J. E. (2004) 'Constitution-Making and Democratic Legitimacy in the EU', in C. Closa and J. E. Fossum (eds), *Deliberative Constitutional Politics in the EU* (Oslo: ARENA report No. 5).

Cohen, J. and Arato, A. (1992) *Civil Society and Political Theory* (Cambridge, Mass.: MIT Press).

Cohen, J. and Arato, A. (1995) 'The Idea of Civil Society', in M. Walzer (ed.), *Toward a Global Civil Society* (Providence, RI: Berhahn Books).

Constantinesco, V. (2004) 'La Cittadinanza dell'Unione: Una "Vera" Cittadinanza?', in S. L. Rossi (ed.), *Il Progetto di Trattato-Costituzione: Verso una Nuovo Architettura dell'Unione Europea* (Milan: Giuffrè).

Corbett, R. (1987[1989]) 'The 1985 Intergovernmental Conference and the Single European Act', in R. Pryce (ed.), *The Dynamics of European Union* (London: Croom Helm).

Corbett, R., Jacobs, F. and Shackleton, M. (2003) *The European Parliament* (5th ed.) (London: John Harper).

Council of Europe (1998) *Conceptual Framework, Methodology and Presentation of Good Practices: Final Report of Activities of the Group of Specialists on Mainstreaming (EG-S-MS)*, Strasbourg, Section on Equality between Women and Men, Directorate of Human Rights.

Craig, P. (2003) 'What Constitution does Europe Need? The House that Giscard Built: Constitutional Rooms with a View', http://www.fedtrust.co.uk

Crossick, S. (2002) 'Involving Civil Society in the Debate; Convention Intelligent', The Convention on the Future of Europe, www.theepc.be, 11 July.

Crossick, S. and Allio, L. (2003) *The Intergovernmental Conference and Business* (Brussels: EPC Issue Paper No. 6).

Crum, B. (2002) *Laying Building Blocks or Just Window-Dressing? The First Half Year of the Convention on the Future of the EU.* http://www.euractiv.com/cgi-bin/cgint.exe?204&OIDN=250498.

Crum, B. (2004a) 'Genesis and Assessment of the Grand Institutional Settlement of the European Convention', *Politique Européenne* 13.

Crum, B. (2004b) 'Politics and Power in the European Convention', *Politics* 24 (1): 1–11.

Crum, B. (2005) 'EU Referendum is Test for Dutch Political Establishment', *EPIN Ratification Monitor – Country Report: The Netherlands*, available at www.epin.org (accessed 4 May 2005).

Dauvergne, A. (2004) *L'Europe en Otage? Histoire secrète de la Convention* (Paris: Saint-Simon).

De Búrca, G. (1996) 'The Quest for Legitimacy in the European Union', *The Modern Law Review* 59: 349–76.

De Búrca, G. (1999) 'The Institutional Development of the EU: a Constitutional Analysis', in P. Craig and G. de Búrca (eds), *The Evolution of EU Law* (Oxford: Oxford University Press).

De Búrca, G. and Walker, N. (2003) 'Law and Transnational Civil Society: Upsetting the Agenda?', *European Law Journal* 9 (4): 387–400.

De Schutter, O. (2001) 'Europe in Search of its Civil Society', in E. O. Eriksen, J. E. Fossum and A. J. Menéndez (eds), *The Chartering of Europe: the Charter of Fundamental Rights in Context* (Oslo: ARENA report No. 8).

De Swaan, A. (2001) *Words of the World* (Cambridge: Polity).

De Witte, B. (1999) 'Direct Effect, Supremacy and the Nature of the Legal Order', in P. Craig and G. de Búrca (eds), *The Evolution of EU Law* (Oxford: Oxford University Press).

De Witte, B. (2002) 'The Closest Thing to a Constitutional Conversation in Europe: the Semi-Permanent Treaty Revision Process', in P. Beaumont, C. Lyons and N. Walker (eds), *Convergence and Divergence in European Public Law* (Oxford: Hart).

De Witte, B. (2004a) The National Constitutional Dimension of European Treaty Revision – Evolution and Recent Debates, The Second Walter van Gerven Lecture (Groningen: Europa Law Publishing).

De Witte, B. (2004b), 'The Process of Ratification of the Constitutional Treaty and the Crisis Option: a Legal Perspective', *EUI Working Papers*, Law 2004/16.

Dehaene, J. L. (2003) 'Seminar European Social Dialogue and Civil Dialogue: Differences and Complementarities', 10 June 2003 (Brussels: EESC Pamphlet Series).

Dehousse, R. (2000) 'Rediscovering Functionalism', in C. Joerges, Y. Mény and J. H. H. Weiler (eds), *What Kind of Constitution for What Kind of Polity? Responses to Joschka Fischer* (Florence: Robert Schuman Centre), pp. 195–202.

Dehousse, R. (2003) 'Beyond Representative Democracy: Constitutionalism in a Polycentric Polity', in J. H. H. Weiler and M. Wind (eds), *European Constitutionalism Beyond the State* (Cambridge: Cambridge University Press), pp. 135–56.

Delanty, G. (1995) *Inventing Europe: Idea, Identity, Reality* (Basingstoke: Palgrave Macmillan).

Della Cananea, G. (2003) 'L'amministrazione europea', in S. Cassese (ed.), *Trattato di diritto amministrative: Diritto ammininistrativo generale* (Milano: Giuffrè).

Della Cananea, G. (2004) 'Procedures in the New (Draft) Constitution of the European Union', *European Review of Public Law* 1 (221).

Deutscher Bundestag (2001) *Die Charta der Grundrechte der Europäischen Union* (Berlin: Zur Sache).

Deutscher Bundestag (2003) *Eine Verfassung für Europa- der europäische Konvent und der deutsche Bundestag* (Berlin: Zur Sache).

Dinan, D. (1994) *Ever Closer Union?* (2nd ed. 1999) (Basingstoke: Palgrave Macmillan).

Dobson, L. and A. Føllesdal (eds) (2004) *Political Theory and the European Constitution* (London and New York: Routledge).

Dougan, M. (2003) 'The Convention's Draft Constitutional Treaty: a "Tidying-Up Exercise" That Needs Some Tidying-Up of its Own'. http://www.fedtrust.co.uk

Drulák, P. (2003) 'Metaphors Europe Lives by: Language and Institutional Change of the European Union', paper for the European Forum 'Constitutionalism in Europe, European University Institute'.

Dryzeck, J. S. (2000) *Deliberative Democracy and Beyond: Liberals, Critics, Contestations* (Oxford: Oxford University Press).

Duff, A (2005) *The Struggle for Europe's Constitution* (London: Federal Trust).

Dupré, C. (2003) *Importing the Law in Post-Communist Transitions: the Hungarian Constitutional Court and the Right to Human Dignity* (Oxford: Hart Publishing).

ECAS (2003) *ECAS Demands More Openness in Finalising the Constitutional Treaty*, 1 September (Brussels).

ECAS (2004) *European Citizens' Initiatives*, November 2004 (Brussels).

ECAS (2005) *50 Questions and Answers on the Treaty Establishing a Constitution for Europe* (Brussels).

ECOSOC (1999) 'Opinion of ECOSOC on "The role and contribution of civil society organisations in the building of Europe"', *CES* 851/1999, 22 September 1999.

ECOSOC (2000) 'Opinion of ECOSOC on the Communication of the Commission, "Promoting the role of voluntary organisations and foundations in Europe"', COM(97) 241 final, *OJ* C 95, 30 March 1998, *CES* 811/2000, 13 July 2000.

ECOSOC (2001) 'Opinion on "Organised civil society and European governance: the Committee's contribution to the drafting of the White Paper"', *CES* 535/2001, 25 April 2001.

Einem, C. (2004) *Die Quadratur der Sterne- So schrieben wir Europas Verfassung (und was daraus geworden ist)* (Wien: Kremayr und Scheriau Verlag).

Elgström, O. (2000) 'Norm Negotiations: the Construction of New Norms Regarding Gender and Development in EU Foreign Aid Policy', *Journal of European Public Policy* 7 (3): 457–76.

Elson, D. (2003) 'Gender Mainstreaming and Gender Budgeting', paper presented at Conference of the Jean Monnet Project on 'Gender Equality and Europe's Future', European Commission, DG Education and Culture, Brussels, 4 March 2003. http://www.europa.eu.int/comm/education/ajm/equality/index.html

Elster, J. (1996) *Argomentare e Negoziare* (Milan: Anabasi).

Elster, J. (ed.) (1998) *Deliberative Democracy* (Cambridge: Cambridge University Press).

Emmanoulidis, J. A. (2004) *Die Institutionellen Reformen in der Verfassung – die neue Machtstruktur der Europäischen Union* (Bertelsmann Stiftung/CAP Verfassungsbriefing, Herbst).

Eriksen, E. O. (ed.) (2005) *Making the European Polity: Reflexive Integration in the EU* (London and New York: Routledge).

Eriksen, E. O. and Fossum, J.-E. (eds) (2000a) *Democracy in the European Union. Integration through Deliberation?* (London and New York: Routledge).

Eriksen, E. O. and Fossum, J.-E. (2000b) 'Post-National Integration', in E. O. Eriksen and J. E. Fossum (eds), *Democracy in the European Union. Integration through Deliberation* (London and New York: Routledge).

Eriksen, E. O. and Fossum, J. E. (2002) 'Democracy through Strong Publics in the European Union?' *Journal of Common Market Studies* 40 (3): 401–24.

Eriksen, E. O. and Fossum, J. O. (2004) 'Europe in Search of Legitimacy: Strategies of Legitmation Assessed', *International Political Science Review* 25 (4): 435–59.

Eriksen, E. O., Fossum, J. E. and Menendez, A. (eds) (2003) *The Chartering of Europe* (Baden-Baden: Nomos Verlagsgesellschaft).

Eriksen, E. O., Fossum, J. E. and Augustín J. Menéndez (eds) (2004) *Developing a Constitution for Europe* (London and New York: Routledge).

ERT (2002) *European Governance for Greater Competitiveness*, November 2002 (Brussels).

Farrell, H. and Héritier, A. (2003) 'Formal and Informal Institutions Under Codecision: Continuous Constitution-Building in Europe', *Governance* 16 (4): 577.

Fioravanti, M. (1992) 'Quale futuro per la "costituzione"?' *Quaderni Fiorentini* 21: 623–37.

Fischer, J. (2000) 'Vom Staatenverbund zur Föderation: Gedanken über die Finalität der Europäischen Integration', lecture given at Humboldt University, Berlin, 12 May.

Fleury, A. and Jilek, L. (eds) (1998) *Le plan Briand d'Union fédérale européenne: perspectivaes nationales et transnationales, avec documents* (Bern: Peter Lang).

Floridia, G. G. (2003) *Il Cantiere della Nuova Europa* (Bologna: Il Mulino).

Føllesdal, A. and Hix, S. (2005) 'Why There is a Democratic Deficit in the EU: a Response to Majone and Moravcsik'. *European Governance Papers* 1(2). http://www.connex-network.org/eurogov/pdf/egp-connex-C-05-02.pdf (accessed 10 March 2006).

Fondation Spaak (1984) *Pour une Communauté Politique Européenne, Traveaux Préparatoires, Volume I: 1952–54; Volume II: 1955–57* (Bruxelles: Bruylant).

Fossum, J. O. (2003) 'Still a Union of Deep Diversity? The Convention and the Constitution for Europe' (Oslo: ARENA working paper No. 21). http://www.arena.uio.no/publications/working-papers2003/papers/wp03_21.pdf

Fossum, J. E. and Menéndez, A. J. (2002) 'The Constitution's gift: a Deliberative Democratic Analysis of Constitution Making in the European Union', paper presented at the CIDEL Conference on 'Deliberative Constitutional Politics in the EU', 19–20 May (Albaraccín, Spain). http://www.arena.uio.no/cidel/workshopZaragoza/JEFossum_AMenendez.pdf

Friese, H. and Wagner, P. (2002) 'Survey Article: the Nascent Political Philosophy of the European Polity', *Journal of Political Philosophy* 10 (3): 342–64.

Furet, F. (1995) 'Europe after Utopianism', *Journal of Democracy* 6 (1): 79–89.

Gerbet. P. (1987[1989]) 'In Search of Political Union: the Fouchet-Plan Negotiations (1960–62)', in R. Pryce (ed.), *The Dynamics of European Union* (London: Croom Helm).

Giering, C. (2003) 'Hohe Hürden auf der Zielgeraden für den EU-Konvent', *Konvent Spotlight* 7. www.eu-reform.de

Ginsburgh, V. and Weber, S. (2005) 'Language Disenfranchisement in the European Union', *Journal of Common Market Studies* 43: 273–86.

Giscard d'Estaing, V. (2002a) 'La dernière chance de l'Europe unie', *Le Monde*, 22 July.

Giscard d'Estaing, V. (2002b) 'Speech for the opening of the academic year at the College of Europe', 2 October (Bruges). http://ue.eu.int/pressdata/EN/conveur/72626.pdf

Giscard d'Estaing, V. (2002c) 'Introductory speech to the members of the Convention on the Future of Europe', 26 February. Available at http://european-convention.eu. int/docs/speeches/1.pdf

Glenn, H. P. (2003) 'La Tradition Juridique Nationale', *Revue Internationale de Droit Comparé* 2 and in D. Nelken and J. Feest (eds), *Adapting Legal Cultures* (Oxford: Hart Publishing).

Gnes, M. (2001) 'Verso la "communitarizzazione del diritto processuale nazionale"', *Giornale di diritto amministrativo* 5 (524).

Göler, D. (2006) *Deliberation – Ein Zukunftsmodell europäischer Entscheidungsfindung?* (Baden-Baden: IEP-Asko Europastiftung, Nomos Verlagsgesellschaft).

Göler, D. and Marhold, H. (2003) 'Die Konventsmethode', *Integration* 26 (4): 317–30.

Greenwood, J. (2002) *Inside EU Business Associations* (Basingstoke: Palgrave Macmillan).

Greenwood, J. (2007) *Interest Representation in the European Union* (Basingstoke: Palgrave Macmillan).

Greve, Morton F. and Jorgensen, K. E. (2002) 'Treaty Reform as Constitutional Politics: a Longitudinal View', *Journal of European Public Policy* 9 (1): 54–75.

Griffith, R. (2000) *Europe's First Constitution: the European Political Community 1952–54* (London: Federal Trust).

Grimm, D. (1995) 'Does Europe Need a Constitution?' *European Law Journal* 1 (3): 282–302.

Guérot, U. (2003) 'EU: Konvent in Zeitnot', *Internationale Politik* 4: 41–8.

Guérot, U., Hughes, K., Lefevbre, M. and Egenhoff, T. (2003) 'France, Germany and the UK in the Convention', EPIN working paper No. 7, July.

Guild, E. (1995) *The Developing Immigration and Asylum Law of the EU* (The Hague: Kluwer Law International).

Haas, E. (1958) *The Uniting of Europe: Political, Social and Economic Forces, 1950–1957* (Stanford: Stanford University Press).

Habermas, J. (1992a) 'Citizenship and National Identity: Some Reflections on the Future of Europe', *Praxis International* 12 (1): 1–19.

Habermas, J. (1992b) 'Further Reflections on the Public Sphere', in C. Calhoun (ed.), *Habermas and the Public Sphere* (Cambridge, Mass.: MIT Press).

Habermas, J. (2001) 'Why Europe needs a Constitution', *New Left Review* 11: 5–26.

Hafner-Burton, E. and Pollack, M. A. (2000) 'Mainstreaming Gender in the European Union', *Journal of European Public Policy, Special Issue: Women, Power and Public Policy in Europe*, guest ed. Sonia Mazey, 7 (3): 432–56.

Hailbronner, K. and Thiery, C. (1998) 'Asylrecht und Einwanderung sowie Überführung des Schengen-Besitzstands aud EU-Ebene', *Europarecht* 5 (583).

Hantrais, L. (1995) *Social Policy in the European Union* (Basingstoke: Palgrave Macmillan).

Hay, D. (1957) *Europe: the Emergence of an Idea* (Edinburgh: Edinburgh University Press).

Heffernan, M. (1998) *The Meaning of Europe: Geography and Geopolitics* (London: Arnold).

Hegel, G. W. F. (1942 [1821]) *Philosophy of Right* (Oxford: Clarendon Press).

Hirschman, A. O. (1993) 'The Rhetoric of Reform', *The American Prospect* 4 (14).

Hirst, P. (1995) 'The European Union at the Crossroads: Integration or Decline?', in R. Bellamy, V. Bufacchi and D. Castiglione (eds), *Democracy and Constitutional Culture in the Union of Europe* (London: Lothian Foundation Press), pp. 45–56.

Höreth, M. (2004) 'Kontinuität oder Pfadsprung: Das institutionelle Dreieck in Europa nach dem Verfassungsvertrag', *Zeitschrift für Politikwissenschaft* 4: 1257–96.

Hughes, J., Sasse, G. and Gordon, C. (2002) 'Saying "Maybe" to the "Return to Europe": Elites and the Political Space for Euroscepticism in Central and Eastern Europe', *European Union Politics* 3.

Hummer, W. (2002) 'Vom Grundrechte-Konvent zum Zukunfts-Konvent: Semantische und andere Ungereimtheiten bei der Beschickung des "Konvents zur Zukunft Europas"', *Zeitschrift für Parlamentsfragen* 2: 323–47.

Hussain, N. (2004) 'Referendums on the EU Constitutional Treaty: the State of Play', Chatham House Briefing Paper 04/01 (October).

Inglewood, R. (1990) *Culture Shift* (Princeton: Princeton University Press).

Jacobs, G. (2000) *Convention on the Future of Europe: Address by George Jacobs, President of UNICE*, 24 June (Brussels).

Jacobs, G. (2003) *Letter to Mr Valéry Giscard d'Estaing, President of the Convention*, 28 May (Brussels).

Jahan, R. (1995) *The Elusive Agenda: Mainstreaming Women in Development* (London: Zed Books).

Joerges, C. (1997). 'The Impact of European Integration on Private Law: Reductionist Perceptions, True Conflicts and a New Constitutional Perspective', *European Law Journal* 3(4): 378–406.

Joerges, C. and Everson, M. (2004) 'Law, Economics and Politics in the Constitution-alization of Europe', in E. O. Eriksen, J. E. Fossum and A. J. Menéndez (eds), *Developing a Constitution for Europe* (London and New York: Routledge), pp. 162–79.

Joerges, C., Mény, Y. and Weiler, J. H. H. (eds) (2000) *What Kind of Constitution for What Kind of Polity? Responses to Joschka Fischer* (Florence: Robert Schuman Centre).

Joerges, C. and Vos, E. (eds) (1999) *EU Committees: Social Regulation, Law and Politics* (Oxford: Hart Publishing).

Jordan, A. (1999) 'The Implementation of EU Environmental Policy: a Policy Problem without a Political Solution?' *Environment and Planning: Government and Policy* 17.

Joseph, J. (2004) *Language and Identity: National, Ethnic, Religious* (Basingstoke: Palgrave Macmillan).

Julios, C. (2002) 'Towards a European Language Policy', in M. Farrell, S. Fella and M. Newman (eds), *European Integration in the 21st Century: Unity in Diversity?* (London: Sage).

Keatinge, P. and Murphy, A. (1987[1989]) 'The European Council's Ad Hoc Committee on Institutional Affairs (1984–85)', in R. Pryce (ed.), *The Dynamics of European Union* (London: Croom Helm).

Kiljunen, K. (2004) *The European Constitution in the Making* (Brussels: Centre for European Policy Studies).

Kirchhof, P. (2003) 'Europa auf dem Weg zu einer Verfassung?' *Zeitschrift für Staats- und Europawissenschaften* 3.

Kleger, H. (ed.) (2004) *Der Konvent als Labor* (Münster–Hamburg–London: LIT-Verlag).

Kohler-Koch, B. (1994) 'Changing Patterns of Interest Intermediation in the European Union', *Government and Opposition* 29 (2): 166–80.

Kokott, J. and Rüth, A. (2004) 'The European Convention and its Draft Treaty Establishing a Constitution for Europe: Appropriate Answers to the Laeken Questions?' *Common Market Law Review* 40.

Kraus, P. (2000) 'Political Unity and Linguistic Diversity in Europe', *European Journal of Sociology* 41 (1).

Kumm, M. (2005) 'To be a European Citizen: Constitutional Patriotism and the Treaty Establishing a Constitution for Europe', in *The European Constitution: the Rubicon Crossed?* (ARENA report No. 3/05), pp. 7–63.

Lacroix, J. (2002) 'For a European Constitutional Patriotism', *Political Studies* 50 (5): 944–58.

Ladeur, K.-H. (ed.) (2002) *The Europeanisation of Administrative Law: Transforming National Decision-Making Procedures* (Aldershot: Ashgate).

Lamassourre, A. (2004) *Histoire Secrète de la Convention Européene* (Paris: Fondation Robert Schuman).

Leinen, J. and Schönlau, J. (2001) 'Die EU-Grundrechtecharta: Visitenkarte für Europa', in S. Kaufmann (ed.), *Grundrechtecharta der Europäischen Union* (Bonn: Europa Union Verlag).

León, M., Diaz, M. and Millns, S. (2003) 'Engendering the Convention: Women and the Future of the European Union'. www.fedtrust.co.uk/Media/Millns.pdf

Lenaerts, K. and Desomer, M. (2003) 'Simplification of the Union's Instruments', in B. de Witte (ed.), *Ten Reflections on the Constitutional Treaty for Europe* (Florence: European University Institute).

Levy, R. (2000) *Implementing European Union Public Policy* (Cheltenham: Edward Elgar).

Liñán Nogueras, D. J. and Roldán Barbero, J. (1993) 'The Judicial Application of Community Law in Spain', *Common Market Law Review* 30.

Lombardo, E. (2003) 'The Participation of Civil Society in the Debate on the Future of Europe. Rhetorical or Action Frames in the Discourse of the Convention?', working paper 3. http://www.unizar.es/union_europea/archivos/workPapers3_UE.pdf

Lombardo, E. and Meier, P. (2006) 'Gender Mainstreaming in the EU: Incorporating a Feminist Reading?' *European Journal of Women's Studies* 13 (2): 151–66.

Longman, C. (2007) 'English as Lingua Franca: a Challenge to the Doctrine of Multilingualism?', in D. Castiglione, and C. Longman, (eds), *The Language Question in Europe and Diverse Societies: Political, Social and Legal Perspectives* (Oxford: Hart).

Ludlow, P. (2002) 'The Laeken Council', *EuroComment*, Brussels – European Council Commentary 1 (1).

Ludlow, P. (2003) 'The Launching of the IGC', *EuroComment Briefing Note* 2.5, 4 October (Brussels).

Ludlow, P. (2004a) 'The European Council and IGC of December 2003', *EuroComment Briefing Note* 2.8, 9 January (Brussels).

Ludlow, P. (2004b) 'The IGC and European Council of June 2004 – In search of a Constitution and a President', *EuroComment Briefing Note* 3.2, 14 July (Brussels).

Luhmann, Niklas (1996) 'La costituzione come acquisizione evolutiva', in G. Zagrebelsky, P. P. Portinaro and J. Lüther (eds), *Il futuro della costituzione* (Turin: Einaudi), pp. 129–66.

MacCormick, N. (1999) *Questioning Sovereignty: Law, State, and Practical Reason* (Oxford: Oxford University Press).

MacCormick, N. (2004) *A Union of its Own Kind? Reflections on the European Convention and the Proposed Constitution of the European Union* (Brussels, Edinburgh: Green, European Alliance Pamphlet).

Madsen, M. R. and Dezalay, Y. (2002) 'The Power of the Legal Field: Pierre Bourdieu and the Law', in R. Banakar and M. Travers (eds), *An Introduction to Law and Social Theory* (Oxford: Hart Publishing).

Madsen, M. R. and Vauchez, A. (2004) *European Constitutionalism at the Cradle. The Impact of the Emergence of a European Legal Space and Discourse. The Briand-Project and the European Convention on Human Rights Revisited*, European Forum 2003/04 Constitutionalism in Europe (San Domenico di Fiesole: European University Institute).

Maduro, M. Poiares (1998) *We, the Court* (Oxford: Hart).

Maduro, M. Poiares (2000) 'Europe and the Constitution', in *What If This is As Good As It Gets?*, Constitutionalism web papers. http://les1.man.ac.uk/conweb/ConWeb No. 5/2000

Maduro, M. Poiares (2003) 'Europe and the Constitution: What If This is As Good As It Gets?', in J. H. H. Weiler and Marlene Wind (eds), *European Constitutionalism beyond the State* (Cambridge: Cambridge University Press), pp. 74–102.

Magnette, P. (2002) 'Why and How Arguing in a Constitutional Convention', paper presented at CIDEL Workshop on 'Deliberative Constitutional Politics in the EU', 19–22 May (Albaraccín, Spain).

Magnette, P. (2003) 'Why and How Arguing in a Constitutional Convention?', Constitution online paper 34/03, Federal Trust (London). www.fedtrust.co.uk

Magnette, P. (2004a) 'When Does Deliberation Matter? Constitutional Rhetoric in the Convention on the Future of Europe', in C. Closa and J. E. Fossum (eds), *Deliberative Constitutional Politics in the EU* (Oslo: ARENA report No.5).

Magnette, P. (2004b), 'Deliberation or Bargaining? Coping with Constitutional Conflicts in the Convention on the Future of Europe', in E. O. Eriksen, J. E. Fossum and A. J. Menéndez (eds), *Developing a Constitution for Europe* (London and New York: Routledge), pp. 207–25.

Majone, G. (1996) *Regulating Europe* (London: Routledge).

Majone, G. (2000) 'The Credibility Crisis of Community Regulation', *Journal of Common Market Studies* 38 (2): 273–302.

Mamadouh, V. (1999) 'Beyond Nationalism: Three Visions of the European Union and their Implications for the Linguistic Regime of its Institutions', *GeoJournal* 48: 133–44.

Mamadouh, V. and Hofman, K. (2001) *The Language Constellation in the European Parliament* (Amsterdam: AME, European Cultural Foundation).

Mancini, G. F. (2000) *Democracy and Constitutionalism in the European Union* (Oxford: Hart Publishing).

Mancini, G. F. and Keeling, D. (1995) 'Legal Culture and Politics in the Life of the European Court of Justice', *Columbia Journal of European Law* 1 (397).

Marschang, B. (1998) 'Mißtrauen, Abschottung, Eigensinn – Entwicklungslinien der europäischen Asylrechts "harmonisierung" bis zum Amsterdamer Vertrag', *Kritische Justiz* 69.

Martín, A. M. (1989) *Derecho comunitario europeo y derecho español* (Madrid: Tecnos).

Marx, K. (1954) *Introduzione alla critica dell'economia politica (1859)* (Roma: Edizioni Rinascita).

Maurer, A. (2003a, July) 'Schließt sich der Kreis? Der Konvent, nationale Vorbehalte und die Regierungskonferenz', *SWP Diskussionspapier*.

Maurer, A. (2003b, October) 'Aufschnüren oder Dynamisieren? Chancen und Risiken der Regierungskonferenz zum EU-Verfassungsvertrag', *SWP-Aktuell* 38.

Maurer, A. (2004, May) 'Die Schlußetappe der Regierungskonferenz', *SWP Diskussionspapier*.

Maurer, A. (2005) 'Ratifikationsverfahren zum EU-Verfassungsvertrag', in Zusammenarbeit mit D. Devrim, A. Crespy, K.-O. Lang, J.-H. Lauer, R. Parkes and A. Stengel (eds), *SWP Diskussionspapier* 2005/05. Berlin

Mazey, S. (2000) 'Introduction: Integrating Gender – Intellectual and "Real World" Mainstreaming', *Journal of European Public Policy, Special Issue: Women, Power and Public Policy in Europe*, guest ed. Sonia Mazey, 7 (3): 333–45.

Mazey, S. and Richardson, J (2001) 'Interest Groups and EU Policy-making: Organisational Logic and Venue Shopping', in J. Richardson (ed.), *European Union: Power and Policy-Making* (London: Routledge), pp. 217–34.

McCluskey, B. (1998) 'A Different Kettle of Fish: the Challenge of Multilingual Translation in Specialist Fields' (speech at the Lisbon Expo). http://europa.eu.int/comm/translation/bulletins/folha/semsdt98/bmcfinal.htm

McCrudden, C. (2000) 'A Common Law of Human Rights?: Transnational Judicial Conversations on Constitutional Rights', *Oxford Journal of Legal Studies* 4.

McCrudden, C. (2003) 'Gender Equality in the Constitutional Treaty: Drafting Suggestions'.   http://europa.eu.int/comm/education/programmes/ajm/equality/contributions_en.html

McKinnon, C. and Castiglione, D. (2003) 'Reasonable Toleration', in C. McKinnon and D. Castiglione (eds), *The Culture of Toleration in Diverse Societies: Reasonable Tolerance* (Manchester: Manchester University Press), pp. 1–11.

Menéndez, A. J. (2004) *A Pious Europe? Why Europe Should Not Define Itself as Christian* (Oslo, ARENA, working paper No. 10). http://www.arena.uio.no/publications/working-papers2004/papers/04_10.xml

Merlingen, M., Mudde, C. and Sedelmeier, U. (2001) 'The Right and the Righteous? European Norms, Domestic Politics and the Sanctions against Austria', *Journal of Common Market Studies* 39 (1): 59–77.

Mill, J. S. (1865) *Considerations on Representative Government* (London: Longman).

Milward, A. (2000) *The European Rescue of the Nation State* (London: Routledge).

Mishler, W. and Rose, R. (2002) 'Learning and Re-learning Regime Support: the Dynamics of Post-communist Regimes', *European Journal of Political Research* 41.

Monar, J. (1998) 'Justice and Home Affairs in the Treaty of Amsterdam: Reform at the Price of Fragmentation', *European Law Review* 23 (320).

Monnet, J. (1976) *Erinnerungen eines Europäers* (Baden-Baden: Nomos Verlasgsgesellschaft).

Moravcsik, A. (1991) 'Negotiating the Single European Act: National Interests and Conventional Statecraft in the European Community', *International Organization* 45 (1): 651–88.

Moravcsik, A. (1993) 'Preferences and Power in the European Community: a Liberal Intergovernmentalist Approach', *Journal of Common Market Studies* 31 (4): 473–524.

Moravcsik, A. (1998) *The Choice for Europe: Social Purpose and State Power from Messina to Maastricht* (London: UCL Press).

Moravcsik, A. (2002a) 'Europe Without Illusions', paper presented at the Third Spaak Foundation, Harvard University Conference, September 2002 (Brussels).

Moravcsik, A. (2002b) 'In Defence of the "Democratic Deficit": Reassessing Legitimacy in the European Union', *Journal of Common Market Studies* 40 (4): 603–24.

Moravcsik, A. (2005a) 'The Constitution is Dead, Long Live the Constitution!', *Prospect* 112, 5 July.

Moravcsik, A. (2005b) 'The European Constitutional Compromise and the Neofunctionalist Legacy', *Journal of European Public Policy* 12 (2): 349–86.

Morgan, G. (2005) *The Idea of a European Superstate: Public Justification and European Integration* (Princeton and Oxford: Princeton University Press).

Müller, W., Bergman, T. and Strøm, K. (2003) 'Parliamentary Democracy: Promise and Problems', in K. Strøm, W. C. Müller and T. Bergman (eds), *Delegation and Accountability in Parliamentary Democracy* (Oxford: Oxford University Press).

Nehl, H. P. (1999) *Principles of Administrative Procedure in EC Law* (Oxford: Hart).

Nic Shuibhne, N. (2002) 'The European Union and Fundamental Rights: Well in Spirit but Considerably Rumpled in Body?', in P. Beaumont, C. Lyons and N. Walker (eds), *Convergence and Divergence in European Public Law* (Oxford: Hart).

Norman, P. (2003) *The Accidental Constitution: the Story of the European Convention* (Brussels: EuroComment).

Nott, S., Beveridge, F. and Stephen, K. (eds) (2000) *Making Women Count: Integrating Gender into Law and Policy-making* (Aldershot: Ashgate).

Nuotio, K. (ed.) (2004) *Europe in Search of 'Meaning and Purpose'* (Helsinki: Forum Iuris, Faculty of Law, University of Helsinki).

Oliver, P. and Roth, W.-H. (2004) 'The Internal Market and the Four Freedoms', *Common Market Law Review* 41 (407).

Olsen, J. (1997) 'Institutional Design in Democratic Contexts', *Journal of Political Philosophy* 5 (3): 203–29.

Olsen, J. (2002) 'Coping with Conflict at Constitutional Moments' (Oslo: ARENA working papers, No. 02/23).

Olsen, T. V. (2004) 'Europe: United Under God? Or Not?', in L. Dobson and A. Føllesdal (eds), *Political Theory and the European Constitution* (London: Routledge).

Oppenheimer, A. (1994) *The Relationship between European Community Law and National Law: the Cases, Vol. 1* (Cambridge: Cambridge University Press).

Oppenheimer, A. (2003) *The Relationship between European Community Law and National Law: the Cases, Vol. 2* (Cambridge: Cambridge University Press).

Pagden, A. (ed.) (2002) *The Idea of Europe: From Antiquity to the European Union* (Cambridge: Cambridge University Press).

Paine, T. (1989) *Political Writings*, ed. B. Kuklic (Cambridge: Cambridge University Press).

Pérez-Solórzano Borragán, N. (2004) 'Organised Business Interests: Lessons from the EU Constitutional Process', *Transnational Associations* 2: 119–24.

Pérez-Solórzano Borragán, N. (2005) 'The Convention Experience: an Exercise in Good Governance?' (Mannheim: The Institutional Shaping of EU–Society Relations CONNEX Research Group 4).

Pernice, I. and Kanits, R. (2004) 'Fundamental Rights and Multilevel Constitutionalism in Europe', *Walter Hallstein-Institut Paper* 7 (4).

Peters, A. (2004) 'European Democracy after the 2003 Convention', *Common Market Law Review* 41 (37).

Phillipson, R. (2003) *English-Only Europe: Challenging Language Policy* (London: Routledge).

Pogány, I. (2003) 'The Impact of EU Enlargement on the Treatment of National and Ethnic Minorities in Central and Eastern Europe, with Particular Reference to the Roma', contribution to Sadurski Workshop in Florence.

Pollak, J. (2005) *The Convention on the Future of Europe: New and Shining?*, EIF-Working Paper No. 7.

Pollak, J. and Slominski, P. (2004) 'Verfassungsverfahren und Repräsentation: Der Konvent als Vorbild demokratischer europäischer Konstitutionalisierung?', in W. Mantl, S. Puntscher-Riekmann and M. Schweitzer (eds), *Der Konvent zur Zukunft der Europäischen Union* (Wien, Köln: Böhlau).

Pryce, R. (ed.) (1989[1987]) *The Dynamics of European Union* (New York: Routledge).

Puntscher-Riekmann, S. and Schweitzer, M. (eds) (2004) *Der Konvent zur Zukunft der Europäischen Union* (Wien: Böhlau).

Rawls, J. (1993) *Political Liberalism* (New York: Columbia University Press).

Richardson, J. (ed.) (2001) *European Union: Power and Policy-Making* (London: Routledge).

Rietbergen, P. (1998) *Europe: a Cultural History* (London: Routledge).

Saurugger, S. (2006) 'The Professionalisation of Interest Representation', in S. Smismans (ed.), *Civil Society and Legitimate European Governance* (Cheltenham and Northampton: Edward Elgar), pp. 260–76.

Scharpf, F.W. (1999), *Governing in Europe: Effective and Democratic?* (Oxford: Oxford University Press).

Scheuing, D. H. (2003) 'Freizügigkeit als Unionsbürgerrecht', *Europarecht* 744.

Schmitter, P. (2000) *How to Democratize the European Union . . . And Why Bother?* (Lanham: Rowman and Littlefield).

Schmuck, O. (1987[1989]) 'The European Parliament's Draft Treaty Establishing the European Union (1979–1984)', in R. Pryce (ed.), *The Dynamics of European Union* (London: Croom Helm).

Schönlau, J. (2003) 'New Values for Europe? Deliberation, Compromise, and Coercion in Drafting the Preamble to the EU Charter of Fundamental Rights', in E.-O. Erikssen, J.-E. Fossum and A. J. Menéndez (eds), *The Chartering of Europe* (Baden-Baden: Nomos Verlagsgesellschaft).

Schönlau, J. (2004) 'Time was of the Essence: Timing and Framing Debates in the European Convention', in C. Closa and J.-E. Fossum (eds), *Deliberative Constitutional Politics in the EU* (Oslo: ARENA, report No 5).

Schönlau, J. (2005) *Drafting the EU Charter: Rights, Legitimacy and Process* (Basingstoke: Palgrave Macmillan).

Schröder, H. (1994) *Jean Monnet und die amerikanische Unterstützung für die europäische Integration 1950–57* (Frankfurt: Verlag Peter Lang).

Schwarze, J. (ed.) (1996) *Administrative Law under European Influence: On the Convergences of the Administrative Laws of the EU Member States* (London: Sweet and Maxwell).

Scott, J. (2002) 'The Culture of Constitution Making? "Listening at the Convention on the Future of Europe"', *German Law Journal* 3 (9). http://www.germanlawjournal.com

Shaw, J. (1999) 'Constitutionalism in the European Union', *Journal of European Public Policy* 6 (4): 579–97.

Shaw, J. (2000) 'Importing Gender: the Challenge of Feminism and the Analysis of the EU Legal Order', *Journal of European Public Policy, Special Issue: Women, Power and Public Policy in Europe*, guest ed. Sonia Mazey, 7 (3): 406–31.

Shaw, J. (2002) 'Process, Responsibility and Inclusion in EU Constitutionalism: the Challenge for the Convention on the Future of the Union', The Federal Trust for Education and Research Working paper 01/02. http://www.fedtrust.co.uk/default.asp?groupid=6

Shaw, J. (2003a) 'Process, Responsibility and Inclusion in EU Constitutionalism', *European Law Journal* 9 (1): 45–68.

Shaw, J. (2003b) 'A Strong Europe is a Social Europe', The Federal Trust for Education and Research Working paper 05/03. http://www.fedtrust.co.uk/default.asp?groupid=0&search=A%20strong%20Europe

Shaw, J. (2003c) 'What's in a Convention?' Institut für Höhere Studien, *Reihe Politikwissenschaft / Political Science Series* 89.

Shaw, J. (2004) 'What Happens if the Constitutional Treaty is Not Ratified?', in I. Pernice and J. Zemanetk (eds), *A Constitution for Europe: the IGC, the Ratification Process and Beyond*, Vol. 5 of the European Constitutional Law Network Series (Baden-Baden: Nomos), pp. 77–96.

Shore, C. (2000) *Building Europe: the Cultural Politics of European Integration* (London: Routledge).

Simitis, S. et al. (1999) *Affirming Human Rights in the European Union – Time to Act* (Luxembourg: Office of Official Publications of the European Communities).

Slaughter, A.-M. (2004) *A New World Order* (Princeton and Oxford: Princeton University Press).

Slaughter, A.-M., Stone Sweet, A. and Weiler, J. H. H. (eds) (1998) *The European Court and National Courts – Doctrine and Jurisprudence: Legal Change in its Social Context* (Oxford: Hart).

Smismans, S. (2003) 'European Civil Society: Shaped by Discourses and Institutional Interests', *European Law Journal* 9 (4): 482–504.

Smismans, S. (2004a) *Law, Legitimacy, and European Governance: Functional Participation in Social Regulation* (Oxford: Oxford University Press).

Smismans, S. (2004b) 'The Constitutional Labelling of "The Democratic Life of the EU" ', in L. Dobson and A. Føllesdal (eds), *Political Theory and the European Constitution* (Abingdon and New York: Routledge), pp. 122–38.

Smismans, S. (ed.) (2006) *Civil Society and Legitimate European Governance* (Cheltenham and Northampton: Edward Elgar).

Snow, D. A. and Benford, R. D. (1988) 'Ideology, Frame Resonance and Participant Mobilisation', *International Social Movement Research* 1: 197–217.

Snow, D. A. and Benford, R. D. (1992) 'Master Frames and Cycles of Protest', in A. D. Morris and C. McClurg-Mueller (eds), *Frontiers in Social Movement Theory* (New Haven: Yale University Press).

Social Partners (2001) *Joint Contribution by the Social Partners to the Laeken European Council*, 7 December.

Sorroza, A. and Torreblanca, J. I. (2005) *Spanish Ratification Monitor Update*, Elcano Royal Institute, Madrid (10 May). www.realinstitutoelcano.org

Stein, E. (1981) 'Lawyers, Judges and the Making of a Transnational Constitution', *American Journal of International Law* 71 (1).

Stone Sweet, A. (2000) *Governing with Judges: Constitutional Politics in Europe* (Oxford: Oxford University Press).

Stone Sweet, A. and Brunell, T. L. (1998) 'Constructing a Supranational Constitution: Dispute Resolution and Governance in the European Community', *American Political Science Review* 92 (63).

Stone Sweet, A., Fligstein, N. and Sandholz, W. (1998) 'The European Courts and the National Courts: a Statistical Analysis of Preliminary References, 1961–1995', *Journal of European Public Policy* 5.

Stuart, G. (2003) *The Making of Europe's Constitution* (London: Fabian Society).

Szyszczak, E. (1996) 'Making Europe More Relevant to its Citizens: Effective Judicial Process', *European Law Review* 21 (351).

Temple Lang, J. (1997) 'The Duties of National Courts under Community Constitutional Law', *European Law Review* 22.

Temple Lang, J. (1998) 'The Duties of National Authorities under Community Constitutional Law', *European Law Review* 23.

Temple Lang, J. (2001) 'The Duties of Co-operation of National Authorities and Courts under Article 10 EC: Two More Reflections', *European Law Review* 26.

Toonen, T. A. J., Steunenberg, B. and Voermans, W. J. M. (2005) 'Saying No to a European Constitution? Dutch Revolt, Enigma or Pragmatism', *Zeitschrift für Staats-und Europawissenschaften/Journal for Comparative Government and European Policy* 3 (4): 594–619.

Triandafyllidou, A. and Fotiou, A. (1998) 'Sustainability and Modernity in the European Union: a Frame Theory Approach to Policy-making', *Sociological Research Online* 3 (1). http://www.socresonline.org.uk/socresonline/3/1/2.html

Tridimas, T. (1999) *The General Principles of EC Law* (Oxford: Oxford University Press).

UNICE (2002) *Convention on the Future of Europe*. *UNICE Comments*, 17 June (Brussels).

UNICE (2003) *UNICE Reaction to Final Draft of the Convention*, 13 June (Brussels).

Van der Mei, A. P. (2002) *Free Movement of Persons within the European Community: Cross-Border Access to Public Benefits* (Oxford: Hart).

Van Parijs, P. (2007) 'Europe's Linguistic Challenge', in D. Castiglione and C. Longman (eds), *The Language Question in Europe and Diverse Societies* (Oxford: Hart).

Van Schlenden, M. P. C. M. (ed.) (1994) *National Public and Private EC Lobbying* (Aldershot: Dartmouth).

Vandamme, J. (1987 [1989]) 'The Tindemans Report (1975–76)', in R. Pryce (ed.), *The Dynamics of European Union* (London: Croom Helm 1987, reprinted London: Routledge), pp. 149–73.

Varouxakis, G. (2000) 'Is the Forgetting of History a Prerequisite for the Emergence of a European "Imagined Community"?', in B. Axford, D. Berghahn and N. Hewlett (eds), *Unity and Diversity in the New Europe* (Oxford: Peter Lang).

Verloo, M. (1999) *Gender Mainstreaming: Practice and Prospects*, report prepared for the Council of Europe, EG (99) 13.

Verloo, M. (2005) 'Mainstreaming Gender Equality in Europe: a Frame Analysis Approach', *The Greek Review of Social Research (Special Issue on Gender Mainstreaming and Equality Policy Frames)* B1 (117): 11–34.

Von Bogdandy, A. (2000) 'The Science of European Law', *European Law Journal* 6.

Von Bogdandy, A. (2004) 'Europäische Verfassung und europäische Identität', *Juristen Zeitung* 59.

Wæver, O. (1993) 'Europe Since 1945: Crisis to Renewal', in K. Wilson and J. van der Dussen (eds), *The History of the Idea of Europe* (London: Routledge).

Walby, S. (1990) *Theorizing Patriarchy* (Oxford: Blackwell).

Walker, Neil (2003) 'The Idea of European Integration and the Finalité of Integration', paper for the 2003–4 European Forum on 'European Constitutionalism', Robert Schuman Centre, Florence: EUI.

Walker, N. (2004a) 'The EU as a Constitutional Project', *Federal Trust Online Constitutional Papers* 19 (4).

Walker, N. (2004b) 'The Legacy of Europe's Constitutional Moment', *Constellations* 11 (3): 368–92.

Walker, N. (2005) 'Europe's Constitutional Momentum and the Search for Polity Legitimacy', *International Journal of Constitutional Law* 4 (2): 211–38.

Walker, N. (forthcoming) 'After the Constitutional Moment', in I. Pernice (ed.), *The Constitutional Treaty* (Baden-Baden: Nomos Verlagsgesellschaft).

Wallace, H. (2003) 'Designing Institutions for an Enlarging EU', in B. de Witte (ed.), *Ten Reflections on the Constitutional Treaty for Europe* (Florence: European University Institute).

Wallace, H. and Young, A. R. (1997) *Participation and Policy-Making in the European Union* (Oxford: Clarendon Press).

Walzer, M. (ed.) (1995) *Toward a Global Civil Society* (Providence, RI: Berhahn Books).

Warleigh, A. (2003) *Democracy in the European Union* (London: Sage).

Wattel, P. J. (2004) 'Köbler, Cilfit and Welthgrove: We Can't Go On Meeting Like This', *Common Market Law Review* 41.

Weiler, J. H. H. (1999) *The Constitution of Europe: Do the New Clothes Have an Emperor?* (Cambridge: Cambridge University Press).

Weiler, J. (2000) 'Foreword', in E. Stein (ed.), *Thoughts from a Bridge: a Retrospective of Writings on New Europe and American Federalism* (Ann Arbor: University of Michigan Press).

Weiler, J. H. H. (2000) 'Fisher: the Dark Side', in C. Joerges, Y. Mény and J. H. H. Weiler (eds), *What Kind of Constitution for What Kind of Polity? Responses to Joschka Fischer* (Florence: Robert Schuman Centre), pp. 235–47.

Weiler, J. H. H. (2001) 'Federalism with Constitutionalism: Europe's *Sonderweg*', in K. Nicolaïdes and R. Howse (eds), *The Federal Vision: Legitimacy and Levels of Governance in the United States and the European Union* (Oxford: Oxford University Press), pp. 54–70.

Weiler, J. H. H. (2002) 'A Constitution for Europe? Some Hard Choices', *Journal of Common Market Studies* 40 (4): 563–80.

Weiler, J. H. H. (2003a) 'In Defence of the Status Quo: Europe's Constitutional *Sonderweg*', in J. H. H. Weiler and M. Wind (eds), *European Constitutionalism Beyond the State* (Cambridge: Cambridge University Press), pp. 7–20.

Weiler, J. H. H. (2003b) *Un'europa cristiana* (Milan: Biblioteca Universale Rizzoli).

Weiler, J. H. H. (2005) 'On the Power of the Word: Europe's Constitutional Iconography', *International Journal of Constitutional Law* 3 (2, 3 special issue): 173–90.

Weiler, J. H. H. and Wind, M. (eds) (2003) *European Constitutionalism Beyond the State* (Cambridge: Cambridge University Press).

Wessels, W. (2004) 'Die institutionelle Architektur der EU nach der Europäischen Verfassung', *Integration* 27 (3): 161–75.

Wiener, A. (1998) *'European' Citizenship Practice: Building Institutions of a Non-State* (Boulder, Col.: Westview Press).

Wiener, A. and Diez, T. (2004) *European Integration Theory* (Oxford: Oxford University Press).

Wilson, K. and van der Dussen, J. (eds) (1995) *The History of the Idea of Europe* (London: Routledge).

Wittgenstein, L. (1967) *Philosophical Investigations*, tr. G. E. M. Anscombe (Oxford: Blackwell).

Wright, S. (1999) 'A Community That Can Communicate? The Linguistic Factor in European Integration', in D. Smith and S. Wright (eds), *Whose Europe? The Turn Towards Democracy* (Oxford: Blackwell).

Wright, S. (2000) *Community and Communication: the Role of Language in Nation State Building and European Integration* (Clevedon: Multilingual Matters).

Wright, S. (2004) *Language Policy and Language Planning: From Nationalism to Globalisation* (Basingstoke: Palgrave Macmillan).

Wright, S. (2005) *Virtually Debating the European Constitution? The Role of Citizens in the Future of Europe* (Granada: ECPR Joint Sessions, Workshop: The Role of Political Agency in the Constitutional Politics of the European Union).

Young, I. M. (1990) *Justice and the Politics of Difference* (Princeton: Princeton University Press).

Young, I. M. (2000) *Inclusion and Democracy* (Oxford: Oxford University Press).

Zagrebelsky, G. (ed.) (2003) *Diritti e Costituzione nell'Unione Europea* (Roma-Bari: Laterza).

Ziller, J. (2003) *La Nuova Costituzione Europea* (Bologna: Il Mulino).

Ziller, J. (2006) 'Le processus des ratifications du traité établissant une Constitution pour l'Europe et la période de réflexion', *EUI Working Papers*, Law 2006/29.

Ziller, J. and Lotarski, J. (2003) 'Institutions et Organes Judiciaires', in B. de Witte (ed.), *Ten Reflections on the Constitutional Treaty for Europe* (San Domenico di Fiesole: Centre for Advanced Studies and the European University Institute).

Index of Names

Index of Subjects